LAW, JUSTICE, AND POWER

Law, Justice, and Power

BETWEEN REASON AND WILL

Edited by

Sinkwan Cheng

STANFORD UNIVERSITY PRESS

STANFORD, CALIFORNIA 2004

Stanford University Press
Stanford, California

Chapter 4 reprinted (with some modifications) from Peter Fenves,
"The Sovereign Sentence: From the Preface to the First Edition of the
First *Critique* to the *Doctrine of Right*," in Peter Fenves, *Late Kant:
Towards Another Law of the Earth*. Reprinted with permission from
Routledge–Taylor and Francis, 2003.

Chapter 6 reprinted (with some modifications) from Nancy Fraser,
"Recognition Without Ethics?" Reprinted with permission from Sage
Publications—Theory, Culture, and Society Ltd., 2001.

Chapter 14 adapted from Julia Kristeva, "Thinking, Willing, and
Judging," in *Hannah Arendt*, translated by Ross Guberman.
Reprinted by permission of Columbia University Press, 2001.
Permission was also granted by Fayard, publisher of Kristeva's
original French text in 1999.

Printed in the United States of America
on acid-free, archival-quality paper.

Library of Congress Cataloging-in-Publication Data

   Law, justice, and power : between reason and will / edited by
Sinkwan Cheng.
      p. cm.
   Includes bibliographical references and index.
   ISBN 0-8047-4885-3 (alk. paper)—
ISBN 0-8047-4891-8 (pbk. : alk. paper)
   1. Sociological jurisprudence. 2. Law—Philosophy.
3. Justice. 4. Law and literature. I. Cheng, Sinkwan.
K376 .L376   2004
340'.1—dc22   2003025167

Original Printing 2004
Last figure below indicates year of this printing:
13 12 11 10 09 08 07 06 05 04

Designed by Eleanor Mennick
Typeset by Heather Boone in 10/12.5 Sabon

For my mother, with love

Contents

Contributors

ALAIN BADIOU is Director of the Department of Philosophy at the École Normale Supérieure. In addition to being a philosopher, Badiou is also a novelist, a dramatist, and a political radical. Among his philosophical writings, the most influential are *L'être et l'événement* (Le Seuil, 1988), his monograph on Saint-Paul (PUF, 1998), his essay on Deleuze (Hachette, 1999), and his recent trilogy *Court traité d'ontologie transitoire*, *Petit manuel d'inesthétique*, and *Abrégé de métapolitique*. His last novel is entitled *Calme bloc ici-bas*, and his recent theatrical pieces *Ahmed le subtil* and *Ahmed philosophe* (published by Actes Sud) have been performed many times in France and elsewhere.

JOHN BRIGHAM is Professor of Political Science at the University of Massachusetts. He has been a member of the Board of Trustees of the (American) Law and Society Association, a Fellow of the International Institute for the Sociology of Law in Onati, Spain, and chair of the Law and Courts Section of the American Political Science Association. He edited, with Christine Harrington, the series *After the Law* (Routledge Press). His most recent books are *The Constitution of Interests: Beyond the Politics of Rights* (1996) and *States, Citizens and Questions of Significance: Proceedings of the Tenth Roundtable on Law and Semiotics* (1997; coedited with Roberta Kevelson).

SINKWAN CHENG is Professor of Liberal Arts at the Maryland Institute, College of Art. Prior to her career in Baltimore, she taught in New York and Berlin. Her awards and honors in the recent three years include a Rockefeller Fellowship, a DAAD Fellowship, a Carl H. Pforzheimer Fellowship, a Mayers Fellowship, and a Franklin Research Grant. She has published widely in *Cardozo Law Review*, *Literature and Psychology*, and *American Journal of Semiotics* on interdisciplinary legal and cultural studies, twentieth-century English and European literature and critical thought, and postcolonial studies. Along with Fredric Jameson, Russell Grigg, and Parveen Adams, she served on the Advisory Board of American-Lacanian-Link. A former member of the editorial board of *Umbr(a) West*, she now serves on the advisory board of *(a)*, a new journal edited by Juliet Flower MacCannell and Dean MacCannell.

PETER FENVES, who holds the Joan and Sarepta Harrison Chair at Northwestern University, is Professor of German, Comparative Literary Studies, and Jewish Studies and Adjunct Professor of Philosophy and Political Science. He is the author of *A Peculiar Fate* (1991), *"Chatter"* (1993), *Arresting Language* (2001), and most recently *Late Kant: Towards Another Law of the Earth,* editor of *Raising the Tone of Philosophy* and *"The Spirit of Poesy,"* and translator of Werner Hachmacher's *Premises.* He has also written numerous articles on literature, philosophy, and political theory.

PETER FITZPATRICK is Anniversary Professor of Law at Birkbeck in the University of London and has taught at universities in Europe, North America, and Papua New Guinea. He has practiced international commercial law both in England and in Australia, of which country he is a national. For many years he worked in the office of the prime minister in Papua New Guinea on development policy, the control of foreign investment, and the establishment of community corporations. However, most of his time has been devoted to academic life. He has published works on law and social theory, and on law, racism, and imperialism, a recent one being *Modernism and the Grounds of Law* (Cambridge University Press, 2001).

NANCY FRASER is a political philosopher whose works have been translated into many languages. She is Henry A. and Louise Loeb Professor of Politics and Philosophy in the Graduate Faculty of the New School for Social Research and coeditor of the journal *Constellations.* She has taught in Paris and Frankfurt and currently holds the Spinoza Chair in Philosophy at the University of Amsterdam. Her books include *Redistribution or Recognition? A Political-Philosophical Exchange* (with Axel Honneth); *Justice Interruptus: Critical Reflections on the "Postsocialist" Condition; Feminist Contentions: A Philosophical Exchange* (with Seyla Benhabib, Judith Butler, and Drucilla Cornell); and *Unruly Practices: Power, Discourse and Gender in Contemporary Social Theory.*

ROBERT GIBBS is Professor of Philosophy at the University of Toronto. He is the coauthor of *Reasoning After Revelation* (with Peter Ochs and Steven Kepnes, 1998), author of *Correlations in Rosenzweig and Levinas* (1992), and coeditor with Elliot R. Wolfson of *Suffering Religion* (2002). He has written extensively on postmodern Jewish thought. His most recent book, *Why Ethics? Signs of Responsibilities* (2000), frames a postmodern ethics of responsibility by way of commentaries on a wide range of intellectual traditions.

MARTTI KOSKENNIEMI is Professor of International Law at the University of Helsinki and Global Professor of Law at the New York University School of Law. He is also a member of the United Nations International Law Commission. Until 1995, he worked as legal advisor with the Finnish Ministry for Foreign Affairs. His main publications are *From Apology to Utopia: The Structure of International Legal Argument* (1989) and *The Gentle Civilizer of Nations: the Rise and Fall of International Law, 1870– 1960* (2002). He has published extensively in the field of international law, legal theory, and the intellectual history of international law.

JULIA KRISTEVA is a well-known figure in the fields of psychoanalysis, semiotics, philosophy, literary criticism, gender studies, and cultural criticism. She is Professor of Linguistics at the Université de Paris VII. Her many publications have been translated into a variety of languages and have made significant impact in Europe, North and South America, Australia, Africa, and Asia. Her most recent work consists of a trilogy called *The Feminine Genius*. Under the titles of *Life, Madness,* and *Language,* the three volumes are devoted, respectively, to examining the lives and works of Arendt, Klein, and Colette.

ERNESTO LACLAU is a political theorist and a philosopher whose works are widely read in different languages in South and North America, Europe, Asia, Africa, and Australia. He is Professor of Politics at the University of Essex, and Professor in the Department of Comparative Literature at the University at Buffalo. He is also Visiting Professor at the New School University. His many publications include *Hegemony and Socialist Strategy* (with Chantal Mouffe), *New Reflections on the Revolution of our Time, Emancipation(s),* and *Contingency, Hegemony, Universality* (with Judith Butler and Slavoj Žižek).

JULIET FLOWER MACCANNELL is Professor Emerita of Comparative Literature at the University of California–Irvine. She has written a number of articles and books on political thought, modern culture, psychoanalysis, and women, including *The Time of the Sign* (with Dean MacCannell; Indiana University Press, 1980), *Figuring Lacan* (Nebraska/Routledge, 1986), *The Regime of the Brother* (Routledge, 1991), and her most recent, *The Hysteric's Guide to the Future Female Subject* (University of Minnesota Press, 2000). She has also edited several collections of critical essays, including *Thinking Bodies* (Stanford, 1994). She is immediate past editor of the *American Journal of Semiotics* and is currently editor of *(a): the journal of culture and the unconscious,* an interdisciplinary journal of art and analysis. In 1995, she was named president of the Society for the Psychoanalysis of Culture and Society. In 1993 and 1994, she chaired the Division on Psychological Approaches to Literature of the Modern Language Association of America. She has recently been visiting graduate professor at Stanford University and at the University of California–Berkeley.

J. HILLIS MILLER is Distinguished Research Professor of English and Comparative Literature at the University of California–Irvine. Before coming to Irvine, he taught at Johns Hopkins University and Yale University. His most recent publications include *Others* (2001), *Speech Acts in Literature* (2002), and *On Literature* (2002). Professor Miller's books and articles have been translated into many languages, including French, Spanish, Portuguese, German, Rumanian, Chinese, Norwegian, and Japanese. He is past president of the Modern Language Association. He has been a member of editorial boards for a number of literary journals, including *Victorian Studies*, *ELH*, *Studies in English Literature*, and *Diacritics*. He has lectured extensively worldwide, including South Africa, New Zealand, and many countries in Europe and Asia.

MAGGIE O'NEILL is Reader in Sociology and Cultural Studies at Staffordshire University, United Kingdom. She was coeditor (with Tony Spybey) of *Sociology*, the official journal of the British Sociological Association until December, 2002. She has published extensively on feminism, prostitution, and the law; responses to child/juvenile prostitution; participatory action research; and ethnomimesis. Her books include *Adorno, Culture and Feminism* (1999)—an edited collection of essays by an international group of feminist scholars on the work and life of Theodor Adorno; *Prostitution: A Reader* (coedited with Roger Matthews, 2002); and *Dilemmas in Managing Professionalism and Gender in the Public Sector* (coedited with Mike Dent and Jim Barry, 2003).

SLAVOJ ŽIŽEK, philosopher and psychoanalyst, is currently Senior Researcher at the Department of Philosophy, University of Ljubljana, Slovenia. His numerous influential writings have been translated into different languages. Among his most recent publications are *Art of the Ridiculous Sublime, Did Somebody Say Totalitarianism?, The Fright of Real Tears*, and *On Belief*.

LAW, JUSTICE, AND POWER

SINKWAN CHENG

INTRODUCTION

Law, Justice, and Power in the Global Age

According to David Hume and J. S. Mill, questions of justice arise in conjunction with conflicts of interest. Had it not been for the limits to human benevolence and the competition for scarce goods, justice would not have been an issue. Justice impacts on our consciousness most concretely when people press claims and justify them by reference to a set of rules (Benn 1967, 298). With the advance of technology in the new millennium, we should, at least in principle, have better resolved the problem of "scarce goods."[1] Why, then, are more claims being pressed, and more demands for justice being made, than ever before?[2] The observations of Amartya Sen and Jean Drèze on famine may help provide a clue: it is not shortfalls in the production of food, they argue, but the absence of legal channels assuring access to it, that causes so many famines in our times. Translated into the terms of justice in general, it is not the shortage of goods, but the politics of *entitlement*[3] in a world of cutthroat competitions, that creates overabundance for a few, scarcity for the majority,[4] and, above all, unhappiness for all in the age of global capital. This unhappiness is marked first and foremost by the feeling of frustration that "I deserve better; I could have gotten what I deserve had it not been for the existence of the Other."[5] As globalization brings people of different races, classes, and genders into close proximity in a system of intense competition, the conflicts of interest escalate.

The increased tension across the globe makes our time an "Age of Extremes"[6]—extreme injustice, extreme uses and abuses of power—which the legal thought of our times must reckon with. The extreme horror of wars (declared or undeclared) and ethnic cleansing are not the only form of cruelty being experienced by our age. As Etienne Balibar points out, "'globalization' of various kinds of extreme violence has [also] produced a tendential division of the 'globalized' world into *life-zones and death-zones*" (2001, 24). This process institutes a "superborder" between the *Übermenschen* (su-

permen) and the *Untermenschen* (subhumans) (18)—with overabundance on
one side, and, on the other, "famines and other kinds of 'absolute poverty'
produced by the ruin of traditional or non-traditional economies" (23).
Global capital destroys welfare, traditional ways of life, and social bonds
(25). Above all, it creates a mass of superfluous human beings—"garbage
humans"—who are "being thrown out of work by the million, while at the
same time . . . being kept *within* the boundaries *of the market*, since the market is an absolute, possessing no *external limits*" (Balibar 1998a, 16–17).
The cruelty of global capitalism is that it allows no alternative and no escape
for the disenfranchised: "the global market is . . . the whole world. When it
excludes you, you cannot leave it, you cannot search for another America, a
place from which to settle and start again" (16–17).

The misery of the *Untermenschen*—the new wretched of the earth—is
perhaps reinforced by global capitalist powers' abuse of "politics as anti-
politics" (Balibar 2001, 26)—the "preventive counter-revolution" or "systematic use of various forms of extreme violence and mass insecurity to prevent collective movements of emancipation that aim at transforming the
structures of domination" (16). The new millennium dawns, therefore, with
a pressing need for fresh strategies to counteract abuses of law, justice, and
power on both global and local levels. This collection brings together prominent international scholars in the disciplines of law, politics, philosophy, sociology, psychoanalysis, linguistics, and literature to contribute original
works on the incommensurable yet inextricable relationships among law, justice, and power. Their innovative analyses of these relationships open new
horizons for political action. The reason for making this volume a transnational project is obvious: the force of globalization needs to be taken up on
its own terms before we can find some wise and appropriate answers to some
of its problematic consequences. An interdisciplinary approach to the subject
at hand is also deemed necessary for our project in light of the fact that laws
in our times are not isolated systems of rules "in books." Ever since law
came to be associated with the popular will in modernity, law "in action"
has penetrated every aspect of culture and daily life. This trend has accelerated in late capitalism when buying and selling—the capitalist ideology of
self-willed, self-imposed contractual transactions—now hold sway over every
aspect of human life, displacing the non-monetary, "non-rational," non-legal
mode of human interaction in traditional societies (see Weber 1978). Only a
multidisciplinary volume would enable us to see how law, as Austin Sarat
puts it, is "everywhere"—both "majestic and ordinary," thoroughly penetrating every aspect of culture and society.

Law, Justice, and Power

"Law in books" often associates law with justice, whereas "law in action" inevitably reveals the operation of a third term—"power"—which breaks up the imaginary economy of the "paper marriage" between law and justice. The premise of this book is that law must be scrutinized in action in order to reveal this hidden complexity in the relationship between law and justice.

Let us begin with the connection between law and justice. At first sight, the two seem inseparable.[7] In Thomas R. Kearns's paraphrase of the common sense association between the two, "Justice without law, where it exists at all, is a precarious good. And without justice, law is an ominous spectre, threatening to violate its own ends." Yet a closer look reveals that the relationship between the two is by no means inevitable. Nor is it "clear and distinct." As Kearns points out, justice "can sometimes be found in a variety of associations and institutions (i.e., in families and between friends) where law is largely absent." Furthermore, utilitarians and Marxists in general disagree that law's (primary) function is to uphold justice. There are "other goods" besides justice that law may be established to protect: for example, security, efficiency, or the interests of a dominant class.

To further complicate the case, many controversies have arisen in the history of legal theory as to which term—*law* or *justice*—should have primacy. For some, *justice* means "the law behind the law, the standard of justice to which positive law must conform" (Pennock 1964, 378). To a believer in natural law, for example, a *law* is legitimate, and carries judicial authority, only when it contains "'rightness,' or correspondence to a standard of justice" (378). For others, such as the legal positivists, "justice" consists primarily of the strict application of existing laws without deviations.

The intricate relationship between law and justice becomes infinitely more complex when power is brought on stage. A consideration of power is indispensable because, whatever ideas we have about law and justice, it is power that makes a real difference in the world—be it catastrophic or providential. Power, in other words, reveals both the oppressive and benevolent faces of the law. Only through power can law act as an oppressive apparatus (see Cartwright 1959). At the same time, it is also through power that law can realize its utopian potential for bringing about a radical reconstruction of society on the principle of justice.[8] To rephrase the relationship of power to law in terms of justice, power is what both enables and destroys the potential of justice within the law. As Pascal puts it, "Justice without force is impotent. Force without justice is tyrannical."

Although power is indispensable to the operation of law, law can also direct the use of power by placing limits on, and controlling abuses of, power.

4

CHENG

This is why legitimacy is always at issue whenever power is being acquired or exercised. The effort to ensure that power operates according to established rules is, in simplistic terms, an endeavor to bring will under the harness of reason, so that the end product of this process—the obedience of the subject—will be submitted to the authority of reason rather than to brute force and raw violence. The sublation of brute force into the power propelling the "civilizing process" (in Elias's sense) informs Max Weber's famous characterization of the state as "upholding the claim to the *monopoly* of the *legitimate* use of physical force in the enforcement of its order" (1978, 54). Becoming "civilized" involves society's surrender of *Gewalt* (that is, violence, power, and force) to the state. As an embodiment of the rational, the state supposedly transforms the violence it takes upon itself into civilization by virtue of the fact that its application of force is *legitimate* and that its end is the protection of a civilized order. But this "civilizing process" becomes more ambiguous as we study concrete cases of law in action. Using imprisonment as his example, Balibar comments that "it is extremely difficult to draw a clear line of demarcation *within* the realm of the law itself . . . between *justice* and *violence*" (1998a, 13). The death penalty, above all, calls attention to "the unavoidable slipping of the exercise of power towards various kinds of institutional cruelty" (Balibar 1998b, 19).

As these examples show, state violence is still violence (and as such cannot be totally assimilated into reason) even though it is codified and labeled as "legitimate." In fact, it is impossible to apply unambiguous labels of "right" and "wrong" to describe the division between power and counter-power, state and revolution, orthodoxy and heresy. As Balibar points out, the dialectical development of the Hegelian World Spirit "is made up of violent deeds and relationships." There remains permanently intertwined with this World Spirit "a manifestation of cruelty, a glimpse of another world, another reality" (Balibar 1998a, 12; translation modified). This "other world" is the realm of *jouissance*—the leftover from the dialectic of violence and counter-violence:

there are forms, or layers, of violence, which do not gravitate around the alternative of power *vs.* counter-power, although they inevitably return to them and *infect them.* . . . This is, if you like, the most "excessive," the most "self-destructive" part of violence. There is a risk of tautology at this point: we designate a certain violence as *self-destructive* or *irrational* because we feel that it overtakes the logic of power and counter-power. (Balibar 1998a, 11)

The dimension of *jouissance* is absolutely crucial to understanding state power, colonial rule, and many other forms of domination—including "legitimate domination." This leftover that exists outside "the logic of power and counter-power" must be taken into account as we negotiate places for law, justice, and power between reason and will, between right and might.

Reason and Will

In jurisprudence, the complex relationship among law, justice, and power is intimately tied to the tension between reason (*ratio*) and will (*voluntas*). To a rationalist, it might seem obvious that law and justice is related through reason, whereas law and power are connected through the will. However, law in practice reveals that reason has no monopoly on justice. Nor is law merely a discourse of reason, since reason is already will, in the sense that reason can itself be a mode of domination and an instrument for imposing the interests of dominant groups. Max Weber, for example, pointed out how the "logically closed" and abstract system of Roman law promoted by university-based Romanists catered to the interests of monarchs and bureaucrats as well as the rising capitalist class concerned with private rights.[9] While it is true that reason is inextricably *entwined* with will, it would be erroneous to disregard their differences. It is important, for example, to be mindful of the fact that power is not merely a product of the will, since reason can also be a source of empowerment. Rights, as we noted before, can be thought in terms of power, even though this power is usually reduced to the normative dimension. By invoking ideals such as justice, reason, and standards of what human life *ought* to be like, individuals acquire the power to demand just and fair treatment.

REASON

A simple way of thinking about the contrast between law as will and law as reason is to invoke the difference between law as command and the rule of law. This simple dichotomy, however, needs to be complicated by a closer look at various traditions of legal thought.

The natural law tradition, beginning with Stoic thinkers Zeno and Chrysippus and continuing as late as Montesquieu and Blackstone, envisions a universe governed by laws exhibiting rationality. This rational-legal order is accessible to all human beings through their innate capacity for reason. Aquinas, for example, defines law as a "*rational* ordering of things which concern the common good" (question 90, art. 4; italics mine). The Western legal tradition has been dominated for centuries by the notion that law is equated with reason: *semblable reason semblable ley* (what seems to be reasonable seems to be law).

In the secular law tradition, the development from the "pre-legal to the legal world" (Hart 1961, 91) was marked by a transition from *asserted* rule to *justified* rule, or from law as command to the rule of law. In this process, legality became identified with reason, which dictates that the force of law should issue from the *authority* of reason, not from the caprice of raw power. It is reason, rather than the whims of some specific monarch, to which the subject of law owes his obedience. In turn, the legal order should also accept the restraints of reason, facilitate public consensus regarding the foundations of civic obligation, and respect the principle of *legality*. The ascendancy of the rule of law hence coincided with the displacement of absolute monarchy by *res publica*—a polity which Rousseau identified with lawfulness or the rule of law: "Any state which is ruled by law I call a republic, whatever the form of the constitution; for then, and then alone, does the public interest govern and then alone is the 'public thing' or *res publica* a reality" (1968, 81–82). Rule-governance and the equality of all before the law contrast sharply with the "patrimonial" state governed by the will of the monarch (see Stahl 1830–33).

Reason also has an important role to play in the positive law tradition. Lawfulness and rule-governance, as Dallmayr pointed out, are supplemented and reinforced in civil society "through the enactment of positive laws backed up by legal magistrates." Stylizing reason into a capacity of formal analysis, Hans Kelsen developed a completely formal or "pure" theory of Law independent of social and political life (Dallmayr 1990, 1452, 1458).

The significant role of reason in modern law can be summed up by invoking Max Weber's theory of legitimate domination, which analyzes law and evolving forms of authority by contrasting the charismatic and the traditional to the "rational-legal" (1978, 215 ff.) Fully developed law according to Weber is a system of rule-governance, characterized by rationality and a related impersonal order.

Important as reason is to law, we must not forget that reason itself is a form of will—a drive to understand and master whatever stands in opposition to the human mind. It is precisely because reason is implicated in will that Weber found human beings of a certain culture—that is, the West, which engendered modernity—to be "*especially* rational," particularly fixated on rules, and favoring effectiveness rather than custom as the preferred means for realizing their goals. What Weber did not develop is that the instrumental rational which dethroned custom in favor of effectiveness was itself motivated by a *Sittlichkeit*, a form of will particularly prominent in the West. "Order," after all, is perhaps not found but made, not disclosed to reason but asserted by acts of will.

WILL

The relations of will to law, justice, and power are complicated by two largely incompatible interpretations of the will in Western culture. On the one hand, the will is conceived as the faculty of choice or decision, by which human beings freely determine their actions. This freedom is predicated on the supposition that human beings, unlike animals, can act on the basis of reason. From the sixteenth century onward, however, another tradition took root—one which holds the will to be a mere locus of action-motivating passion common to animal and human beings. From this perspective, the will is no longer a locus of agency or freedom. This trend became especially prominent with the empiricists.[10] However, the initial impulse for this understanding of the will came from the Augustinian-Calvinistic conception that original sin severely damaged human beings' practical rationality. As a result of the Fall, human action became as appetite-driven as animal action; the human will lost its status as a rational appetite or a locus of free agency (see Calvin 1960, book 2, chapter 2; Pink 1998, 720–24).

Both concepts of the will have had a tremendous impact on law, justice, and power. Insofar as the will is understood as rational appetite and the locus of free agency and self-determination, law is concomitantly perceived as emanating from the popular will. Law as the expression of popular will provides the legitimate foundation for the nation-state. Thus when Europe translated the universal text of Roman law into national codes of vernacular law, the national codes came to "represent the spirit of the people in an authoritative and accessible written form which would bind its administrators and judges to the popular will" (Goodrich 1994, 322). Compliance with law no longer meant submission to arbitrary rules but of "giving oneself the law" in the sense Kant elaborated in his concept of autonomy.[11] Embracing the optimism of a republican, Hegel upheld the state as the highest stage in the moral evolution of human beings. Law in this sense emerged from the will of the state as a rational association. The state embodied concretely, as a living institution, the autonomous, rational will of human beings.

The association of law with popular sovereignty in political modernity presents a particularly difficult problem for international justice, since any foreign intervention into state affairs would by implication become an attack on the unity and integrity of state sovereignty, on popular will, on freedom, autonomy, and justice. The legality of international law is thus called into question.[12] As John Ford describes it, "Where external independence is regarded as a further facet of the internal superiority of the sovereign, the constraints of international law can no more be considered properly legal than the constraints of natural law, and international law can at best be considered to have delegated authority" (1998, 58).

Will as action motivated by passion has played no less prominent a role than will as rational appetite in the history of law. Cicero, for example, recognized the importance of rhetoric for effecting the practical goals of philosophy, even as he stressed at the same time human beings' natural capacity for reason. The rhetorical culture of the ancient Romans was sensitive to how the discourse of reason is already a discourse of mastery: the discourse of reason, in their view, asserts *dominion* and carves out a *domain* for the speaking subject.[13] The Romans' awareness of how law and justice are always inflected by particular interests and the will to domination has persisted into the present. For instance, the New Rhetoric movement, starting in the mid-1940s by Chaim Perelman and Lucy Olbrechts-Tyteca, revives the legacy of Aristotle and the Roman jurists, emphasizing the use of discursive techniques in legal arguments to move an audience to certain decisions or actions. This rhetorical view of law flies in the face of legal rationalism's valorization of transparency and intersubjective communicative ethics.

The involvement of law with *Sittlichkeit* or mores is another way that the unreflective aspects of the will become intertwined with issues of justice and power. Hermann Kantorowicz, for example, protested that the "ought"—that is, the moralizing element of all laws—is culturally determined, not universal. Legal evolutionism and historical jurisprudence provide perhaps the best illustrations of *Sittlichkeit*-oriented legal thinking. In the English-speaking world, Henry Sumner Maine was among the most renowned legal evolutionists to link different "stages" of law to the social developments that produced them. A more mystical connection between law and culture was established in German romanticism, which identified law with the cultural unity of a people. Friedrich Karl Savigny, generally regarded as the founder of historical jurisprudence (Stone 1950, chapter 18), held law to be the expression of national distinctiveness and the spirit and genius of the institutions of a people (*Volksgeist*), with *Volksgeist* resonating both race and culture.

The ideological dangers of historical jurisprudence notwithstanding, Savigny's ideas help draw attention to the discrepancy between the positive norms of the state, and the de facto norms which emerge from the institutions of society at large—a gap that reveals how the formalized reason of positive law fails to reflect the "living law." Picking up this clue from Savigny's writings, the Austrian jurist Eugen Ehrlich capitalizes on the living law as "the *de facto* normative pattern that develops as competing social interests are resolved within the many groups and institutions constituting the 'inner order' of a society" (Mayhew 1968, 60). Law needs to be attentive to *Sittlichkeit* for the practical reason that, in order to function effectively, it must recognize itself as a materialist practice with its own social reality. The legal establishment must also take social mores into consideration for ethical reasons. Long before the advent of multiculturalism, the view that law needs to be sensitive to custom and mores was already in place. Guizot and Hegel, for example, were aware of the need to create institutions that reflected people's passions, interests, and values. Without this sensitivity to will, law could become unjust and even tyrannical. In fact, any attempt to colonize the will by reason risks perverting the will. Reason is reason only when it maintains a heterogeneity to the will. The attempt to totalize law with reason at the expense of will can easily transform reason itself into a perverse will. Lacan, among others, has important insights on this subject.[14] The danger of total-izing will with reason can be seen in the dynamics of imperialism, colonial-ism, and their contemporary transformations—dynamics which are no mere by-products of "the white man's hypocrisy." The transformation of pure rea-son into perverse will enables us to see how, even when "the white man's mission" is carried out for the most "just" reasons combined with the most sincere intentions, the result is still often violence and cruelty.[15]

In short, despite attempts by "legal purists" such as Hans Kelsen to con-struct a completely formal theory of law independent of social and political life, the interlacing of law and will renders "'the social' . . . both impossible to differentiate from 'the legal' yet as constitutively law's 'outside'" (Brown 1998, 496).[16] In fact, even if law attempts to resolve normative problems through purely positivistic means, one must not overlook how the *rituals* of textual interpretation are culturally and socially embedded.

LAW AND THE DIALECTIC OF REASON AND WILL

A discussion of law in terms of the dialectic of reason and will is un-avoidable because law is as much a set of normative principles as a material practice. Law is not law unless it is both. In philosophical terms, law is con-cerned with both speculative and dialectical reason, and practical reason is precisely what is at issue in the dialectic of reason and will. In between rea-son and will, practical reason becomes the battleground for whether reason should guide custom, or whether it is a product of custom itself. In this di-alectic, reason may set the grounds for action, but it may also be perceived as a mere slave to passion (as Hume maintained), a rationalizing instrument in the service of the will.

It is not the intent of this volume to produce a definitive answer to these questions. Its goal is rather to investigate the new dynamics and configura-tions of reason and will, and the new forms of their entwinement with law, justice, and power in the twenty-first century.

Responses and Challenges to the New Millennium

TRENDS AND COUNTER-TRENDS

The dominant trend of legal studies in the twentieth century could be characterized as a turn away from "law in books" to "law in action." The beginning of the new millennium has seen a continuation of this focus on law's association with will rather than law as pure reason. This volume is not content to merely follow this fashion. It seeks instead to set a new tone for the study of law, justice, and power as they relate to reason and will—a goal it seeks to accomplish by 1) further teasing out the critical potential in current legal scholarship, and 2) indicating new directions for legal thought by calling attention to various blind spots in contemporary approaches to law.

The focus on the entwinement of law with will rather than reason is evident in many aspects of contemporary legal studies. The notion that law is a field of dissensus and conflict arising from cultural differences and class stratification seems to have gained ground on theories founded on consensus and common values. The return to *Sittlichkeit* in discussions of multiculturalism and human rights in the late twentieth century, the revival of interest in Carl Schmitt in discussions of international law, the attention to the quotidian and micropowers in the sociology of law, the ethical and rhetorical turns in legal theory, and the role of psychoanalysis in challenging traditional understanding of the law, are all telling evidence that the relationship of justice to law can no longer be approached merely in terms of reason.

Cultural and sociological studies of law inspired by Marx and Foucault call attention to the ways power serving private interests is often rationalized by, and as, law. It is important, however, to remember that the will does not only produce violence. The will can also generate power in the service of justice. In fact, reason without will is impotent. Moreover, will sometimes can reach a justice that lies beyond reason—as in the case of love and forgiveness. This is not to say, however, that reason should be subjugated to the will. The temptation to elevate will above reason, exemplified in postmodernist thinking, needs to be subjected to rigorous examination, even as one should be mindful of the many contributions postmodernism has made to law and democracy. The horror of the triumph of the Will in the Nazi movement, the elation the Nazis experienced by exalting (their version of) the Hegelian Spirit (in contradistinction to "the mind") and the Nietzschean Will, their utter contempt for "the imbecility of reason" they associated with liberal democracy, should be enough to warn us against prematurely hypostatizing will above reason. Justice cannot be upheld without reason. To ignore reason and the universalism associated with it means giving up the grounds on which we can talk about universal human rights and equality. A one-dimensional insistence on cultural relativism and identity politics risks giving legitimacy to General Westmoreland's "multicultural" claim during the Vietnam War that extreme measures against "Orientals" were not morally unacceptable because "Life is plentiful, life is cheap in the Orient. As the philosophy of the Orient expresses it, life is not important" (Davis 1985). We must not prematurely dismiss the importance of reason if we are to carry on struggles for justice and democracy. Governance by law (in the sense of reason) instead of by "men" can at least establish a basic democratic framework where human beings can, at least in principle, recognize right and not might, and where they can associate with each other as rational beings of equal dignity.

While differences between reason and will need to be maintained in order to avoid colonizing the will with reason, hard-and-fast distinctions between the two have to be problematized. Even if one sets aside Lacan's observation that "pure reason" can become a perverse will, it would be naive to insist that law is solely a discourse of reason. Fruitful and critical discussions of law, justice, and power can come about only when we acknowledge the value of both reason and will, and engage them in an ongoing process of mutual interrogation and defamiliarization. Rousseau and Kant have both attempted to reconcile reason and will within the concept of autonomy. Habermas offers a discursive model, steering between facticity and validity to achieve a similar objective. While benefitting from these great thinkers' insights, contributors to this volume at the same time seek strategies for negotiating places for law, justice, and power between reason and will, between right and might—with special attention to the *Sittlichkeit* of the new millennium.

CONTRIBUTIONS MADE BY THE VOLUME

The book is organized under seven topics. Part I, "The 'New World Order' Between State Sovereignty and Human Rights," launches the discussion into the new millennium by addressing the pressing issue of the (im-)possibility of (trans-)national justice in the "New World Order."

The year 1989 marked not only the end of the Cold War but also the "second death" of a balance of world powers which originated in Europe in 1648 with the Treaty of Westphalia. Established to prevent wars and hegemonic dominance, this balance arrangement was destroyed by the two World Wars. What ensued was the birth of a new kind of "balance"—a "'balance' of super-powers"—between the USA and the USSR. This second balance came to an end in 1989. Since that time, the global triumph of capitalism has taken place alongside a drive toward universalism in international politics, such as the rising popularity of human rights above state sovereignty, and of "morality" above politics. Morality, associated with human reason, is deemed universal. By contrast, politics is suspected of complicity with the particular wills of power elites. Various humanitarian operations have thus taken place on behalf of "a law that ranks higher than the law which protects the sovereignty of states" (Havel 1999; quoted in Žižek's essay in this volume). The tensions involved in such undertakings between state sovereignty and human rights, between legality and morality, make it incumbent on us to subject such applications to rigorous examination.

To illuminate the debate over which should have primacy—human rights or state sovereignty—Part I includes two kinds of transnational "humanitarian" operations: military interventions and refugee policies. Three scholars from four disciplines—philosophy, psychoanalysis, international law, and sociology—contribute to this debate. The first two essays take the Kosovo campaign as a point of departure, whereas the last essay turns to the 1999 British Immigration Act regarding refugees from Bosnia-Herzegovina and Afghanistan. The first two contributors, Slavoj Žižek and Martti Koskenniemi, observe how political and military interventions—made in the name of reason, law, and justice—are in reality often complicitous with the will to domination. Žižek diagnoses the NATO operation's complicity with global capitalism, and critiques high-sounding moral claims such as depoliticized "universal human rights" for blurring the boundaries between private and public in political discourse. In a similar spirit, Koskenniemi questions NATO's substitution of "moral duty" for law in justifying the campaign in Kosovo. Unlike Žižek, however, Koskenniemi maintains the necessity of an ethical politics, despite the impossibility of fully realizing such a goal in a divided and agnostic world. Koskenniemi thus proposes a law whose tentative universality is derived from the absence of any external objective structure; as such, it can "remain open for the articulation of any moral impulse" and "any conception of what is just." Moving the focus from military interventions to the opening of state borders to asylum seekers, Maggie O'Neill relies on, and is much more affirmative of, human rights and morality than the first two contributors. Her chapter focuses on the interrelationships among citizenship, (human) rights, power, and the law as they are experienced in the United Kingdom by asylum seekers from Bosnia-Herzegovina and Afghanistan.

The "New World Order" and the disruption of political and legal boundaries across nation-states were well prepared by colonialism.[17] Part II, "Colonialism and the Globalization of Western Law," uses the retrospective insight gained from the global age to throw new light on law and colonialism. Peter Fenves's essay explores how the formation of *res publica* simultaneously caused the nation-state to transgress its own boundaries by "deporting justice" to colonies. Focusing on Kant's rejection of *Machtspruch* (sovereign sentence) for *Rechtspruch* (legal decision), might for right, Fenves demonstrates how the *Machtspruch* was reintroduced to preserve the state when strict legality threatened an avalanche of executions. In such a state (of) emergency, *Machtspruch* was reinstated to deport "disruptive elements" to colonies—the "under-house" instead of the "slaughter-house." The *Machtspruch*, outlawed by the court of reason, thus turned out to be the "higher" reason making possible the rule of law. The West's "progress" from the rule of might to the rule of right, in other words, was dependent on the existence of colonies outside the dominant countries' legal jurisdiction yet under their executive authority.

My own essay examines how Western law, which reforms and deforms the colonized's culture and consciousness (for instance, their relationships to labor, land, time, and marriage), can also be mobilized in the colonized's struggle for independence. I contrast two differing forms of strikes carried out by the men and women in Forster's *A Passage to India* and investigate how the men appealed to, while the women rejected, the proprietary rhetoric of Western law and the foundation it provided for the British colonial structure. My analysis of strategies of resistance to colonial law uses the insights of Lacanian psychoanalysis to develop a notion of law defining the subject in terms of his/her lack, in contrast to liberal law which defines the subject in terms of his/her possessions.

Part III, "Legal Pluralism and Beyond," moves from external to "internal" colonialisms, from the global operations of law to its local administrations, by addressing the rising importance in legal studies of the "local" and the pragmatic in such domains as multiculturalism, gender studies, and the quotidian. While supportive of the politics of legal pluralism, the essays in this section go beyond the contributions of twenty-first-century scholarship. Nancy Fraser opens the conversation by arguing that justice today requires both redistribution and recognition of the values held by diverse cultural and historical groups. These values are also known as the will of different peoples—a will associated with *Sittlichkeit* (ethics) and "the good"—in contradistinction to reason and its association with *Moralität* (morality) and "the right." Contrary to identity politics, however, Fraser seeks for marginalized groups a justice which would recognize differences without falling into the trappings and constraints of *Sittlichkeit*. In the process of rethinking recognition on the basis of the right rather than the good, of reason rather than will, Fraser destabilizes the distinction between morality and ethics.

John Brigham also writes in response to the disintegration of the grand theory of law, but he concentrates instead on the pragmatic turn in legal theory. Foucault and Foucauldian legal scholarship serve as a focal point for Brigham's comments on informal law—the operation of normative control in areas traditionally considered to be outside the domain of law (Goodrich 1994, 324). While criticizing the tendency of Foucauldian scholarship to trivialize the state and the law and their concrete articulations of power, the essay also credits Foucault's legacy for drawing attention to the cultural mechanisms through which the law is imposed and the way it operates through various practices of everyday life. Brigham's goal is to transcend "the traditional conception of legal pluralism to a constitutive perspective that is in the best tradition of Foucault."

Part IV, "New Ethical and Philosophical Turns in Legal Theory," brings the discussion from the *empirical* other of legal pluralism to both the *concrete* Other[18] and the *radically singular* subject in Continental ethics and philosophy. This section marks the concerted efforts of four legal, political, and philosophical thinkers to explore new ways of going beyond Enlightenment notions of law, justice, and power. Ernesto Laclau, Robert Gibbs, and Peter Fitzpatrick challenge the Kantian notion of autonomy in ways that surpass contemporary academic appropriations of Levinasian ethics. Alain Badiou, on the other hand, rethinks the (dis-)connections between philosophy and politics in a manner that enables him to radically revise the Enlightenment principle of equality. For him, equality is "a universal capacity for political truth" that is nevertheless subjective and performative, with "neither a guarantee nor a proof."

In taking up the ethical turn in legal theory, the first three essays demonstrate how this volume is by no means content with uncritically hypostatizing ethics above norms. Contributors to this volume, in other words, are sensitive to the fact that departure from the duty to apply pre-existing laws declared to subjects of law in advance results in its own form of injustice. Instead of prematurely privileging equity above legality, heteronomy over autonomy, the three authors seek to engage these ideas in a rigorous process of mutual interrogation, all the while vigilant that, as responsible thinkers, they have to respond to both demands of justice.

In this spirit, Ernesto Laclau explores both the continuities and discontinuities between norms and ethics. While refusing to treat ethics and norms as independent of each other, Laclau warns against the totalitarian practice of collapsing the two. He advocates establishing an impossible but necessary relationship between the two registers via a "radical investment of the ethical into the normative"—radical because "there is no way of logically moving from ethical experience to norm," and the relationship is one of investment because "there is nothing which could be called an ethical normativity." This radical investment renders the normative order heterogeneous to itself. In so doing, Laclau goes beyond the Enlightenment idea of autonomy by proposing a subject that "emerg[es] from the undecidable game between autonomy and heteronomy . . . for which there is no universality but universalization, no identity but identification, no rationality but partial rationalization of a collective experience."

In resonance with Laclau's critical response to the Enlightenment tradition of justifying the rule of law on the basis of autonomy, Robert Gibbs proposes a philosophy of law based on ethics and "responsibility for *others*" (my italics). He analyzes three thinkers—Levinas, Luhmann, and Lyotard—focusing on their shared attempt to contest the *self*-grounding of universal law. Beginning from an asymmetric ethics of responsibility for the Other, Gibbs explores the ways that both norms and laws can serve to balance particular responsibilities and to hold open the future for the Other. Focusing on judicial procedure (the right to a hearing and to appeal) and deliberative democracy (seen from the viewpoint of an ongoing revision of legislation), Gibbs offers a way to justify law starting from particular and extreme responsibilities. His goal is to investigate alternative ways of justifying both norms and laws.

Like Laclau and Gibbs, Peter Fitzpatrick is interested in heightening law's responsiveness to justice. Fitzpatrick's discussion of the death penalty lends particular urgency to the confrontation of law with ethics in the domains of death. Death shares with law a tone of finality, but death also subverts the closed finality of law by confronting it with an absolutely unknown that is beyond the legal order: "Death denies and dissolves [the legal] order and makes something else possible, something unknowable without any assurance beforehand." Existing at the limits of law, death is both within law's horizon and yet beyond it.[19] Working to serve law at its limit by making manifest law's authority to make a "final" decision, death paradoxically challenges law at the same time: the finality involved in death penalty confronts law with an absolute responsibility to ensure that its decision "be made and brought to bear in as open, accountable, and revisable a manner as possible." Speaking from the standpoint of a new philosophy, Alain Badiou takes up a somewhat different task in his engagement with the Enlightenment paradigm of law, justice, and power. Rather than relying on the language of abstract universals, he rethinks equality in terms of the radically singular and the performative. While justice pertains to an "egalitarian recognition of [all people's] capacity for truth," Badiou also maintains that "equality means that the political actor is represented under the sole sign of his specifically human capacity." Justice in this way is characterized as the "*seiz[ing] of*] the egalitarian axiom inherent in a veritable political sequence" by philosophy—the latter realized as a comportment to thought and truth. Equality cannot be positivized as an objective of action; rather, it is an *axiom* of action. This axiom, Badiou emphasizes, is performative. Justice which "seizes the latent axiom of a political subject" hence "designates necessarily not what must be, but what is."

Part V, "The 'Inhuman' Dimension of Law: Poststructuralist Assessments," turns from ethics and philosophy to investigating a linguistically generated "inhuman" dimension of law, using the insights of deconstruction and Lacanian psychoanalysis. Focusing on Benjamin's *Zur Kritik der Gewalt*, J. Hillis Miller identifies *Schicksal* (roughly translated as "fate") to be the cause of the incommensurability among law, justice, and power. *Schicksal*, or the "mystical foundation of authority"—as Derrida (1990), following Montaigne and Pascal, names this problematic—is wholly other to human reason; it both disrupts and makes possible binary oppositions. At times associated with *divine* will and at others with mythical violence (a binary opposition which breaks down), *Schicksal* is as resistant to *human* will as it is to reason. Miller traces this "inhuman" dimension to the fact that the "ground of authority is a foundation immanent to language as speech act." The mystical foundation of law, in other words, is the immanence of an abyss "within performative utterances that is covered over by the word *Schicksal*, as in a judge's pronouncement of a verdict for capital punishment that determines the luckless criminal's fate."

Juliet Flower MacCannell explores the "inhuman" dimension of the law by tracing manifestations of the drive in theories of law from Aristotle to Hobbes, the demise of which tradition she credits to Rousseau—the main subject of her discussion. By offering a concept of law invested in freedom rather than order, MacCannell argues, Rousseau liberates the political subject from the hidden fantasies that had perpetually destroyed the law of order from within. By corresponding Rousseau's analysis of the flaw in classical legal theory (in the *Second Discourse*) to Freud's work of "construction" in psychoanalysis, MacCannell's study gives us new insight into political freedom. It also enriches our understanding of freedom in the psychoanalytic sense: freedom in both cases involves the impossible struggle for freedom from fantasy.

MacCannell's essay draws attention to the insights psychoanalysis has to offer to legal studies. The possibility of cross-fertilizations between law and psychoanalysis has taken hold in both disciplines since the last decade of the twentieth century—a dialogue partly prompted by the fact that both invoke the concept of "law." "Law" has different referents in the two fields, and it is important not to confuse them, but neither is it accurate to set them entirely apart—for example, by assigning them to separated domains such as "internal *versus* external law." Even though psychoanalytic law is not the same as judicial law, the former is a by-product which escapes, or is left over from, judicial law. Psychoanalytic law thus relates to judicial law in terms of what Kant and Hegel would call "limit" rather than "boundary."[20] Far from existing in two separate realms called the "internal" and the "external," the two laws bear to each other a (non-)relation of what Lacan and Jacques-Alain Miller would call *extimité*. This (non-)relation renders psychoanalytic law a particularly strategic tool for reading with, and against, judicial law.[21] Love and perversion, for example, operate "outside the limits of the law."[22] They are the *unheimlich* other to judicial law and as such can de-*familiar*ize the latter for us. Employing the insights of psychoanalysis, Julia Kristeva—the author of the essay in Part VI, "Psychoanalysis: Justice Outside the 'Limits' of the Law"—urges us to think anew the relationship between law and justice.

Kristeva turns to two kinds of "good will"—forgiveness and promise—which open a different avenue to justice and power from outside the limits of the law. In her psychoanalytic explication of Arendt's political philosophy, Kristeva points out how forgiveness is the only power that can release the human subject from the facticity of the past with which the judgment of law is concerned. Contrasting justice to mercy with their respective emphases on equality and singularity, Kristeva concurs with Arendt that "to judge and to forgive are but the two sides of the same coin" because "every judgment is open to forgiveness." While forgiveness releases human beings from the facticity of the past, promise protects human beings from the unpredictability of the future. Promise in the forms of legislation and the "mutual promise 'act in concert'" delivers human beings from the sense of insecurity that goads them to acts of domination.

Forgiveness, aimed at the person and not the deed, is an act of love. Kristeva's essay has a powerful message to deliver: "Whereas forgiveness is opposed to vengeance, the promise is opposed to domination." With this message, the volume concludes with an essay which welcomes the new millennium on a note of love, forgiveness, and promise.

NOTES

I would like to thank Austin Sarat for graciously permitting me to use the title "Law, Justice, and Power" for this volume and this chapter—"Law, Justice and Power" being a title he uses for his series with Dartmouth/Ashgate Press. I would also like to acknowledge my debt to the Law and Society Association, of which Professor Sarat was the president, for sponsoring my participation at their Summer Institute in 1997. The abundant good work of the Association has been crucial to refining my legal scholarship and inspiring me to undertake this project. Special thanks are also due to all contributors to this volume for their excellent work and their collaborative efforts on this volume.

1. Globalization has, for example, "trebl[ed] world per capita income since 1945" (Scholte 1996, 53).

2. The number and complexity of lawsuits, both collective and individual, have increased drastically in the past few decades. Clare Dyer reports on March 27, 1999, that "Negligence claims against general practitioners have gone up 13-fold between 1989 and 1998, according to figures released last week by the Medical Protection Society. . . . Compensation awards and settlements also rose steeply: while the highest settlement in 1989 was £777000, in 1998 it was £1.7m ($2.7m)" (1999, 830). Despite this upsurge in litigation, unfortunately, those most in need of justice are often the ones who do not have the means to demand it. Oftentimes, it does not even occur to the most disenfranchised in society that they are entitled to, or deserving of, justice.

3. "*Entitlement*," of course, is a legally charged term. Sen defines *entitlement* as follows: "The entitlement of a person stands for the set of different alternative commodity bundles that the person can acquire through the use of the various *legal* channels of acquirement open to someone in his position" (1990, 36; my italics). On Sen's entitlement approach, see also his works in 1977 and 1981.

4. Jean Drèze and Amartya Sen draw attention to the vast number of famine victims in our times as a result of "the political economy of hunger": "Despite the
widespread opulence and the unprecedentedly high real income per head in the
world, millions of people die prematurely and abruptly from intermittent famines,
and a great many million more die every year from endemic undernourishment and
deprivation across the globe" (1990, 1). Etienne Balibar repeatedly highlights how
global capital induces massive reproletarianization by dismantling social and devel-
opmental programs:

> One kind of effect [of globalization] is simply to generalize material and moral
> insecurity for millions of potential workers, i.e., to induce a massive proletarian-
> ization or reproletarianization (a new phase of proletarianization which crucially
> involves a return of many to the proletarian condition which they had more or
> less escaped, given that insecurity is precisely the heart of the "proletarian con-
> dition"). This process is contemporary with an increased mobility of capital and
> also humans, and so it takes place across borders. (2001, 24–25)

5. Among the deprived, such sentiments would seem well justified. But ironically,
it is the "haves," rather than the "have-nots," who tend to be consumed by the
ressentiment against "the neighbor who stole my *jouissance*," as Lacan would put it.
The "ethic" of capitalism is superegoistic: the more one has, the more one wants.
This is why capitalism is characterized by what Marx diagnosed as a constant revolution of the means of production. "Giving famishes craving" is one way to account
for the tremendous energy generated by this structural imbalance of capitalism.

6. This is a term appropriated from Eric Hobsbawm.

7. This is especially true in many European languages outside English. The medieval concept that an unjust law is no law (invoked by Martin Luther King in his
"Letter from City Birmingham Jail") obviously comes from the fact that in Latin (as
well as in French, German, Italian, and Spanish), the word for *law* (*jus, droit,
Recht, diritto*, and *derecho*) stands for what an English speaker would render as
"*just* law," "*right* law," or "*justice.*" Even when these terms are used to denote
"law" in the narrow sense of the word, they carry with them a rather strong con-
notation of *rightness* (Pennock 1964, 378).

8. Sociological jurisprudence, for example, is committed to using the power of
law for social reforms and the realization of democracy. Important spokesmen of
this school include Rudolf von Jhering (1872) and Roscoe Pound (1911–12). Philip
Selznick provides a telling illustration of the indispensable role of power to the operation of law: "A tax is *illegal* if it violates an authoritative order, and it is *nonlegal*
if it lacks appropriate authority . . . legality presumes the emergence of authoritative
norms whose status as such is 'guaranteed' by evidence of other, consensually vali-
dated, rules" (1968, 52).

9. Similar critiques targeting the Roman law of private property had also been
made by Rousseau and the early Hegel.

10. Hume, for example, defines the will as follows: "By the *will*, I mean nothing
but *the internal impression we feel and are conscious of, when we knowingly give
rise to any new motion of our body, or new perception of our mind*" (1978, "Of
Liberty and Necessity," book 2, part 3, section 3 of *Treatise of Human Nature*).

11. Justice thus emerges as "the sum of the conditions under which individual

wills can be conjoined in accordance with a universal law of freedom" (Attwooll 1998, 511).

In light of Kant's concept of autonomy as a reconciliation of will and reason, I part company with Fredrich Julius Stahl's (1830–33) purely formal definition of the rule of law. By identifying the *Rechtsstaat* exclusively with reason, Stahl set the rule of law in opposition not only to "patrimonial" law but also to the law associated with popular will.

12. The urgency of such issue in our global age is precisely what Part I of this volume undertakes to address.

13. See Part V of this volume, devoted to discussing law, justice, and power between philosophy and rhetorics.

14. See Parts VI and VII in this volume.

15. See Part II of this volume.

16. See Part III of this volume.

17. Bill Ashcroft, Gareth Griffiths, and Helen Tiffin have commented on the relationship between colonialism and globalization, although they omit the fact that colonialism was from its onset a legal as well as a military, political, and economic enterprise. Law provided the "legitimacy" and foundation for the political and administrative structures of the colonial state. The observation of Ashcroft et al. goes as follows: "The importance of globalization to post-colonial studies comes . . . from its demonstration of the structure of world power relations which stands firm in the twentieth century as a legacy of Western imperialism" (2000, 112).

18. The "concrete" in Continental philosophy does not refer to the merely empirical. Hegel criticized the merely empirical as "abstract" (see, for example, Hegel's discussion of empiricism at the beginning of *Phenomenology*). For Hegel, empirical data remain abstract until they have been mediated into the Absolute. In similar spirit, Marx maintained that the commodity makes sense only within a system of references—that is, the market (see *Capital*). Note also that the "concrete" and the "radically singular" in existentialism and contemporary French thought do not equal the empirical. For further elaborations on this subject, please see n. 33 in Chapter 5 of this volume.

19. It would be interesting to perform a Levinasian move here and seize on death as a way of opening law to ethics (see Levinas, *God, Death, and Time* [2000]; *Entre nous* [1991]; and *De l'existence à l'existant* [1978]). Fitzpatrick's demand that law be hyperresponsible in the face of its inadequate response to the death of the other, however, would differ in context and emphasis from Levinas's discussion of death as what interrupts absolutely my self-mastery.

20. See Kant's *Critique of Pure Reason* and *Prolegomena*; see also Hegel's *Phenomenology* and *Logic*. In brief, "limit" could be described as a "reflection-into-itself" of the boundary.

21. My strategy of reading one thought with, and against, another is adopted from Lacan's "Kant *with* Sade" (my italics).

22. This expression is appropriated from the end of Lacan's *Seminar XI* (commonly known as *The Four Fundamental Concepts of Psychoanalysis*). See also Juliet Flower MacCannell's development of this idea in her article "Love Outside the Limits of the Law" (1994).

WORKS CITED

Ashcroft, Bill, Gareth Griffiths, and Helen Tiffin. 2000. *Post-colonial studies: The key concepts*. London: Routledge.
Attwooll, Elspeth. 1998. Legal idealism. In *Routledge encyclopedia of philosophy*, ed. Edward Craig et al., 5:510–14. London: Routledge.
Balibar, Etienne. 1998a. Violence, ideality, and cruelty. *New Formations* 35:7–18.
———. 1998b. Specters of violence. Paper presented at the School of Criticism and Theory, Cornell University, July 14.
———. 2001. Outlines of a topography of cruelty: Citizenship and civility in the era of global violence. *Constellations* 8, no. 1:15–29.
Benn, Stanley I. Justice. 1967. *Encyclopedia of philosophy*. 4:288–302.
Brown, Beverley. 1998. Legal discourse. In *Routledge encyclopedia of philosophy*, ed. Edward Craig et al., 9:496–99. London: Routledge.
Calvin, Jean. 1559, 1960. *Institutes of the Christian religion*. Trans. F. L. Battles. Ed. J. T. Mitchell. Philadelphia: Library of Christian Classics.
Cartwright, Dorwin. 1959. A field theoretical conception of power. In *Studies in social power*, ed. Dorwin Cartwright, 183–220. Ann Arbor: Research Center for Group Dynamics, Institute for Social Research, University of Michigan.
Dallmayr, Fred. 1990. Hermeneutics and the rule of law. *Cardozo Law Review* 11, no. 5–6:1449–69.
Davis, Peter, dir. 1974, 1985. *Hearts and minds*. Videocassette. Los Angeles: Embassy Home Entertainment.
Derrida, Jacques. 1990. Force de loi: Le "fondement mystique de l'autorité" / Force of law: The "mystical foundation of authority." *Cardozo Law Review* 11, no. 5–6:920–1045.
Drèze, Jean, and Amartya Sen. 1989. *Hunger and public action*. Oxford: Oxford University Press.
———, eds. 1990. *The political economy of hunger*. New York: Oxford University Press.
Dyer, Clare. March 27, 1999. GPs face escalating litigation. In *British Medical Journal* 318 (7187): 830.
Ford, John D. 1998. Sovereignty. In *Routledge encyclopedia of philosophy*, ed. Edward Craig et al., 9:56–59. London: Routledge.
Goodrich, Peter. 1993, 1994. Law. In *The Blackwell dictionary of twentieth-century social thought*, ed. William Outhwaite and Tom Bottomore, 321–25. Oxford: Blackwell.
Hart, H. L. A. 1961. *The concept of law*. Oxford: Clarendon.
Havel, Vaclav. 1999. Kosovo and the end of the nation-state. *New York Review of Books* (June 10): 6. Quoted from Slavoj Žižek, NATO as the left hand of god?, in this volume.
Hegel, Georg Wilhelm Friedrich. 1977. *Phenomenology of spirit*. Trans. A. V. Miller. Oxford: Clarendon Press.
———. 1969. *Hegel's science of logic*. Trans. A. V. Miller. Atlantic Highlands, NJ: Humanities Press International.
Hobsbawm, Eric. 1996. *The age of extremes: A history of the world, 1914–1991*. New York: Vintage-Random.

Hume, David. 1739–40, 1978. *Treatise of human nature.* Ed. L. A. Selby-Bigge. Oxford: Oxford University Press.

Jhering, Rudolf von. 1872. *Der Kampf um's Recht.* Wein: Manz.

Kant, Immanuel. 1998. *The critique of pure reason.* Trans. and ed. Paul Guyer and Allen W. Wood. New York: Cambridge University Press, 1998.

———. 1977. *Immanuel Kant: Prolegomena to any future metaphysics that will be able to come forward as science.* Trans. and ed. Gary Hatfield. Cambridge: Cambridge University Press.

Lacan, Jacques. 1978. *The four fundamental concepts of psycho-analysis.* Trans. Alan Sheridan. Ed. by Jacques-Alain Miller. New York: Norton. Translation of *Le Séminaire de Jacques Lacan,* vol. 11, *Les quartre concepts fondamentaux de la psychanalyse.* Paris: Éditions du Seuil. 1973.

———. 1989. Kant with Sade. Trans. James B. Swenson Jr. *October* 51:55–104.

Levinas, Emmanuel. 1978. *De l'existence à l'existant.* Paris: J. Vrin.

———. 1991. *Entre nous: Essais sur le penser-a-l'autre.* Paris: Bernard Grasset. Trans. as *Entre nous: On thinking of the other.* 1998. Trans. Michael B. Smith and Barbara Harshav. New York: Columbia University Press.

———. 1993. *Dieu, la mort et le temps.* Paris: Bernard Grasset. Trans. Bettina Bergo as *God, death, and time.* 2000. Stanford: Stanford University Press.

MacCannell, Juliet Flower. 1994. Love outside the limits of the law. *New Formations* 23:25–42.

Marx, Karl. 1957–62. *Capital.* Ed. Frederick Engels. Moscow: Foreign Language Publishing House. 3 vols.

Mayhew, Leon H. 1968. The legal system. In *International encyclopedia of the social sciences,* ed. David L. Sillis, 9:59–66. New York: Macmillan.

Pennock, J. Roland. 1964. Law. In *A dictionary of the social sciences,* ed. Julius Gould and William L. Kolb, 378–80. New York: Free Press–Macmillan.

Pink, Thomas. 1998. Will. In *Routledge encyclopedia of philosophy,* ed. Edward Craig et al., 9:720–25. London and New York: Routledge.

Pound, Roscoe. 1911–12. The scope and purpose of sociological jurisprudence. *Harvard Law Review* 24:591–94, 25:489–516.

Rousseau, Jean-Jacques. 1762, 1968. *The social contract.* Trans. M. Cranston. Harmondsworth, UK: Penguin.

Sarat, Austin. 1988. " . . . The law is all over": Power, resistance, and the legal consciousness of the welfare poor. *Yale Journal of Law and the Humanities* 1:343–70.

Scholte, J. A. 1996. Beyond the buzzword: Towards a critical theory of globalization. In *Globalization: Theory and practice,* ed. E. Kofman and G. Youngs, 43–57. London: Pinter.

Selznick, Philip. 1968. The sociology of law. In *International encyclopedia of the social sciences,* ed. David L. Sillis, 9:50–58. New York: Macmillan.

Sen, Amartya. 1977. Starvation and exchange entitlements: A general approach and its application to the great Bengal famine. *Cambridge Journal of Economics* 1, no. 1:33–59.

———. 1981. *Poverty and famines.* Oxford: Oxford University Press.

———. 1990. Food, economics and entitlements. In *The political economy of hunger,* ed. Jean Drèze and Amartya Sen, 34–52. New York: Oxford University Press.

Stahl, Fredrich Julius. 1830–33. *Die Philosophie des Rechts nach Geschichtlicher Ansicht*. Heidelberg: Mohr.

Stone, Julius. 1946, 1950. *The province and function of law: Law as logic, justice, and social control—A study in jurisprudence*. Cambridge: Harvard University Press.

Weber, Max. 1968, 1978. *Economy and society*. Trans. Ephraim Fischoff, Hans Gerth, A. M. Henderson, et al. Ed. Guenther Rother and Claus Wittich. Berkeley: University of California Press.

Part I

THE "NEW WORLD ORDER" BETWEEN
STATE SOVEREIGNTY AND HUMAN RIGHTS

SLAVOJ ŽIŽEK

1 NATO *as the* Left Hand of God?

The Impasse of the Left

The winner in the contest for the greatest blunder of 1998 was a Latin American patriotic terrorist who sent a letter bomb to a U.S. consulate to protest against the Americans interfering with local politics. As a conscientious citizen, he wrote his return address on the envelope; however, he did not put enough stamps on it, so the post office returned the letter to him. Forgetting what he had put in it, he opened it and blew himself up—a perfect example of how, ultimately, a letter always arrives at its destination. And is not something quite similar happening to the regime of Slobodan Milosevic with the recent NATO bombing? For years, Milosevic was sending letter bombs to his neighbors, from the Albanians to Croatia and Bosnia, keeping himself out of the conflict while igniting fire all around Serbia—finally, his last letter returned to him. Let us hope that the result of the NATO intervention will be that Milosevic will be proclaimed the political blunderer of the year.

There is a kind of poetic justice in the fact that the west finally intervened apropos of Kosovo—let us not forget that it all began there, with Milosevic's ascension to power. This ascension was legitimized by the promise to amend the underprivileged situation of Serbia within the Yugoslav federation, especially with regard to the Albanian "separatism." Albanians were Milosevic's first target; afterward, he shifted his wrath onto other Yugoslav republics (Slovenia, Croatia, Bosnia), until finally the focus of the conflict returned to Kosovo—as in a closed loop of destiny, the arrow returned to the one who shot it by way of setting free the specter of ethnic passions. This is the key point worth remembering: Yugoslavia did not start to disintegrate when the Slovene "secession" triggered the domino effect (first Croatia, then Bosnia, Macedonia . . .); it was already disintegrating at the time of Milosevic's constitutional reforms in 1987, depriving Kosovo and Vojvodina of their limited autonomy. The fragile balance on which Yugoslavia rested was irretrievably disturbed. From that moment onward, Yugoslavia continued to live only be-

cause it hadn't yet noticed that it was already dead—it was like the proverbial cat in the cartoons walking over the precipice, floating in the air, and
falling only when it becomes aware that it has no ground under its feet.

As to this key point, even such a penetrating political philosopher as
Alain Badiou insists that the only Yugoslavia worth of respect was Tito's
Yugoslavia, and that in its disintegration along ethnic lines, all sides are ultimately the same: "ethnic cleaners" of their own entity—Serbs, Slovenes,
or Bosnians:

The Serb nationalism is worthless. But in what is it worse than others? It is more
broad, more expanded, more armed, it had without any doubt more occasions to
exercise its criminal passion. But this only depends on circumstances. . . . Let us
suppose that, tomorrow, the KLA of the Kosovar nationalists will take power: can
one imagine that one Serb will remain in Kosovo? Outside the victimizing rhetorics,
we haven't seen one good political reason to prefer a Kosovar (or Croat, or Albanian, or Slovene, or Muslim-Bosnian) nationalist to the Serb nationalist. . . . Sure,
Milosevic is a brutish nationalist, as all his colleagues from Croatia, Bosnia, or Al-
bania. . . . From the beginning of the conflict, the Westerners have effectively only
taken side, and in an awkward way, of the weak (Bosnian, Kosovar) nationalism
against the strong (Serb and subsidiary Croat) nationalism.

The ultimate irony of such leftist nostalgic longing for the lost Yugoslavia
is that it ends up identifying as the successor of Yugoslavia the very force
that effectively killed it: the Serbia of Milosevic. In the post-Yugoslav crisis
of the 1990s, it was the ("Muslim") Bosnia which can be said to stand for
the positive legacy of the Titoist Yugoslavia—the much-praised multiculturalist tolerance—: the Serb aggression toward Bosnia was (also) the aggression of Milosevic, the first true post-Titoist (the first Yugoslav politician
who effectively acted as if Tito were dead, as a perceptive Serb social scientist put it more than a decade ago), against those who desperately clung to
the Titoist legacy of ethnic "brotherhood and unity." No wonder that the
supreme commander of the "Muslim" army was General Rasim Delic, an
ethnic Serb; no wonder that, all through the 1990s, "Muslim" Bosnia was
the only part of ex-Yugoslavia in whose government offices Tito's portraits
were still hanging. To obliterate this crucial aspect of the Yugoslav war, and
to reduce the Bosnian conflict to the civil war between different "ethnic
groups" in Bosnia, are not neutral gestures, but gestures that adopt the
standpoint of one of the sides in the conflict: Serbia.

To justify their avoidance of the inexorable political choice, many leftists
resort to the "what if . . ." game (a thoroughly fictional alternative scenario). The favored options here are the fate of the last federal government
of Ante Markovic and the recognition of Slovenia and other "secessionist"
republics: instead of choosing the "secessionist" path that set in motion the
overall destruction, Slovenia and Croatia should have fully supported the
Markovic government and thus made possible a unified, peaceful, demo-

cratic, market-oriented Yugoslavia. The west should not have recognized
Slovene and Croat independence so quickly, because this recognition set the
civil war in motion. Both these arguments advocate a thoroughly nonreal-
istic option: Markovic never had a chance in the face of Milosevic's nationalist populism; the advocacy of the nonrecognition of Slovenia and other
"secessionists" is not only factually wrong (in this case, the war would have
been even more bloody and protracted because it would render the resistance to the Serb Army more difficult), it also relies on a fatal misreading of
the situation: the true "separatist" was none other than Milosevic himself,
who undermined the fragile balance that kept together Tito's Yugoslavia,
and, paradoxical as it may sound, the separation from him was, for the others, the only way to save what was positive in the idea (that is, the political
project) of Yugoslavia.

However, resorting to such fictional scenarios enables us to assume a
comfortable position, one in which we can avoid taking sides in the actual
conflict. Furthermore, if one accepted the game of (non)recognition, then
the only consistent ethicopolitical stance of the "great powers" in 1991
would have been to conclude that Yugoslavia as a federal state, as a sovereign international political subject, ceased to exist once the federal bodies
lost efficiency and legitimacy, and consequently to withdraw diplomatic
recognition from all post-Yugoslav entities, inclusive of the Serb-dominated
new "Yugoslavia," and to set minimal political conditions (democratic political life, respect of the minority rights, and so on) for the recognition of
its parts as sovereign states.

This, of course, does not mean that in ex-Yugoslavia, the worst possible
scenario was played out. There is a subgenre of science fiction, the alternative history, in which history plays out differently. The hero may intervene in
the past in order to prevent some catastrophic event from occurring, yet the
unexpected result of his intervention may be an even worse catastrophe, as
in Stephen Fry's chillingly amusing *Making History*, in which a scientist intervenes in the past, making Hitler's father impotent just before Hitler's conception, so that Hitler is not born. As one can expect, the result of this intervention is that another German officer of aristocratic origins takes over
the role of Hitler, develops the atomic bomb, and wins the World War II. . . .
And, *mutatis mutandis*, the same goes for ex-Yugoslavia: it might have been
worse. Instead of Milosevic, there might have been a more intelligent nationalist politician who would successfully play the game of presenting himself to the West as the main proponent of stability in the region.

Perhaps, after a delay of ten years, this can happen now. The partisans
of global liberal capitalism see the choice that confronts ex-Yugoslav republics as that between embracing Western liberal capitalism or persisting
in their ethnic self-enclosure. But what if this is a false alternative and there
is a third choice—the combination of the two that Vesna Pesic, member of

the Serb democratic opposition, called the possible "Russification" of Serbia? What if, after Milosevic, we'll get a new ruling elite, composed of the corrupted nouveaux riches and members of the present political class, who will present themselves to the West as "pro-Western" (in order to get Western financial support), while endlessly postponing true democratic changes, justifying it by special circumstances, and (while, in internal politics, actually following the nationalist line) claiming that if the west withdraws its support from it, the nationalist hard-liners will take over again?

This phenomenon is more general than it may appear. In a lot of third world states, the ideological interpellation of the ruling elite is double: the elite in the cities resort to liberal-democratic interpellation while simultaneously interpellating individuals (especially in remote areas) as members of an exclusive ethnic community. And the illusion of a lot of political agents, from patronizingly benevolent Western interveners to Mandela, is that it is possible to simply suspend the ethnic identification, this alleged source of "tribal ethnic savage violence," and directly impose the regime of universal democratic citizenship. As the experience from Bosnia to Kenya demonstrates, this solution doesn't function: in this case, the catastrophic outcome is that the main political options get overdetermined (or invested, colored) by ethnic differences: a certain political orientation is identified with members of a certain ethnic community.

So, back to Serbia, the proof of Milosevic's hegemony is that, until now, no political force, not even the most "democratic" one, was able to formulate an all-inclusive platform interpellating and including Albanians. Their exclusion was silently accepted by everyone—that is, all parties concerned shared a substantial nationalistic agenda. Even if some most radical circles of the Serb "democratic opposition" unambiguously admitted and condemned Serb crimes against Albanians (for that, they deserve full recognition), they were unable to propose a political platform that would not only condemn the violence against Albanians as object-victims, but also actively interpellate them as political subjects, making them part of a common movement. In clear contrast to it, and notwithstanding the presence of the "regressive" political tendencies in other ex-Yugoslav republics, in all of them, there are serious political forces that advocate a platform that also addresses the ethnic Other. That is, in them, there is no nationalist consensus. And this is probably the minimum criterion of democratic politics in ex-Yugoslavia: the absence of a nationalist consensus between power and opposition.

The ultimate cause of the opposition to the NATO bombing of Yugoslavia in some leftist circles is their refusal to confront the impasse of today's left. This refusal also explains the properly uncanny appeal of negative gestures like the spectacular retreat of the German superminister Oskar Lafontaine: the very fact that he stepped down without giving a reason, combined with his demonization in the predominant mass media (from the front-page headline of *The Sun*—"The most dangerous man in Europe"— to the photo of him in *Bild*, portraying him in profile, as in a mug shot), made him an ideal projection for all the fantasies of the frustrated left that reject the predominant Third Way politics. If Lafontaine were to stay, he would save the essentials of the welfare state, restore the proper role to the trade unions, reassert the control of politics over the "autonomous" financial politics of the state banks, even prevent the NATO bombing of Yugoslavia. . . . Although Lafontaine's elevation to a cult figure has its positive side (it articulates the utopian desires for an authentic left that would break the hegemonic Third Way stance of accepting the unquestioned reign of the logic of the capital), suspicions should nonetheless be raised that there is something false about it. Very simply, if Lafontaine were effectively in the position to accomplish at least some of the above-mentioned goals, he would simply not step down. Rather, he would go on with his job. The cult of Lafontaine is thus possible only as a negative gesture: it is his *stepping down* that created the void in which utopian leftist energies can be invested, relying on the illusion that, if external circumstances (for example, Schroeder's opportunism) were not preventing Lafontaine from doing his task, he would effectively accomplish something. The true problem, however, is this: what would have happened if Lafontaine had not been forced to step down? The sad but most probable answer is that either nothing of real substance would have happened (he would have been gradually "gentrified," coopted into the predominant Third Way politics, as had already happened with Jospin in France), or his interventions would have triggered a global economic-political crisis forcing him—again—to step down and discrediting Social Democracy as unable to govern. (In this respect, Lafontaine is a phenomenon that parallels the leaders of Prague in spring 1968: in a way, the soviet intervention saved face. It provided the illusion that, if they could remain in power, they would effectively give birth to a "socialism with a human face," to an authentic alternative to both Real Socialism and Real Capitalism.)

Human Rights and Their Obverse

Does this mean that one should simply praise the NATO bombing of Yugoslavia as the first case of an intervention—not into the confused situation of a civil war, but into a country with full sovereign power? True, it may appear comforting to see the NATO forces intervene not for any specific economic-strategic interests, but simply because a country is cruelly violating the basic human rights of an ethnic group. Is not this the only hope in our global era—to see some internationally acknowledged force as a guarantee that all countries will respect a certain minimum of ethical (and, one hopes, also health, social, ecological) standards? This is the message that Vaclav Havel tries to bring home in his essay, significantly titled "Kosovo and the End of the Nation-State"; according to Havel, the NATO bombing of Yugoslavia

places human rights above the rights of the state. The Federal Republic of Yugoslavia was attacked by the alliance without a direct mandate from the UN. This did not happen irresponsibly, as an act of aggression or out of disrespect for international law. It happened, on the contrary, out of respect for the law, for a law that ranks higher than the law which protects the sovereignty of states. The alliance has acted out of respect for human rights, as both conscience and international legal documents dictate. (6)

Havel further specifies this "higher law" when he claims that "human rights, human freedoms, and human dignity have their deepest roots somewhere outside the perceptible world. . . . while the state is a human creation, human beings are the creation of God" (6). If we read Havel's two statements as the two premises of a judgment, the conclusion that imposes itself is none other than that the NATO forces were allowed to violate the existing international law because they acted as a direct instrument of the "higher law" of God himself. If this is not a clear-cut case of "religious fundamentalism," then this term is devoid of any minimally consistent meaning. There are, however, a series of features that disturb this idyllic picture: the first thing that cannot but arouse suspicion is how, in the NATO justification of the intervention, the reference to the violation of human rights is always accompanied by the vague but ominous reference to "strategic interests." The story of NATO as the enforcer of the respect for human rights is thus only one of the two coherent stories that can be told about the bombings of Yugoslavia, and the problem is that each story has its own rationale. The second story concerns the other side of the much-praised new global ethical politics in which one is allowed to violate the state sovereignty on behalf of the violation of human rights. The first glimpse into this other side is provided by the way the big Western media selectively elevate some local "warlord" or dictator into the embodiment of Evil: Sadam Hussein, Milosevic, up to the unfortunate (now forgotten) Aidid in Somalia. At every point, it is or was "the community of civilized nations against. . . ." And on what criterion does this selection rely? Why Albanians in Serbia, but not also Palestinians in Israel, Kurds in Turkey, and so on? Here, of course, we enter the shady world of international capital and its strategic interests.

According to Project CENSORED (Carl Jensen, *Censored 1999*), the top censored story of 1998 was that of a half-secret international agreement in working, called the Multilateral Agreement on Investment (MAI). The primary goal of MAI is to protect the foreign interests of multinational companies. The agreement will basically undermine the sovereignty of nations by assigning power to the corporations that is almost equal to that of the countries in which these corporations are located. Governments will no longer be able to treat their domestic firms more favorably than foreign firms. Furthermore, countries that do not relax their environmental, land-use, and health and labor standards to meet the demands of foreign firms may be accused of acting illegally. Corporations will be able to sue sovereign states if they impose ecological or other standards that they deem too severe. Under NAFTA (which is the main model for MAI), Ethyl Corporation already sued Canada for banning the use of its gasoline additive MMT. The greatest threat is, of course, to the developing nations that will be pressured into depleting their natural resources for commercial exploitation. Renato Ruggerio, director of the World Trade Organization, the sponsor of MAI, is already hailing this project, elaborated and discussed in a clandestine manner, with almost no public discussion and media attention, as the "constitution for a new global economy." And in the same way in which, already for Marx, market relations provided the true foundation for the notion of individual freedoms and rights, this is also the obverse of the much-praised new global morality celebrated even by some neoliberal philosophers as signaling the beginning of a new era in which the international community will establish and enforce some minimal code that prevents sovereign states from engaging in crimes against humanity, even within its own territory. The recent catastrophic economic situation in Russia, far from being the heritage of old socialist mismanagement, is a direct result of this global capitalist logic embodied in MAI.

This other story also has its ominous military side. The ultimate lesson of the last American military interventions, from Operation Desert Fox against Iraq at the end of 1998 to the renewed war against Iraq in 2003, is that they signal a new era in military history—battles in which the attacking force operates under the constraint that it can sustain no casualties. When the first stealth fighter fell in Serbia, the emphasis of the American media was that there were no casualties—the pilot was saved! (This concept of "war without casualties" was elaborated by General Colin Powell.) And was not the counterpoint to it the almost surreal way CNN reported on the war: not only was it presented as a TV event, but the Iraqis themselves seem to treat it this way. During the day, Bagdad was a "normal" city, with people going about their business, as if war and bombardment were unreal, nightmarish specters that occurred only during the night and did not take place in effective reality.

Let us recall what went on in the final American assault on the Iraqi lines during the Gulf War: no photos, no reports—just rumors that tanks with

bulldozer-like shields in front of them rolled over Iraqi trenches, simply bury-
ing thousands of troops in earth and sand. What went on was allegedly considered too cruel in its sheer mechanical efficiency, too different from the
standard notion of heroic face-to-face combat, with images that would per-
turb too much. Public opinion could not handle it, so a total censorship
blackout was strictly imposed. Here we have the two aspects joined together:
the new notion of war as a purely technological event, taking place behind
radar and computer screens, with no casualties, and extreme physical cruelty
too unbearable for the gaze of the media—not the crippled children and
raped women, victims of caricaturized local ethnic "fundamentalist war-
lords," but thousands of nameless soldiers, victims of efficient technological
warfare. When Jean Baudrillard made the claim that the Gulf War did not
take place, this statement could also be read in the sense that such traumatic
pictures that stand for the Real of this war were totally censored.

There is another, even more disturbing aspect to be discerned in this vir-
tualization of the war. The usual Serb complaint is that instead of confronting them face to face, as befits brave soldiers, NATO was cowardly
bombing them from distant ships and planes. And, effectively, the lesson
here is that it is thoroughly false to claim that war is made less traumatic if
it is no longer experienced by the soldiers (or presented) as an actual encounter with another human being to be killed, but as an abstract activity
in front of a screen or behind a gun far from the explosion, like guiding a
missile on a warship hundreds of miles away from its target. Although this
kind of distance makes the soldier less guilty, it is open to question whether
it effectively causes less anxiety. Take, for example, the strange fact that soldiers often fantasize about killing the enemy in a face-to-face confrontation,
looking him into the eyes before stabbing him with a bayonet (in a kind of
military version of the sexual false memory syndrome, they even often "remember" such encounters when they never took place). There is a long literary tradition of elevating such face-to-face encounters as an authentic war
experience (see the writings of Ernst Juenger, who praised them in his mem-
oirs of the trench attacks in World War I). So what if the truly traumatic
feature is not the awareness that I am killing another human being (to be
obliterated through the "dehumanization" and "objectivization" of war
into a technical procedure), but, on the contrary, this very "objectivization," which then generates the need to supplement it by the fantasies of
authentic personal encounters with the enemy? It is thus not the fantasy of
a purely aseptic war run as a video game behind computer screens that protects us from the reality of the face-to-face killing of another person; it is,
rather, this fantasy of a face-to-face encounter with an enemy killed in a
bloody confrontation that we construct in order to escape the trauma of the
depersonalized war turned into an anonymous technological apparatus.

The Ideology of Victimization

What all this means is that the impasse of the NATO intervention in Yugoslavia is not simply the result of some particular failure of strategic reasoning, but depends on the fundamental inconsistency of the very notion on which this intervention relies. The problem with NATO acting in Yugoslavia as an agent of "militaristic humanismism" or even "militaristic pacifism" (Ulrich Beck) is not that these terms are Orwellian oxymorons (reminding us of "peace is war" slogans from his *1984*), which, as such, directly belies the truth of its position (against this obvious pacifist-liberal criticism, I rather think that it is the pacifist position—"more bombs and killing never brings peace"—which is a fake, and that one should heroically endorse the paradox of militaristic pacifism); it is neither that, obviously, the targets of bombardment are not chosen out of pure moral consideration, but selectively, depending on unadmitted geopolitical and economic strategic interests (the obvious Marxist-style criticism). The problem is rather that this purely humanitarian-ethic legitimization (again) thoroughly depoliticizes the military intervention, changing it from an intervention into humanitarian catastrophe grounded in purely moral reasons, not an intervention into a well-defined political struggle. In other words, the problem with "militaristic humanism/pacifism" resides not in "militaristic," but in "humanism/pacifism": in the way the "militaristic" intervention (into the social struggle) is presented as a help to the victims of (for example, ethnic) hatred and violence, justified directly in depoliticized universal human rights. Consequently, what we need is not a "true" (demilitarized) humanism/pacifism, but a "militaristic" social intervention divested of the depoliticized humanist/pacifist coating.

Even the large majority of those who opposed the NATO bombing silently accepted this moralistic logic and merely complained that this logic was not fully implemented, that there were other (strategic, geopolitical) interests behind it. The typical stance of a moralist opponent to the NATO bombardment of Yugoslavia was that he supports the moral consideration for human rights, but deplores the concrete way in which NATO militarily intervened (bombing bridges and civilian objects). What I am tempted to do is to reverse this commonplace: the NATO intervention ultimately did bring about some good results (refugees are returning; the Milosevic rule is for the first time seriously threatened), but what was problematic about it was precisely its depoliticized humanitarian legitimization, the most outstanding expression of the new moral tone that pervades contemporary political discourse more and more.

To get a taste of this falsity, it is sufficient to compare this recent moral tone with the great emancipatory movements based on the universalist moral appeal epitomized by Mahatma Gandhi and Martin Luther King. Gandhi and King led movements directed not against a certain group of people but against concrete (racist, colonialist) institutionalized practices. Their movements involved a positive, all-inclusive stance that, far from excluding the "enemy" (whites, English colonizers), made an appeal to their moral sense and asked them to do something that would restore their own moral dignity. As Wendy Brown astutely demonstrated, the predominant form of today's "politically correct" moralism, on the contrary, is that of the Nietzschean ressentiment and envy: it is the fake gesture of the disavowed politics, of assuming a "moral," depoliticized stance in order to make a stronger political case. We are dealing here with a perverted version of what, in the good old days of dissidence, Havel called the "power of the powerless": one manipulates one's powerlessness as a stratagem in order to gain more power in exactly the same way that today, in our politically correct times, in order for one's voice to gain authority, one has to legitimize oneself as being some kind of a (potential or actual) victim of power. This stance is not assertive, but controlling, leveraging, bridling—like the "ethical committees" in the sciences popping up everywhere today, which are mainly concerned with how to define the limits and prevent things (say, biogenetic engineering) from happening. So, in this perspective, every actual act is bad: when Serbs cleanse Kosovo of Albanians, it's bad; when NATO intervenes to prevent it, it's bad; when the KLA strikes back, it's bad—every excuse is good because it allows us to claim that of course we await an act, we want an act—but a proper moralistic act, the conditions for which are simply never here—like the proverbial falsely enlightened husband who, in principle, agrees that his wife can take lovers but complains of every actual lover she chooses, "You can have lovers, but not *this* one. Why did you have to pick this miserable guy?"

The ultimate cause of this moralistic depoliticization is, of course, the retreat of the great leftist historical-political narratives and projects. In this constellation, rationally convinced that the radical change of the existing liberal-democratic capitalist system is no longer even imaginable as a serious political project, but nonetheless unable to fully renounce their passionate attachment to the prospect of such a global change, the disappointed leftists invest the thwarted excess of their political energy that cannot find satisfaction in the moderate changes within the system, into the abstract and excessively rigid moralizing stance. So the choice is: either we resignedly renounce this "excessive" stubborn attachment to the prospect of global change and "maturely" accept our postpolitical universe of particular pragmatic solutions, or we risk a thorough repoliticization that would translate the false moralist zeal back into a radical ethicopolitical commitment.

A May 12, 1999, report by Steven Erlanger on the suffering of the Kosovo

Albanians in the *New York Times* perfectly renders this logic of depoliticized victimization (A13). Its title is telling: "In One Kosovo Woman, an Emblem of Suffering"—the subject to be protected (by the NATO intervention) is from the outset identified as a powerless victim of circumstances, deprived of all political identity, reduced to bare suffering. Her basic stance is that of excessive suffering, of traumatic experience that blurs all differences: "She's seen too much, Meli said. She wants a rest. She wants it to be over." As such, she is beyond any political recrimination—an independent Kosovo is not on her agenda; she just wants the horror to be over: "Does she favor an independent Kosovo? 'You know, I don't care if it's this or that,' Meli said. 'I just want all this to end, and to feel good again, to feel good in my place and my house with my friends and family.'" Her support of the foreign (NATO) intervention is grounded in her wish for all this horror to be over: "She wants a settlement that brings foreigners here 'with some force behind them.' She is indifferent about who the foreigners are." Consequently, she sympathizes with all the sides in an all-embracing humanist stance: "There is tragedy enough for everyone," she says. "I feel sorry for the Serbs who've been bombed and died, and I feel sorry for my own people. But maybe now there will be a conclusion, a settlement for good. That would be great." Here we have the ideological construction of the ideal subject-victim to whose aid NATO intervenes: not a political subject with a clear agenda, but a subject of helpless suffering, sympathizing with all suffering sides in the conflict, caught in the madness of a local clash that can only be pacified by the intervention of a benevolent foreign power, a subject whose innermost desire is reduced to the almost animal craving to "feel good again."

The ultimate paradox of the NATO bombing of Yugoslavia is thus not the one about which Western pacifists complain (by bombing Yugoslavia in order to prevent ethnic cleansing in Kosovo, NATO effectively triggered a large-scale cleansing and thus created the very humanitarian catastrophe it wanted to prevent), but a deeper paradox involved in the ideology of victimization: the key aspect to take note of is NATO's privileging of the now discredited "moderate" Kosovar faction of Ibrahim Rugova against the "radical" Kosovo Liberation Army. What this means is that NATO is actively blocking the only and obvious alternative to the ground intervention of Western military forces: the full-scale armed resistance of the Albanians themselves. (The moment this option is mentioned, fears start to circulate: KLA is not really an army, just a bunch of untrained fighters; we should not trust KLA because it is involved in drug trafficking and/or is a Maoist group whose victory would led to a Khmer Rouge or Taliban regime in Kosovo. . . .) Now, with the agreement on the Serb Army's withdrawal from Kosovo, this distrust against the KLA resurfaced with a vengeance: after a couple of weeks in which it seemed that the U.S. army was seriously counting on the KLA against the Serb forces, the topic of the day is again the "danger" that, after the Serb army's withdrawal, the KLA will—as the NATO sources and the media like to put it—"fill in the vacuum" and take over. The message of this distrust, again, cannot be clearer: it's OK to help the helpless Albanians against the Serb monsters, but in no way are they to be allowed to effectively cast off this helplessness by way of asserting themselves as a sovereign and self-reliant political subject, a subject with no need for the benevolent charge of the NATO "protectorate."

In short, while NATO is intervening in order to protect the Kosovar victims, at the same time, it is taking care that they will remain victims, not an active politicomilitary force capable of defending itself. The strategy of NATO is thus perverse in the precise Freudian sense of the term: it is itself (co)responsible for the calamity against which it offers itself as a remedy (like the mad governess from Patricia Highsmith's "Heroine", who sets the family house on fire in order to be able to prove her devotion to the family by bravely saving the children from the raging fire). What we encounter here is again the paradox of victimization: the Other to be protected is good *insofar as it remains a victim* (which is why we are bombarded with pictures of helpless Kosovar mothers, children, and the elderly, all telling moving stories of their suffering); the moment it no longer behaves as a victim but wants to strike back on its own, it suddenly, magically turns into a terrorist/fundamentalist/drug-trafficking Other.

The uncanny phenomenon that is strictly correlative to this logic of victimization is the blurring of the line of separation between private and public in the political discourse: when the German defense minister Rudolph Scharping tried to justify the NATO bombing of Yugoslavia, he did not present his stance as something grounded in a clear, cold decision. Rather, he went deep into rendering his inner turmoil public, openly evoking his doubts, his moral dilemmas regarding this difficult decision. So if this tendency catches on, we shall no longer have politicians who will publicly speak the cold, impersonal official language, following the ritual of public declarations, but rather will share their inner turmoils and doubts with the public in a unique display of "sincerity." Here, however, the mystery begins: one would expect this "sincere" sharing of private dilemmas to act as a countermeasure to the predominant cynicism of those in power: is not the ultimate cynic a politician who, in his public discourse, speaks in a cold, dignified language about the high politics, while privately he entertains a distance toward his statements, well aware of particular pragmatic considerations that lie behind these high-principled public statements? It thus may seem that the natural counterpoint to cynicism is the "dignified" public discourse. However, a closer look soon reveals that the "sincere" revealing of inner turmoils is the ultimate, highest form of cynicism. The impersonal "dignified" public speech counts on the gap between public and private. We are well aware that when a politician speaks in the official dignified tone, he speaks as the stand-in for the Institution, not as a psychological individual (that is, the Institution speaks through him), and therefore nobody expects him to be "sincere" because that is simply not the point (in the same way, a judge who passes a sentence is not expected to be "sincere," but simply to follow and apply the law, whatever his sentiments). On the other hand, the public sharing of the inner turmoils, the coincidence between public and private, even and especially when it is psychologically "sincere," is cynical—not because such a public display of private doubts and uncertainties is faked, concealing the true privacy. What this display conceals is the objective sociopolitical and ideological dimension of the decisions, so the more this display is psychologically "sincere," the more it is "objectively" cynical in that it mystifies the true social meaning and effect of these decisions.

So how are we to break out of this deadlock? A year or so ago, on Austrian TV, there was a roundtable discussion about Kosovo with a Serb, a Kosovar Albanian, and a German-speaking pacifist. The Serb and the Kosovar were arguing in a clear and "rational" way (rational, of course, if one accepts the underlying politicoideological premise of their respective reasoning): the Serb for the Serb right to retain their hold over Kosovo, the Kosovar for the right of the Albanian majority there to freely decide their fate. However, the pacifist basically ignored their arguments and just repeatedly insisted that they should renounce violence and promise not to shoot and kill each other, that they should strive to replace intolerance and hatred with the tolerant acceptance of the Other. . . . In the midst of these pacifist's ruminations, the Serb and the Kosovar, the two sworn enemies, quickly, almost imperceptibly, exchanged their glances in an amused and perplexed way, as if, in an unexpected gesture of solidarity, saying to each other: "What is this idiot talking about? How can he be so stupid as not to understand *anything at all*?" And my point is that if this brief moment of solidarity could have been somehow operationalized (to put it in an ironically brutal way, if the Serb and the Kosovar were to tell to each other: "Do we really have to take this crap? Let's just shoot the idiot and go on . . ."), there would be some real hope for Serb-Kosovar relations. That is to say, how are we to interpret this exchange of gazes? The obvious way would be to read it as the sign of the obscene solidarity of "primitive" ethnic murderers directed against a sincere civilized pacifist: "Let him go—the idiot doesn't know what pleasure ethnic hatred can bring!" However, what if the perplexity of the two ex-Yugoslavs rather expressed their awareness of how the pacifist's attitude itself displayed a patronizing, racist ignorance?

The point here is not to get a cheap laugh at the pacifist's sincere effort, but rather to bring to light its hidden arrogance. Michael Ignatieff, with whose liberal approach I otherwise profoundly disagree, recently drew attention to the term "protectorate" used to describe the immediate political status of Kosovo: as if the international community were dealing with immature people who had to be disciplined and protected from their destructive impulses by a benevolent outside force. For the same reason, one should reject the multiculturalist pacifist appeals to tolerance. They also involve a gesture of disabling the other, as if we are dealing with fighting children who should be taught to treat each other kindly. Again, paradoxical and counterintuitive as it may appear, one should therefore reject the patronizing diagnostic of Yugoslav war(s) in terms of "ethnic" or "nationalist" conflicts—the struggle was between different political options. This perception ("ethnic conflict") is itself a distortion that involves an a priori moral patronizing judgment (the people are "immature," all sides are the same, the need for protectorate . . .) and is thus part of the moralizing depoliticization of the situation.

The Carnival in the Eye of the Storm

The "disavowal of reality" in the NATO-Yugoslav war was double: the Serb counterpart to the NATO fantasy of war without casualties, of a precise surgical operation ideologically sustained by the ideology of global victimization, was—in the first weeks of the NATO bombardment—the faked carnivalization of the war, which involved the total disconnection from the reality of what went on down in Kosovo. So, on the one hand, we had the more and more openly racist tone of the Western media reports on the war: when three American soldiers were taken prisoners, CNN dedicated the first ten minutes of the news to their predicament (although everyone knew that nothing would happen to them!), and only then reported on the tens of thousands of refugees, the burned villages, and new ghost town of Pristina. And the Serb counterpoint to it was the obscenities of the state propaganda: they regularly referred to Clinton not as "the American president," but as "the American Fuehrer"; two of the posters on their state-organized anti-NATO demonstrations were "Clinton, come here and be our Monica!" (that is, suck our . . .), and "Monica, did you also suck out his brain?" This is where the NATO planners got it wrong, caught in their schemes of strategic reasoning, unable to forecast that the Serb reaction to bombardment will be recourse to a collective Bakhtinian carnivalization of the social life.

The standard topic of critical psychiatry is that a "madman" is not in himself mad, but rather functions as a kind of focal point in which the pathological tension that permeates the entire group (family) to which he belongs finds its outlet. The "madman" is the product of the group pathology, the symptomatic point in which the global pathology becomes visible—one can say that all other members of the group succeed in retaining (the appearance of) their sanity by condensing their pathology in (or by projecting it onto) the sacrificial figure of the madman, this exception who grounds the global order of group sanity. However, more interesting than this is the opposite case, exemplified by the life of Bertrand Russell. He lived until his death in his late 90s a long, normal life, full of creativity and "healthy" sexual satisfactions, yet all the people around him, members of his larger family, seemed to be afflicted with some kind of madness. He had love affairs with most of the wives of his sons, and most of his sons and other close relatives committed suicide. It is thus as if, in a kind of inversion of the standard logic of group sanity guaranteed by the exclusion of the "madman," here, we have the central figure who retained (the appearance of) his sanity by way of spreading his madness all around him, onto all his close relatives. The task of critical analysis here, of course, is to demonstrate how the true point of madness of this social network is precisely the only point that appears "sane": its central paternal figure who perceives madness everywhere around himself, but is unable to recognize in himself its true source.

And does the same not hold for the predominant way the Serbs perceive their role today? On the one hand, one can argue that, for the West, Serbia is a symptomatic point in which the repressed truth of a more global situation violently breaks out. On the other hand, Serbs behave as an island of sanity in the sea of nationalist/secessionist madness all around them, refusing to acknowledge even a part of responsibility. It is illuminating to watch the Serb satellite state TV that targets the foreign public: no reports on atrocities in Kosovo are presented, and refugees are mentioned only as people fleeing the NATO bombing. The overall idea is that Serbia, the island of peace, the only place in ex-Yugoslavia that was not touched by the war raging all around it, is attacked by the NATO madmen destroying bridges and hospitals.

No wonder, then, that the atmosphere in Belgrade in the first weeks of the war was carnivalesque in a faked way—when they were not in shelters, people danced to rock or ethnic music on the streets, under the motto "With music against bombs!", playing the role of the defiant victims (because they know that NATO does not really bomb civilian targets). Although it may fascinate some confused pseudoleftists, this obscene carnivalization of the social life is effectively the other, public, face of ethnic cleansing: while in Belgrade people defiantly dance on the streets, three hundred kilometers to the south, genocide of monstrous proportions is taking place. So when, in the nighttime, crowds are camping out on the Belgrade bridges, participating in pop and ethnic music concerts held there in a defiantly festive mood, offering their bodies as the live shield to prevent the bridges from being bombed, the answer to this faked pathetic gesture should be a very simple one: why don't you go to Kosovo and start a rock carnival in the Albanian parts of Pristina? And when people are wearing papers with a target emblem printed on them, the obscene falsity of this gesture cannot but strike the eye: can one imagine the real targets, years ago in Sarajevo or now in Kosovo, wearing such signs?

What is this almost psychotic refusal to perceive one's responsibility grounded in? There is a well-known Israeli joke about Clinton visiting Bibi Netanyahu. When, in Bibi's office, Clinton saw a mysterious blue phone, he asked Bibi what it was. Bibi answered that it allowed him to dial God up there in the sky. Upon his return to the United States, the envious Clinton demanded that the Secret Service provide him such a phone at any cost. In two weeks, they delivered it and it worked—but the phone bill was exorbitant: $2 million for a one-minute talk with God. So Clinton furiously called Bibi and complained: "How can you afford such a phone, if even we, who support you financially, cannot? Is this how you spend our money?" Bibi calmly answered: "No, it's not that—you see, for us Jews, that call counts as a local call!"

The problem with Serbs is that, in their self-perception, they tend more and more to imitate Jews and identify themselves as the people for whom the phone call to God counts as a local call. That is to say, in the last years, the Serb propaganda promoted the identification of Serbia as the second Israel, with Serbs as the chosen nation and Kosovo as their West Bank where they fight, in the guise of "Albanian terrorists," their own intifada. They went as far as repeating the old Israeli complaint against the Arabs: "We will pardon you for what you did to us, but we will never pardon you for forcing us to do to *you* the horrible things we had to do in order to defend ourselves!" The hilariously mocking Serb apology for shooting down the stealth bomber was, "Sorry, we didn't know you were invisible!" One is tempted to say that the answer to Serb complaints about the "irrational barbaric bombing" of their country should be, "Sorry, we didn't know you are a chosen nation!"

When the Western powers continuously repeat that they are not fighting the Serb people, but rather their corrupt leaders, they rely on the (typically liberal) wrong premise that Serbs are victims of their evil leadership personified in Milosevic, that they are manipulated by him. The painful fact is that the Serb aggressive nationalism enjoys the support of the large majority of the population—no, Serbs are not passive victims of nationalist manipulation, they are not Americans in disguise, just waiting to be delivered from the nationalist spell. On the other hand, this misperception is accompanied by the apparently contradictory notion according to which Balkan people are living in the past, fighting old battles again and again, perceiving recent situation through old myths. I am tempted to say that these two cliches should be precisely turned around: not only are people not "good," because they let themselves be manipulated with obscene pleasure, but there are also no "old myths" that we need to study if we are really to understand the complex situation, just the *present* outburst of racist nationalism that, according to its needs, opportunistically resuscitates old myths. To paraphrase the old Clintonian motto: no, it's not the old myths and ethnic hatreds, it's the *political power struggle,* stupid!

Where, in all this, is the much-praised Serb "democratic opposition"? One shouldn't be too hard on them: in the present situation of Serbia, of course, any attempt at public disagreement would probably trigger direct death threats. On the other hand, one should nonetheless notice that there was a certain limit that, as far as I know, even the most radical Serb democratic opposition was never able to trespass: the farthest they can go is to admit the monstrous nature of Serb nationalism and ethnic cleansing, but nonetheless to insist that Milosevic is ultimately just one in a series of the nationalist leaders who are to be blamed for the violence of the last decade: Milosevic, Tudjman, Izetbegovic, Kucan—they are ultimately all the same. I am not claiming, against such a vision, that one should put all the blame on Serbs. My point is just that instead of such pathetic apolitical generalizations ("they are all mad, all to blame"), one should, more than ever, insist on a concrete political analysis of the power struggles that triggered the catastrophe. And it is the rejection of such an analysis that accounts for the ultimate hypocrisy of the pacifist attitude toward the Kosovo war: "the true victims are women and children on all sides, so stop the bombing; more violence never helped to end violence—it just pushes us deeper into the vortex."

So what should the Serb "democratic opposition" do? Let us recall Freud's late book on Moses and monotheism: how did he react to the Nazi anti-Semitic threat? Not by joining the ranks of the beleaguered Jews in the defense of their legacy, but by targeting its own people, the most precious part of the Jewish legacy, the founding figure of Moses—that is, by endeavoring to deprive Jews of this figure, proving that Moses was not a Jew at all—this way, he effectively undermined the very unconscious foundation of the anti-Semitism. And is it not that Serbs should today risk a similar act with regard to Kosovo as their precious object-treasure, the cradle of their civilization, that which matters to them more than everything else and which they are never able to renounce? Therein resides the final limit of the large majority of the so-called democratic opposition to the Milosevic regime: they unconditionally endorse Milosevic's anti-Albanian nationalist agenda, even accusing him of making compromises with the west and "betraying" Serb national interests in Kosovo. In the course of the student demonstrations against Milosevic's Socialist Party falsification of the election results in winter 1996, the Western media who closely followed the events and praised the revived democratic spirit in Serbia rarely mentioned the fact that one of the regular slogans of the demonstrators against the special police forces was "Instead of kicking us, go to Kosovo and kick out the Albanians!" For this very reason, the sine qua non of an authentic act in Serbia today would be precisely to renounce the claim to Kosovo, to sacrifice the substantial attachment to the privileged object. (What we have here is thus a nice case of the political dialectic of democracy: although democracy is the ultimate goal, in today's Serbia, any direct advocacy of democracy that leaves uncontested nationalistic claims about Kosovo is doomed to fail—*the* issue, apropos of which the struggle for democracy will be decided, is that of Kosovo.)

The Second Way

The conclusion that imposes itself is thus that what we have here, in the NATO-Yugoslav conflict, is a political example of the famous drawing in which we recognize the contours either of a rabbit head or of a goose head, depending on our mental focus. If we look at the situation in a certain way, we see the international community enforcing minimal human rights standards on a nationalist neocommunist leader engaged in ethnic cleansing, ready to ruin his own nation just to retain power. If we shift the focus, we see NATO, the armed hand of the new capitalist global order, defending the strategic interests of the capital in the guise of a disgusting travesty, posing as a disinterested enforcer of human rights, attacking a sovereign country that, in spite of the problematic nature of its regime, nonetheless acts as an obstacle to the unbridled assertion of the New World Order.

How, then, are we to think these two stories together, without sacrificing the truth of each of them? A good starting point would be to reject the double blackmail implied in their contrast (if you are against NATO strikes, you are for Milosevic's protofascist regime of ethnic cleansing, and if you are against Milosevic, you support the global capitalist New World Order). What if this very opposition between enlightened international intervention against ethnic fundamentalists, and the heroic last pockets of resistance against the New World Order, is a false one? What if phenomena like the Milosevic regime are not the opposite to the New World Order, but rather its symptom, the place at which the hidden truth of the New World Order emerges? Recently, one of the American negotiators said that Milosevic is not only part of the problem, but rather *the* problem itself. However, was this not clear from the very beginning? Why, then, the interminable procrastination of the Western powers, playing for years into Milosevic's hands, acknowledging him as a key factor of stability in the region, misreading clear cases of Serb aggression as civil or even tribal warfare, initially putting the blame on those who immediately saw what Milosevic stands for and, for that reason, desperately wanted to escape his grasp (see James Baker's public endorsement of a "limited military intervention" against Slovene secession), supporting the last Yugoslav prime minister Ante Markovic, whose program was, in an incredible case of political blindness, seriously considered as the last chance for a democratic market-oriented, unified Yugoslavia, and so on? When the West fights Milosevic, it is *not* fighting its enemy, one of the last points of resistance against the liberal-democratic New World Order; it is rather fighting its own creature, a monster that grew as the result of the compromises and inconsistencies of the Western politics itself. (And, incidentally, it is the same as with Iraq: its strong position is also the result of the American strategy of containing Iran.)

In the last decade, the west followed a Hamlet-like procrastination toward Balkan, and the present bombardment effectively has all the signs of Hamlet's final murderous outburst in which a lot of people unnecessarily die (not only the king, his true target, but also his mother, Laertius, and Hamlet himself), because Hamlet acted too late, when the proper moment had already passed. We are clearly dealing with a hysterical acting out, with an escape into activity, with a gesture that, instead of trying to achieve a well-defined goal, rather bears witness to the fact that there is no such goal, that the agent is caught in a web of conflicting goals. This also accounts for the insufficiency of the otherwise correct statement that, at the Rambouillet negotiations in the early spring of 1999, the Western proposal put Yugoslavia in an untenable position, effectively stripping it of its sovereignty: it demanded that the NATO ground troops be granted free access not only to Kosovo, but to the military facilities in all of Yugoslavia; the free use of all transport facilities; the exemption from being prosecuted by the Yugoslav authorities for any crimes committed; and so on—in short, an effective occupation of Yugoslavia. Does this not raise the suspicion that, at least for the United States, the Rambouillet meeting was from the very beginning not considered a serious negotiation? Was not the goal from the very beginning to put Serbs in a position to reject the western nonnegotiable proposal and thus to provide the blueprint for the bombing by putting the blame on the Milosevic's "stubborn rejection of the peace proposal"? However, although this observation is in itself adequate, one should nonetheless take note that its "excessive" character derives not from any direct "malevolence" or aggressive intent of the west, but from the simple and quite understandable frustration at being duped for so many years by Milosevic's maneuver (recall the humiliations the UN forces were exposed in Bosnia, when they were even used as the protective shield against possible air attacks). The Western "cornering" of Yugoslavia in Rambouillet can only be properly grasped as the delayed acting out that tried to recompense for the long years of Western frustrations—its "excessive" character signals that previous unresolved tensions and frustrations were displaced onto it.

One thing is for sure: the NATO bombardment of Yugoslavia did change the global geopolitic coordinates. The unwritten pact of peaceful coexistence (the respect of each state's full sovereignty—that is, noninterference in internal affairs, even in the case of the grave violation of human rights) is over. However, the very first act of the new global police force usurping the right to punish sovereign states for their wrongdoings already signals its end, its own undermining, because it immediately became clear that the universality of human rights as its legitimization is false (that is, that the attacks on selective targets protect particular interests). The NATO bombardment of Yugoslavia also signals the end of any serious role of the UN and the Security Council: it is NATO, under U.S. guidance, that effectively pulls the strings. Furthermore, the silent pact with Russia that held until now is broken: in the terms of this pact, Russia was publicly treated as a superpower and was allowed to maintain the appearance of being one, on the condition that it did not effectively act as one. Now Russia's humiliation is open, any pretense of dignity unmasked: Russia can only openly resist or openly comply with western pressure. On the other hand, the oscillations in the West's relationship toward Russia also betrayed the confusion of their global strategy in the Balkans: because the western bombardment was a violent *passage a l'acte* lacking a clearly defined goal, after humiliating Russia, it had to turn again to Russian diplomacy to mediate the political solution of the crisis. The further logical result of this new situation will be, of course, the renewed rise of anti-Western resistance from Eastern Europe to the third world, with the sad consequence that criminal figures like Milosevic will be elevated into the model fighters against the New World Order.

So the lesson is that the alternative between the New World Order and the neoracist nationalists opposing it is a false one: these are the two sides of the same coin—the New World Order itself breeds monstrosities that it fights. This is why the protests against bombing from the reformed communist parties all around Europe, inclusive of PDS (Party of Democratic Socialism), are totally misdirected: these false protesters against the NATO bombardment of Serbia are like the caricatured pseudoleftists who oppose the trial against a drug dealer, claiming that his crime is the result of social pathology of the capitalist system. The way to fight the capitalist New World Order is not by supporting local protofascist resistances to it, but to focus on the only serious question today: how to build transnational political movements and institutions strong enough to seriously constrain the unlimited rule of the capital, and to render visible and politically relevant the fact that the local fundamentalist resistances against the New World Order, from Milosevic to le Pen and the extreme right in Europe, are part of it?

According to the media, when, at a recent meeting of the leaders of the western great powers dedicated to the politicoideological notion of the Third

Way, the Italian prime minister, d'Alema, said that one should not be afraid of the word "socialism," Clinton and, following him, Blair and Schroeder, could not restrain themselves and openly burst out laughing—this anecdote tells a lot about the problematic character of today's talk about the Third Way. The curious enigma of the second way is crucial here: today, which is the second way? That is to say, did the notion of the Third Way not emerge at the very moment when, at least in the developed west, all other alternatives, from true conservativism to radical Social Democracy, lost in the face of the triumphant onslaught of the global capitalism and its notion of liberal democracy? Is the true message of the notion of the Third Way therefore not simply that there is no second way, no actual alternative to the global capitalism, so that, in a kind of mocking pseudo-Hegelian negation of negation, this much-praised Third Way brings us back to the first and only way? The Third Way is simply global capitalism with a human face—that is, an attempt to minimize the human cost of the global capitalist machinery, the functioning of which is left undisturbed.

Let us then hope that—out of simple necessity, because for these countries, in the long run, this is their only means of survival—Russia or another country like it will invent a true and simple *second* way—a way of breaking the vicious circle of global capitalism versus nationalist closure.

WORKS CITED

Badiou, Alain. "La Sainte-Alliance et ses serviteuirs." 2001. Unpublished; available on the Internet.
Brown, Wendy. "Toward a Genealogy of Contemporary Political Moralism." In *Liberalism Out of History*, 7–33. Princeton, NJ: Princeton University Press, 2001.
Havel, Vaclav. "Kosovo and the End of the Nation-State." *New York Review of Books* 46 (June 10, 1999): 10.
Jensen, Carl. *Censored 1999: The News that Didn't Make the News.* New York: Seven Stories Press, 1999.

2 *Legal Universalism*

BETWEEN MORALITY AND POWER
IN A WORLD OF STATES

On March 24, 1999, as the North Atlantic Treaty Organization
(NATO) launched its seventy-eight-day-long series of air strikes in the territory of Serbia-Montenegro, Javier Solana, the secretary-general of NATO,
made a press statement in which he reiterated that his organization was
"not waging a war against Yugoslavia" and that he had "no quarrel with
the people of Yugoslavia." The actions were "directed against the repressive
policy of the Yugoslav leadership." As the justification of operation "Allied
Force," he stated, "We must stop the violence and bring an end to the humanitarian catastrophe now taking place in Kosovo. We have a moral duty
to do so."[1] The Kosovo campaign has become a symbol of what is "new"
in the post-1989 world order, a more or less anguished focus for debates
about the respective roles of power, law, and justice in a world conventionally understood to be ambivalently poised between "globalization" and
"fragmentation." Positions about Operation Allied Force did not arrange
themselves neatly in traditional right-left oppositions: *Realpolitik* and solidarity could both mean intervention and nonintervention. Liberals who
supported the action were apprehensive about whether that committed
them to the democratic euphoria of their states and the globalization of capitalism that seemed indissociable from it. The anti-imperialist left was em-
barrassed to find that its traditional opposition to the use of military force
by the West compelled it to support the Milosevic regime and the archaic
privileges of sovereignty.[2] I wish here to focus on the absence of any mention of law from Solana's statement, and his reference instead to a "moral
duty," an absence that reflects oddly on the official western emphasis on the
rule of law in political transition. Many lawyers have suggested that the
bombing may have been illegal but nonetheless morally necessary.[3] Although perhaps pleasurable in its tragic aspects, such a conclusion tears

wide open the fragile fabric of diplomatic consensus and exposes the aporia of a normative structure deferring simultaneously to the impossibility of ethical politics in a divided and agnostic world and the impossibility not to assess political action in the light of some ethical standpoint.

Initially, the move to "morality" may seem easy to understand. Among legal experts, the international law governing the use of force in 1999 was relatively simple and uncontested. The prohibition on the use of force in article 2(4) of the UN charter admitted of only two exceptions: use of force in self-defense (article 51) or through the authorization of the Security Council (article 42).[4] Judged against these provisions, it was very difficult to justify the bombing. But should that be the end of the matter? Surely, as Antigone has taught us, there are more important things than obedience. Obsession about formal legality has been subjected to devastating criticisms by a whole generation of postwar "realist" thought. Hans J. Morgenthau, the founder of international relations at United States universities in the 1950s, dismissed the formal prohibition of war in the Covenant of the League of Nations as an "attempt to exorcise social evils by the indefatigable repetition of magic formulae," an outright harmful inducement for passivity in face of aggression (Morgenthau, "Positivism," 260). But Morgenthau would not have endorsed Solana's reference to "moral duty" either. On the contrary, he would have seen it as a hypocritical smokescreen over an act whose principal motive was the drive for power. From the right-wing Weimar jurist Carl Schmitt—one of Morgenthau's sources of inspiration—to much of left commentary on Kosovo today, talk about "moral duty" has been understood to veil the singularity of political decisions that act as the *pouvoir constituant* of concrete international orders (Schmitt, *Der Nomos*, 200 et seq.).[5] In 1999, that order would no longer accept formal sovereignty as a plausible defense for activities that the NATO powers saw as fundamentally unacceptable. If so, then Solana's moral duty would reveal a form of imperialism from which the project of cosmopolitan right always tried to save us.

Among the many problems of "Kosovo" lies that of the justification of constraint in the conditions of moral skepticism. The idea of cosmopolitan right—universal law based on agreement between free republics—arose from the experience that moral principles were intangible, subjective, and prone to misuse by those in positions of authority. This is why western legal thought has read the Westphalian peace of 1648 as the starting point of cosmopolitan modernity. If now knowledge of "moral duty" has become finally available—we have become reenchanted—then there is no reason for despair. Empire is our fate, but a benevolent empire that is merely the institutional reflection of what has already been decreed by morality. But when did empire not claim that it was merely implementing the dictates of some higher order? Surely it is hard to believe that the dualisms that have, since Augus-

tine, been inscribed in western political consciousness as a distinction between a divine and a temporal realm have suddenly ceased producing what
Sloterdijk calls "Christianized state-cynicism," the drive to explain the enslavement of others as their liberation from vice (234–38). As the war on terror and the American occupation of Iraq continue, many critics—not least
"old European" critics—have sought refuge from something akin to the old
ius publicum Europaeum: sovereignty, formal independence, international
law and organization.[6] But nostalgia for a melancholy system of formal
equality between equally evil sovereignties is hardly warranted. Between imperial cynicism and bureaucratic stasis, how can we choose? Does the standpoint of "morality" and "humanity" automatically project the adversary as
the one who is immoral or inhuman and justify the taking of extreme measures? Is there room for a cosmopolitan right that can distinguish between
imperialism and solidarity, a concept of the universal that is not just another
particularity distinguished only by the force of its technologies of hegemony?

A Prehistory of Western Legal Universalism

European legend finds in Stoic philosophy the view of the world as
governed by a single normative code: natural law. Irrespective of ethnic or
cultural difference, human beings belong together in a single cosmopolitan
space. The character of the *cosmopolis* has been explained differently in different ages, the explanations reflecting changing understandings of Europe's
own identity and the value contemporaries have given to European institutions. In Cicero's *De re publica* and *De legibus* (54–51 BCE), the idea of a single true law based on the right reason became a philosophical defense of Roman empire. If "all nations at all times will be bound by this one eternal and
unchangeable law" and this law underlay Roman political institutions, the
way to Empire was firmly set: "Do we not see that the best people are given
the right to rule by nature herself, with the greatest benefit to the weak?" (Cicero 71, 73). Law was not simply the praetor's edict or the legislator's whim,
but reflected the one reason that differentiated humans from animals and
made them resemble gods. The political implication was clear: reason being
the law, all people sharing reason, they also share the law (including "procedures of justice")—"and those who have these things in common must be
considered members of the same state" (Cicero 113).[7] The one who understands this "is not bound by human walls as the citizen of one particular spot
but a citizen of the whole world as if it were a single city" (Cicero 127).
Rome is law, law is reason, reason is universal: Rome is universal.

In the Justinian Code, and in Augustine, reason changes color, and so
does empire. Irrespective of the changing places of its political boundaries,

the *Respublica Christiana* saw itself as enacted by God to govern the affairs of believers and nonbelievers alike. Again, no separate defense for the Crusades was needed: proselytism arose naturally from belief in the one God whose representative on Earth was the Catholic church. If there was doubt about the justice of the war—and there often was, as the jurist-theologian Francisco de Vitoria speculated at the beginning of the sixteenth century— then the prince should accept the verdict of his advisers, assumed to be Christian elders. There was no "morality" here that would have been separate from the dictates of the faith: even acting justly would be a sin if it were done for reasons other than faith.[8] The famous debate at Valladolid in 1550 between the humanist scholar Juan Ginés de Sepúlveda and the Dominican theologian Bartolomé de Las Casas may have vindicated the latter's view that the Indians, like the Spanish, were in possession of a soul and governed by God's universal law. That conclusion also provided a public defense for Spanish trade and proselytizing as well as a language of rectitude through which the Indians would henceforth be disciplined (Anghie 321). Las Casas was no less colonialist than Cortés, as Tzvetan Todorov has shown, and the opposition between the principle of love and the principle of economic interest that we see in their juxtaposition permanently affected the understanding of the ambivalence of Empire (Todorov 168–82 and passim).

So when in 1608 the Dutch lawyer Hugo de Groot (Grotius) defended the capture by his cousin, Jacob van Heemskerk, of a Portuguese vessel with a cargo the value of which was not far off the total annual budget of the English government at the time, and did this in terms of a natural law of private relationships, he was engaging in an already firm tradition of projecting as universal the principles of European law, especially those of possessive individualism: the right of every man, everywhere, to seize upon property not already belonging to another, and to protect it by all means available.[9] As far as the Indians were concerned, Grotius wrote in 1625, war could be lawfully waged on them if they were in breach of natural law, even if that breach were not to occasion an injury to oneself (Grotius, vol. 2, Ch. 20, sect.40). And as the Swiss legal consultant Emmerich de Vattel published in 1758 what professional men have since early nineteenth century regarded as the first modern treatment of international law, he merely updated a tradition that spoke of universal law in terms of two sets of relationships: those between European states and those that Europeans entertained with others. Taking his distance from the Spanish conquest, this acquaintance of Voltaire and admirer of Locke conceived his law as providing the right of possession on the basis of the cultivation of the soil: "while the conquest of the civilized Empires of Peru and Mexico was a notorious usurpation, the establishment of various colonies upon the continent of North America might, if done within just limits, have been entirely lawful" (Vattel 36, 85–88). However noble the American savage was, the enlightened mind could not think that his idleness could found a claim for the possession of a whole continent. Thus when Chief Justice Marshall in a series of famous decisions in the 1820s approved of the right of Indian occupancy as against enterprising colonists in the United States, he also gave the federal government the right to extinguish it in the interests of ordered expansion.[10]

This familiar narrative of universal law seems discontinuous, fragile, far removed from the density of the principles of Western Enlightenment through which legal modernity has sought to vest meaning to its past. A few passages from the writings of a few jurists at several centuries' intervals provides a poor foundation for the intuition about historical progress being about uniting (or perhaps reuniting) mankind under a single, cosmopolitan regime. Pitching his objectives much higher, Kant famously dismissed Grotius and his like as "sorry comforters"; the French socialist Pierre-Joseph Proudhon, writing in a lonely exile in Brussels in 1861, had this to say about the profession of Grotius and Vattel: "Leur prétendu science de droit des gens, que dis-je? le corps entier du droit, tels qu'ils l'ont concu et exposé, est un échafaudage de fictions auxquels ils n'ajoutent pas eux-mêmes créance" (9).

Law as Civilization

Modern legal internationalism was born out of the activities of a handful of liberal lawyers in the aftermath of the Franco-Prussian war. In September 1873 eleven men met at the town hall of Ghent in Belgium to set up the *Institut de droit international*, the first professional society of international lawyers. As article 1 of its statute, they defined the mission of the institute and of their profession to be "the organ of the juridical conscience of the civilized world." By the end of the century, chairs of international law had been established at most European universities. The Hague Conferences of 1899 and 1907 signaled to many contemporaries that European societies had definitely embarked on the path toward peace under law that was indissociable from the progress of a *civilization* to which the lawyers became an "organ." Europeans were bound not because there was a super state to police them but because "their moral nature imposes upon them the duties of good faith, of concession of redress for wrongs, of regard for the personal dignity of their fellows, and to a certain extent sociability" (Hall 45). The rules of European law were like the rules of a Victorian social club, derived from the culture of civilized men. But if law was cultural in this way, then of course it could not be applied beyond Europe. As Cambridge professor John Westlake saw it, the native did not possess legal sovereignty because he did not possess the (cultural) *concept* of sovereignty (247–48). The native did enjoy a private right of property that enabled him to trade with Europeans on European terms as well as "human rights" that integrated him as a proper object of the *mission civilicatrice*. But native communities differed from European states as well as from each other in such radical ways that, as the Institute's almost twenty-year study on whether European customary international law could be applied in "the Orient" concluded, no general rules on relations with them could be laid down (Twiss 301–11; Bulmerincq 259–63).

Modern legal universalism started in the late nineteenth century by an argument that played on a crude distinction between "civilized," "half-civilized," and "savage" nations that reflected the educated European common sense at the time. This idea found other legal expressions in Sir Henry Sumner Maine's casual distinction between "progressive" and "stationary" cultures, and the Swiss-German political theorist Johann Caspar Bluntschli's speculations about the "Aryan" state as the highest form of social organization (Maine 18–20; Bluntschli 82–90).[11] The lawyers may have disagreed about how rapidly progress would lead into "the civilization of the Orient," and whether there were intermediate stages in the process, but it was impossible not to think in terms of a universal history, and that it meant that everyone would come to resemble Europeans.

But the non-European community could never really become European, no matter how much it tried, as Turkey had always known and as Japan was to find out, to its bitter disappointment. The Ottoman Empire's celebrated entry into the realm of European public law in 1856 had little consequence to the dismissive treatment that European powers gave to the protests of the Sublime Porte as they encroached gradually deeper into its decaying imperial realm. The existence of a "standard of civilization" was a myth in the sense that there was never anything to gain (see Gong). Every concession was a matter of negotiation, every status dependent on agreement, quid pro quo. Here was the paradox: if there was no firm standard for civilization, then everything depended on what Europeans approved. What Europeans approved, again, depended on the degree aspirant communities were ready to play with European rules. But the more eagerly the non-Europeans wished to prove that they played with European rules, the more suspect they became. In order to attain equality, the non-European community must accept Europe as its master—but to accept a master was proof that one was not equal.

Between Ideology and Power: The Social Concept of Law

No doubt, the concept of civilization hardly provided a solid foundation for universal law. Besides, by the end of 1918, little was left in Europe of the assumption that civilization necessarily coincided with what took place in Europe. Among European populations, the imperial euphoria was over. Such disappointments gave vent to the old theory about cosmopolitan law not being a proper law at all but a utopia perhaps reassuring to European elites but useless in the government of international order. To defend the idea of a universal law, lawyers responded by two techniques: by adopting a rationalist political theory that depicted law in terms of self-legislation by states, and by moving to sociology that was grounded on the assumption of (economic) interdependence.

Georg Jellinek, Max Weber's friend from Heidelberg, claimed that international law was no different from domestic public law. Both arose from self-legislation by the state. This argument was received by analogy from Kantian ethics and founded both the domestic *Rechtsstaat* as well as the re-. ality of international law. A truly autonomous self legislated to itself, its autonomy being conclusive explanation for why it is bound. Analogously, sovereignty meant the state's capacity to legislate for itself (by treaty) and to be bound by the law thus legislated (Jellinek). But why would the state legislate for itself? Because of the "nature of the living conditions of the international world" (*"Natur der Lebensverhältnisse"*). A state could only attain its purposes by collaborating with others. If Jellinek still accepted the theory of interdependence as an article of his liberal faith, the Swiss jurist Max Huber, future president of the Permanent Court of International Justice, sketched in 1911 a historical sociology under which "progress" would consist everywhere of an increasing awareness of the need of cooperation and its institutionalization. The functional "unions" of the last years of the nineteenth century would gradually transform into general-purpose organizations that would pave the way for world federation (Huber).

A sociological theory of cosmopolitan law was developed in the 1920s and 1930s especially in France in relation to debates about the nature of the League of Nations. Durkheim had assumed that even modern, industrial societies would cohere through the work of organic solidarity that compelled individuals to cooperate not in spite but precisely because of increasing specialization and division of labor. Autonomy fostered interdependence. The philosophy of "solidarism" that became an article of faith for the liberals of the Third Republic taught universal integration as an objective social necessity, gradually making obsolete the archaic forms of statehood. From such premises lawyers derived a syndicalist federalism in which the League would become a global coordinator of the activities of the "professions," which, in the Comtean image, would replace states as the centers around which modern individuals everywhere would construct their identities (Hayward 19–48; Borgetto).[12] There was little distance between "solidarism" and the theory of cosmopolitan right based on a shared civilization. Both looked at what European modernity had to offer and generalized that into a theory of universal progress. The Paris professor Georges Scelle, for instance, saw no intrinsic merit in national self-determination, assumed that for cultural and other reasons the populations of the colonies would prefer to be ruled by the French, and depicted the mandates system in the League as a form of educating the natives to see the benefits of economic and technological modernity. Not all lawyers were solidarists. Some still espoused a Christian naturalism, and others followed Kant's arguments to ground their universalism. Both read positive law "backward" as a manifestation of humanitarian principles or axioms of formal order. By the 1930s the increasing number of treaties and legal processes—arbitration and adjudication—made it seem plausible to imagine the international world as governed by a positive world law. The League Covenant was a world constitution, and juristic arguments about general principles and domestic law analogies guaranteed that no gaps existed in the normative framework projected more as a matter of professional imagination than formal legislation.[13]

Deformalization

As the League slowly fell apart in the 1930s, little of these explanations preserved credibility. Rationalistic or sociological points about solidarity provided no more stable a foundation for a universal law than civilization had done. Among many others, E. H. Carr mocked the hypocrisy behind the assumption of a harmony of interests behind the facade of international politics, that "peculiar combination of platitude and falseness" that dominated the rhetoric or jurists and politicians in the interwar era (Carr 53).

In economic life, harmony may have been plausible as long as the economies kept expanding; but little of that was visible after 1929. The jargon of solidarity became an instrument of dominant powers to convince others that unless they yielded, retaliation would follow. The "supposedly absolute and universal principles" declared by Wilson, Briand, or Eden "were not principles at all, but the unconscious reflexions of national policy based on a particular interpretation of national interest at a particular time . . . as soon as the attempt is made to apply these supposedly abstract principles to a concrete political situation, they are revealed as the transparent disguises of selfish vested interests" (Carr 87–88). Waiting to be indicted among the war criminals in Nuremberg, the same sentiment was echoed by Carl Schmitt in his analysis of the end of the European age, published in 1950 as the *Nomos der Erde im Völkerrecht des Jus Publicum Europaeum*. The classical law of equality between European nations whose great merit had been the limitation of (European) war as a war between "just enemies" had collapsed in face of an economically driven, sea-based Anglo-American moral universalism. The new morality had no content that would be independent from the policies of the States invoking it:

> Of course, everyone is for law, morality, ethics and peace; no one will want to commit injustice; but *in concreto* the relevant question is always who shall decide what in this case is law, what counts as peace, what is a threat or disturbance of peace, with what means it shall be restored, when a situation has become normal or "peaceful" and so on. (Schmitt, "Zu Friedrich Meinecke," 50; my translation)

Behind the moral principles were American (and Soviet) interests. The turn from formal law to morality intensified hostilities, giving the friend-enemy antagonism the quality of almost theological struggle in which there would be no compromise. In a war waged in the name of humanity the enemy would appear as an enemy of humanity *tout court* against which no measures would be excessive (Schmitt, *Concept of the Political*, 51, 54).

Many such ideas were shared by Morgenthau, whose 1951 analysis of the international transformations was practically identical with Schmitt's. He too saw the European order being replaced by a technological and moral undermining of traditional diplomacy. The quality of the international order did not depend on law but on "the existence of national communities capable of preserving order and realizing moral values within the limits of their power" (Morgenthau, *In Defense*, 38). Like Schmitt, Morgenthau interpreted international law and international institutions—the allocation of international problems to technical and legal experts—as an attempt at neutralization and depoliticization of what were in fact political choices: the policy of law was the policy of the status quo powers. The liberals had never understood the fundamental nature of the desire for power and had therefore been bitterly disappointed. Instead, their use of moral and legal language intensified conflicts and made settlement more difficult. "Peace-loving nations" came into constant conflict with "criminal" ones. The result would be a "fight to the death or to 'unconditional surrender of all those who adhere to another, a false and evil, 'ideal' and 'way of life'" (Morgenthau, *Politics Among Nations*, 182–83).

Much of Morgenthau's discussion of the primacy of power in international affairs suggests a future international order based on a balance between large spaces (*Grossräume*), as proposed by Schmitt, and his emphasis on the role of the statesman resembles Schmitt's decisionism. There is, however, an important difference between the attitudes of the two Weimar jurists on the role of law. For Schmitt, law merely ratified what was decreed by the "concrete order." For Morgenthau, despite his acerbic critiques of liberal legalism, law continued to be removed from the facts of power. "Power," he wrote, "engenders that revolt against power, which is as universal as the aspiration of power itself." This revolt was expressed in "ethics, mores and law"—all three constituting the substance of which political ideologies were "but a reflection": "Superior power gives no right, either moral or legal, to do with that power all that it is physically capable of doing" (Morgenthau, *Politics Among Nations*, 169, 170). "Realism" saw law either as a completely epiphenomenal ratification of the concrete order, or as an expression of the revolt of private conscience. Between power and private morality, where is law?

Legal Instrumentalism

The critiques of law rehearsed by Schmitt and Morgenthau in the 1950s and 1960s brought about international relations as an academic discipline whose policy relevance was guaranteed by its alignment with the anti-ideological American foreign policy elites around Henry Kissinger and George Kennan (Hoffmann 3–24; Smith 189–206). At the same time, the consolidation of legal realism at American law schools transformed international law's image from that of a formal structure of intersovereign relationships into a policy science. Cosmopolitan right did not contain any determined image of universal society. Instead, it deferred to political processes of interpretation and application. Because of its "normative-ambiguity," law was defensible only as a means of social engineering (McDougal 143–44, 188–91). Men such as Harold Lasswell from Chicago or Myres S. McDougal from Yale taught of law in fully instrumental terms: instead of a collection of formal rules, it was to be seen as a process of decision making to further what they called the "goal values of human dignity." The lawyer became an anticommunist policy adviser whose universalism was that of a free world confronting the dark empire (McDougal and Lasswell 42–154).[14]

Such instrumentalization was evidenced by the development that Weber had analyzed as the deformalization of law in complex modernity. As the forms of international communication and interdependence diversified, they became increasingly regulated by informal, flexible understandings and expectations between dominant actors. International standards enshrined broad notions of equity and reasonableness, the protection of good faith and legitimate expectations. From the 1980s, international economic and environmental treaties, for example, were concluded as "framework agreements" laying down procedures for negotiation and information exchange and avoiding clear-cut substantive obligations.[15] Human rights standards were defined in terms of complex systems of rules and exceptions, and the doctrine of "interdependence and indivisibility" introduced contextual balancing standards into their administration.[16] Economic and political conditions varied endlessly. Each regulation could therefore always only be ad hoc. The desired objective was everything: any rule completely deferred to it.

At the same time, legal regulation started to emerge from the most varied sources. Decisions by transnational companies on standards and criteria came to play an increasing normative role and international business
was conducted under a privately created *lex mercatoria*—an "extremely indeterminate" set of "broad principles that change in their application from
case to case" (Teubner 21). Governmental agencies—ministries, other regulatory agencies, even courts—were disaggregating and coordinating their
behavior through informal international networks (Slaughter 183–97).
These developments were paralleled by the rise in the international relations academia of a study of international "regimes"—that is, informal systems of norms, principles, expectations, and practices that explained international cooperation from fundamentally realistic premises.[17] As a result,
cosmopolitan right was reduced into a tool in the hands of those whom
power and accident had put in decision-making positions. This is the context where Solana's call for *moral duty* finds its application—as a fallback
position of a consciousness that has "deconstructed" all structure and for
which, therefore, only the singularity of the decision remains. Here it aligns
with contemporary cosmopolitan moral theory.

The Imperialism of "Moral Duty"

Initially, the call for morality to direct the international decision
maker seems no different from the naturalism of Las Casas, or Grotius. As
such, it would be vulnerable to the Enlightenment critique of the manipu-
lability of the postulated moral sensibilities, their being just the political
preferences of the law appliers, a new Middle Ages. But the instrumental-
ists of the postrealist era claim that that although that would be true of ordinary morality, it is not so in regard to moral norms that transgress the
preferences of single individuals, clans, or nations. These are norms—such
as universal human rights—the universality of which results from their having been derived through a purely formal system of reasoning, Cicero's
recta ratio resuscitated. Because reason (in contrast to preference) is universal, these commands enjoy universal validity. That is to say, every thinking person, state, or people would choose them—or would have reason to
choose them—from behind a "veil of ignorance" about the particular interests or preferences that person, group, or state might have.[18] Even the
Serbians, or the Iraqi, if they only understood their interests properly,
would endorse them. This is why they constitute an effective and legitimate
justification for international action.

It follows that a person, group, or state that does not share them is not
only of another opinion (or preference), but also has made a mistake about

something that that person, group, or state should think rational for itself, too. Universalizability in moral theory leads automatically to expansion as political practice. If my principle is valid because it is universal, then I not only may but perhaps must try to make others accept it as well. If I engage in contacts with others, I need not be open to their preferences because I already know that mine are valid for them too. The object of my encounter can only be the transformation of the way they see the world, having them accept my principles too (because they are not really "mine" but universal).[19]

But this is, as many critics since Hegel have argued, an impossible position. No actual person, state, or people lives in abstraction from particular histories, contexts, and qualities.[20] Irrespectively of the logical merits of an argument about rules to which everyone has reason to agree because they have been derived in a noncontextual way, that position has never been open to anyone, and it is doubtful whether the principles thus invented would actually be persuasive.[21] If, however, one persists in thinking that this is what one must assume as right in order to avoid the otherwise compelling conclusion that one is simply imposing one's own preferences on others, then the temptation emerges to interpret one's own behavior in this light. Consensus on a formal language is mistaken for political agreement. One claims to be fighting a just war, or obeying "moral duty"—and the result is empire in either of two forms.

First case is the one where the decision maker believes that his or her preferences fulfill the criteria postulated by the theory about universal (rational) norms. In such case, every deviating position will appear as irrational, or at least as partially subjective, historically conditioned, politically biased, an atavistic residue from religious, ethnic, or other such particular moralities.[22] It may be taken into account for strategic reasons, but it enjoys no independent normative validity vis-à-vis the decision maker. In due course, with increasing enlightenment (defined as gradual acceptance of the noncontextual position), it would be given up, or at least it would loosen its obsessive hold on those who still cling to it. In a deep sense, having such preference demonstrates ignorance and error, induced perhaps by "evil" manipulation by the leaders of that other community when measured against the norms or policies that have been demonstrated as universally valid. These positions might be called *rational imperialism.*[23]

In the second alternative, the decision maker shares the view that the only legitimate norm is one that enjoys noncontextual validity but does not think that he or she (or anyone else) is now in possession of it. Every empirical position is contextually and historically based. "How do I know that my understanding of human rights is the right one?" If I have no response to such question, then I either fall into apathy or have nothing to say against the one who accuses me of imperialism. But if I do possess a substantive response, then I have found God, and I have no longer any need for the fallback position that formal law is. The course I am likely to follow, however, is to persist in making justifications that refer back to the non-contextual assumption—although I have no idea as to why I might be entitled to do that, or at least no means to translate my intuitions into the language of public policy. This will produce the same outcome as the former alternative, with the significant twist, however, that the decision maker is now acting in bad faith. He or she does not think that the policy enjoys the noncontextual validity that the theory of legitimate decision making requires. But deviating preferences are still overruled by their particularism. This could be called *cynical imperialism*.[24]

Now both of these positions are distinctly *imperialist* in the sense that other positions are overruled not because of their merits, but as lacking the special character (noncontextuality) of the norms the decision maker holds. They are not just different but at a different level of seriousness or justifiability altogether: "irrational" where the decision maker's is "rational," "subjective" or "passionate" against the decision maker's "objective" or "reasonable" position.[25] Because they are so, there never is—and can never be—dialogue between the decision maker and those with different preferences. Equality is excluded. Only imperialism remains, as Schmitt wrote more than sixty years ago, describing the new order through the discriminatory concept of war. The different-thinking Other becomes not just my adversary, but an enemy of humanity because he fails to accept what I know is true of all humanity. Therefore, as John Rawls writes now, the nonliberal, nondecent state is the *outlaw* state (90).

A world where decision makers learn that one is entitled to think one's preferences justified only if they are justified for everyone else, too, is bound to tragedy, or imperialism, or both. Gliding from a "continuous discomfort of a perpetually uneasy conscience" involved in acting upon preferences that one knows others do not (necessarily) share, to identifying those preferences as universal is, as Morgenthau observed, the most human of inclinations (*Politics Among Nations* 193).[26] If nobody's positions are justifiable in the way demanded by the theory of rational coercion, and that because of this, nobody had a justifiable claim for allegiance, then all decision making in a deformalized context will always appear as the use of arbitrary power. For Morgenthau, the only exit from hypocrisy or cynicism was to adopt a tragic posture on life as struggle between incompatible but equally valid (because equally arbitrary) preferences. Independently of the availability or desirability of *that* option, many people follow another itinerary. Once the critique of formalism has broken the constraint of rules, and the quest for the fabled moral norms that dictate rational choices for everyone has turned into an unending political controversy,[27] they turn away from that task in frustration and fall back on intuition—justifying this nonetheless as if it had been produced by contemplation of a moral theory that everyone has the reason to accept.

To escape the megalomania of the first path and the cynicism awaiting at the end of the second, the tempting alternative is to turn back to "realist" political science, and to accept as correct, and controlling, not only its critique of formalism but also its political agenda. Do not its complex moral ponderings, multifactor calculations, dependent and independent variables, graphs, or quixotic discourses suggest an altogether deeper mode of understanding than formal rules or moral pathos do? In this way, the antiformalist technique, and the indeterminacy of the search for "moral duty" that accompanies it, leads into accepting as authoritative the styles of argument and substantive outcome that "realist" political science has been able to scavenge from the moral battlefield. Thoroughly instrumental as that political science is, and located at predominantly United States universities, this avenue is only a step removed from underwriting the preferences of the Western foreign policy elite.

Critical Universalism: What Room for Law?

The justification of Operation Allied Force by reference to a "moral duty" is not least problematic because of the hypocrisy involved. Why would moral duty apply here but not to the north-south relationship, the spectacular decrease of development assistance in the 1990s, the death in the third world of 30,000 children per day as a result of poverty-induced disease? As Western lawyers and politicians concentrate on great crises, war, and terrorism, they overlook the fact that, for example, in 1998, 588,000 deaths were caused by wars, whereas 18 million resulted from starvation from preventable diseases. The decade covering the end of the Cold War and the establishment of the World Trade Organization was discussed as one of cooperation and institutional innovation. And yet, while an enormous amount of material resources was freed in the west, the world's richest countries (members of the OECD) reduced their official development aid (ODA) in 1987–97 from 0.33% of their combined GNPs to 0.24%.[28] Judged against such and many comparable statistics, the rhetoric of morality in Kosovo or that of the "just war" against terrorism since 2001 seems misplaced.[29] The suffering caused by Western ways of life becomes invisible because the west's political discourse is already saturated by a sense of moral superiority created by Kosovo and the victimization resulting from September 11. No doubt, that sense is a reflex of the west's moral failures in the twentieth century. But the guilt of nations is very unevenly dispensed. Events related to World War II in

Europe are increasingly covered—but little of colonialism or slavery and the slave trade.[30] The determination to strike in Serbia in 1999 still contrasts strikingly to the passivity in Rwanda in the spring of 1994. But the fact of hypocrisy and double standards is not a conclusive argument either for or against action such as Kosovo. One may engage in the right action inconsistently or for the wrong motives. Obsessed with coherent principles or pure motives, critics of the NATO action have sometimes let their concern with the moral status of western states or statesmen overrule their ability to assess Kosovo in its singularity. Outside the partisan concerns of liberal and left critics, the problem of Kosovo was about the possibility of universal justice in the conditions of moral agnosticism. This problem has been highlighted by the way the war against terror was expressly launched as a crusade against "evil." The "moral duty" of Kosovo found its hidden underside in the violent rejection of the one to whom the moral light shines differently.

Here in conclusion, I would only wish to trace an argument that will seek to show—perhaps in a rather standard liberal fashion—why those problems lead back to international law, albeit a law that would no longer pretend to be undeconstructible in the way old naturalist or positivist theories claimed. The skeptics were right to hold that international law does not contain a transparent ideal of the good society (to replace moral doubt). But they were wrong to suggest that it thus was either a conservative obstacle toward the attainment of just causes or an instrument for those in power to realize their political agendas. Both views separate "moral duty" from law and relegate it to the status of a preexisting, private datum whose entry into the political is either prevented or facilitated by the law's objective technique. This involves a misunderstanding of law, political justice, and their relationship, and it undermines the skeptical criticism itself.

For if the law is indeterminate, then there is nothing that may obstruct or realize any purposes, only an ideological obfuscation that makes the work of hegemony appear as obedience to the law. In such case, reference to "moral duty" might appear as a sobering affirmation that in the absence of an objective legal order I can only act on the basis of moral impulse. Undoubtedly, such impulse may often emerge as a work of ressentiment, or an attempt to manipulate public debate. But even as it is felt honestly, it will remain a matter of the private conscience, perhaps as "the experience of the undecidable" (Derrida 26). In the public realm, however, decision needs to be taken. To refer in such case to moral duty is to back down from the political to the private. In the conditions of moral skepticism, it is the arrogance of fait accompli: this is what I have decided, this is how I will act. As Schmitt and others have pointed out, such attitude casts the enemy—the Serbs, the Taliban, Saddam Hussein—as someone with whom there is no political community and so no political antagonism. Instead, the struggle is existential: this is what "I" do. My being what "I" am is defined by this act. The norm—moral duty—now becomes a datum on which I depend for my identity: there is nothing to discuss, no compromise to make, no measure excessive.

This is a world of solipsism, and of empire, as Hans Kelsen, Schmitt's antagonist and one of the past century's most brilliant legal thinkers, pointed out (*Problem der Souveränität* 151 et seq.). Not merely universality but all community is excluded. In the moral world, only I exist. But the social world by definition involves an encounter. The moral meets with the political in the passing of the judgment.[31] Because it thinks morality not trustworthy, classical political theory refers the judgment to law. But what if law (like any economic, social, or moral structure) is indeterminate? What if law is not an objective and neutral representative of something (legislative will, community interest) beyond itself? This is what political theory considers a scandal. But it need not be. For only if the law does not already represent some external ("objective") structure can it remain open for the articulation of any moral impulse, any subjectively felt violation, any conception of what is just. Only then it can pretend to universality.

The judgment cannot be reduced to the law. But a judgment that nevertheless refers to law thereby also refers to what is shared and thus beyond the solipsism of the moral impulse. It calls for the acceptance or rejection of what has been decided by reference to standards assumed to be shared within a community and thus *becomes itself an aspect of the work toward it*. As international law has the aspiration of universality, it compels those that make claims under it to make those claims in a universal way. Even as the claims, as Ernesto Laclau has observed, often have to do with the recognition of particular identities (typically claims of self-determination, sovereignty, human rights), they do this in terms of articulating a lack suffered by the subject in universal terms: to be full in my identity, this is what I need (Laclau 20–35, 48–51). To argue about whether the NATO bombing violated Serbia's legal rights (sovereignty, independence) involves an assessment of the status of the 500 to 1,000 Serbians that were killed by Operation Allied Force (there is no single authoritative number) by reference to a universal standard—and thus that those deaths were not of aliens but of members of the human community, equal to the Kosovars or, indeed, of NATO pilots.[32] However much a violation is felt as a special wrong by the person suffering it, the ability to claim redress through law requires the translation of that special wrong into a species of a universal wrong—a wrong that would be equally condemnable, whoever had suffered it. This is the meaning of the legal isolation of the Guantánamo prisoners, too. To be outside of law (in this case, both of U.S. and international law) is to be excommunicated from membership in a moral and political community and thus ultimately from one's sharing of the universal quality of a human being.

In other words, a universal community is not only presumed but constructed by an international law that precisely due to its indeterminacy does not a priori exclude the articulation of any violations—and the aspirations of justice that different communities have—into a public discourse. When invoked as a public defense of one's acts, "moral duty" or "fight against evil" do not allow this. Only the judgment of the legal correctness of one's act provides a point of passage from moral or religious duty—the nondetermined decision—to political justice. Even as always a weak, deconstructible opening, it still remains the only such opening. International law's merit lies in its artificiality. It does not presume the existence of a prepolitical community or structure that it would only be called on to "reflect." This is where the constructions of international law surveyed above failed, fixing themselves into a determined image of "civilization," a particular form of "progress," a certain interpretation of "reason" and thus appeared as unjust mechanisms of exclusion—exclusion of the non-European, the preindustrial, the nonstate, and so on.[33] This is why, too, lamenting about the lack of a European demos as a purported precondition for a democratic European Union is such a mistake. The task of European law is to *construct* such demos: imagined by the law on which its identity is based (Weiler 337–48). Legal structure does not realize a prepolitical justice but acts as the surface on which the search for justice is conducted. But of course justice is constantly deferred; the work of politics is never ending, the limits of community are in constant flux. We need law because we are not the same, because we need closeness while preserving distance, recognition without assimilation. At its best, this is what positive law gives by its refusal to be merely a translation of something beyond itself.

A judgment that would be fully determined would not be an act of justice—but nor would it be an act of law. A fact of the structure reproducing itself, it would have no room for freedom or democracy. It would presume a community of automatons, the ultimate totalitarian utopia. But a judgment that invokes "moral duty" or "fight against evil" reduces (in conditions of skepticism) the political to the private, makes others appear as merely raw material for the decision makers' emotions.[34] To exit from such unappealing alternatives, it is necessary to advance beyond the jurisprudence of positivism and naturalism. There is no irreducible opposition between moral right or wrong as determining what a person should do, or "social justice" as what politics should attain, and "law." In its indeterminate being, law provides the path from morality to justice, solipsism to universality, if always only in a temporary, and deconstructible, sense. Kelsen was right to insist on the independence of law from morality and sociology; but he was wrong to think that this was all there was to say. The separation was meaningful as part of a theory of knowledge, the aim to define them by reference to the ways in which they can be known. This was of course Kelsen's project—to create law as science.[35] But inasmuch as we do not share that project, we are no longer tied with a concept of law that is premised on an absolute contrast to morality or justice. From outside epistemology, it is possible to understand law *as the justice that comes*.[36] Then law's indeterminacy would be merely another name for the becoming-of-justice that it performs, the realization-in-society that it brings about, always partially, always through political controversy. The important point here is that there is no more "authentic" form of justice or community than these. The work of justice and community never ends and is a work carried out through law: an open-ended, indeterminate, conflictual, and ambivalent law, a law proper for the conditions of freedom and democracy.

So finally, the reference to "moral duty" by NATO's secretary-general in 1999 was unobjectionable insofar as it expressed a sense that the judgment did not simply reproduce some preexisting normative structure. But it fell short of an acceptable defense to the extent that it referred back to the decision maker's private conscience, perversely either casting the secretary-general as God or appearing as a cynical dismissal of any need to explain. The absence of law from Solana's statement in 1999, or from America's actions in Iraq in 2003 was their great problem; it closed the door for evaluating the action by reference to standards other than those that NATO or the White House had unilaterally applied. It closed the door for examining the use of power in terms of struggle toward just conditions of public life. Each attack was reduced to an impulse, a reflex symptom of political structures resigned to private ressentiment.

NOTES

1. NATO Press release (1999) 041 (March 24, 1999).

2. For an elaborate discussion of these dilemmas, cf. Michel Feher, *Powerless by Design*.

3. E.g., Simma, 1–22. For useful discussions of the international lawyers' reaction, cf. Schieder, 663, 691–98; and Corten, 223–59.

4. For a recent overview, cf. Christine Gray, *International Law*.

5. Recourse to ethics in the justification of Kosovo as a prelude to "ethic cleansing" is a central theme in Virilio, *Stratégie de la déception*, e.g., 31.

6. For one of the more interesting and complex reactions in this vein, see Giovanna Borradori, *Philosophy in a Time of Terror*.

7. Cicero: "Those who have been given reason by nature have also been given right reason, and therefore law too, which is right reason in commands and prohibitions" (117).

8. Vitoria, *De indis*, second relectio, sect. 25, 174. Cf. further Koskenniemi, *From Apology to Utopia*, 73–83.

9. For a recent discussion, cf. Tuck, *Rights of War and Peace*, 78–108.

10. *Johnson vs. McIntosh*, 21 US (1822), 579.

11. For this argument in much more depth, cf. Koskenniemi, *Gentle Civilizer*, 12–97.

12. For a strong statement by a leading solidarist lawyer, cf. Scelle, *Précis du Droit des gens*.

13. Cf. in particular Lauterpacht, *Function of Law*; and commentary in Koskenniemi, *Gentle Civilizer*, 354–412.

14. Cf. McDougal and Lasswell, 42–154; and for a useful analysis, Rosenthal, *L'Étude*.

15. For a good example, cf. the 1982 UN Convention on the Law of the Sea and the analysis in Kennedy, *International Legal Structures*, 201–44.

16. I have made this argument in general terms in "The Politics of International Law," 1–32; and in regard to human rights in "The Effect of Rights on Political Culture," 99–116.

17. The classic is Keohane, *After Hegemony*.

18. For a recent reformulation, cf. Rawls, *Law of Peoples*, 32–33.

19. This is the objective of the foreign policy of "liberal peoples" in Rawls, *Law of Peoples*, 92–93.

20. The argument from a hypothetical choice situation must build on the dubious assumption that the individual self can exist in abstraction from its (historically contingent) properties or the ends it pursues. Cf. Sandel, *Liberalism and the Limits of Justice*, 50–65.

21. That a minimal morality offered by the hypothetical choice will be unresponsive to the aspirations of any "dense" culture is argued in Walzer, *Interpretation and Moral Criticism*, 11–18.

22. This is how the conflicts in the 1990s in Africa or the former Yugoslavia were characterized so as to play down the political element involved and to justify the "international community's" apparently neutral (and often ineffective) involvement in "managing" them. Cf. Feher, *Powerless by Design*, 45–47, 54–68.

23. Much of "democratic fundamentalism" comes under this heading, giving no independent normative standing for sovereignty or the effective control of a government over a population. It deduces the unacceptability of a regime immediately from its having not been instituted by determined rituals of popular consultation. Often it concludes that there must be a right (or even a duty) of intervention by others to oust such regime from office. For two recent critiques, cf. Roth, *Governmental Illegitimacy*, esp. 34–35, 413–30; and Marks, *Riddle of All Constitutions*. Both suggest that to posit a right to democracy may raise more problems than it resolves, inasmuch as "[s]uch a 'right' either is indeterminate or entails the imposition of specific liberal-democratic worldview that has yet to find general acceptance." Roth, *Governmental Illegitimacy*, 424.

24. In Tzvetan Todorov's classic study, the distinction between rational and cynical is expressed in the opposition of Las Casas and Cortès, the former being a colonialist out of love, the latter using the language of love in search of private gain. *Conquest of America*, 174–76.

25. Framed in such a way, the opposition enacts the Enlightenment story of reason against myth. The exclusion of the unreasonable preference becomes then less a political maneuver than a necessary step toward truth and progress, a prepolitical

operation that simply clears the ground for (rational, universal) politics. What the depiction fails to accept is that myth might be only another form of reason. Cf. Descombs, *Barometer of Modern Reason*, 144, and the discussion of the "profound ambiguity of the French Revolution . . . when a particular community [that is, the French] presumed to speak for humanity as a whole," 134. Descombs' discussion builds on themes in Lyotard, *Differend*, 145–47. Lyotard points out, in a Schmittian vein, that "[a]fter 1789, international wars are also civil wars," 146.

26. Moral universalism as a psychological trap imposing excessive demands on its proponents—and thus leading to brutalization and cynicism—is a consistent theme in critiques of Kant. For a controversial recent argument about morality as "the last refuge of Eurocentrism," cf. Enzensberger, *Civil War*, 59, 61. Jürgen Habermas has retorted that if moralization is mediated through a legal order, brutalization will not occur. As Habermas readily admits, this assumes the presence of "an authority that judges impartially and fulfils the conditions of neutral criminal punishment." But if the critique of legal formality is right—and that is the argument's starting point—the defense becomes a non sequitur. Habermas, too, accepts that a "deception" follows from unmediated moralism, for instance in the form of a "fundamentalism of human rights," 147, 145–49. In the absence of a defense of formalism, Habermas has nothing to say to Enzensberger's critique (which follows points made by Hegel as well as by Carl Schmitt).

27. Thus Tesón, for instance, suggests that international law problems about humanitarian intervention should be answered by recourse to philosophy: "I will suggest that moral philosophy is necessarily a part of the articulation of legal propositions." This then leads him to the position where the "ultimate justification of the existence of a state is the protection and enforcement of the natural rights of the citizens." If they fail, then "foreign armies are morally entitled to help victims of oppression in overthrowing dictators, provided that the intervention is proportionate to the evil which it is designed to suppress," *Humanitarian Intervention*, 6, 15. The replacement of legal argument by philosophy here seems both empty and superfluous. Surely the references to "natural rights," "victims of oppression," and "proportionality" have failed to deal with the lawyer's professional insecurity; surely it is precisely the vagueness of those notions where the lawyer's problem lies—and can hardly be resolved by restating them.

28. Thomas Pogge, "Priorities of Global Justice," 13–14.

29. Jean Bethke Elshtain, *Just War against Terror*.

30. For a recent overview, cf. Barkan, *Guilt of Nations*.

31. For a useful discussion of the point of passage from the "experience of the undecidable" to the judgment as "madness," cf. Critchley, 19, and especially 33–37.

32. It is for this reason impossible to accept the dismissal by the International Court of Justice of its jurisdiction to indicate interim measures over the Serbian claims made under the 1948 Convention on Genocide in 1999 because there had been, allegedly, no prima facie evidence of "intent to destroy" as required by the Convention. The Serbians were denied a voice, their deaths unadjudicated, dismissed. For the full argument, cf. Koskenniemi, "Evil Intentions," 180–207.

33. Cf. my "Wonderful Artificiality of States," 22–28.

34. This is decisionism, of course, but a decisionism as ironically described in Schmitt, *Political Romanticism*.

35. Cf. Kelsen, *Introduction to the Problems of Legal Theory*.

36. For this argument, I draw inspiration from Minkkinen, *Thinking Without Desire*.

WORKS CITED

Anghie, Antony. "Francisco de Vitoria and the Colonial Origins of International Law." *Social and Legal Studies* 5 (1996): 321–36.

Barkan, Elazar. *The Guilt of Nations: Restitution and Negotiation of Historical Injustices*. New York: Norton, 2000.

Bluntschli, Johann Caspar. "Arische Völker und Arische Rechte." In *Gesammelte kleine Schriften*, 1:63–90. Nördlingen: Beck, 1879.

Borgetto, Michel. *La notion de fraternité en droit public francais: Le passé, le present et l'avenir de la solidarité*. Paris: LGDJ, 1991.

Borradori, Giovanna, ed. *Philosophy in a Time of Terror: Dialogues with Jürgen Habermas and Jacques Derrida*. Chicago: Chicago University Press, 2003.

Bulmerincq, August. "Rapport." In *Annuaire de l'Institut de droit international*, 259–63. 1888–89.

Carr, Edwin Hallett. *The Twenty-Years' Crisis 1919–1939*. 2nd ed. London: Macmillan, 1981.

Cicero. *On the Commonwealth and on the Laws*. Edited by James E. G. Zetzel. Cambridge: Cambridge University Press, 1999.

Corten, Olivier. "Les amibiguités de la référence au droit international comme facteur de légitimation portée et signification d'une déformalisation du discours légaliste." In *Droit, légitimation et politique extérieure: l'Europe et la guerre du Kosovo*, edited by Olivier Corten and Barbara Delcourt, 223–59. Brussels: Bruylant, 2000.

Critchley, Simon. "Deconstruction and Pragmatism—Is Derrida a Private Ironist or Public Liberal?" In *Deconstruction and Pragmatism*, edited by Chantal Mouffe, 19–37. London: Routledge, 1997.

Derrida, Jacques. "Force of Law: The 'Mystical Foundations of Authority.'" In *Deconstruction and the Possibility of Justice*, edited by Drucilla Cornell, Michel Rosenfeld, and David Gray Carlson, 3–67. New York: Routledge, 1992.

Descombs, Vincent. *The Barometer of Modern Reason: On the Philosophies of Current Events*. Oxford: Oxford University Press, 1993.

Durkheim, Emile. The Division of Labor in Society. Introduction by Lewis A. Coser. Translated by W. D. Hawkes. New York: The Free Press, 1984.

Elshtain, Jean Bethke. Just War Against Terror: The Burden of American Power in a Violent World. New York: Basic Books, 2003.

Enzensberger, Hans Magnus. *Civil War*. London: Granta, 1994.

Feher, Michel. *Powerless by Design: The Age of the International Community*. Durham, NC: Duke University Press, 2000.

Gong, Gerrit W. *The Standard of "Civilization" in International Society*. Oxford: Clarendon, 1986.

Gray, Christine. *International Law and the Use of Force*. Oxford: Oxford University Press, 2001.

Grotius, Hugo. *De jure belli ac pacis*. Vol. 3. Oxford: Oxford University Press, 1925.

Habermas, Jürgen. "Kant's Idea of Perpetual Peace, with the Benefit of Two Hundred Years' Hindsight." In *Perpetual Peace: Essays in Kant's Cosmopolitan Ideal*, edited by James Bohman and Matthias Lutz-Bachmann, 113–53. Cambridge, MA: MIT Press, 1997.

Hall, W. E. *A Treatise on International Law*. 4th ed. Oxford: Clarendon, 1895.

Hayward, J. E. S. "The Official Social Philosophy of the French Third Republic: Léon Bourgeois and Solidarism." *International Review of Social History* 6 (1961): 19–48.

Hoffmann, Stanley. "An American Social Science: International Relations." In *Janus and Minerva: Essays in the Theory and Practice of International Politics*, 3–24. Boulder, CO: Westview, 1987.

Huber, Max. *Die soziologischen Grundlagen des Völkerrechts*. 1911. Berlin: Rothschild, 1928.

Jellinek, Georg. *Die rechtliche Natur der Staatenverträge: Ein Beitrag zur juristischen Construktion des Völkerrechts*. Vienna: Hölder, 1880.

Kelsen, Hans. *Das Problem der Souveränität und die Theories des Völkerrechs: Beitrag zu einer reinen Rechtslehre*. 2nd ed. Tübingen: Mohr, 1928.

———. *Introduction to the Problems of Legal Theory*. Translated by Bonnie Litschewski Paulson and Stanley L. Paulson. Oxford: Clarendon, 1992.

Kennedy, David. *International Legal Structures*. Baden: Nomos, 1987.

Keohane, Robert. *After Hegemony: Cooperation and Discord in World Political Economy*. Princeton, NJ: Princeton University Press, 1984.

Koskenniemi, Martti. "The Effect of Rights on Political Culture." In *The EU and Human Rights*, edited by Philip Alston, Mara Bustelo, and James Heenan, 99–116. Oxford: Oxford University Press, 2000.

———. "Evil Intentions or Vicious Acts? What is *Prima Facie* Evidence of Genocide?" In *Liber Amicorum Bengt Broms*, 180–207. Helsinki: Finnish Branch of the International Law Association, 1999.

———. *From Apology to Utopia: The Structure of International Legal Argument*. Helsinki: Lakimiesliiton Kustannus, 1989.

———. *The Gentle Civilizer of Nations: The Rise and Fall of International Law 1870–1960*. Cambridge: Cambridge University Press, 2001.

———. "The Politics of International Law." *European Journal of International Law* 1 (1991): 1–32.

———. "The Wonderful Artificiality of States." *Proceedings of the American Society of International Law* 88 (1994): 22–28.

Laclau, Ernesto. *Emancipation(s)*. London: Verso, 1996.

Lauterpacht, Hersch. *The Function of Law in the International Community*. Oxford: Clarendon, 1933.

Lyotard, Jean-Francois. *The Differend: Phrases in Dispute*. Translated by Georges van den Abbeele. Minneapolis: University of Minnesota Press, 1988.

Maine, Henry Sumner. *Ancient Law*. 1861. Reprint, London: Dorset Press, 1986.

Marks, Susan. *The Riddle of All Constitutions*. Oxford: Oxford University Press, 2000.

McDougal, Myres S. "International Law, Power and Policy: A Contemporary Conception." *Recueil des cours de l'Académie de droit international* 82, no. 1 (1953): 143–64, 188–91.

McDougal, Myres S., and Harold Lasswell. "Legal Education and Public Policy: Professional Training in the Public Interest." In *Studies in World Public Order*, edited by Myres McDougal et al., 42–154. New Haven, CT: New Haven Press, 1987.

Minkkinen, Panu. *Thinking Without Desire: A First Philosophy of Law*. Oxford: Hart, 1999.

Morgenthau, Hans J. *In Defense of the National Interest: A Critical Examination of American Foreign Policy*. New York: Knopf, 1951.

———. *Politics Among Nations: The Struggle for Power and Peace*. New York: Knopf, 1948.

———. "Positivism, Functionalism and International Law." *American Journal of International Law* 34 (1940): 261–84.

Pogge, Thomas. "Priorities of Global Justice." *Metaphilosophy* 32 (2991): 6–24.

Proudhon, Pierre-Joseph. *La guerre et la paix: Recherches sur la constitution du droit des gens*. In *Oeuvres Complètes*, Nouvelle édition, Paris: Libraire des sciences politiques et sociales, Marcel Rivière, 1927.

Rawls, John. *The Law of Peoples, with the "Idea of Public Reason" Revisited*. Cambridge, MA: Harvard University Press, 1999.

Rosenthal, Bent. *L'Étude de l'oeuvre de Myres Smith McDougal en matière de droit international*. Paris: LGDJ, 1970.

Roth, Brad. *Governmental Illegitimacy in International Law*. Oxford: Clarendon, 1999.

Sandel, Michael. *Liberalism and the Limits of Justice*. Cambridge: Cambridge University Press, 1982.

Scelle, Georges. *Précis du Droit des gens: Principes et systématique*. 2 vols. Paris: Sirey, 1932–34.

Schieder, Siegfrid. "Pragmatism as a Path Towards a Discursive and Open Theory of International Law." *European Journal of International Law* 11 (2000): 663–98.

Schmitt, Carl. *The Concept of the Political*. Translated by Georg Schwab. 1934. Reprint, Cambridge, MA: MIT Press, 1996.

———. *Der Nomos der Erde im Völkerrecht des Jus Publicum Europaeum*. 1950. 3rd ed. Berlin: Duncker & Humblot, 1988.

———. *Political Romanticism*. 1925. Translated by Guy Oakes. Cambridge, MA: MIT Press, 1986.

———. "Zu Friedrich Meinecke's 'Idee der Staatsräison' (1926)." In *Positionen und Begriffe im Kampf mit Weimar-Genf-Versailles 1923–1939*, 45–52. Berlin: Duncker & Humblot, 1988.

Simma, Bruno. "NATO, the UN and the Use of Force: Legal Aspects." *European Journal of International Law* 10 (1999): 1–22.

Slaughter, Anne-Marie. "The Real New World Order." *Foreign Affairs* 76 (1997): 183–97.

Sloterdijk, Peter. *Critique of Cynical Reason*. Translated by Michael Eldred. Minneapolis: University of Minnesota Press, 1987.

Smith, Steve. "Paradigm Dominance in International Relations: The Development of International Relations as a Social Science." *Millennium* 16 (1987): 189–206.

Tesón, Ferdinand. *Humanitarian Intervention: An Inquiry into Law and Morality*. New York: Transnational, 1988.

Teubner, Gunther. "Global Bukowina: Legal Pluralism in the World Society." In

Global Law Without a State, edited by Gunther Teubner, 3–30. Aldershot, UK: Ashgate, 1997.

Todorov, Tzvetan. *The Conquest of America: The Question of the Other.* Translated by Richard Howard. New York: Harper-Collins, 1984.

Tuck, Richard. *The Rights of War and Peace: Political Thought and the International Order from Grotius to Kant.* Oxford: Oxford University Press, 1999.

Twiss, Sir Travers. "Rapport." In *Annuaire de l'Institut de droit international,* 301–11. 1879.

United Nations Development Programme. *Human Rights and Human Development: The Human Development Report 2000.* New York: United Nations Development Programme, 2000.

Vattel, Emerich de. *Droit des gens ou principles de la Loi Naturelle, appliqués à la conduite et aux affaires des nations et des Souverains* 1:7.81. 1758. Translated as *The Law of Nations* by Joseph Chitty, 1863.

Virilio, Paul. *Stratégie de la déception.* Paris: Galilée, 1999.

Vitoria, Francisco de. *De indis et de jure belli relectiones.* Carnegie Endowment for International Peace. 1696. Reprint, Washington, DC: Classics of International Law, 1917.

Walzer, Michael. *Interpretation and Moral Criticism.* Cambridge, MA: Harvard University Press, 1987.

Weiler, J. H. H. *The Constitution of Europe.* Cambridge: Cambridge University Press, 1999.

Westlake, John. "Le conflit Anglo-Portugais." *Revue de droit international et de législation comparée* 18 (1891): 247–48.

3 Global Refugees

(HUMAN) RIGHTS, CITIZENSHIP, AND THE LAW

> History is the subject of a structure whose site is not
> homogeneous empty time, but time filled by the presence
> of the now [*Jetztzeit*].
> —Walter Benjamin, *Illuminations*, 252–53

This chapter combines sociocultural theory, experience (life history accounts/cultural memory), and action/praxis (art forms) to explore and better understand the experiences of being in exile, a refugee, an asylum seeker in the United Kingdom between the twentieth and twenty-first centuries. The discussion will revolve around the interrelationship between citizenship, (human) rights, power, and the law focusing on the lived experiences of people from Bosnia-Herzegovina living in "exile" in the UK. In re-presenting the "voices" of "refugees" living in the UK, issues around nationalism, "otherness," "displacement," the development and reconstruction of communities and "citizenship," and the mediating power of the law will be explored. This chapter draws on ethnographic research conducted over a period of twelve months with a Bosnian community in the Midlands, United Kingdom.

The research methodology stems from contemporary sociocultural research (Taussig 1993; O'Neill et al. 2001), especially participatory action research (Fals Borda 1988; Mies 1993; Mienczakowski 1995; Whyte 1989). In the process of developing intertextual research with "refugees"[1] and "asylum seekers," I do not aim to or claim to speak for the people I work with, but rather to speak with them, from multiple standpoints, and to open up intellectual and practical spaces for them to speak for themselves. This work as a work in progress, as "micrology," aims to create intertextual social knowledge as ethnomimesis (O'Neill 2001) and can help us avoid accepting reified versions of "reality" and re-present the complexity of lived experience and lived relations in postmodern times. The research also supports processes of community development (social regeneration, social renewal) and cultural citizenship in collaboration with the Bosnians. The participants in the research are the cocreators of the research. Life history narratives are re-presented in photographic form. The life story narratives and photographs re-present three key themes that emerged from the life stories of those involved in the research:

1. Experiences before the war—dislocation marked by postcommunist citizenship in "Yugoslavia" that reconstituted "citizenship" on a kinship or community basis, that is, for the Serb leader only Serbs were allowed "citizenship" and the protection of law.
2. Experiences during the war—displaced and abstracted from history, citizenship, and the law—separated from families and friends—living in refugee camps, and for some, concentration camps.
3. Experiences of living in the UK—relocating and rebuilding communities.

The research is both transgressive and regressive. Working together with the Bosnians in the Midlands over a twelve-month period through participatory action research (PAR) proved to be transgressive across three levels of praxis. The first level is textual, performed through documenting their life stories as testimony to the evil, suffering, and genocide they encountered at the hands of the government, army, police, employers, hospitals, medics, and former friends and neighbors. The second level is visual, performed through the production of art forms to re-present their life stories with the help of freelance artists, saying the unsayable and imagining a better future. The third level combines the visual and textual elements, and supports and fosters processes of community development.

The project could also be defined as regressive in that the artistic outcomes (a traveling exhibition) may facilitate the transformation of pain into enjoyment—where suffering can simply be consumed/enjoyed and something of its horror removed. "When genocide becomes part of the cultural heritage in themes of committed literature, it becomes easier to play along with the culture that gave birth to murder" (Adorno 1980, 189). However, the research does not simply memorialize the testimonies of participants. By retelling, rewriting, reconstructing, reimagining the loss, displacement, and experiences of exile faced by the people involved, and by re-presenting their stories or testimonies through art forms, processes of regeneration and reconstruction emerge, and they act as a spur to processes of community development. Challenging and resisting dominant images and stereotypes of "refugees" and "asylum seekers" and making this work available to as wide an audience as possible can also serve to raise awareness, as well as educate and empower individuals and groups. Dominant images and stereotypes include those of victim, passivity, and dependence and do not reflect the courage or resistance, as well as the need for building self-esteem, self-identity, and cultural identity, in the face of tragedy and loss (see Harrell-Bond 1999; Adelman 1999).

This chapter is therefore concerned with the interrelationship and the mediation between the "micrology" of lived experience and broader structures of power, domination, and violence within the context of postmodern times, detraditionalization, and what Stejpan Mestrovic (1997) calls "postemotionalism" and compassion fatigue. In postemotional society, a "new hybrid of intellectualized, mechanical, mass produced emotions has appeared on the world scene" (26). Following Hannah Arendt (1970) and Keith Tester (1992), the interrelation between thinking, feeling, and doing is crucial to counter postemotionalism in the administered society. Moreover, the interplay between critical thought, artistic praxis, and social action is one source of resistance to and transformation of the disempowering and reductive social and psychic processes that Mestrovic (1997) speaks about so clearly in his work.

The project is emancipatory, critical, and reflexive. By both narrativizing and re-presenting/reimagining history, this essay draws on PAR with a Bosnian community in the Midlands within the context of the Asylum and Immigration Acts of 1999 and 2002. The vital importance of opportunities for social renewal, for creating "citizenship," for reimagining identities and communities against the backdrop of British law is this chapter's focus. The role and purpose of PAR, the vital role of the arts in processes of social inclusion, and the civic role and responsibility of the university are also discussed.

Citizenship and Community:
Law and Patterns of Exclusion

> Here, abroad, nothing of that is left, we have been catapulted
> out of history, which is always the history of a specific area on
> the map, and we have to cope with, to use an expression of an
> exiled writer, "the unbearable lightness of being."
> —Czeslaw Milosz, *Joseph Koudelka*, 1–3

At the point of reception into the UK, asylum seekers abstract from history, but then history returns as the history of the culturally repressed. Cultural repression comes out in the troubles they experience in the UK. The 1999 and 2002 Asylum Acts instantiate in law a rational individualist diaspora. They are instrumental thinking in operation. The Asylum Acts engender a "culture of disbelief" toward asylum seekers—it is very difficult to prove asylum status.

For example, the 1999 Act enabled the British government to prepare removal documents and deportation orders before the decision on an asylum claim was made. An extension of carriers liability was introduced to include fines of £2,000 per head imposed on any international carrier—airline or shipping company—for every passenger coming in without valid documents. This covers all road, rail, sea, and air services; and includes a new civil penalty aimed at any carrier bringing "clandestine entrants" into the country; again, £2,000 per illegal immigrant is levied, and their vehicles are impounded until fines are paid. The Act extends criminal offenses that cover trying to enter or remain in the UK using "deception" to include asylum seekers and their representatives who "knowingly" make false statements on their behalf.

Asylum seekers can now be sent back to a third "safe" country if they traveled through it to reach the UK. They are dispersed in clusters predominantly to the northwest, northeast, and midlands. They have one-choice accommodations: no choice. They live on vouchers, to be exchanged at certain supermarkets (not the cheapest), and a no-change policy for the vouchers is in existence, although the government has recently been moved to review this in the face of the overwhelming evidence and reaction against this policy; or asylum seekers are given board and lodgings but no cash; and they have no rights to employment. The vouchers are worth 70 percent of state benefit. Female asylum seekers face further problems, as the UN conventions are based on a masculinist state and legal system that provides no flexibility toward the particular experiences and needs of women seeking asylum (see Crowley, 1997).

The 2002 Nationality, Immigration, and Asylum Act introduced a further raft of legislation that erodes the basic human rights of people seeking asylum in the UK. The fundamental right to protection and sanctuary has been significantly and seriously reduced, partly the result of the impact of sections 55 and 57, which came into force on January 8, 2003. The new measures deny automatic access to food, shelter, and clothing to destitute asylum seekers; and they leave already vulnerable people, which may include pregnant women, children, and those with special needs, exposed to victimization, bullying, and harassment.

Before the latest act, asylum seekers who applied for asylum as "in-country" applicants usually turned up at refugee and voluntary sector organizations and applied for emergency accommodation. This was then given, and arrangements for screening were made. Screening can take time to arrange. Since January 8, 2003, asylum seekers must claim asylum immediately at the port of arrival. Screening interviews will have to take place first, and if successful, a government agency, the National Asylum Support Service, will supply a letter to confirm whether the individual or family is eligible for support. If they do not have a letter, they won't get support. Decisions on support will only be made at the Asylum Support unit in Croyden. Press releases from the Refugee Council suggest that only eight to ten staff members are available there! If a decision is negative, there is no right to appeal.

The reality is that pregnant women may not be entitled to support until after their babies are born; people with disabilities or special needs will have to wait for assessment from the local authority—and it may take at least six weeks before support is granted; families could be without shelter overnight or longer while the Home Office considers their case for support; and teenage children claiming to be under eighteen and above fifteen who are not believed by the Home Office (that is, age-dispute cases) could be denied support.

The measures will lead to a massive surge in homelessness. Estimates based on figures for 2002 suggest that 45,000 refugees will have rights to housing, and basic needs will be removed because refugees do not claim their status immediately upon arrival. The reasons that 45,000 people did not claim at the point of arrival (but rather were asylum in-country applicants; according to the Refugee Council, the majority applied within 10 days) last year were as follows: there were no facilities to do so; fear; trauma; fear of authorities; and lack of language skills and support.

In 1996 similar measures were attempted but were defeated by a High Court ruling.

The state wants individual tourists to enter Britain—not families dispersed and separated—not families, not communities, not "Others." For those seeking asylum, their postkinship diaspora—archaic depths loss of kinship, loss of history, loss of politics—combines with the experience of cultural repression. Concepts of what constitutes "citizenship" and "community" can be explored through patterns of inclusion and exclusion.

The British government appears to see the "asylum issue" first and foremost in terms of firm and tough responses that will deter potential asylum seekers rather than as a human rights issue. Asylum seekers are objectified, faceless, and nameless in most of the media coverage of the issue. In a memo by Tony Blair leaked to the press, he wrote, "We are perceived to be soft. . . . We need to be highlighting removals," and a later memo read, "We do need to be seen to care; and to act" (Natasha Walter, *Independent Newspaper*, July 31, 2000). The "removal" policy for asylum seekers from Afghanistan has increased dramatically since the government was severely criticized in the press by the conservative opposition party for being "soft" on the people from Afghanistan when those aboard the hijacked plane that landed at Heathrow made asylum applications. Before this debacle, more than 90 percent of asylum applications from Afghanistan were allowed. In June 2000, Amnesty International claimed that only 30 percent of Afghan asylum seekers were being accepted. Afghanistan is second (after Iraq) in the top ten countries of origin from asylum applicants in the UK (*Inexile*, April 2001); it is a country where very serious human rights abuses occur daily.

Kushner and Knox (1999) state that Britain is "becoming a country committed to asylum without the possibility of entry" and of being a "haven for the oppressed without the presence of refugees" (1999, 417). As "outsiders," asylum seekers have few rights. Denied citizenship, they have to cope with racism, poor living conditions, poverty, and the problems of communicating in a new language (for some), as well as the sorrow and pain that is a part of the experience of seeking exile.

One aspect of this pain is the loss of kinship. Many people from Bosnia who made it to Red Cross camps and who were then sent to "safety" in Europe and the United States were separated from family members during this process of removal and relocation. From the community of Bosnians in the Midlands, we find the following examples. An elderly man sent his wife to her sisters in Croatia when war broke out. He later survived the journey to a UN camp in Croatia but was not allowed to stay in Croatia because he did not have the necessary papers. From the safety of the refugee camp in Croatia, he was offered a choice of the United States or England. He chose England, but he never saw his wife again: she died while the Red Cross in England were arranging papers for her to join him. A mother was allowed to go to Sweden because her sister was there; but from the same Red Cross camp in Croatia, her daughter was given the choice of America or England. She chose England to be nearer Bosnia, to be near to where she imagined her teenage son was. She had encouraged her son and daughter to leave when children were being taken from schools by Serbian soldiers and "used as target practice." She was reunited with her son in England after three years, and eventually, after a further two years, she visited her daughter in Norway and met her grandchildren for the first time. She said:

With every war you can only expect the worse. Every war is bringing only unhappiness, killing, destroying, dead innocent people . . . All the families are separated, not one family is living together now . . . but now we are not longing for what we had in the past, possessions, houses and belongings. We are longing now for the families that are now in three or four different countries.

Laila, forced to flee from Afghanistan four years ago, told the Refugee Council: "My relatives are scattered all around the world, all in other countries. I have a brother in Germany, a sister in Australia, an uncle in Canada and another uncle I have just discovered in Pakistan" (*Inexile*, December 2000, 16).

Renewed Methodologies for
Social Justice and Inclusion

Renewed methodologies that incorporate the voices and images of "refugees" and "asylum seekers" through scholarly/civic research as participatory research not only can serve to enlighten and raise our awareness of

certain issues, but could also produce critical reflexive texts that may help
to mobilize social change. The interrelationship between social research and
praxis is fraught with tensions. The tension between a modernist ethos of
resistance and transformation through participation as praxis (working
with research participants toward social renewal); and a postmodern ethos
of hybridity, complexity, and intertextuality (anti-identitarian thinking, re-
presenting the complexity of lived experience through performative praxis,
working across genres and borders) is uneasy but re-presents the complex
dynamics of this work, and it uncovers important messages about the complexity of everyday life. Ethnomimesis as performative praxis seeks to speak
in empathic ways with people, re-presented here through the photographic
text in ways that counter postemotionalism, valorizing discourses, and the
reduction of the Other to a cipher of the oppressed/marginalized/exploited
(see Mestrovic 1997).

Our work seeks to understand, express, and reimagine the complexity of
loss, longing, exile, *and* reconstruction—renewal through a combination of
life history work; reimagining through artistic forms; and community development. This is a dialectical/constellational project rather than one that deals
in binaries. Hillis Miller (1992) describes this process well when he argues
against binaries, as in the reversibility of the politicizing of art into the aes-
theticizing of politics; and for a cultural studies that promotes the performative over the merely theoretical (1992, 16). Arguing for new forms of consolidation and solidarity, Hillis Miller, like Drucilla Cornell, Juliet Flower
Maccannell, Shierry Nicholsen, John Berger, Theodor Adorno, and Walter
Benjamin, looks to art and aesthetics as one means to reimagine and renew
our social worlds.

Evoking Adorno's concept of the "new" in *Aesthetic Theory* and Benjamin's "*Jetztzeit*," Hillis Miller illustrates "how works of art bring something new into the world rather than reflecting something already there.
This something new is constitutive rather than being merely representa-
tional or, on the other hand, a revelation of something already there but
hidden. Works of art make culture. Each work makes different the culture
it enters" (1992, 151). In relation to this focus on the "new," for Shierry
Nicholsen (1997, 1999), the importance of drawing on Adorno today is
his focus on the role of the subject and subjective experience, particularly
the imaginary and imagination. As I have argued elsewhere (see O'Neill
1999), the usefulness of Adorno's oeuvre is that his work gives voice to the
critical, moral, and creative potential of nonidentity thinking, *Kulturkritik*,
and the social role of art in dialectical tension with the role of subjective experience, within the context of a social world marked by identity thinking
and instrumental reason. The exemplars of instrumental reason and identity thinking are none more obvious than in the psychic and social processes

that led to war in Bosnia. They are also present in the British government's response to asylum seekers, as enshrined in the 1999 and 2002 Asylum and Immigration Acts.

The university also has a central role in challenging and changing instrumental reason, and I am in full agreement with both Hillis Miller and Zygmunt Bauman on the subject. Hillis Miller (1992) sees the university as an instrument of power—"it is political through and through" (see 18–19)—and furthermore, the "elaboration of questions of responsibility and justice is a major task of cultural studies today" (54). Bauman has argued for the emancipatory role of sociology and the sociologist as an active agent in societal transformation through working with, not legislating on or for. PAR as ethnomimesis, is, I would argue, a suitable response to both Hillis Miller and Bauman. PAR provides a renewed focus on the role and purpose of academic involvement in the public sphere, especially in relation to facilitating processes of social inclusion and regeneration *with* and for the communities involved in the research. The impact of this research on social policy (by the inclusion of the stereotypical "subjects" of research usually seen as "outsiders" or "outlaws") may appear to be small scale but has much wider repercussions in terms of the impact on the groups and wider communities involved. For example PAR promotes individuals/group self-esteem and facilitates the development of skills, empowerment, and ownership of a stake in creating change, in creating praxis (see Fals Borda 1988).

PAR: ETHNOMIMESIS AS PERFORMATIVE PRAXIS

The splinter in your eye is the best magnifying glass.
—Adorno, *Minima Moralia*, 50

Adorno's statement above encourages us to focus on what is ordinarily overlooked: the small scale, the minutiae of lived experiences. In focusing on the small scale, we can often reach a better understanding of the bigger picture. For Adorno, it is only by trying to say the unsayable, what is "outside of language," the mimetic, the sensual, the nonconceptual, that we can approach a "politics" that undercuts identity thinking/identitarian thinking and crisscrosses binary thinking/territories and resists appropriation.

PAR as ethnomimesis explores renewed methodologies for doing cultural studies in the twenty-first century by developing hybrid texts, by drawing on the interrelation/intertextuality between art and ethnography in the service of social renewal (rebuilding and reimagining communities). Ethnomimesis mimesis (a combination of ethnographic work and artistic re-presentations of the ethnographic work through participatory action research) is therefore a process and a practice, but it is ultimately rooted in principles of equality, democracy, and freedom, as well as what Jessica Benjamin (1993) describes (drawing on Hegel, Kant, and Adorno) as a dialectic of mutual recognition.

The key concept used here to express the re-presentation of life stories in artistic form is "mimesis" and the dialectic of mimesis and constructive rationality. Following Adorno, "mimesis" does not simply mean naive imitation, but rather feeling, sensuousness, and spirit; the playfulness of our being in the world in critical tension to constructive rationality; reason; the "out-there" sense of our being in the world. Hilde Heynon writes, "Mimesis, however, is not simply equivalent to a visual similarity between works of art and what they represent. The affinity Adorno refers to lies deeper. It can be recognized, for example, in an abstract painting that, in mimetic fashion, depicts something of reality's alienating character" (1999, 175). Taussig understands "mimesis as both the faculty of imitation and the deployment of that faculty in sensuous knowing" (1993, 68).

Ethnomimesis is both a practice (a methodology) and a process aimed at illuminating inequalities and injustice through sociocultural research and analysis; but it also seeks to envision and imagine a better future based on a dialectic of mutual recognition, care, respect for human rights, cultural citizenship, and democratic processes. But more specifically, human rights are contested constructs whose meaning is established in practice as well as through moral, political, and legal debate (see Forsythe 2000). For example, nongovernmental organizations such as Amnesty International, Red Cross, and Save the Children have proved themselves very effective at campaigning, educating, and generating the development of change. Human Rights Watch performs an increasingly important global role in detailing and making public the gross violations of human rights across the continuum of loss of citizenship through torture, slaughter, and genocide. As a matter of human rights, the principles of the "truth and reconciliation commissions" in El Salvador and South Africa are important role models to help understand, counter, and prevent the atrocities committed against individuals and groups.

Perhaps as Forsythe (2000, 228) suggests, we need to take a case-by-case response when dealing with human rights violations, be it criminal proceedings, diplomacy, or truth and reconciliation, although it seems to me that we need to be acutely aware of the fact that the world's refugee crisis will continue to worsen until the international community addresses the root causes of conflict.[2] Borrowing from Kushner and Knox (1999), who quote Auschwitz survivor Rabbi Hugo Gryn, the asylum issues are indeed an index of our spiritual and moral civilization.

How you are to the one to whom you owe nothing, that is a grave test and not only as an index of our tragic past. I always think that the real offenders at the half way point of the century were the bystanders, all those people who let things happen because it didn't affect them directly. I believe that the line our society will take on this matter on how you are to people to whom you owe nothing is a signal. (416)

Re-presenting social research through art forms can create multivocal, dialogical texts and can make visible "emotional structures and inner experiences" (Kuzmics 1997, 9) that may "move" audiences through what can be described as "sensuous knowing" or mimesis (Taussig 1993). As a researcher, interpretive ethnography grounded in the stories of the cocreators of the research (participatory research) rooted in critical theory is my chosen method. This method privileges their voices and triangulates their voices with cultural texts re-presenting and imagining the "refugee experience" through "feeling forms" (Witkin 1974).

The point about such methodologies is that they deal *with* the contradictions of oppression *and* the utter complexity of our lived relations at the turn of the new century—within the context of technologization and globalization, and indeed, within the context of what Paul Piccone calls "the permanent crisis of the totally administered society" (1993, 3). Renewed methodologies such as ethnomimesis can serve to

1. Rememorialize.
2. Focus our attentions on history and the unspeakable—genocide/refugee.
3. Focus our attentions on the transgressive acts, everyday resistances, and hope for the future.
4. Focus our attentions on the democratic processes and possibilities for citizenship, rights, and freedom within the realm of relative unfreedom, marked by the instrumental reason and "postemotionalism" that exists in the west.

CITIZEN RIGHTS AND HUMAN RIGHTS

The research that is documented here seeks to facilitate art forms that speak of the complexity of diversity and cultural heritage in our communities as a key element in processes of social inclusion, and regeneration through cultural citizenship. The concept of citizenship used is that defined by Jan Pakulski (1977). Cultural citizenship is the right or presence and visibility (as opposed to marginalization), the right to dignifying representation (rather than stigmatization), and the right to identity and maintenance of lifestyle (instead of assimilation to the dominant culture). Denied actual citizenship, asylum seekers deserve the respect, dignity, and rights to identity and maintenance of lifestyle mediated by sociocultural structures and processes through the major institutions and organizations that make up "society"—especially law, education, health, welfare services, and media.

At the start of the twenty-first century, Britain is criticized by human rights groups for coming near the bottom of the league table regarding the granting of asylum applications—and the latest asylum and immigration acts, characterized as firm but fair by Jack Straw, have created a tier of destitute people. In Britain in 2003, the asylum process is in chaos. The compulsory dispersal system introduced in April 2000 to relieve the pressure on London boroughs and the southeast aimed to disperse 65,000 people across the UK by April 2001. Clearinghouses in London and Kent monitored the accommodations available in other areas. People were dispersed purely on the availability of housing stock. To date, the Home Office figures show that by September 2002, 44,815 people had been dispersed, the majority to the northwest, Yorkshire and Humberside, and the West Midlands. Local councils in the dispersal areas and refugee groups have warned the government that asylum seekers are drifting back to London, or simply choosing to remain in the capital, where they have no access to housing but where they do have access to support from their communities.

Amanda Sebestyen of the Asylum and Legal Fund (*Guardian*, December 31, 2000) stated that government claims to have cut the asylum backlog to under 70,000 were boosted by a 40 percent rise in the numbers of asylum seekers rejected for not filling in the forms correctly. In December 2000 the Refugee Council reported that there were 62,965 asylum applications from January to October 2000. Decisions granted include the following: 8,540 given refugee status; 9,990 given exceptional leave to remain; and 38,320 refusals. A total of 19,370 were refused on grounds of noncompliance. January 2002 to September 2002 saw 27,585 applications for asylum, and of these, 2,805 were granted asylum and 18,730 were refused, 5,610 on grounds of noncompliance. This figure is likely to grow substantially in 2003, under the new, more punitive asylum regime. "Noncompliance" is failure to support the asylum claim within the given time period of fourteen days, or failure to attend an interview. A case worker in Leicester reported that "in seven out of ten cases the travel warrant is not arriving" (*Inexile*, December 2000, 6). Another case worker said, "Sometimes the Immigration Nationality Directorate (IND) sends letters with the wrong date of interview to the wrong address. Or, the National Asylum Support Service (NASS) don't arrange the travel warrant on time. The end result is the same—[the] asylum seeker fails to turn up for [the] interview and they are refused asylum" (7).

The problems asylum seekers face, as documented by the Refugee Council, are as follows: widespread indiscriminate detention, poverty, substandard housing, poor access to health care, and lack of training and employment possibilities. In addition, they are required to use a voucher system that deprives them of a stake in the cash economy and marks them out as different and thus open to racist acts. Racist acts include abuse, incivility, violence, and murder. Opposition to asylum seekers is marked by racism alongside profiteering. Increasingly complex procedures enable a token refugee policy while the global refugee situation continues to escalate. Stereotyping, prejudice, fear of "the other," and sociocultural discrimination abound.[3] Grave concern about the measures contained in the latest Asylum and Immigration Acts of 1999 and 2002 have been documented by the Refugee Council, Refugee Action, and Amnesty International, as well as by refugee groups, academics, politicians, and journalists.

The Identity of "Refugee" or "Asylum Seeker"

Needless to say, the identity of "refugee" or "asylum seeker" is problematic within the context of dislocation and attempts at relocation in a climate of "disbelief." It shifts, as Kushner and Knox (1999) document, from proud and self-sufficient to shameful and a crime; it represents failure. "Catapulted out of history," it is very difficult to feel at home in the new world. Finding new rhythms in time and space, and quelling the anxiety of the unfamiliar and the loss of orientation take time.

The Bosnians achieve this in part in the context of a postkinship diaspora by developing and building a community association in mutual recognition with the wider community or communities they live alongside. The right to presence and visibility is marked by the sharing of the cultural traditions of food, music, and dancing (the community association successfully bid for some funds to hold a cultural festival to celebrate Eid, inviting the wider communities living locally to attend). The right to dignifying representation is evident in the newsletter that the association creates and the promoting of the traditional folk dancing and folk music. The groups perform in civic events, and the folk group leader teaches dance and runs workshops in local schools. The right to identity and maintain a lifestyle is important within the context of being included, recognized, and respected by the wider multiethnic community. The community association provides an anchor, a place for regular meetings on "club" afternoons. The chair of the Association said:

We have our meetings . . . we share conversation, thoughts and feelings . . . it means a lot . . . we can relax from everything . . . we are still under pressure and always will be from what happened . . . we can never forget what happened and when we talk amongst ourselves . . . no one can understand what we went through . . . and talking to others who understand . . . it is good to have someone to share . . . it is easier to cope.

The weight of evidence from history, from experience, is that refugee groups revitalize our cities, arts, culture, economy, and polity. In reimagining and renewing the social order along democratic principles, the key themes of our collaboration include the development of participatory action research and processes of community development, the vital role of the arts in social regeneration/social inclusion/building communities, the role of creative inclusion in facilitating spaces for the voices of marginalized peoples, and the importance of taking a grassroots approach to facilitating cultural citizenship.

Drucilla Cornell draws on Stuart Hall to describe cultural identity as a matter of "becoming" as well as of "being," belonging to the future as much as to the past and subject to the continuous play of history, culture, and power. And, she tells us, "far from being grounded in mere recovery of the past, which is waiting to be found and will secure our sense of our selves in eternity, identities are the names we give to the different ways we are positioned by, and position ourselves within the narratives of the past" (2000, 55). These narratives of the past are situated within a broader historical story.

The Camp as an "Artificially Designed Order": Law, Power, and Injustice in the Twentieth Century

Holocaust survivor Rabbi Hugo Gryn stated just before his death in 1996 that historians "will call the twentieth century not only the century of great wars, but also the century of the refugee. Almost nobody at the end of the century is where they were at the beginning. It has been an extraordinary period of movement and upheavals" (Kushner and Knox 1999, 1). The extraordinary period of war, exile, and resettlement for those participating in the research in the Bosnia-Herzegovina Midlands is embedded in the history of the Federal Republic of Yugoslavia. In 1993, the U.S. committee for refugees said,

In B-H [Bosnia-Herzegovina] the most extreme elements of the nationalist Serb community—aided and abetted by their patron in Serbia (Milosevic) have chosen to wipe out, liquidate, remove rather than live with those who are somehow "different." Their methods are crude, but effective: artillery barrages of civilian centres; forced population movements; appropriation of property. Those who survive and are not driven out face imprisonment, rape, forced separation from family. Nationalist Croat forces and, to a lesser extent, troops of the mostly Muslim Bosnian army have also committed violent heinous acts. (Hughes et al. 1995, 511)

Hughes et al. tell us that largely through mass rallies and state-controlled media, people were taught to hate those who were different. "It all began with 'sweet' stories about national states, national rights, life within ethnic boundaries. . . . Nationalism was constructed on a highly imagined community inhabited by people whose identities had little to do with accurate history, geography or real attributes" (1995, 511). This imagined community was founded on a kinship basis and the idea of a single Serb nation and the nationalistic hatred of "others." The war that ensued was literally unspeakable in its structure and outcomes for individuals, families, and communities—and for humanity in a global sense. One of the contributors to the research, a man living in the Midlands with his wife and youngest son, said,

Muslim people were not even allowed to go to the market . . . you were not allowed to have anything . . . you could not have a car . . . I had a big house . . . the people just came and said I need this . . . took the cars . . . everything . . . we could not even sleep in the house . . . in 1994 56 people were killed in one day in their homes . . . the Serbs would come and shoot them . . . a Serb soldier was killed and they were just going into houses and shooting people . . . 10 women and children for one soldier were killed . . . they were running away . . . even in the daytime you were never sure . . . people had to leave their homes . . . someone would come and say we need your house . . . this is no longer your house . . .

Muslims were thrown out of their houses. Those who escaped death were sent to the camps. Supplies to the region and the camps were sporadic, and the people suffered because of this. The International Red Cross and UN High Commission for Refugees were instrumental in securing the safety of the people in camps and evacuating them to Croatia and "to other parts of unwilling Europe" (Glenny 1996, 208). A woman, now living with her husband in the East Midlands, described her experience:

Serbs were coming to our houses and they would just say I need that—a piece of furniture—and there is nothing you can do. What is the worse you know these people they were your friends before and they would pretend that they don't even know you. The worse thing is that you can't do anything to stop them. You can only watch them taking your things away. The worse was with the children. All the children over 18 it was terrible, they would take them away, beat them or kill them.

Muslim and Croat women were herded into schools, hotels, warehouses, and camps and raped repeatedly. The EC commission estimated that 20,000 women were raped. Evidence shows clearly that women on all sides were raped and also documents the rape of men (see Glenny 1996; Langer 1997; Rape Survivors Special Report in *Marie Claire*, November 1994).

A man now living in the Midlands who survived the Omarska concentration camp said:

Conditions in Omarska and Kerater . . . it was terrible hard . . . indescribable what they were doing . . . lots of people died from beating . . . or no food . . . they lost so much weight . . . some could hardly walk anymore . . . there was like an epidemic . . . nits . . . some people were very hurt as well . . . and on some occasions they were cutting a cross in the skin on the chest . . . and there was nothing to put on . . . sometimes they got maggots in the wounds . . . there were a few soldiers that were OK but most were really nasty . . . sometimes they would cut someone's ear just to check if the knife is sharp enough . . . and you had to watch . . . after all that time they were not even scared anymore . . . they were waiting every day to have their turn. . . . and in Kerater the people who survived that . . . they were in like a big hall . . . first they put gas in . . . and they closed the door . . . like there was a big hole they put the gas in . . . and no-one could come out they were shouting and banging . . . 108 people in one moment.

Elaine Scarry (1985) writes that whatever pain achieves it is unsharable, that pain does not resist language but actively destroys it, and that the political consequences are dire, for they lead to misconceptions. "The failure

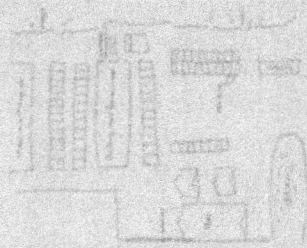

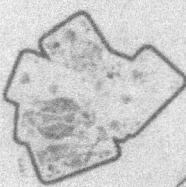

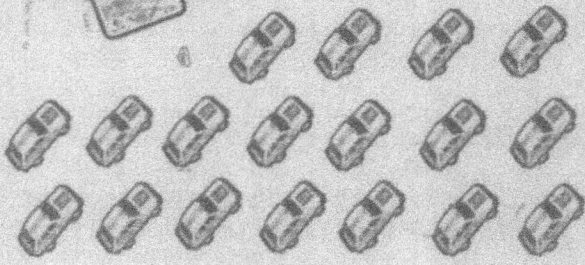

to express pain will work to allow its appropriation and conflation with debased forms of power; conversely the successful expression of pain will always work to expose and make impossible that appropriation and conflation" (14). It is not my intention to develop an analysis of pain and suffering, but rather to illuminate the need to express pain and suffering as part of the complex processes of living with exile and of "becoming," as well as the need politically to empathize with pain and suffering as the outcomes of war and torture to counter the postemotionalism that is dominant in contemporary representations of war in the west in relation to the former Yugoslavia, Rwanda, Sri Lanka, Nigeria, Afghanistan, Iraq—and the list goes on. This is particularly necessary in relation to countering the binary divide between some Arab nations and the United States, supported uncritically by the UK, in part as a consequence of U.S. foreign policy.

Objectification is linked to materialism—people are objectified. This is identity thinking in operation. The concept of Adorno and others of the "authoritarian personality" can help us to understand processes of ethnic antagonism, prejudice, and discrimination in relation to negative responses to refugees and asylum seekers. The "authoritarian society" is perhaps better understood as authoritarian patterns of thought, where prejudice operates through stereotypical thinking and scapegoating, fear, anxiety, and projection. Bauman (1995, 192) asks how our century will go down in history: will "it be under the 'Age of Camps?'" Part of a response may be found in his answer as to why the camps were possible: by our ability "to separate action and ethics, of what people do from what people feel or believe, of the nature of the collective deed from the motives of individual actors (accomplishments of modern civilization . . . : the ability to act at a distance, the neutralization of the moral constraints of action) and the pursuit of artificially designed order" (195).

Camps as totalitarian regimes are organized on principles of total order, containment, surveillance—instrumental reason in operation. They are, in Bauman's words, "distillations of an essence diluted elsewhere, condensations of totalitarian domination and its corollary, the superfluity of man, in a pure form difficult to achieve elsewhere" (1995, 201). Figure 1, "Timeline," was created by Enis and Adnan, who were, respectively, aged nine

FIGURE 1. *(Opposite)* "Timeline" was produced by Enis and Adnan, supported by artist Simon Cunningham, a freelance artist working for City Arts, a community arts organization in Nottingham, UK. The project Global Refugees was coordinated by Maggie O'Neill and Bea Tobolewska and combined participatory action research and participatory arts. This work is ongoing support by the AHRB (Arts and Humanities Board). Copyright 1999, City Arts. Reproduced with kind permission.

and ten when war broke out and fifteen and sixteen when they completed this image. The camp as a highly organized functional system is transgressed by the hand-drawn symbols of the machinery of war: bombs, land mines, tanks. The images writ large are images from their childhood—toy cars, a Walkman, a dictionary, the alphabet—stark reminders that challenge the very notion of the camps and the clinical image/plan/order of the camp that otherwise we may take as a given.

Genocide involves classifying or categorizing a group and is enacted through a "categorial killing" (Bauman 1995, 203). The victims are killed not for what they have done, but for the group they belong to. They have no "selves"; their identity is equated with, as Bauman states, disease; they are guilty of being "identified." One contributor illustrates this point as follows:

Where I used to live most of the people were Muslim . . . even though it was multi-ethnic (in the former Yugoslavia you didn't really know who was who) . . . then they started ethnic cleansing (and they started to bomb the village) . . . and after two days because the Serbs had bases all around the people couldn't go anywhere . . . they couldn't run away . . . women and children died . . . they were just firing on people and they didn't have anywhere to run . . . the people who survived were taken to the concentration camps, Omarska, Trnopolye, and Kerater.

Listening to the voices of peoples seeking asylum encourages us to engage with ethics, with people as similar to our "selves," within a moral order and conscience based on thinking and feeling and compassion. Thus, precluding the possibility of objectifying, classifying, and categorizing as faceless, nameless, less than our "selves," may inspire praxis instead of the adoption of a bystander role. The worry is that during the twenty-first century, there will be an increase, not decrease, in war and crimes against human rights; and increased breakdown of law, justice, and protection of peoples. The importance of empathy, of working *with* groups, not on or for them, cannot be overestimated.

Ethnomimesis: Narrativization and Visual Re-Presentation

Thus our stories are a necessary response to our awesome origins; they are a self-shaping recollective practice that binds nature to culture. Our two knowledges of the world and soul can never entirely separate. Every tale is a story of ourselves becoming gods of an imaginative order where creation and recreation are the twin comets of an infinitely deferred world collision.
—O'Neill, *Incorporating Cultural Theory: Maternity at the Millennium*, 177–78

The life history interviews with the participants in the research throw up a number of major themes: the pain and suffering of dislocation from identity, society, and citizenship; abstracted from the law *unheimlich*, living in concentration camps and/or then Red Cross camps/waiting to be relocated; and finally the processes of relocation in the UK and building communities.

ABSTRACTED FROM HISTORY AND THE LAW

I think everyone suffered so much and it was so hard to watch, after all family by family were leaving slowly. Some people were leaving; some were disappearing. Every day we had an opportunity to see funerals. There were funerals in a day that we saw and a few that we didn't see. We as a Muslim people we couldn't even go outside much. . . . In the part where we lived it was very difficult to live because every day we were expecting only the worse and also whose turn it was that day.

My neighbours next door, they left their hot lunch on the table and Serbs came and sat down to eat their lunch. My neighbours had to leave without anything, they were even laughing at them and teasing them that lunch was delicious. This family was, the man was 81 years old and his wife was 70 something. That was terrible. They got out of their home and they just sat on the street. They didn't have anywhere to go to. In the end they ended up together with everyone else in the field where camp was made with nylon tent. Some people didn't even make it to the camp, we don't even know where they are. I just hope that no one would have to go through that any more.

RELOCATION: FINDING RHYTHMS OF SPACE AND TIME AND BUILDING COMMUNITIES

We just want to show to English people that we have our traditions, education and culture and give them a chance to see us in a different way and they can get to know us better. I think that they can learn that we are friendly people and nice nation and that war is not the only way to remember us.

Figure 2 was developed by Fahira over a period of seven weeks. The image was developed as an installation of a box of goodies on the theme of "good neighbor" and digitally photographed. The "bread" was made by the artist and photographed along with the "keys." Both are symbolic of a life saved and a humanity greater than the experiences of pain, suffering, and the outcomes of war. This re-presentation, anchored by the text in figures 3 and 4, challenges the binaries of Serb and Muslim, self and Other thus transgressing the process of labeling, objectification, and dehumanization that emerges as a process and product of instrumental reason, war, and genocide in particular.

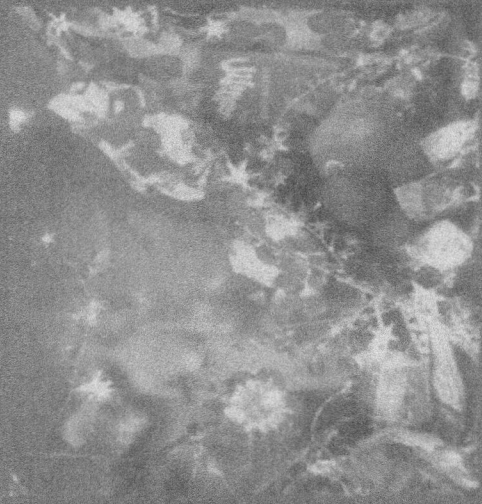

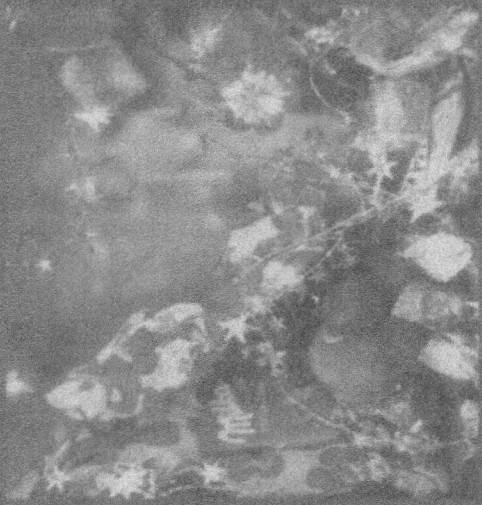

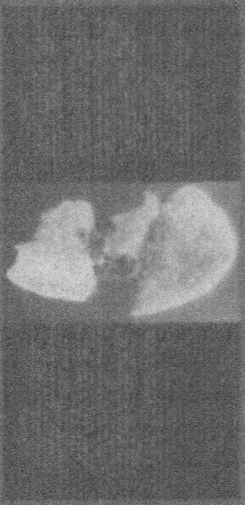

Beyond the Judicial Terrain: Ethical/Moral
Responsibilities, Individually and Collectively

Bruno Bettleheim's experiences in the camps (1981) taught him that he "had gone much too far in believing that only changes in man could create changes in society. I had to accept that the environment could, as it were, turn personality upside down, and not just the small child, but in the mature adult too" (1981, 15). He began to see that "soon how a man acts can alter what he is. Those who stood up well in the camps became better men, those who acted badly soon became bad men" (16). Bettleheim made a very important point in his account and analysis of the consequences of living under extreme fear and terror. The external symptoms of neurosis and psychotic breakdown (rooted in the inner difficulties of man) reflect back the nature of society, showing up "what ails all of us in some measure at present, and warn us of things to come . . . they can also inform us about which forces an age looks to for solving the difficulties it is failing to master" (1981, 52).

We must therefore address psychic processes *and* social processes in trying to understand the global refugee crisis. Moreover, in trying to find ways of caring for, respecting, and supporting the needs of internally and externally displaced peoples,[4] we must actively seek ways of preventing civil unrest, conflict, and war. Hence the vital importance placed in this text on the interrelationship between what Bauman (1995) calls autonomous individuality and collective responsibility. The sharing of collective responsibilities is a moral imperative in current times. Clearly there is an urgent need to develop interventionary strategies based on collective responsibility and what Benhabib (1992) has called a "civic culture of public participation and the moral quality of enlarged thought" (1992, 140)[5] in response to what has been called the global refugee crisis.

How can interpretive research and ethnomimesis address this? The experiences of the people concerned must be listened to and acknowledged, and advocacy networks must be developed to operationalize their voices through participatory action research. Recovering and retelling people's

---

FIGURE 2. *(Opposite)* This image was produced by Fahira, supported by artist Karen Fraser, a freelance artist working for City Arts, Nottingham, UK, on the Global Refugees project. The image on the theme of "good neighbor" re-presented Fahira's thanks to her neighbor, who effectively saved her from certain death by allowing Fahira and her family to hide in the Serbian neighbor's flat when Serbian soldiers were looking for Muslims during the war in Bosnia. Copyright 1999, City Arts. Reprinted with kind permission.

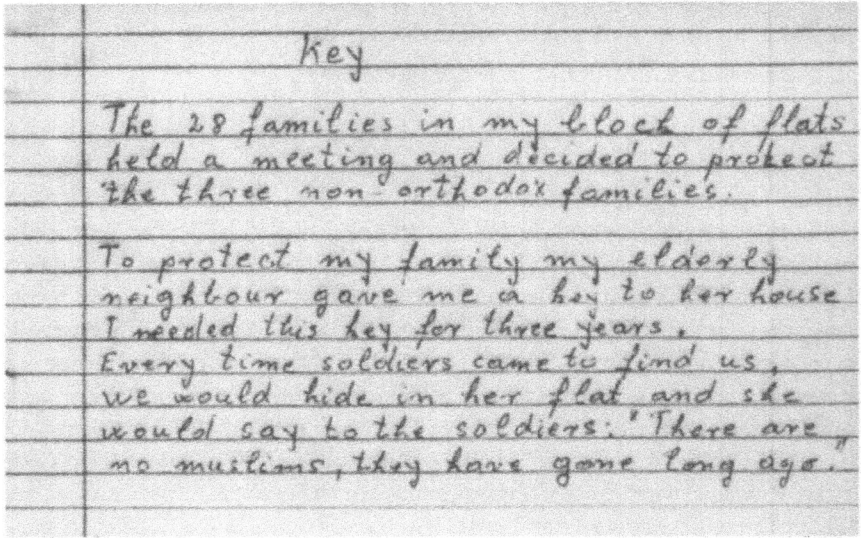

Key

The 28 families in my block of flats held a meeting and decided to protect the three non-orthodox families.

To protect my family my elderly neighbour gave me a key to her house I needed this key for three years. Every time soldiers came to find us, we would hide in her flat and she would say to the soldiers: "There are no muslims, they have gone long ago."

FIGURE 3. The "key" image and narrative is cropped from Fahira's artwork and tells of the importance of the neighbor's key to Fahira and her family. Copyright 1999, City Arts. Reprinted with kind permission.

subjectivities, lives, and experiences is central to attempts to better understand our social worlds with a view to transforming these worlds. Such work reveals the resistances, strengths, and humor of people seeking asylum, as well as knowledge of and a better understanding of the legitimation and rationalization of power, domination, and oppression. Re-presenting lived experience through PAR as ethnomimesis can help to illuminate the necessary mediation of autonomous individuality and collective responsibility involved in performative praxis. Drawing on Shierry Nicholsen's work, the photographs presented here have the capacity to arouse our compassion while not letting us forget that what we are seeing is socially constructed meaning. Through re-presenting the unsayable, the images help to "pierce" us, bringing us into contact with reality in ways that we cannot forget—ways that counter the "postemotionalism" of contemporary "me"-dominated society that Mestrovic (1997) details so carefully in his work.

The civic role of the university is also a key factor, as is the role of academics and social researchers as interpreters and facilitators within the context of an institutional organization that has a degree of status and power in society, as well as access to channels of communication and audiences able to influence social policy through the combination of the theoretical and the performative. Our work in the Midlands envisions/imagines a renewed social sphere for asylum seekers and refugees as citizens of Europe,

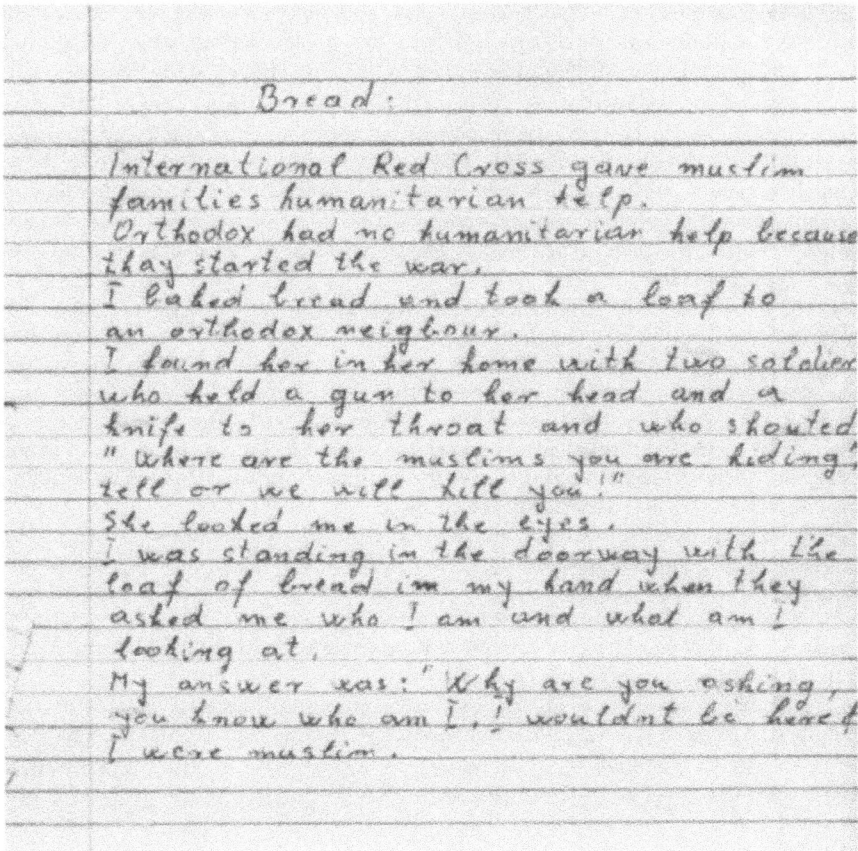

Bread:

International Red Cross gave muslim families humanitarian help. Orthodox had no humanitarian help because they started the war. I baked bread and took a loaf to an orthodox neighbour. I found her in her home with two soldiers who held a gun to her head and a knife to her throat and who shouted "Where are the muslims you are hiding! tell or we will kill you!" She looked me in the eyes. I was standing in the doorway with the loaf of bread in my hand when they asked me who I am and what am I looking at. My answer was: "Why are you asking, you know who am I. I wouldn't be here if I were muslim.

FIGURE 4. The "bread" image is cropped from Fahira's art work and shows the text in English. The narrative and image of the gift of bread serve to anchor the image and story in the reader's imagination. Copyright 1999, City Arts. Reprinted with kind permission.

with our eyes firmly fixed on the "becoming" of equality, freedom, and democracy, through processes of cultural citizenship and mutual recognition in the spheres of polity, economy, and culture.

NOTES

Special thanks to the Bosnia-Herzegovina Community Association and all those who contributed to and facilitated the work. Thanks to the City Arts for supporting the work and to the artists who worked with us: Bea Tobolewska, Simon Cunningham, Karen Fraser, and Maggy Milner. Thanks to the AHRB for funding the development of this work and to John O'Neill, Chris Rojek, and Sinkwan Cheng for their critical comments and support. The themes and ideas documented in this chapter are the author's and are not necessarily representative of the contributors to the research.

1. See article 1(a) of the 1951 Convention Relating to the Status of Refugees. Protection as at the heart of the responsibility that the international community bears toward refugees: in order to be granted protection, individuals have to show that they have a well-founded fear of persecution on account of race, religion, nationality, political opinion, or membership of a political group. Acts or fear of persecution must have been perpetrated by the government or groups that the government cannot control.

2. The outgoing UN High Commissioner Sadako castigated governments for picking and choosing refugee problems to support, depending on strategic interest or public pressure. An example she uses is the support for those fleeing Kosovo but the scant attention paid to the hundreds of thousands uprooted in Sierra Leone and Guinea-Bissau (*Inexile*, December 2000, 3). Moreover, it has to be understood by the British government that asylum applicants do not necessarily think about benefit levels when seeking asylum, but rather whether or not their particular community has an established presence in the country.

3. We must now be aware of and respond compassionately to the obvious risks to Arab and Muslim refugees and asylum seekers in the West following the demonization of, and retaliation against, Arab/Muslim peoples in the wake of the tragic acts of terrorism in the United States on September 11, 2001.

4. See Cohen and Deng's work at the Brookings Institution, Washington, available at http://www.brook.edu.

5. Benhabib (1992) outlines Arendt's interpretation of Kant's theory of reflective judgment, seeing in it a model for intersubjective validity where judgments have to be submitted to the public realm. Judgment involves certain narrative and interpretative skills that together constitute the capacity for an "enlarged mentality" (53–54).

WORKS CITED

Adleman, H. 1999. Modernity, globalization, refugees and displacement. In *Refugees: Perspectives on the experience of enforced migration*, ed. A. Ager, 83–110. London: Continuum.
Adorno, T. W. 1978. *Minima Moralia: Reflections from a damaged life*. Trans. E. F. N. Jephcott. London: Verso.
———. 1980. Commitment. In *Aesthetics and politics*, trans. and ed. Ronald Taylor, 177–95. London: Verso.
———. 1984. *Aesthetic theory*. Trans. Christian Lendhart. London: Routledge and Kegan Paul.
Arendt, H. 1970. *On violence*. New York: Harcourt Brace.
Bauman, Z. 1995. *Life in fragment: Essays in postmodern morality*. London: Sage.
Benhabib, S. 1992. *Situating the self*. Cambridge: Polity Press.
Benjamin, W. 1992. *Illuminations*. London: Fontana Press.
Benjamin, J. 1993. *The bonds of love: Psychoanalysis, feminism and the problem of domination*. London: Virago Press.
Bettleheim, B. 1981. *The informed heart: A study of the psychological consequences of living under extreme fear and terror*. Harmondsworth, UK: Penguin.

Cornell, D. 2000. *Just cause: Freedom, identity, and rights*. Lanham, MD: Rowman and Littlefield.

Crowley, H. 1997. *Women asylum seekers: A legal handbook*. London: Immigration Law Practitioners Association, and Refugee Action

Fals Borda, O. 1988. *Knowledge and people's power: Lessons with peasants in Nicaragua, Mexico and Colombia*. New York: New Horizon.

Forsythe, D. T. 2000. *Human rights in international relations*. Cambridge: Cambridge University Press.

Glenny, M. 1996. *The fall of Yugoslavia*. London: Penguin.

Harrell-Bond, B. 1999. Refugees' experiences as aid recipients. In *Refugees: Perspectives on the experience of enforced migration*, ed. A. Ager, 136–68. London: Continuum.

Heynon, H. 1999. Mimesis, dwelling and architecture: Adorno's relevance for a feminist theory of architecture. In *Adorno, culture and feminism*, ed. Maggie O'Neill. London: Sage.

Hillis Miller, J. 1992. *Illustration*. London: Reaktion Books.

Hughes, D., et al. 1995. Feminist resistance in Serbia. *European Journal of Women's Studies* 2, no. 4.

Inexile: The magazine of the Refugee Council. 2000–2001. (The magazine is produced six times a year. Address: The Refugee Council, 3 Bondway, London SW8 1SJ.)

Kushner, T., and K. Knox. 1999. *Refugees in an age of genocide*. London: Frank Cass.

Kusmics, H. 1997. State formation, economic development and civilisation in North Western and Central Europe. *Geschichte und Gegenwart* 16, no. 2:80–91.

Langer, J., ed. 1997. *The bend in the road: Refugees writing*. Nottingham, UK: Five Leaves Press.

Mestrovic, S. 1997. *Post emotional society*. London: Sage.

Mienczakowski, J. 1995. The theater of ethnography: The reconstruction of ethnography into theater with emancipatory potential. *Qualitative Enquiry* 1, no. 3:360–75.

Mies, M. 1993. Towards a methodology for feminist research. In *Social research: Philosophy, politics and practice*, ed. M. Hammersley, 64–82. London: Sage.

Milosz, M. 1988. On exile. In *Exiles*, ed. J. Koudelka. London: Thames and Hudson.

Nicholsen, S. 1993. Walter Benjamin and the aftermath of the aura: Notes on the aesthetics of photography. *Antioch Community Record*. February 12, 1993. Personal communication to the author.

———. 1997. *Exact imagination: Late work on Adorno's aesthetics*. Cambridge: MIT Press.

———. 1999. Adorno, Benjamin and the aura: An aesthetics for photography. *Adorno, culture and feminism*, ed. Maggie O'Neill, 41–65. London: Sage.

O'Neill, J. 2002. *Incorporating cultural theory: Maternity at the millennium*. Albany, NY: SUNY Press.

———. 2001. *Prostitution and feminism: Towards a politics of feeling*. Cambridge: Polity Press.

O'Neill, M., et al. 2002. Renewed methodologies for social research: Ethno-mimesis as performative praxis. *Sociological Review* 50, no. 1 (February 2002): 69–88.

Pakulski, J. 1977. Cultural citizenship. *Citizenship Studies* 1:73–86.

Piccone, P. 1993. Beyond pseudo-culture? Reconstituting fundamental political concepts. *Telos* 95 (Spring).

Scarry, E. 1985. *The body in pain: The making and unmaking of the world.* New York: Oxford University Press.

Taussig, M. 1993. *Mimesis and alterity.* London: Routledge.

Tester, K. 1992. *The inhuman condition.* London: Routledge.

Whyte, W. F. 1989. Advancing scientific knowledge through participatory action research. *Sociological Forum* 4, no. 3:367–85.

Witkin, R. 1974. *The intelligence of feeling.* London: Heinemann.

Part II

COLONIALISM AND THE
GLOBALIZATION OF WESTERN LAW

4 *The Sovereign Sentence*

KANT AND THE DEPORTATION
OF JUSTICE

Infallibility

Sovereigns have at their disposal an uncommon form of speech: sovereign sentences. By means of such sentences, a sovereign can arrest legal processes and dismiss cases from the arena of judicial competence. Sovereign sentences remain outside of the legal order, even though they possess the force of law. By virtue of their extralegal status, they cannot be considered generally applicable rules, much less universally valid principles. Each sovereign sentence is applicable only to a single case and applies only once. The singularity of the sentence corresponds to the uniqueness of the sovereign who pronounces it. Sovereignty can even be understood as the power to issue sovereign sentences, which, for their part, recreate the condition of their own accomplishment: the condition, namely, of sovereignty as exemption from legal processes and judicial procedures. In other words, only a sovereign can pronounce a sovereign sentence; it does not belong to common forms of discourse. Once such a sentence has been pronounced, however, no word can be spoken in response; arguments are in vain, discussion is at an end. Whatever has been sentenced must be enacted, and this "must" cannot be gainsaid, for if a sovereign sentence were not immediately enacted—without delay and without appeal to a law by means of which it would be legitimated—it would prove to have been something other than a sovereign sentence. Success, in other words, is one of its constitutive criteria. Sovereigns can falter, of course, but sovereign sentences cannot. Any apparent failure of such a sentence is only evidence of a faltering sovereign. To this extent, sovereign sentences are infallible. By virtue of their infallibility, moreover, they cannot be counted among common forms of "speech acts." However much misery they may bring, their enactment cannot be "infelicitous."[1] Because they cannot fail, however, they cannot be judged successful either—regardless of how much felicity they may bring. For the same reason, and despite their incomparable power, it is doubtful whether sovereign sentences can be considered one form of "speech act" among others. Just as sovereigns remain outside the legal order over which they dispose, sovereign sentences escape the category into which they obviously fall.

"Sovereign sentence" is not among the technical terms of Anglo-American juridical discourse—which is not to say that the phenomenon of an infallible "speech act" is unknown, unrecognized, or insignificant. Yet it does suggest that an exposition of this idea can be more fruitfully undertaken within a context of a juridical discourse that not only recognizes this phenomenon but also accords it a stable name. Such is the case in Prussia, particularly during the years in which its jurists begin to reflect on its newly acquired status as a kingdom. The name for a "sovereign sentence" is *Machtspruch*: the "saying" (*Spruch*) in which "power" (*Macht*) expresses itself without recourse or reference to the processes and procedures of the "legal order" (*das Recht*): "The propositions '*Princeps legibus solutus*' and '*Quod principi placuit legis habet vigorem*' stand in close connection with each other. Advisors and attendants of the king already found these sentences in the *corpus iuris civilis* and thereby forged a theory, according to which law in its entirety is subject to the sovereign."[2] Retranslation of *Machtspruch* into the Latin legal lexicon from which this newly devised theory develops might yield phrases like *decretum principis* and *sententia definitiva*; but a better interpretation of the word, which has no exact Latin or English equivalent, would be captured by two other terms: *fatum* and *fiat*.[3] Because a *Machtspruch* has the power to make what it says come true, it corresponds to *fatum* in the original sense of the word—"what has been said"—and comes true for this very reason. Only those who can immediately create the conditions for the truth of their speech escape the sphere of fate, fortune, and fallibility. Because a *Machtspruch* is immediately enacted, moreover, its force is equal to that of the original jussive of *Genesis*: *y'hi or*, which is to say, in Latin, *fiat lux* or, in English, "let there be light" (Genesis 1:3). No word can be said in response to this command, for nothing precedes its enunciation. The first word is in this sense also the final one. Every subsequent *Machtspruch*—if any *Machtsprüche* can be called "subsequent"—remains like the first: at once first and last.

Although the term *Machtspruch* suggests a stark exercise of unprincipled power, its use in specific legal circumstances moves in the opposite direction: toward justice—more exactly, toward a sphere of justice that frees itself of cumbersome, confusing, and often conflicting legal procedures and processes. Whenever the outcome of a juridical process appears unjust—or is unjustly delayed—the sovereign may choose to pronounce a *Machtspruch* as an extralegal remedy. According to the principal jurists in the court of Friedrich Wilhelm I (the first Prussian king), a sovereign may reject any legal decision that he deems unjust; considerations of equity require nothing less. Defined as an indispensable means *"ex plenitudine potestatis principis jus subditis quaesitum auferre,"*[4] the *Machtspruch* enjoyed a secure position in Prussian juridical discourse until the middle years of the eighteenth century, at which time its validity as a solution to mishandled civil suits began to come under increasing scrutiny for two reasons: some poorly planned sovereign sentences caused even greater confusion than the decision of the courts they overruled, and certain principles of *Aufklärung*-inspired administration captured the attention of both royal jurists and the kings they served. In 1765, Philipp Joseph von Jariges, Friedrich II's high chancellor, anonymously published a treatise modeled on Montesquieu's *L'Esprit des Loix* (1755), in which the alteration finds an apt expression. The sole German term that makes its way into the French pamphlet is *Machtspruch*, which serves as a translation of the phrase around which the entire endeavor revolves: *"décision arbitraires et immédiates du sovereign."* Jariges concludes his pamphlet by firmly rejecting sovereign sentences, regardless of their underlying motive or overall intention: "sovereign sentences, even the most equitable, are illegal and contrary to the constitution of the state."[5] In 1780, Friedrich the Great himself echoes his former high chancellor's opinion and goes one step further: "I am very far from presuming to render immediate decisions. That would be a sovereign sentence [*Machtspruch*], and you know that I abhor them."[6]

By the last decade of the eighteenth century, Friedrich II's antipathy achieves a well-articulated conceptual framework. During the time in which Carl Gottlieb Svarez sought to convince the Prussian royal family to bring into effect the massive codification of Prussian law that he coauthored under the title *Allgemeines Landrecht*,[7] he also held a series of lectures on jurisprudence for the crown prince. For Svarez, nothing is more important for the edification of princes than the following lesson. Instead of retaining the prerogative to pronounce *Machtsprüche*, according to Svarez, the sovereign should resolve to accept under all conditions the *Rechtsprüche* (legal decisions) of his courts:

The regent who wants to nullify or alter the verdicts of his courts by sovereign sentences [*Machtsprüche*] acts in opposition to one of his first duties, the protection of everyone in his domain. . . . Sovereign sentences produce neither rights nor obligations. . . . As a result, there is no wiser principle for the security of property and for the freedom of Prussian subjects than the following highly beneficent one: that the juridical circumstances of these subjects only be investigated and decided according to those laws of the State that derive from the courts established by the State; that sovereign sentences never have a juridical effect; and that the sovereign himself never want to issue such sentences, nor allow his ministers to do so.[8]

From the perspective of a *Rechtspruch*—and the jurists who guard the independence of juridical principles and procedures—every *Machtspruch* appears wholly arbitrary, even tyrannical, for each one depends on the "magisterial right" of the prince to present himself as the highest master of the land. From the perspective of the *Machtspruch*, by contrast, the *Rechtspruch* appears insufficient, if not outright impotent, for the strength of its pronouncements are ultimately dependent on the ability of the sovereign to exert his power. The antinomy between "might" and "right," *Macht* and *Recht*, plays itself out in terms of their respective modes of speech—with the proviso that "might" in this case presents itself as the guardian of that unformalizable quality of justice which "right" is prepared to forfeit so as to preserve its continuity, coherence, and integrity: "Only in the eighteenth century did anyone dare maintain that the *Rechtspruch* of a court could not be nullified and declared invalid by a *Machtspruch* of the sovereign."[9] If Svarez can be understood as a representative voice of legal reasoning, then one can say that the *Machtspruch* had entirely relinquished its "rights" by the end of the eighteenth century. *Rechtsprüche* alone are justifiable from the perspective of enlightened jurists, lawmakers, and princes. Whatever sovereigns may represent in relation to their own states, and whatever they may do in relation to other ones, they have no say in the legal order, whose "potentate" they are—which is to say that the legal order can operate safely, without concern for the threat of unprincipled, case-by-case interventions of princely power.

Echoing the King

As long as the threat of a *Machtspruch* has not been fully extinguished, no legal process can be sure that it will have the last word, and if the legal process cannot be sure of having the last word, it cannot be certain that it will have the first one either. Investigations can be suspended, trials interrupted, and outcomes revoked. The mere acceptability of a *Machtspruch* menaces legal proceedings and juridical processes from start to finish. Only by doing away with this threat can the legal order secure itself as an order in its own right. In his lectures to the crown prince—to say nothing of the general code of law he helped prepare—Svarez presents himself as an uncompromising proponent of the *Rechtspruch*. The legal order must dismiss from its midst the menacing prospect of an internal agent of judicial disintegration and legal incoherence. A decade earlier, as if in anticipation of Svarez, Kant had done the same. So completely does Kant cast himself into the role of enlightened jurist that the treatise upon which he hopes to secure a sure path for the science of metaphysics not only begins with a critique of such sentences, but justifies its now-famous title by demonstrating the degree to which this critique is the point of departure for a philosophico-juridical review of finite—and therefore eminently fallible—

reason. No sentence can be allowed to escape the jurisdiction of an "Areopagus" (1:222) that Kant, repeating the gesture that opens the *Universal Natural History*, institutes under the rubric "critique of pure reason." Because sovereign sentences, by definition, are exempt from legal reasoning, they must be silenced from the start. If the "court of reason" were to accept any *Spruch* other than a *Rechtspruch*, it would immediately cease to be an autonomous tribunal in which it sets out to investigate cases, "deduce" rights, and pronounce decisive verdicts.[10]

Sometimes Kant indicates that the chaos of war is the disastrous alternative to the court of reason that he is in the processing of establishing; but at other times—less famously, although more closely in line with the legal reasoning of a Jariges or a Svarez—he insists that the alternative to the court of reason is an unstable court of justice menaced by the threat of uncivil sentences issued by unstable sovereigns. Under this lamentable condition, war becomes a civic affair: reason, which champions the *Rechtspruch*, comes into irresolvable conflict with power, which expresses itself in *Machtsprüche*. Nothing is more important for the vast project of philosophical review and doctrinal codification that Kant first begins to outline in the *Critique of Pure Reason*, therefore, than the dismissal from its inception of the danger posed by, to cite Jariges again, "*décision arbitraires et immédiates du sovereign.*" A few months after Friedrich the Great makes known his profound distaste for sovereign sentences, his "most loyal servant" (1:219) does the same. Echoing the king, as the king echoes his counselors, Kant makes an antipathy to *Machtsprüche* into the basic mood of a philosophical project that seeks to show the means and manner by which all of us—princes and subjects alike—give laws to nature:

However much they may think to make themselves unrecognizable by exchanging the language of schools for a popular tone, these so-called indifferentists, insofar as they think anything at all, always fall without fail back into metaphysical assertions, which they yet professed so much to disdain. Yet, this indifference, occurring amidst the flourishing of all sciences and directed precisely at those sciences whose cognitions, if there were any, we could least do without, is a phenomenon deserving our attention and reflection. It is obviously the effect not of the thoughtlessness of our age, but of its ripening *power of judgment*, which no longer puts up with illusory knowledge, and it is a demand addressed to reason to take over once again the most difficult of all its occupations, namely self-knowledge, and to institute a tribunal [*Gerichtshof*], by which reason may secure its legitimate claims [*gerechten Ansprüchen*] while at the same time dismissing all groundless presumptions—not by sovereign sentences but, rather, according to its eternal and immutable laws, and this is none other than the *critique of pure reason* itself [dagegen aber alle grundlose Anmaßungen, nicht durch Machtsprüche, sondern nach ihren ewigen und unwandelbaren Gesetzen, abfertigen könne, und dieser ist kein anderer als die Kritik der reinen Vernunft selbst]. (A xii)

In these well-known words of the first preface to the first *Critique*, Kant expresses himself with exceptional lucidity: the philosophico-juridical review of reason that he has just initiated will not accept any sovereign sentences. No *dictum*, in other words, that, by fiat, constitutes irrevocable *fatum* will enter into the halls of metaphysical jurisprudence. The integrity of philosophical discourse, like that of its juridical counterpart, thus rejects sovereign sentence outright. To do otherwise would be to open the tribunal of reason to an alien power that would also have the air of strange familiarity. Such is the paradoxical character of the *Machtspruch*: it defies the legal order for the sake of what this very order is supposed to establish, protect, and represent—namely, justice. In the same way, the *Machtsprüche* that Kant rejects in the opening gesture of the first *Critique* would defy the court of human reason for the sake of a "higher" reason. Whereas sovereign sentences are infallible inasmuch as they create the conditions for their own accomplishment, the sentences whose source lies in human reason are not. On the contrary, these sentences are highly fallible, so much so that they demand vigilant self-critique. The sole space in which the "peculiar fate of human reason" (A vii) can be heroically borne—which is not to say "overcome"—is a closed courthouse. By proclaiming "no sovereign sentences," Kant encloses the tribunal of reason once and for all.

But the courthouse within which finite reason adjudicates its claims is not absolutely sealed. Twice Kant breaks his promise to forbid sovereign sentences. The first break—which cannot be analyzed here—takes place in the first publication that appears under Kant's name after the completion of "my entire critical enterprise" (5:170), namely "On the Failure of All Philosophical Attempts at Theodicy" (1791). The second break, which is the subject of this essay, occurs in the first of the two "doctrinal" works Kant promises to complete after having brought his "critical enterprise" to a close, namely the *Metaphysical Foundations of the Doctrine of Right* (1797). Whereas "On the Failure of All Philosophical Attempts at Theodicy" makes failure into one of its themes, the *Doctrine of Right* begins by conceding that it is, at least in part, a failure. Even after the long delay—privately promised in 1765, publicly promised in 1790, delivered some seven years later[11]—the sections that include the acceptance of a sovereign sentence remain unfinished: "the later sections (concerning public right) are currently subject to so much discussion and are nevertheless so important that they can well justify for some time a delay in rendering the decisive judgment" (6:209). This postponement is undeniably odd: a "decisive judgment" on matters of great importance will be delayed because they are now under discussion; but there is room for discussion only because a "decisive judgment" has yet to be rendered. As long as discussion continues, "decisive judgment" will be delayed, and as long as a "decisive judgment" about matters of general importance remains outstanding, discussion will continue. Only one kind of sentence can break into this vicious circle—a sentence that neither discusses nor judges, but that instead dismisses both juridical judgments and general discussion: in other words, the sentence issued solely by a sovereign.

"The Spectacle of a Slaughter-House"

One of the major dimensions of "Public Right" is the right of the state to punish those who break its laws. The principle of punishment enunciated in the *Doctrine of Right*, like all of its principles, derives from the application of the categorical imperative to external relations among persons. In this case, punishment can never serve merely as a means—deterrence of crime, for example, or rehabilitation of criminals, as another—but must always also be an end in itself: in particular, the preservation of the moral personality of the condemned criminal. Therefore, penal law, for Kant, must operate entirely under the law of retribution (*jus talionis*): "all other principles are fluctuating and unsuited for a sentence of pure and strict justice, for extraneous considerations are mixed into them" (6:332).[12] Nevertheless, in a single circumstance, an exception to the law of retribution is acceptable: when the rigorous execution of the penal law threatens the very existence of the state that it is instituted to protect. In this singular circumstance, the sovereign can—and indeed must—arrest the legal process, interrupt the juridical procedure, enter the courthouse, and dismiss its "decisive judgment":

All those who murder, commit murder, order it, or are also commanded, or participates in it, they must suffer death. Justice as an Idea of judicial power [*richterlichen Gewalt*] wills this in accordance with universal laws that are grounded *a priori*.—If, however, the number of accomplices (*correi*) to such a deed is so great that the state, in order to have no such criminals in it, could soon come to be without subjects; and if the state still does not want to dissolve itself, that is, to pass over into the state of nature, which is far worse because it is then entirely bereft of external justice (especially if it does not want to deaden the people's feeling by the spectacle of a slaughter-house [*vornehmlich durch das Spektakel einer Schlachtbank das Gefühl des Volks abstumpfen*]), then the sovereign must also have it in his power [*der Souverän in seiner Macht haben*], in this case of necessity (*casus necessitatis*), to make himself into the judge (to represent one) and pronounce a judgment [*den Richter zu machen (vorzustellen) und ein Urteil zu sprechen*], which, instead of capital punishment, recognizes another punishment for the criminals, by which the population is still preserved, such as deportation [*Deportation*]: this cannot be done in accordance with public law, but it can be done by a sovereign sentence [*Machtspruch*], that is, by an act of the magisterial right [*Majestätsrechts*] which, as clemency, can always be exercised only in singular cases. (6:334)

Nothing Kant ever published is stranger than this paragraph. The sovereign deports the populace of his state in order to preserve its population and thereby keep intact the feeling of its people. It is difficult to imagine the circumstance to which Kant refers, and yet, in its own way, few passages of his work come closer to representing—albeit in an oblique manner—those historical catastrophes that, from the perspective of both sanguine *Aufklärung* principles and its melancholic counterparts, are wholly unimaginable: a country becomes so saturated with *correi*,[13] so filled with murderers and accomplices to murderer, that the proper execution of well-founded legal procedures would constitute a grave threat to its very existence. The state commits suicide by rigorously enacting its principles of justice. This circumstance is so strange, moreover, that the "deportation" Kant recommends even enters into his own formulation. The sovereign does not simply act as judge, he also (in parentheses) "*represents* himself" as one. The parentheses around *vorzustellen* (to represent) indicate at the very least that the act in which the sovereign arrests the juridical process is also *play-acting*. Those before whom the sovereign represents himself as judge—without being one—appear in the previous parentheses: "the people," whose "feeling" would be "deadened by the spectacle of a slaughter-house."

The deadening of feeling corresponds to mass execution undertaken by the legal authorities. Not only does the sole sovereign sentence Kant accepts into his *Doctrine of Right* serve to preserve the state by deporting its people; it also prevents the people who escape deportation from falling prey to an enigmatic anesthetization. When the feeling of the people is deadened, it does not die; rather, it survives—as something other than itself, as something other than "a" people. For, as Kant emphasizes at the very inception of his *Doctrine of Right*, feeling is an indispensable element of the phenomenon we call "life": "the *faculty of desire* is the faculty to be, by means of one's representations, the cause of the objects of these representations. The faculty of an entity to act in accordance with its representations is called *life*. First, *pleasure and displeasure*, susceptibility to which is called *feeling*, is always connected with desire or aversion; but the converse does not always hold" (6:211). A people without feeling is no longer either alive or dead; it falls into an indeterminate zone in which the first article of legal reasoning—that distinguishing life from death—is itself moribund. And if the first principle is moribund, so, too, are all the subsequent ones.[14] Once the distinction between life and death comes into question, so too does the difference between extralegal violence and legally sanctioned coercion: "juridical power" may now be indistinguishable from "juridical violence." And even if this is not the case, even if the law can distinguish its violence from the violence it seeks to punish, the execution of its verdicts still appears to the people as a "spectacle of a slaughter-house," which is to say, as a stark display of state-controlled cannibalism.[15] In strict accordance with the principles of justice, the legal order thus becomes in effect—regardless of its intention—indistinguishable from the murderous *correi* that it condemns to death.

Only someone outside of, and immune from, the demonic cycle of this potential spectacle can arrest the proceedings. This is the function of the sovereign, who is summoned to halt the legal process by virtue of his own internal immunity from its judgments. Even if the sovereign were also a member of the *correi*—and who doubts it?—it would make no difference, for he is still exempt from judicial rulings. And the sovereign in Kant's strange scenario does not simply arrest these procedures and processes; he does so in the form of a *counterspectacle*—not the "spectacle of a slaughter-house," to be sure, but a dramatic display of himself as judge. By casting himself in this inappropriate role, however, the sovereign violates the very separation of powers that, according to Kant, allows a state to make good on the very idea of legality and thus become the *res publica* toward which all juridical programs and legal philosophies should tend.[16] There is therefore a choice of spectacles: either a show of legally sanctioned mass slaughter or a display of the sovereign coming on stage in stolen attire.

Kant chooses the latter. The choice does not go without saying, however, for everywhere else in his reflections on legal principles, he not only insists on the strict separation of powers but also advocates the merciless enforcement of the law of retribution. He thus writes a short essay "On a Supposed Right to Lie on the Basis of Philanthropy" (1797) in which he strenuously argues for the proposition that everyone must always tell the truth, under every conceivable circumstance, even when murderers knock at the door and demand to know the whereabouts of their enemies. The prospect of a friend's murder, according to Kant, does not generate any right—not even an "emergency right" to mislead homicidal interrogators.[17] The prospect of mass slaughter under the direction of legal authorities, by contrast, generates such a right; more exactly, it gives rise to a supposed right: not a "real" right that could be unambiguously pronounced, but only the right of an exceptional figure to represent himself as someone else in the exceptional circumstance of potential civil war. The sovereign may not be precisely lying when he represents himself as judge, but he is still mendacious, for he has no right to be who or what he presents himself as. Only a few paragraphs after his approval of a sovereign sentence, Kant concedes this point:

Of all the rights of a sovereign, the *right to grant clemency* to a criminal (*ius aggratioandi*), either by lessening or entirely remitting punishment, is certainly the slipperiest: in order to show the splendor of his majesty and yet, thereby, to do injustice to a high degree [*um den Glanz seiner Hoheit zu beweisen und dadurch doch im hohen Grade unrecht*].—With regard to crimes of subjects against one another, it is absolutely not for him to exercise his right, for here the absence of punishment (*impunitas criminis*) is the greatest injustice against his subjects. He can make use of it, therefore, only when a wrong is done *to himself* (*crimen laesae maiestatis*). But not even then, if lack of punishment could endanger the people's security.—This right is the only one that deserves the name *magisterial right*. (6:337)

So slippery is the right to grant clemency that Kant himself almost slips up. In this paragraph, which explains the idea of "magisterial right" invoked in the previous one, the exercise of an uncommon right is acceptable only in those circumstances where the life of the sovereign has been endangered. In the earlier discussion, however, the sovereign is allowed to commute the legally valid decision of the court under completely different conditions: when crimes have been committed by subjects against one another—and indeed committed on an unprecedented scale. If every exercise of magisterial right is "unjust to a high degree," then the supreme degree of injustice is reached in this instance. The exercise of this right is outright wrong. Drawing on Prussian legal tradition, Kant proposes a sovereign sentence as the remedy for a legal situation in which the unchecked juridical process would give rise to injustice: the people in this case would be sickened by the sight of so great a slaughter. But Kant does not—and cannot—present the sole *Machtspruch* that he accepts into his *Doctrine of Right* as an interruption of the juridical process for the sake of a higher justice; on the contrary, the pronouncement of this sentence must still be considered wrong, perhaps even as wrong as the wretched crime committed by those revolutionaries who, according to a footnote of the *Doctrine of Right*, carried out the "formal execution" of their sovereign—one of those mysterious crimes that "cannot be forgiven either in this world or the next" (6:321).[18] Unforgivable and yet acceptable in the same stroke: such is the paradox of the sovereign sentence that preserves the population and spares the feelings of the people by deporting a sizable portion of the populace.

The pronouncement of the sovereign sentence is not done for the sake of justice, only for the sake of its appearance. By pardoning criminals who commit crimes *lèse majesté*, a sovereign "demonstrates the splendor of his majesty," which is to say: he reveals the extent to which he remains exterior to the sphere of law from which judge and judged cannot escape except on pain of death. When the sovereign pronounces a sovereign sentence that commutes the sentence of subjects who have done harm to other subjects, he too enters into this sphere—as both judge *and* judged. This "and" marks the absorption of civil divisiveness into the person of the sovereign, who, for his part, cannot fail to appear (even to himself) as a split personality. Because the crimes in question are against his subjects, not himself, the sovereign cannot even appeal to the dubious right of majesty as the basis for the commutation. Casting himself into the legal sphere, the sovereign appears as outlaw—but only under the condition that this self-casting produces a spectacle in which the sovereign plays all parts of the drama. The resolution of this spectacle, however, demands *real* outcasts, who, for their part, cannot be produced at will. The earth must be divided in a very special manner in order for the drama to resolve itself. More exactly, the state in question must have at its disposal certain zones that are both inside and outside its legal order. Drawing on the Roman legal tradition, Kant calls such zones "provinces." Outside of a country's legal jurisdiction and yet nevertheless within its executive power, provinces express, consolidate, and confirm the "split personality" of the sovereign. As judge and outlaw, the sovereign transposes the condemned into places where the juridical authorities can be arrested under any conceivable circumstance—where, in other words, the "doctrine of right" ceases to function. The obverse of the highly conspicuous tribunal of reason at the opening of the *Critique of Pure Reason* is the equally inconspicuous "province" that makes its way into those sections of the *Doctrine of Right* that, as Kant concedes in its preface, shy away from a "decisive judgment."

Colonialism

None of the three *Critique*s says anything about provinces of the critical enterprise. The introduction to the *Critique of Judgment* lays out the "domain of philosophy in general" by delineating the spaces into which the "field" of concepts is divided into "territories," "domains," and "domiciles"—without any provinces or colonies. In a passage of the *Prolegomena to Any Future Metaphysics*, Kant does, to be sure, describe pure mathematics as the "the most valuable province" in the "whole field of *a priori* cognitions" (4:272); but this curious remark, which casts some light on the sovereignty of philosophy, remains undeveloped. Only in the *Doctrine of Right*—and only after allowing for the pronouncement of a deportation order as "sovereign sentence"—does Kant pay any attention to the concept of province. Yet even here the attention is directed not so much toward the complexities of this concept as the usefulness of provinces for the resolution of conflicts in the homeland. A province, more exactly, is the destination of deportees. As opposed to exile, in which the "lord of the land withdraws all protection" (8:338), deportation requires certain ambiguous but by no means vague geographic zones in which subjects are removed from the juridical authorities of a state without escaping the exercise of its power.

The following three passages from Kant's *Doctrine of Right*, taken together, comprise his scattered account of provinciality:

A country (*territorium*) whose inhabitants are citizens of one and the same commonwealth [*eines und desselben gemeinen Wesens*] already through its constitution, that is, without having to perform any juridical act (therefore by birth), is called a *fatherland* [Vaterland]; a country of which they are not citizens apart from this condition is called *a foreign land* [Ausland]; and this is called a province [*Provinz*] (in the sense in which the Romans used this word), if it makes up a part of the country's dominion [*Landesherrschaft*]; because it does not constitute an integrated part of the realm (*imperii*), a place of *residence* for fellow citizens, but only its possession as an under-house [*als eines Unterhauses*], the province must honor the dominant country as a motherland [*Mutterland*]. (6:337)

In the case of a crime committed by a subject which makes all community with his fellow citizens harmful to the state [the lord of the land] also has a right of *banishment* to a province outside the country [*das Recht der Verbannung in eine Provinz im Auslande*], where he will not participate in the rights of a citizen, that is, *deportation*. (6:337–38)

A colony or province is a people that has its own constitution, its own legislation, and its own land, on which those who belong to another state are only foreigners, even though this other state has supreme executive power [*oberste ausübende Gewalt*] over the colony or province. The state having that executive authority is called the mother state [*Mutterstaat*]. The daughter state is dominated by the latter but nevertheless governs itself (by its own parliament, possibly with a viceroy presiding over it) (*civitas hybrida*). This was the relation Athens had with respect to various islands and that Great Britain now has with regard to Ireland. (6:348).

By virtue of its relation to the provinces over which it exercises executive authority, the fatherland turns into a motherland: it can give birth—not to a son-land, of course, which might challenge the fatherland but, rather, to a daughter-land, which cannot. Nor can the daughter-land give birth to its own daughter-lands, for, as a hybrid, it remains barren. An island is a particularly propitious place for a *civitas hybrida* because it is de facto isolated, and its intercourse can therefore be effectively controlled. The constitutions of such places are not "mixed," as this term is traditionally understood in political philosophy; rather, each has its own constitution, its own legislation, and its own "land" (*Boden*), but they all remain subject to a "supreme executive power" that can at any moment and under any pretense interrupt its legal processes and arrest its juridical procedures. In other words, the spatiality of the provinces corresponds to the language of the sovereign sentence. In still other words—those of Hannah Arendt—its spatiality corresponds to "government by decree."[19] And "government by decree" operates in reverse as well: returning from the daughter-land to fatherland, as the sovereign sends his subjects to the provinces by means of a sovereign sentence. In order for the exceptional pronouncement of a sovereign sentence to be issued inside the fatherland, therefore, sovereign sentences must already serve as the rule (in both senses of the term) within its daughter-lands. Kant could not have appealed to a sovereign sentence in the catastrophic circumstance he describes unless he could assume that the sovereign who makes this pronouncement had at his disposal an "outlandish" place where the issuing of sovereign-like sentences goes without saying.

By pronouncing the sovereign sentence in which the condemned are deported, the sovereign imports the spatiality of the province into the "fatherland." *Imported* may not be the right term, however, for the sole sovereign sentence Kant authorizes *realizes* the general condition of sovereignty: *everyone* in the state is *in principle*, if not in fact, deported to the provinces, for everyone is shown to subject to executive decree—except the sovereign, who, in reverse, casts himself as a judge. Those inside the legal order, in short, are cast outside, and the sole outsider casts himself as one of the insiders. And the country as a whole is transported—not in the sense that all "fellow citizens" are shipped off to some island, but insofar as the fatherland turns into a territory where "government by decree" becomes acceptable—neither legally valid nor otherwise legitimate, still less just, but acceptable all the same. And the same can be said of the colonial condition about which Kant writes in the sections on "public right," for he unambiguously condemns their existence in the earlier—and more fully developed—sections on "private right": "Lastly, it can be still be asked whether, when neither nature nor chance but simply our own will brings us into the neighborhood of a people that holds out no prospect of a civil union with it, we should not be authorized to found colonies by force, if necessary, in order to establish a civil union with them and bring these human beings (savages) into a legal condition. . . . But it is easy to see through this veil of injustice (Jesuitism), which would any means to good ends. Such a way of acquiring land is therefore to be repudiated" (6:266)—not so conclusively repudiated, however, as to disappear entirely from the sphere of "public right."

Accordingly, an otherwise unimaginable "under-house" (6:337) becomes the dominant model of legal architecture; its counterimage is the slaughter-house. Kant, whose architectonic imagination perhaps expresses itself nowhere more subtly, does not quite say that the fatherland turns into its own "under-house," without any home, properly speaking, but he comes very close. For the acceptability of a *Machtspruch* depends on the prospect of progressive depopulation. This prospect comes from two apparently conflicting sources: the conspiratorial *correi* and the juridical power that condemns the conspirators to death. As an extralegal remedy—and as a show of might—the sovereign substitutes his own sentence for that of the courts. Yet this substitution also reveals the condition under which the *Machtspruch* can be pronounced: the motherland must be divided into a fatherland, where the powers are rigorously separated, and daughter-lands, where sovereign sentences—under whatever name—can be issued by self-concealing agents of "public right." The condition for the possibility of an acceptable sovereign sentence, in other words, is a separation of the state into two rigorously divided zones: one in which "executive decrees" are everywhere acceptable, and another in which a sovereign sentence is acceptable for the purpose of thwarting the spectacular of mass slaughter. On the basis of this division of the earth into heterogeneous zones of "public right," Kant goes against the demand that he issues at the very beginning of the "critical enterprise." The cost of this concession is high: no longer is the sovereign alone able to pronounce sovereign sentences; on the contrary, anonymous administrators of the provinces can do so—and indeed can, without saying anything, make sovereign sentences with a regularity and ease that would be unacceptable for any sovereign who wants to maintain the appearance of being sovereign. The infallibility of these decrees alters in turn: no longer are they infallible because they, like the command *fiat lux*, recreate the conditions of their accomplishment but, on the contrary, because no one—not even the sovereign who represents himself as such—is in a position to say that they have failed. Or, for that matter, succeeded. Instead of either success or failure, sovereign sentences appear in the guise of fate, as sheer "natural" force.

Another Historical Sign

Kant's inconspicuous acceptance of a single—and singularly weird—*Machtspruch* can be understood as something like an "historical sign" (*Geschichtszeichen*). In a contemporaneous account of the conflict between the philosophical and the juridical faculties of the university, Kant explicitly identifies such a sign: the distant spectators of the revolution in France. By publicly expressing their sympathy for one party in the conflict—a sympathy that "closely borders on enthusiasm" (7:85)—these spectators courageously expose themselves to the danger that emanates from the regimes in which they live. There is only conceivable reason they would universally do something so contrary to their self-interest: out of respect for the mere idea of right.[20] Whatever horrors the Revolution may bring—and Kant does not deny that it, too, may turn into a "spectacle of a slaughter-house"—the state founded on the idea of law appears to its foreign spectators as a genuine *res publica*, that is, as a fatherland in which executive and legislative powers are rigorously separated. Because a "public thing," by definition, grants the legislature the right to decide who is an enemy and who a friend, its declarations of war are no longer *Machtsprüche*. The inevitable result of this transformation of executive *Machtspruch* into legislative *Rechtspruch*, according to one of Kant's more famous political-historical theses, is a gradual elimination of aggressive warfare, at least among fellow "republics."

By contrast, in the *other* historical sign—the acceptance of a sovereign sentence into the philosophico-juridical forum that began by excluding sovereign sentences from its midst—the executive power does not supplant the legislative; rather, the sovereign enters into the legal sphere as judge and thereby makes himself into an internal outlaw. The condition for this counterspectacle is the rigorous division of the earth into zones where the rule of law alone governs legal procedures and zones where it does not. Whereas the historical sign Kant explicitly identifies indicates constant progress of the human species toward the realization of the immanent idea of legality,[21] the latter points toward the geographical *condition* of such progress: the establishment of zones outside the reach of the legal order and yet inside the sphere of executive power. The strangeness of the sole circumstance for which Kant proposes a sovereign sentence as an extralegal remedy, moreover, determines the time that corresponds to these "outlandish" zones: when states threaten to destroy themselves by executing their laws; or, less dramatically, when unchecked legal processes and automated juridical procedure threaten to deaden the feeling of the people, and thereby make "the people" into a remnant of itself.

NOTES

1. The terms *infelicity* and *speech act* are drawn, of course, from the work of John Austin, who characteristically would not concern himself with the "uncommon"—noble or especially sovereign—speech acts; see Austin, *How to Do Things with Words*.

2. Hans Hattenhauer, *Die geistesgeschichtlichen Grundlagen*.

3. For a brief analysis of the term "*Machtspruch*," see Jacob and Wilhelm Grimm, *Deutsches Wörterbuch*, 13:1415.

4. See Adolf Stölzel, *Brandenburg-Preußens Rechtsverwaltung*, 2:15. Stölzel's work is an indispensable resource for research into the character of Prussian law. An abbreviated account of the concept of the *Machtspruch* can be found in the last two chapters of Stölzel's *Fünfzehn Vorträge*, 157–82; see also Eberhard Schmidt, "Rechtssprüche und Machtsprüche." Schmidt's study, which relies heavily on Stölzel's documentation, is compromised by its premises, which largely correspond to those of the regime under which it was written. Stölzel is an unabashed and outspoken antagonist of the sovereign sentence. Near the end of his voluminous work, he blames much of the ills of the Prussian administration of justice on its tendency to admit sovereign sentences (or executive mandates) into its calculations: "Those '*Machtsprüche*,' which in the course of the eighteenth century convulsed the structure of the Prussian legal state, produced the demand for complete separation of supreme-judicial and royal powers. This demand found nourishment partly from France, partly from the Rhein, which exercised its influence eastward" (*Brandenburg-Preußens* 2:684–85). Schmidt criticizes Stölzel for misunderstanding the character of sovereign sentences in the early decades of the eighteenth century and, more generally, for failing to discern the reason for their initial acceptance and gradual rejection: beginning with Friedrich II, Prussian kings lost their self-confidence and forgot that they alone could speak in the name of "popular" justice.

5. Anonymous (attributed to Philipp Joseph von Jariges), *Réflections philosophiques*, quoted in Stölzel, *Fünfzehn Vorträge*, 249. (The publisher, Decker, is the court publisher.) The attribution of the pamphlet to Jariges, who also served as the secretary for the Prussian Royal Academy of Sciences, derives from Johann Ludwig Klüber, *Oeffentliches Recht*, 888.

6. Quoted in Stölzel, *Fünfzehn Vorträge*, 178.

7. See Hattenhauer, ed., *Allgemeines Landrecht für die Preussischen Staaten von 1794*. For analyses of the conditions and consequences of the *Allgemeines Landrecht*, see Hattenhauer's introduction to his edition; Reinhart Koselleck, *Preußen zwischen Reform*; and more briefly, Theodore Ziolkowski, *Mirror of Justice*, 187–214.

8. Quoted from Adolf Stölzel, *Carl Gottlieb Svarez*, 312–14.

9. Hattenhauer, ed., *Geistesgeschichtlichen Grundlagen*, 20. The most famous case of a royal *Machtspruch* is the one with which Friedrich II concluded the trial of the miller, Günther Arnold, resident of Pommerzig (Neumark), against Count Schmettau. The king was of the opinion that the judges in the case were partial to the count and nullified their decision; when it was reinstated, he had them imprisoned (1779). After the king's death in 1786, the trial was resumed, and they were set free. The negative connotations of *Machtspruch* in the latter part of the eighteenth century were in large measure due to the controversy over the Arnold affair; see Stölzel, *Fünfzehn Vorträge*, 170–82.

10. In the second edition of the *Critique of Pure Reason*, Kant emphasizes the legal character of the term "deduction" (B 113): in the course of a legal action, the *quid juris* (unlike the *quid facti*) proceeds as a "deduction." Except in the case of the *Critique of Pure Reason*, where references are to the 1781 edition ("A") and the 1787 revision ("B"), citations of Kant refer to *Immanuel Kants Gesammelte Schriften*, ed. Königlich-Preußische [later Deutsche] Akademie der Wissenschaften zu Berlin. All references to Kant are in parentheses in the text, and all translations are my own.

11. As early as 1765, Kant mentions to Lambert that he plans to publish shortly a "metaphysical first principles of practical world-wisdom [*Weltweisheit*]" (10:53). A detailed account of Kant's changes in plans for a treatment of moral topics from 1765 to the publication of the second *Critique* in 1787 can be found in Lewis White Beck, *Commentary on Kant's "Critique of Practical Reason"*; a succinct presentation of the many delays between the letter to Lambert and the eventual appearance of the *Doctrine of Right* can be found in Bernd Ludwig's edition of the *Metaphysische Anfängsgründe der Rechtslehre*, esp. xiv–xxv. For a discussion of Kant's tendency toward delay, see Fenves, *Late Kant*, 1–4; and for an analysis of the use of the term *Machtspruch* in "On the Failure of All Philosophical Attempts at Theodicy," see *Late Kant*, 47–74.

12. For a lucid analysis of Kant's doctrine of punishment, see Susan Meld Shell, *Rights of Reason*, esp. 160–62.

13. The term *correi* derives from *correus*, "partaker in guilt, joint criminal," and it is defined in the *Digest* of Justinian (34, 3, 3, §3).

14. On the zone of indetermination and its relation to life (understood in a manner quite different from its exposition in Kant's work in general and his *Doctrine of Right* in particular), see the provocative study of Giorgio Agamben, *Homo Sacer*.

15. Elsewhere in the *Doctrine of Right*, Kant associates certain royal actions with cannibalism (6:345); even more devastating remarks can be found in *Toward Eternal Peace* (8:354–55). For further discussion of these passages, see Susan Meld Shell, "Cannibals All."

16. For Kant's most extensive analysis of republicanism, see the "first definitive article for eternal peace" in "Toward Eternal Peace": "*Republicanism* is the political principle of separation of the executive power (the government) from the leg-

islative power" (8:352). In this brief discussion, Kant does not mention juridical power. His silence corresponds to a curious passage in Montesquieu's *L'Esprit des Loix* (from whom he derives this definition), according to which the juridical power should be *"invisible et nulle"* (cited in Carl Schmitt, *Die Diktatur*, 109–110; see also Schmitt's discussion of the separation of powers in *Verfassungslehre*, 182–87). Kant takes Montesquieu's enigmatic remark concerning the invisibility of juridical power literally, so to speak, for he, too, makes it invisible, as it—in keeping with its basic obligation—merely subsumes cases under laws that are elsewhere legislated and enforced.

17. For an analysis of "On the Supposed Right to Lie," see Fenves, *Late Kant*, 117–21.

18. For a more extensive analysis of this remarkable footnote in the *Doctrine of Right*, see Fenves, *Peculiar Fate*, 271–76.

19. Hannah Arendt, *Origins of Totalitarianism*, 243; on the relation of the linguistic mode of decree and imperial expansion, see Susannah Y. Gottlieb, *Regions of Sorrow*, 44–50.

20. For Kant's identification the "historical sign," which is likewise its interpretation *as* a sign, see the second section of the *Conflict of the Faculties* (7:49–94); on the character of this sign and its interpretation, see Michel Foucault, "Un cours inédit"; Jean-Françoise Lyotard, *L'Enthousiasme*; and Fenves, *Peculiar Fate*, 170–285.

21. See the subsection of the *Conflict of the Faculties* that responds to the question "What Proceeds [*Ertrag*] Will Progress Toward the Better Throw Forth?": "Not an ever-growing quantity of *morality* with regard to intentions but an increase in the products of *legality* in dutiful actions whatever their driving springs" (7:91).

WORKS CITED

Agamben, Giorgio. *Homo Sacer: Sovereign Power and Bare Life*. Translated by Daniel Heller-Roazen. Stanford: Stanford University Press, 1998.

Arendt, Hannah. *The Origins of Totalitarianism*. Rev. ed. New York: Harcourt Brace Jovanovich, 1979.

Austin, John. *How to Do Things with Words*. Edited by J. O. Urmson and Marina Sbisà. Cambridge: Harvard University Press, 1975.

Beck, Lewis White. *A Commentary on Kant's "Critique of Practical Reason."* Chicago: University of Chicago Press, 1960.

Fenves, Peter. *Late Kant: Towards Another Law of the Earth*. London: Routledge, 2003.

———. *A Peculiar Fate: Metaphysics and World-History in Kant*. Ithaca: Cornell University Press, 1991.

Foucault, Michel. "Un cours inédit." In *Dits et écrits: 1954–1988*, 4:679–88. Paris: Gallimard, 1994.

Gottlieb, Susannah Y. *Regions of Sorrow: Anxiety and Messianism in Hannah Arendt and W. H. Auden*. Stanford: Stanford University Press, 2003.

Grimm, Jacob and Wilhelm, eds. *Deutsches Wörterbuch*. Rev. ed. Gustav Rosenhagen and the Arbeitstelle des Deutsches Wörterbuches zu Berlin. Leipzig: Hirzel, 1954.

Hattenhauer, Hans, ed. *Allgemeines Landrecht für die Preussischen Staaten von 1794*. Frankfurt am Main: Metzner, 1970.

———. *Die geistesgeschichtlichen Grundlagen des deutschen Rechts*. 3rd ed. Heidelberg: Müller, 1983.

Jariges, Philipp Joseph von (published anonymously). *Réflections philosophiques et historiques d'un jurisconsulte, adressées à son ami à Turin sur l'ordre de la procédure et sur les décisions arbitraires et immédiates du sovereign*. Berlin: Decker, 1765.

Kant, Immanuel. *Gesammelte Schriften*. Edited by Königlich-Preußische [later Deutsche] Akademie der Wissenschaften zu Berlin, 29 vols. to date. Berlin: Reimer; later, De Gruyter, 1990–.

———. *Metaphysische Anfängsgründe der Rechtslehre*. Edited by Bernd Ludwig. Hamburg: Meiner, 1986.

Klüber, Johann Ludwig. *Oeffentliches Recht des Teutschen Bundes und der Bundes-Staaten*. 2nd ed. Frankfurt am Main: Andreä, 1822.

Koselleck, Reinhart. *Preußen zwischen Reform und Revolution: Allgemeines Landrecht, Verwaltung, und soziale Bewegung zwischen 1791 bis 1848*. Stuttgart: Klett, 1967.

Lyotard, Jean-Françoise. *L'Enthousiasme: la critique kantienne de l'histoire*. Paris: Galilée, 1986.

Schmidt, Eberhard. "Rechtssprüche und Machtsprüche der preussischen Könige des 18. Jahrhunderts." *Berichte über die Verhandlungen der Sächsischen Akademie der Wissenschaften zu Leipzig* 95 (1943): 3–48.

Schmitt, Carl. *Die Diktatur: Von den Anfängen des modernen Souveränitätsgedankens bis zum proletarischen Klassenkampf*. 1924. Reprint, Berlin: Duncker & Humblot, 1989.

———. *Verfassungslehre*. Munich: Duncker & Humblot, 1928.

Shell, Susan Meld. "Cannibals All: The Grave Wit of Kant's Perpetual Peace." In *Violence, Identity, and Self-Determination*, edited by Hent de Vries and Samuel Weber, 150–61. Stanford: Stanford University Press, 1997.

———. *Rights of Reason: A Study of Kant's Philosophy and Politics*. Toronto: University of Toronto Press, 1980.

Stölzel, Adolf. *Brandenburg-Preußens Rechtsverwaltung und Rechtsverfassung, dargestellt im Wirken seiner Landesfürsten und Obersten Justizbeamten*. Berlin: Vahlen, 1888.

———. *Carl Gottlieb Svarez. Ein Zeitbild aus der zweiten Hälfte des achtzehnten Jahrhunderts*. Berlin: Vahlen, 1885.

———. *Fünfzehn Vorträge aus der Brandenburglich-Preußischen Rechts- und Staatsgeschichte*. Berlin: Vahlen, 1889.

Ziolkowski, Theodore. *Mirror of Justice*. Princeton: Princeton University Press, 1997.

5 The Female Body as a Post-Colonial Site of Political Protest

THE HUNGER STRIKERS VERSUS
THE LABOR STRIKERS IN
FORSTER'S 'A PASSAGE TO INDIA'

In Forster's *A Passage to India*, Aziz, a Muslim medical doctor, is falsely accused of having made a sexual advance on a British woman. Given the power differential between the colonizer and the colonized in British India, it seems that his "conviction [is] inevitable" (239). Not surprisingly, the British find themselves confronted by a series of protests from the Indians before the trial:

> The Sweepers had just struck, and half the commodes of Chandrapore remained desolate in consequence—only half, and Sweepers from the District, who felt less strongly about the innocence of Dr. Aziz, would arrive in the afternoon, and break the strike, but why should the grotesque incident occur? And a number of Mohammedan ladies had sworn to take no food until the prisoner [Aziz] was acquitted; their death would make little difference, indeed, being invisible, they seemed dead already, nevertheless it was disquieting. (238)

Forster's ironical stance toward the British is evident. The narrator expresses the annoyance experienced by the British when the Sweepers leave the commodes uncleaned and articulates the disquietude they feel when faced with the Mohammedan women's hunger strike. But he is obviously criticizing the British even as he is speaking for them. *A Passage to India* is full of similar examples of Forster's ironic swipes at the British[1]—a point overlooked by certain post-colonialist critics such as Edward Said, who misconstrues Forster as unambiguously supporting and "elaborat[ing] the already existing [British colonial] structure of attitude and reference without changing it" (205). But Said's misplaced critique diverts attention from another level of collusion: the more involuntary or "unconscious" colonialist text inhabiting Forster's novel despite his humanist intentions and liberal sympathy toward the natives.

In spite of Forster's evident disapproval of British colonialism, he does not seem to be much interested in the Indians' own objections to their colonizer—a point underlined by the fact that Forster seems to totally forget the protesters after this point. This is especially evident in his treatment of the Indian women, who make their sole entry onto the stage of political action in this scene but then sink back into oblivion. One begins to wonder whether Forster is not also participating in the colonial economy of forgetfulness by overlooking the significance of this struggle of the colonized, especially the colonized women, for a political voice. For Forster, that is, the Indians, and especially the Indian women protesters, are as "invisible" and half-dead as the Mohammedan women in general are for the British he criticizes.[2] The *insignificance* of this passage in the novel, in other words, reveals the *significance* of Forster's colonial and sexist unconscious.

My project then, will begin where Forster's "ends." By focusing on the above passage, I will highlight and develop what Forster's author-ity seems to have repressed: namely, the ways the native men and women remake and unmake the legal structure sustaining British colonialism as they carry out their struggle against their colonizer. In challenging British colonialism, the protesters are at the same time confronting modern law,[3] the proprietary rhetoric of which provides the basis for the colonizer's political, economic, and military expansion,[4] and inaugurates such political notions in the colony as subjecthood, citizenship, and legitimacy.[5] The advent of the property-owning subject and contractual labor—foregrounded by the Sweepers' labor strike in Forster's passage, for example—illustrates a new understanding of persons and relationships brought about by the Western legal notion of property in the process of colonization. It is precisely these legal categories, as we shall see, that the Sweepers try to manipulate against the colonizer. In contrast to the Sweepers, the Mohammedan women hunger strikers reject this possessive notion of personhood, and along with it the values and institutions which create and impose this modern subjectivity.

The two strikes, in other words, raise concrete legal and political questions about authority and legitimacy which Forster's aesthetically couched criticism fails to address.[6] Read as an exploration of different modalities of political protest, the above passage redirects abstract discourses about power and politics, oppression and opposition—discourses crucial to discussions of colonialism and post-colonialism—to their concrete legal basis. More importantly, focusing attention on the two kinds of protests brings out a contrast between the men and the women in their resistance to the administrative and political structure of the colonial government.[7] By examining the different ways the men and women strikers position themselves with regard to British liberal law, I will argue that the women perform a more radical disruption of the modern legal order underpinning British colonialism. The male strikers protest against British injustice by withholding their labor and as such are still operating within the economy of bourgeois law which defines the subject in terms of his[8] possessions, including his proprietorship of his body and his labor. The Mohammedan women, on the other hand, reject this modern law of possession with their hungry bodies—a political act which confronts the subject of possession with the subject of lack, and in so doing disrupts the liberal law of property by a law parallel to the Lacanian law of desire. Drawing inspiration from Lacan, Benjamin, and Hamacher's discussions of an unconditional law that originates in a violation of law,[9] I will argue that the Mohammedan women hunger strikers inaugurate a law which can be called an "ethical violence *par excellence*" and "the political as such."[10] This theoretical configuration, as I will demonstrate, makes possible a new way of understanding the female body as a post-colonial site of political protest.

Let me start by analyzing the difference between the two strikes described by Forster in the passage above. The men refuse to work; the women refuse to eat. The first group refuses to clean up and clean *out* waste and excrement. The second refuses to take *in* any food. The Indian men carry on a form of dirty protest directed toward the physical infrastructure of colonial rule. The female Mohammedans' hunger strike, on the other hand, has its roots in the Muslim religious practice of fasting which aims to bring about the purification and cleansing of the soul (see Wagtendonk 24). The two genders also have different ways of positioning their bodies within each of their particular protests. The Sweepers strike by withholding their bodies from civil services. But by doing so, their bodies become detached and protected from the consequences of their political actions. The women, by contrast, weave their bodies and their protest into one inseparable entity. Dauntlessly throwing their bodies in front of the modern machine[11] of British colonialism, their protest is penetrated through and through by a death drive that refuses assimilation into the colonial ordering of bodies and subjects. In Lacanian terms, the women position themselves within the Real and as such disrupt both the symbolic and imaginary constructions of colonial subjectivity. The strike carried out by the men, by contrast, avoids the encounter with the Real in which life and death join each other.

The differences between the strikes carried out by the men and the women can be seen as a manifestation of the tension between the subject of property and the subject of lack, the bourgeois law of possession and the psychoanalytic law of desire. In refusing to work, the Sweepers are operating within the framework of the liberal law tradition which constructs a subject as the sum of his possessions—his body and his labor being part of the "property" which he can freely alienate or withhold.[12] The Sweepers gain the "right" to strike only by first acknowledging their labor to be a commodity. As the Russian legal historian Evgenii Bronislavovich Pashukanis points out, within the paradigm of modern law, the precondition of the workers' rights (including the right to withhold their labor) is the commodification of their bodies and their labor.[13] The Sweepers and their rights are marketable and transferable,[14] which is why one Sweeper can be easily exchanged for, and replaced by, another. As Forster points out, the Sweeper-Strikers will soon be replaced by their less sympathetic "colleagues" from the District.

The Sweepers are hence caught in a vicious dilemma. By asserting their right to strike, they trap themselves inside a tradition which subsumes rights under property, and which gives greater protection to property than it does to human rights.[15] If the target of their protest is British colonial injustice, the moral underpinnings[16] of their strike are undermined by its vehicle—that is, contractual law—since contractual law concerns itself with property claims at the expense of morality. The Mohemmadan women's hunger strike, on the other hand, resists this "economy" of rights absolutely.[17] Contractual law necessitates that the protection of property can be *alienated* from the protection of morality; the labor strikers can *detach* their bodies from the consequences of their political action. The women hunger strikers, by contrast, demonstrate with their hungry bodies the *inseparability* of human existence from moral good. The Lockean tradition maintains an "ownership" relationship between the subject and his/(her) life. As such, it creates a split between the owner and the owned, thereby objectifying and commodifying human existence. Forster's Mohammedan women, on the other hand, view their bodies not as legal possessions but as an integral whole with moral values. Non-participants in the "freely"-buying and "freely"-selling exchange economy of the modern subject, the Mohammedan women's comportment toward death threatens the positive law of the British colonial court from the uttermost limit of human existence.[18] The women strikers' death drive, in other words, disrupts bourgeois law's jealous guardianship of external boundaries with the internal limit[19] revealed by the law of desire.[20] What emerges from the women's protest is no longer a subject of property, but what Lacan calls a subject of lack—the subject barred by desire ($). In the next section, I will examine this desiring subject by using Lacan's interpretations of the Sadean concept of the "second death" as well as the Kantian idea of the unconditional and irrecognizable moral obligation. I will also be drawing on Benjamin's messianic time and his politics of quotation, as well as Hamacher's notion of the "afformative."[21]

To the British, the Mohammedan ladies, hardly visible behind their purdahs, "seemed dead already" (238).[22] Why, then, should they find their hunger strike "disquieting"? If anything, these women's ghastly existence can only be made more ghastly by their hunger strike. Like Melville's apparitional figure Bartleby, Forster's Mohammedan ladies are already dead even while they are living. Forster's hunger strikers are thus occupying a space "between-two-deaths." They are like Antigone who, as Lacan points out, "tells us that her soul died long ago and that she is destined to give up help" (*Ethics of Psychoanalysis* 270). In Žižek's terms, these figures have the status of "the *objet petit a*, the sublime object placed in the interspace between the two deaths" (*Sublime Object* 145). It is in this interspace that the women hunger strikers challenge the bourgeois determination of personhood. To paraphrase Padraig O'Malley's analysis of the Irish hunger strike, the Mohammedan women in Forster's novel confront the public with the following question: what does it mean when these "merciless[23] young [strikers] would prefer to do right by denying life instead of affirming it, whose sense of victimhood had become such an integral part of their personality that they needed to reaffirm it by destroying identity itself?" (O'Malley 6). Despite British liberal law's apparent valorization of the subject's right to life, the Mohammedan women demonstrate that, under the British colonial judicial system, the only authentication of one's existence resides in a radical destruction of it, and the choice of death becomes the only way of affirming one's identity. The unambiguous definition of personhood upheld by British law loses its clarity and distinctness when confronted by the Mohammedan women "camping out"[24] in the interspace between two deaths. This space is like a Möbius strip where death merges into life, and powerlessness becomes power. Prior to the Mohammedan women's entry into the interspace opened up by their hunger strike, they were living a death-in-life and as such were neglected by the British. By contrast, they become most alive in the consciousness and conscience of their colonizers as they commit themselves to a cause of comportment toward death.

But there is some-*Thing* even more disturbing occupying the space of suspension between two deaths. As Žižek points out, "This place between two deaths, a place of sublime beauty as well as terrifying monsters, is the site of *das Ding*, of the real-traumatic kernel in the midst of the symbolic order" (*Sublime Object* 136). Like Antigone, the strikers have crossed the uttermost limit of human existence into the realm of the sacred and the profane. In this space, the women strikers are transformed from being associated with food, nurturing, and the source of life[25] to a pitiless and fearless "Thing" like Antigone, herself the em-*bodi*-ment of the death drive and of the positivization of the *objet a*. In other words, the women hunger strikers have gone beyond their association with biological life and the imaginary order to the realm of the Real and of the death drive. Having exceeded the bounds of human life, the Mohammedan women hunger strikers have become, like Antigone, "raw" and "uncivilized" (Lacan, *Ethics of Psychoanalysis*, 263/306 [English/French original]). These "terrible, self-willed victim[s]" who "disturb us" with their raw inflexibility (Lacan, *Ethics of Psy-*

choanalysis, 247) can be compared to the IRA hunger strikers as portrayed by Padraig O'Malley. Both the IRA and the Mohammedan women hunger strikers have hardened themselves into a fearless and pitiless Thing: "And who were they [the hunger strikers], I wondered, who could *harden* themselves to abandon life with a casual disregard for the terminal consequences of their actions, eyes fixed on a star in a galaxy of patriot ghosts imploding in their imaginations, . . . minds impervious to the importunings of those who did not inhabit their closed universe" (6; my italics).

The "hardening" of the human into "the Thing" (*das Ding*) has to do with the strikers overstepping the *até*—a word Lacan ties to *atrocious* (*Ethics of Psychoanalysis* 263/306). It is no accident, then, that the British find the Mohammedan women's "crossing of the limit" "disquieting" (238). No violation of human legality can be as *atrocious* and intransigent as going beyond the human order and the bounds of the symbolic. However, as Weber points out, the *até* is a limit which has its "origin" in "the violation of a limit, a delimitation" (146). By breaching the limit, the hunger strikers are also "'camping' out at the most extreme limits of human existence in order to mark it precisely as a limit, as a horizon that as such cannot be inscribed 'in any signifying chain' . . . but that *allows signification and law and order to take place*" (Weber 152; my italics). In other words, the Mohammedan women's violent "strike" at the modern law's proprietary concept of the "right to life" simultaneously inaugurates a more originary signifying order and founds a more originary legality than those imposed on India by the British.

The hunger strikers' protest against British injustice are hence reminiscent of the caesura opened up by Benjamin's revolutionary strike.[26] As Hamacher explains, this "counter-rhythmical interruption" would be "the critical, the moral, the pure word: a wordless one belonging to no spoken language because it would be its impartability, the very possibility of language and social life themselves" (125). In other words, the Mohammedan women's "absolute crime" is actually "ethical violence *par excellence*" (Hamacher 115).[27] By violating the limit, the hunger strikers are delimiting the scope of human law, making possible the articulation of law itself. In going beyond modern law and its self-appointed role as the Guarantor of "Human Justice," the Mohammedan women strikers are actually grounding themselves in a more originary "origin" of law—namely, "the breach," an alterity that turns out to be the enabling condition of law and justice (see Weber 153). Like Benjamin's revolutionary strike, the Mohammedan women effect "an overthrow" which their strike "not so much causes as accomplishes."[28] To borrow from Hamacher again, the Mohammedan women's hunger strike is not enacted as a particular form of politics, but as a manifestation of "the political as such" (122).

The radicality of the Mohammedan women's hunger strike is also evident in the light of Benjamin's idea of "deposing"[29] (*Entsetzung*)—a notion Benjamin associates with the revolutionary strike. In contrast to the Sweepers, the Mohammedan women's hunger strike, like Benjamin's politics of "deposing," insists that "legal contracts are not the norm for all social and political interaction" (Hamacher 114). To appropriate Hamacher's vocabulary, the politics and violence of the Mohammedan women are "pure"[30] because they manifest a form of *justice* independent of "law's changing power of imposition" (110). This act of deposing—also termed by Benjamin "pure immediate" and "revolutionary" violence, as well as "the highest manifestation of pure violence by humanity"—is, as Hamacher describes it, an "absolute *imperformative* or *afformative* political event"[31] and a "political *a-thesis*" (115). Like Benjamin's "destructive character" ("Destructive Character" 301–3) or "the expressionless" ("*das Ausdruckslose*" in his essay "Goethes Wahlverwandtschaften," *Gesammelte Schriften* 1:181), the Mohammedan women's depositive political act is characterized by "interruption" and "objection," and, along with them, the appearance of the "sublime violence of truth"[32] (Hamacher 124). To adopt Žižek's language, the Mohammedan women's "death drive" and the space they occupy between two deaths point to "the possibility of the total 'wipe-out' of historical tradition opened up by the very process of symbolization/historicization as its radical, self-destructive limit" (*Sublime Object* 135–36). The destruction (in a Benjaminian sense) of the British symbolic order[33] by the Mohammedan women's "afformative" action is hence not confined to the colonizer's positive forms of law. The foundation of British colonial historiography is also severely destabilized. To demonstrate how the Mohammedan women's hunger strike carries the potential of pushing the linear narrative of colonial historiography to its self-destructive limit, I would like to weave into my discussion here Walter Benjamin's politics of quotation.

The Mohammedan women's hunger strike has its roots in Islam. Although Muslims fast regularly, fasting is practiced even more unrelentingly in states of emergency when the consciousness of the pious becomes heightened toward the allusion of the political back to the religious, and the foundation of human power in the divine.[34] The confrontation of the British's concepts of *time*, progress, and modernity by the colonized's appeal to the *timeless* power of divine justice is further complicated by the ghosts reawakened through the intertextualized bodies of the hunger strikers—ghosts from both the past and the future that explode the linear narrative of human progress legitimizing British colonialism. As Maud Ellmann observes, "hunger strikes . . . unsettle chronological accounts of history because they represent what Seamus Heaney calls the 'afterlife' of former protests, former macerations. By hungering, the protesters transform their

bodies into the 'quotations' of their forbears and reinscribe the cause of . . .
nationalism in the spectacle of starving flesh" (14). In their act of self-starvation, the Mohammedan women's bodies call up "ghosts of past and future fasts" (Ellmann 14). These "intertextual and even intergastrical allu-
sions" (Ellmann 14) do not just challenge liberal law's notions of the
bounded body and the subject-individual, they also blast the bourgeois experience of time as a rational, unidirectional progress. Through the bodies
of the strikers, the ghosts of past and future fasts intervene into and explode
the homogeneous, empty time of the British colonial mythical narrative of
human progress with a Benjaminian *jetztzeit*.[35] The hunger strike, in fact, is
a spectral moment when proposopoeia emerges as citation (Balfour 645),
when the strikers's bodies are transformed into quotations of those of their
forbears and of the generations to come like a "tiger's leap" into the past
and into the future. In this context, then, the Lacanian between-two-deaths
can be rewritten as in-the-midst-of-countless-deaths. Here the "dead"
emerge as the most intensely alive and articulate by speaking through the
bodies of the hunger strikers who are seemingly already dead.[36]

   From this perspective, the hunger strikers' bodies become "part objects"
and "part narratives" referring to the absent whole, warning of the possibility of a complete erasure of ethnic history and ethnic space if the British
were to triumph. Hence, it is the Mohammedan women strikers, rather
than their male counterparts, who would be better able to "bring about a
true state of emergency." Žižek describes this revolutionary sense of urgency most effectively in his Lacanian analysis of Benjamin's "On the Concept of History" (*Über den Begriff der Geschichte*):

revolution is an affair of life and death; more precisely: of the *second, symbolic
death*. The alternative opened up by the revolution is that between *redemption*,
which will retroactively confer meaning on the "scum of history" . . . —or what
was excluded from the continuity of Progress—and the *apocalypse* (its defeat),
where even the dead will again be lost and will suffer a second death: "*even the
dead* will not be safe from the enemy if he wins" (Theses VI). (*Sublime Object*, 144)

The "second, symbolic death" in the case of India would be the eternal si-
lencing of the Indians, and of the Muslim women in particular—their identity already in the process of being erased by the British's metonymic reduction of the Muslim women to their purdahs.

   The Mohammedan women's hunger strike, then, confounds the distinctions between life and death, and with it the homogenous categorization of
time into past, present, and future. Their protest amounts to being a violent
"strike" on time, an explosion of British imperial historiography and linear
narrative. Their political protest carries the potential of instantiating a revolution in the Benjaminian sense. As Žižek describes it, such a revolution

is not part of a continuous historical evolution but, on the contrary, moments of "stasis" when the continuity is broken, when the texture of previous history, that of the winners, is annihilated, and when, retroactively, through the success of the revolution, each abortive act, each slip, each past failed attempt which functioned in the reigning Text as an empty and meaningless trace, will be "redeemed," will receive its signification. (*Sublime Object*, 143)

Transposed to Lacanian terms, the Mohammedan women's "afformative" protest can be explained as "a *creationist* act, a radical intrusion of the 'death drive': erasure of the reigning Text, creation *ex nihilo* of a new Text by means of which the stifled past 'will have been'" (Žižek, *Sublime Object*, 143–44).

In short, the Mohammedan women are hardly visible, yet the British find their hunger strike disquieting. The reason is, not unlike the ghosts, the Mohammedan women hardly *ex-ist*, but they *in-sist*.[37] That is how they participate in a social and political system that denies them political participation. Their insistence, by extension, points out a direction for all Indians (and perhaps all colonial subjects)—male or female, Hindus or Muslims—a direction for their intervention into a political system that denies them political representation. The fact is, the Mohammedan women are not the only ones who suffer from invisibility in the British eyes, nor are they the only ones whom the British refuse to acknowledge in their exercise of a right to dissent publicly. The British also willfully turn their eyes from the Indian men who attempt to assert their right to defend their liberties and their duty to oppose injustice. Thus, the Mohammedan women are not the only Indians being effaced, fragmented, and metonymized into the purdahs they wear. (Often in the novel, the purdah stands in for the invisible Mohammedan lady.) The purdah as a metonymy is woven into the fabric of British imperialism and comes to envelope all Indians—be they female or male, Muslims or Hindus. The British's violent reduction of the natives to a metonymic object which the colonizer stereo-*types* on the colonized's body (for example, the purdah)[38] has quite successfully "protected" the colonizer from seeing his colonial other face to face. That is why time and again, the Indians in the novel are reported to be totally incomprehensible to the British.[39]

The Mohammedan women's hungry bodies hence become a powerful mouthpiece for all Indians—past, present, or future—which brings into view yet another critical difference between the men and women strikers. Since bourgeois law is so bound up with property, it is necessarily territorial and exclusive—hence the close association of bourgeois law with the "bounded body." Casting oneself as a proprietary subject with a bounded body involuntarily sets the "self" against "the other." How is it possible, then, for the Sweepers to be speaking for Aziz—another "body"—committed as they are in their labor strike to the liberal law paradigm? In fact, how

can they possibly speak for any-*body* other than their own? The labor strikers are thus caught in a vicious cycle. Their bodies and that of Aziz's perpetually evade each other—a condition evidenced in the Sweepers' *with-*
drawal of their bodies from the public in the very protest carried out on
behalf of Aziz's *imprisoned body.*

The theoretical framework of bourgeois law thus makes it difficult for
the subject to speak on behalf of another. By excluding the other from the
possessive subject, the law of property inevitably undermines the grounds
for collective actions—political actions in particular—such as protests and
strikes. As Macpherson puts it, "to insist that a man's labour is his own, is
not only to say that it is his to alienate in a wage contract; it is also to say
that his labour, and its productivity, is something for which he owes no debt
to civil society" (221). The consequence is, "the individual was seen neither
as a moral whole, nor as part of a larger social whole, but as an owner of
himself" (3).

The Mohammedan women, on the other hand, are capable of acting for
the other because they ek-sist outside themselves. They are not subjects under bourgeois law, and they do not rely on any qualitative confines to confer upon them an identity. They submit themselves instead to the law of internal limit which is the "reflection-into-itself" of the boundary.[40]
Consequently, the Mohammedan women are not bound by an opposition
between "self" and "other." Rather, their state of being can be characterized as "in-me-more-than-me" (*plus moi-même de moi-même*)—a phenomenon which Lacan in his *Ethics of Psychoanalysis* associates with an "excess" of identity at the origin of the self (198).[41] It is this excess which
renders the subject of internal limit—the barred subject—capable of receiv-
ing and relaying the message of the other. At first sight, one might wonder
how the British injustice to the Indians—and to Aziz in particular—can be
represented by the Mohammedan women. Given the difficulties faced by
the male strikers in speaking *for* Aziz, how could the women be expected to
succeed? If all individuals, as bourgeois law proposes, are separated from
each other, the women would be even more separated from Aziz than the
men given the gender differences. The ordeals undergone by the women
during the hunger strike are by no means identical to those experienced by
Aziz in prison. How do these women—and each of these individual
women—come to stand in for, and to stand up for, Aziz? The answer lies
precisely with the "in-me-more-than-me"—what Lacan and Jacques-Alain
Miller call the "extimate"—relationship between the hungry bodies of the
Mohammedan women and the imprisoned body of Aziz.

As Allan Feldman points out in *Formations of Violence*, hunger strike
turns the body "inside out."[42] The British *im*pose boundaries on Aziz's
body, marking him out as a criminal-subject to be isolated from other indi-

viduals. By starving themselves, the Mohammedan women turn their empty stomachs to the outside world, thereby *ex*posing the colonial injustice which has *im*prisoned (both literally and metaphorically) Aziz and other Indians. Through self-starvation, the Mohammedan women also *external*ize the torture and sufferings which each Indian has been forced to carry with*in* his or her own body. The Muslim women's hunger strike, in other words, put on *ex*hibition the prison and other forms of state violence which the British colonial government *im*plants within every-body in India.[43] Feldman's analysis of the inversion of the roles of the captor and the captured assumed by the hunger strikers and the state is pertinent here:

Starvation of the flesh in the hunger strike was the inverting and bitter interiorization of the power of the state. Hunger striking to the death used the body of the [strikers] to recodify and to transfer state power from one topos to another. . . . The act of self-directed violence interiorized the Other, neutralized its potency, enclosed its defiling power, and stored it in the corpse of the hunger striker for use by his support community. (237)

In other words, it is the ob-scenity[44] of the British colonial law that is being captured, imprisoned, and made a spectacle of to the public by the empty stomachs of the Mohammedan women. Note, too, that while Aziz the *man* is taken prisoner by the colonial government, it is the Mohammedan *women* who take prisoner the injustice of British colonial law by using their bodies. Equally important is the women's seizure of the *body* as the site of their political protest in response to the British colonial officials's intention to hijack Aziz's identity through an act of *"incorporeal* transformation"[45]— an act which would transform Aziz from a colonial subject to a criminal subject if the British were to succeed. As a purely symbolic act, incorporeal transformation can take place only by short-circuiting the body—in this case by refusing to acknowledge the body as a material Thing. The declaration of Aziz by British law as a prisoner *instantaneously* transforms Aziz into a prisoner only because such transformations take place completely independently of the material body. To borrow the formulation of Deleuze and Guattari, one can say that British colonial law generates "acts which are only noncorporeal attributes or the 'expressed' of a statement" (80). Through self-starvation, the Mohammedan women bring into view the body of the *Real*—the material "Thing"—and as such disrupt the violence of the colonial *symbolic* order. Their hunger and comportment toward death exemplify "the actions and passions affecting [the] bodies" (Deleuze and Guattari 80). In Lacanian language, the women hunger strikers' bodies are absolutely singular and resistant to the violence of symbolic abstractizations because theirs are "bodies of the drive."

By giving us the notion of a limit which has its "origin" in "the violation of a limit,"[46] and the principle of an absolute that originates in the violation of the absolute, the psychoanalytic law of desire provides us with a way to conceive of legality from a space outside of the contemporary dichotomies of the self and the other, the public and the private. As my analysis shows, bourgeois law holds the body captive within its boundaries, and it is through this law that the British imprison and colonize their Indian subjects. By contrast, the subject of desire presents a body which is thoroughly "traversed by the other, and traverses in this movement the limits of one's identity."[47] Desire, in other words, gives us a law which defines relationships in terms of an "inoperative community" rather than in terms of possession, prohibition, and power. A psychoanalytic reading of the differences between the men's strike and the women's strike in Forster's novel hence gives us an-Other body and an-Other legality for reconsidering questions of resistance in the context of colonialism and its aftermath. It imparts to us new possibilities of configuring social differences and identity. In sum, it presents us with a gift of absolute Alterity in thinking about the legal foundation of national consciousness, and the (im-)possibility of resistance to/through law.

NOTES

I want to thank the Law and Society Association for funding my participation in a most stimulating summer institute in 1997, during which I refined my thoughts on law and colonialism. I would also like to acknowledge my debts to J. Hillis Miller for his suggestions on revising this project.

This essay has been presented as a lecture at various institutions. I would like to thank, in particular, my audience for their stimulating questions at the University of Colorado on January 26, 1999, and at the University of Rhode Island on February 4, 1997.

1. See, for instance, his description of Adela's resumption of her "morning kneel to Christianity" before the trial: "Just as the Hindu clerks asked Lakshmi for an increase in pay, so did she implore Jehovah for a favorable verdict. God who saves the King will surely support the police" (234).

2. The only Indian woman who comes close to "having a face" in A Passage to India is a dead woman—that is, Aziz's deceased wife, whose face is frozen within a photographic frame. She can be considered the most prominent Indian woman in the novel. Even then, Forster gives but a vague description of her face: "The lady faced the world at her husband's wish and her own, but how bewildering she found it, the echoing contradictory world!" Forster "puts her face" away as readily as he drops the subject about the Indians' protest. Immediately following the above description, Forster, through his character Aziz, locks away for good the face of the dead woman: "'Put her away, she is of no importance, she is dead,' said Aziz gently. 'I showed her to you because I have nothing else to show. . . . '" (126).

3. Following many scholars in the field of legal theory, I use the terms bourgeois law, liberal law, and modern law interchangeably. However, like Jane Collier, Bill Maurer, and Liliana Suárez-Navaz, I favor Pashukanis's term bourgeois law in my

chapter. As Collier et al. point out, the term *bourgeois law* "identifies the primary creator and beneficiary of law as an individual who 'owns' property, even if only in 'his' person" (2).

4. Peter Fitzpatrick dissects the colonial logic of modern law by highlighting the narrative of evolution underlying modern law's claim to superiority over "primitive law"—a claim that legitimizes the conquest of the "lawless savages" by modern (Western) law and order. Henry Sumner Maine and Lewis Henry Morgan, for example, portray "primitives" as being ruled by irrational "customs" instead of submitting themselves to the rule of law.

5. Drawing on John Delaney's scholarship, I would like to call attention here to the role of the legal concept of property in the colonizing process as it *re*forms and *de*forms culture and consciousness—a concept which inaugurates in the colonies new relations to "the self" (for instance, our propriety rights to our selves and our bodies), to everyday life (such as ideas of home, work, and community), and to culture (notions of cultural differences and the polarization of the "we" and the "they"). It is important, at the same time, to keep in mind the role played by the idea of property in the process of decolonization, since it is the notion of property that makes possible arguments about liberty, personhood, agency, and power.

6. The urgency for performing a careful reading of the two strikes in Forster's novel becomes all the more pressing when we consider the way Forster's negligence has been duplicated by his critics. This passage has been ignored not only in writings on Forster by Barbara Harlow, Hunt Hawkins, Jeffrey Heath, Judith Scherer Herz, and Frances Singh, but also in criticism of *A Passage to India* and British colonialism by Edward Said, Sara Suleri, and Abdul JanMohammed. This lack of attentiveness, even from post-colonialist scholars well-known for their sensitivity to the colonial implications of seemingly insignificant details in Western canonical works, is worth noting. As I argue elsewhere, this silence marks part of a more general blindness among post-colonialist critics toward the crucial place of law within the operations of colonialism and its aftermath.

7. Homi Bhabha examines in "Of Mimicry and Man" the colonizer's project to mold the colonized into a "reformed recognizable Other" (*Location of Culture*, 87–88). As I will argue in this chapter, the women strikers are more radical in resisting this colonial imposition than their male counterparts.

8. I am confining myself to the male pronoun in order to call attention to the gender bias of the subject of the liberal law tradition. Associating the bourgeois subject with a "he" also highlights the gender issue in my discussion of the differences between the two kinds of strikes.

9. Despite some rather significant divergences in their theoretical positions (a subject which is regretfully beyond the scope of this chapter), these three thinkers have some overlapping ideas in their radical notions of law.

10. These formulations are borrowed from Werner Hamacher, 115.

11. Instead of accepting the breakup of old orders and identities by modern law, Forster's Mohammedan women confront Western bourgeois law with a Muslim tradition which weds a religious practice of purification to a political protest.

Later on, I will discuss how the Mohammedan women hunger strikers base their protest on an *atemporal* law—that is, a law in defiance of modernity and the homogeneous empty *temporal* schema in which modernity is produced. In a way, the Mohammedan women can be understood as "laying siege to time itself . . . vandalizing the ideas of sequence, rhythm, and chronology" (Ellmann 119). The women's "vandalism" of chronology has significant political implications in a (post—)colonial context, given the important roles played by the ideas of progress and evolution in legitimizing colonialism.

12. See Locke's famous statement: "every man has a 'property' in his own 'person'. . . . The 'labour' of his body and the 'work' of his hands . . . are properly his" (204).Other members of this dominant tradition in modern British legal thoughts include Hobbes, Blackstone, and Adam Smith.

13. See Pashukanis's *Law and Marxism*: "At the same time . . . that the product of labour becomes a commodity and a bearer of value, man acquires the capacity to be a legal subject and a bearer of rights" (112). C. B. Macpherson also points out the intimate connection between commodity and various modern legal concepts surrounding the subject such as rights and freedom: "It cannot be said that the seventeenth-century concepts of freedom, rights, obligation, and justice are all entirely derived from this concept of possession, but it can be shown that they were powerfully shaped by it." In a society of possessive individualism, Macpherson observes, "freedom is a function of possession" (3).

Pashukanis and Macpherson have both come under the influence of Marx's critique of rights. See Karl Marx's "On the Jewish Question" and *Communist Manifesto*.

14. See Frederick Pollock's "Locke's Theory of the State" for a critique of Locke's endeavor to subsume all human rights under Property (90).

15. Roscoe Pound makes the following charges against English liberal law in his *Social Control Through Law*: "If, therefore, the law secures property and contract more elaborately and more adequately than it secures personality, it is not because the law rates the latter less highly than the former, but because legal machinery is intrinsically well adapted to securing the one and intrinsically ill adapted to securing the other" (60). See also McIlwain's *Growth of Political Thought*, where the author observes that English liberty is based on the control of purse strings (394). For additional critical assessements of the Lockean legacy or liberal law in general, see J. W. Gough, *John Locke's Political Philosophy*; and Arthur L. Goodhart, *English Law and the Moral Law*.

16. Note that while the Sweepers' strike only provokes feelings of annoyance ("why should the grotesque incident occur?" [238]), it is the women's hunger strike that presses on the British's conscience. The British find their strike "disquieting," an unwitting acknowledgment of the moral impact of the Muslim women's political protest.

17. Since the intake of food is a primary gesture of the subject's appropriation of the outside world, the Mohammedan women's political abstention from food is already a challenge to the ideology of the modern legal subject of possession.

18. In choosing self-starvation to defy an unjust political system, the Mohammedan women associate human existence with moral good rather than with property. As such, their protest is a challenge to British liberal law's *proprietary* concept of the "right to life."

19. I borrow the terms "*ex*ternal boundaries" and "*in*ternal limitations" from Hegel. Later on, I will elaborate on these two concepts in relation to a Lacanian distinction between "*ex*istence" and "*in*sistence."

20. I will soon turn to discuss the Mohammedan women's hunger strike in light of the death drive.

21. Drawing from Hamacher, I will undertake to demonstrate the ways the Mohammedan women hunger strikers disrupt Western possessive individualism by operating neither inside nor outside the modern law "given" to the Indians by the British.

22. The purdah is a recurring figure in the novel. Its significance will become apparent later in my essay.

23. In his discussion of Antigone's death drive, Lacan also emphasizes Antigone's mercilessness and "rawness." (See "The Essence of Tragedy" in *The Ethics of Psychoanalysis*.)

24. I borrow this expression from Samuel Weber's "Breaching the Gap."

25. As a result of their role as mothers, women have been traditionally associated with feeding and nurturing in many cultures. Women are thus often linked to nature, biological existence, "mere life," and the imaginary order. In *Holy Feast and Holy Fast*, Caroline Bynum discusses medieval European women's role in the preparation and distribution of food, but her discussion of medieval Europe seems to have wide applicability to other cultures as well: "[Women] . . . distributed food, both prosaically and miraculously. . . . women had many ways of manipulating and controlling self and environment through food-related behavior, for food formed the context and shapes of women's world—of their responsibilities and privileges—more fundamentally than it did the world of men" (208).

26. In his "Critique of Violence," Benjamin thinks of "proletarian general strike" in terms of pure political violence. As Hamacher points out, the form of justice pertaining to the Benjaminian proletarian strike is independent of "the law's changing power of imposition" (110). Benjamin's proletarian strike is hence much closer to the Mohammedan women's hunger strike than the Sweepers' strike.

27. See Lacan's "Kant with Sade" and his *Ethics of Psychoanalysis* for a discussion of the paradoxical relationship between Sade's absolute crime and Kant's categorical imperative. Samuel Weber briefly alludes to the connection as follows:

> the secularized Christian conception of an immanence of nature capable of recuperating and reappropriating its own finitude is called into question by the artifice of the absolute crime of what is called 'the second death' (Weber 142–43). Another and related point for Lacan is to be found in Kant—first of all, in his moral philosophy, which, in separating the moral law from intuition and cognitive experience, endows moral obligation with an "unconditional" character that is independent of its possible realization. This, Lacan remarks, has the effect of anchoring moral obligation in a cognitive void, one that will turn out in the light of psychoanalysis to have been the site of desire. (143)

Note also the parallel between, on the one hand, Benjamin's revolutionary strike which breaks absolutely the mythical cycle between law-founding and law-preserving violence, and, on the other, the Sadean "second death" which is a "crime against nature subverting the 'natural' opposition of 'death' and 'life'" (Weber 144).

28. Benjamin, *Gesammelte Schriften*, 2:194.

29. This particular translation is adopted from Hamacher. The notion is appealing for its ability to get beyond the binary opposition of positing and its opposite:

> Deposing is not posited. It is not the opposite of positing and cannot be defined as the negation—determinate or indeterminate—of a position as long as the logic of

negation is governed by the premises of positional or propositional logic. Accordingly, Benjamin does not simply regard deposing as a historical consequence of unsuccessful political or legal impositions, but as the event of a "pure immediate violence . . . beyond the law," that is, as the manifestation of a violence independent in principle from positing (*Gesammelte Schriften* 2:202). Moreover, as "pure immediate" violence, deposing is neither a historical nor even a causal consequence, but rather the absolute precondition of every historical positing violence. The afformative character of political deposing, therefore, does not stand opposed to particular legal positings; it lies beyond position and opposition and is—as athetical, immediate mediacy—the precondition for both, without, however, being expressible, representable or presentable in either of them. (Hamacher 128, n. 12)

30. In Lacanian terms, the Mohammedan women's strike embodies pure desire.

31. The "afformative" is a neologism invented by Hamacher to discuss the revolutionary strike described by Benjamin in "Critique of Violence": "*Afformative* is not *aformative*; afformance 'is' the event of forming, itself formless, to which all forms and all performative acts remain exposed. (The Latin prefix *ad-*, and accordingly *af-*, marks the opening of an act, and of an act of opening, as in the very appropriate example of *affor*, meaning 'addressing,' for example when taking leave.) But of course, in *afformative* one must also read *aformative*, as determined by *afformative*" (Hamacher 128, n. 12).

32. Benjamin, "*Goethes Wahlverwandtschaften*," in *Gesammelte Schriften* 1:181.

33. The "strike" on the symbolic order by the Mohammedan women's "ethical violence *par excellence*" is significant. It points out a direction for understanding the way the psychoanalytic law of desire singularizes each individual in terms of his/her lack—a subject which I regretfully will not have time to discuss in detail in this chapter. Despite liberal law's focus on the "individual subject," the list of non-individualized attributes (such as "liberty," "agency," "accountability") indiscriminately assigned to every subject is an indication that the symbolic order as bourgeois law frames it is still general, or, in Hegelian terms, "abstract" (see n. 18 in my introduction to this volume). The suspension of the symbolic order by the women's hunger strike hence amounts to a suspension of the abstractness and generality of the liberal law of possession. The women strikers' destruction of bourgeois law's symbolic act of conferral allows their radical singularity—their uniqueness which always remains *other* to any external determining order—to emerge. This singularity is similar to what Levinas envisions for his notion of rights—a kind of rights capable of expressing the alterity or absoluteness of every human being:

Rights that, independently of any *conferral, express the alterity or absolute of every person, the suspension of all reference* . . . ; an alterity of the *unique* and the incomparable, due to the belonging of each one to mankind, which, *ipso facto and paradoxically*, is annulled, precisely to leave each man *the only one* of his kind. A tearing loose and a suspension—or freedom—which is no mere abstraction. It marks the absolute identity of the person, that is, of the non-interchangeable, incomparable and unique. A uniqueness beyond the individuality of multiple individuals within their kind. A uniqueness not because of any distinctive sign that would serve as a specific or individuating difference. . . . It remains *concrete* [my italics], precisely in the form of the various rights of man, claimed unconditionally, under the various necessities of the real, as various modes of freedom. (1993: 117)

Note, however, that Levinas's position on liberalism is very different from mine.

34. See Wagtendon 9.

35. See the fourteenth thesis in Benjamin's "On the Concept of History": "History is the subject of a structure whose site is not homogeneous, empty time, but time filled by the presence of the now [*Jetztzeit*]. Thus, to Robespierre ancient Rome was a past charged with the time of the now which he blasted out of the continuum of history. The French Revolution viewed itself as Rome returned. It cited Rome the way fashion cites costumes of the past. Fashion has a flair for the topical, no matter where it stirs in the thickets of long ago; it is the tiger's leap into the past. The jump, however, takes place in the arena where the ruling class gives the commands. The same leap in the open air of history is the dialectical one, which is how Marx understood the revolution." (I follow here Balfour's slight modification of Zohn's translation. Balfour, by translating "*zitieren*" as "cite" rather than "evoke," is both more accurate and better conveys Benjamin's politics of quotation. See Balfour 645–46, n. 43.)

36. Indeed, *A Passage to India* is haunted throughout by ghosts—the ghostly presence of Mrs. Moore at the trial, the ghost of the man killed by Nawab Bahadur's car (an accident resulting from the colonization of India by Western technology and modern industrial economy [106]), the ghostly echoes which Adela desperately struggles to "exorcise" (267). Elsewhere, I discuss at length the tension between a "detective story" and a "ghost story" in *A Passage to India*. The detective story follows the paradigm of bourgeois law and attempts to locate a responsible subject-agent for each incident. This rational narrative, however, is constantly haunted by a ghost story—one that makes guilt unlocalizable and leaves mysteries unresolvable. The repeatedly thwarted attempts of Fielding to resolve the mystery of the caves is a case in point.

37. The term *insist* is adopted from Lacan's *Encore Seminar* (translated as *On Feminine Sexuality: The Limits of Love and Knowledge, 1972–1973*, by Bruce Fink.) I contrast "insistence" to "existence" in order to highlight the differences between the liberal law of possession and the psychoanalytic law of desire. *Existence* falls on the side of male logic, not only for its connection to the sovereign subject of existentialism, but also for its intimate relation to the way the subject asserts itself in modern law—that is, in terms of self-possession and *ex*ternal boundaries. *In*sistence, by contrast, singularizes a subject by foregrounding *in*ternal limitations. Following the law of desire, insistence disrupts the idea of existence by constantly referring itself back to the persistence of trauma.

The Mohammedan women, of course, do not exist as subjects in bourgeois law. For the British, they are "hardly visible" (238). Nonetheless, their dignity insists despite the exclusion of their "existence" by the British colonial judicial system. Note that "insistence" is by no means a passive, "reactive" politics. Prevented from participation by the exclusive and colonial male logic, the Mohammedan women respond with a inclusive female logic which Joan Copjec calls "the logic of absolute all." See also Renata Salecl's *Spoils of Freedom*, where she develops a logic of radical democracy on the basis of Lacan's discussion of sexuation (133).

38. Allan Feldman in his *Formations of Violence* makes a most telling observa-

tion about the perniciousness of the British colonizer's practice of reducing the colonized's body into codified fragments:

> The act of violence transposes the body whole into codified fragments: body parts or aspects which function as metonyms of the effaced body and of larger totalities. The violent reduction of the body to its parts or disassociated aspects is a crucial moment in the political metaphorization of the body . . . a material as much as it is a linguistic practice: (1) Metonymic displacement and substitution (parts replacing the whole) express the political instrumentation of the body and thus mark a shift from prior usages of the body, from its prepolitical semantic status. (2) The distillation of the body into parts is the miniaturization of the body. This miniaturization is a mimesis of the concentration of politico-historical codes in the body altered by violence. The body marked by violence encapsulates certain political purposes, mediations, and transformations. (69–70)

Feldman further warns that the "essentialization of ideological codes in the body prepares for the violent dematerialization of the body as the prescribed site for the lodgement and dislodgement of such codes" (71).

39. The devastating confusion experienced by the British in response to the echoes in the caves is a definitive symbol of the British's inability to appreciate, much less understand, India. Among the British characters, even those who demonstrate much good will toward India (such as Fielding, Adela, and the novel's narrator) are, in general, not exempted from a blindness toward their "colonial other." Adela, for example, assumes all Muslims to be the same and offends Aziz by asking in her *"honest, decent,* inquisitive way: 'Have you one wife or more than one?'" (169; my italics). In their anxiety to understand "the real India," these characters desperately try to impose their cognitive framework with its stereotypical categories in an attempt to understand (and thus appropriate) Indian culture. The more anxious they are to "know" India, the less capable they are of appreciating India. Adela, for instance, despairs over her inability to apprehend India by means of her intellect: "How can the mind take hold of such a country?" (150). Likewise, the narrator feels threatened by the fact that the reputation of the Marabar Caves "does not depend upon human speech" (137). In their attempt to "understand" India, both are trying to master India and colonize it with their Western "sense." Both experience frustrations because the Other resists being captured and evaluated by the Western rational subject.

40. These concepts are adopted from Kant's *Critique of Pure Reason* and *Prolegomena,* and Hegel's *Phenomenology* and *Logic.* See also Žižek's explanation of these ideas in *For They Know Not What They Do* (109).

41. Lacan highlights a certain lexical redundancy in the etymological development of the French word *même* from the Latin *metipsemus,* which he interprets as a linguistic indication of a certain repetition that lies at the "heart" of the self (*Ethics of Psychoanalysis* 198 / 233).

42. Note, however, some major differences between the hunger strikes of the IRA and that of Forster's Mohammedan women. In Forster's novel, for example, the strikers were not themselves the prisoners. Unlike the IRA hunger strike, there is no coincidence between the hungry bodies and imprisoned bodies in *A Passage to India.* This is to say, what goes on in Forster's novel is a different "inversion of the body" requiring a different method of examination. To highlight the differences between

Feldman's study and mine concerning the relationship between the hungry body and the imprisoned body, let me quote the following from *Formations of Violence*: "The symbiosis between prison discipline and political resistance culminated in a *literal inversion* of the body, in a dissected body turned inside out. . . . The margins between prison and body were submerged and erased; the cell became the extended body of the prisoners, and their bodies became their temporary prison" (166).

43. This shows yet another way the law of internal limitations—that is, the psychoanalytic law of desire—can contribute to feminist studies. As the feminist legal theorist Zillah R. Eisenstein points out, the law of bounded bodies discriminates against women whose "boundaries" become unclear in cases such as pregnancy. The question of pregnancy is highly pertinent to our analysis here, since the women hunger strikers are pregnant with the ghosts of other hunger strikers. In their self-starvation, the women strikers also demonstrate how they are pregnant with sufferings from injustice. As such, they make evident that the bodies of the Indians are always already shot through by the injustice of the British. Their message hence amounts to the following: in reality, there is no "Indian subject" possible as liberal law prescribes it, since the boundaries of the natives' bodies have always been invaded through and through by British violence.

44. In addition to its conventional meaning, the word "ob-scenity" is hyphenated here to recall how "obscene" can also imply "off-stage" in Lacanian usage.

45. This term is adopted from Deleuze and Guattari's *A Thousand Plateaus* (80–85). Deleuze gives as an example of incorporeal transformation "the judge's sentence that transforms the accused into a convict" (80).

46. See Samuel Weber's explication in "Breaching the Gap" (146).

47. This is a formulation borrowed from Christopher Fynsk (xviii).

WORKS CITED

Balfour, Ian. "Reversal, Quotation (Benjamin's History)." 106 (1991): 622–47.
Benjamin, Walter. "Critique of Violence." In *Reflections: Essays, Aphorisms, Autobiographical Writings*, translated by Edmund Jephcott and edited by Peter Demetz, 277–300. New York: Schocken, 1978.
———. "The Destructive Character." In *Reflections: Essays, Aphorisms, Autobiographical Writings*, translated by Edmund Jephcott and edited by Peter Demetz, 301–3. New York: Schocken, 1978.
———. "Goethes Wahlverwandtschaften." In *Gesammelte Schriften*, edited by Rold Tiedemann and Hermann Schweppenhäser, 1:i:123–201. Frankfurt am Main: Suhrkamp, 1974.
———. *Gesammelte Schriften*. Frankfurt am Main: Suhrkamp, 1972–89.
———. "Theses on the Philosophy of History." In *Illuminations*, translated by Harry Zohn and edited by Hannah Arendt. New York: Helen and Kurt Wolff-Harcourt, Brace, and World, 1968.
Bhabha, Homi. *The Location of Culture*. London: Routledge, 1994.
Bynum, Caroline. *Holy Feast and Holy Fast: The Religious Significance of Food to Medieval Women*. Berkeley: University of California Press, 1987.
Collier, Jane, Bill Maurer, and Liliana Suárez-Navaz. "Sanctioned Identities: Legal Constructions of Modern Personhood." *Identities: Global Studies in Culture and Power* 2, no. 1–2 (1995): 1–27.

Copjec, Joan. "Sex and the Euthanasia of Reason." In *Supposing the Subject*, edited by Joan Copjec, 16–44. London: Verso, 1994.

Deleuze, Gilles, and Félix Guattari. *A Thousand Plateaus: Capitalism and Schizophrenia*. Translated by Brian Massumi. Minneapolis: University of Minnesota Press. Translation of *Mille plateaux*, 1980. Vol. 2 of *Capitalisme et schizophrenia*. Paris: Les Éditions de Minuit, 1987.

Eisenstein, Zillah R. *The Female Body and the Law*. Berkeley: University of California Press, 1988.

Ellmann, Maud. *The Hunger Artist*. Cambridge: Harvard University Press, 1993.

Feldman, Allan. *Formations of Violence: The Narrative of the Body and Political Terror in Northern Ireland*. Chicago: University of Chicago Press, 1991.

Fitzpatrick, Peter. "Custom as Imperialism." In *Law, Society, and National Identity in Africa*, edited by Jamil M. Abun-Nasr, Ulrich Spellenberg, and Ulrika Wanitzek. Beitrage zur Afrikaforschung, 1:15–30. Hamburg: Helmut Buske Verlag, 1990.

———. *Mythology of Modern Law*. London: Routledge, 1992.

Forster, E. M. *A Passage to India*. 1924. Reprint, San Diego: Harcourt Brace, 1984.

Fynsk, Christopher. "Experiences of Finitude." Foreword to *The Inoperative Community*, by Jean-Luc Nancy, vii–xxxv. Theory and History of Literature 76. Minneapolis: University of Minnesota Press, 1991.

Goodhart, Arthur L[ehman]. *English Law and the Moral Law*. London: Stevens, 1953.

Gough, J[ohn] W[iedhofft]. *John Locke's Political Philosophy: Eight Studies*. 2nd ed. Oxford: Clarendon Press, 1973.

Hamacher, Werner. "Afformative, Strike: Benjamin's 'Critique of Violence.'" Translated by Dana Hollander. In *Walter Benjamin's Philosophy: Destruction and Experience*, edited by Andrew Benjamin and Peter Osborne, 110–38. Warwick Studies in European Philosophy. London: Routledge, 1994.

Harlow, Barbara. "Law and Order in *A Passage to India*." In *A Passage to India*, edited by Tony Davies and Nigel Wood, 65–89. Theory in Practice Series. Buckingham: Open University Press, 1994.

Hawkins, Hunt. "Forster's Critique of Imperialism in *A Passage to India*." *South Atlantic Review* 48 (1983): 54–65.

Heath, Jeffrey. "A Voluntary Surrender: Imperialism and Imagination in *A Passage to India*." *University of Toronto Quarterly* 59 (1989–90): 287–309.

Hegel, Georg Wilhelm Friedrich. *Phenomenology of Spirit*. Translated by A. V. Miller. Oxford: Clarendon Press, 1977.

———. *Hegel's Science of Logic*. Translated by A. V. Miller. Atlantic Highlands, NJ: Humanities Press International, 1969.

Herz, Judith Scherer. "Listening to Language." In *"A Passage to India": Essays in Interpretation*, edited by John Beer, 59–70. London: Macmillan Press, 1985.

———. *"A Passage to India": Nation and Narration*. Twayne Masterwork Studies 117. New York: Twayne Publishers, 1993.

Herz, Judith, and Robert K. Martin, eds. *E. M. Forster: Centenary Revaluations*. Toronto: University of Toronto Press, 1982.

JanMohammed, Abdul. "The Economy of Manichean Allegory: The Function of Racial Difference in Colonialist Literature." *Critical Inquiry* 12 (1985): 59–87.

Reprinted in *"Race," Writing, and Difference*, edited by Henry Louis Gates Jr., 18–106. Chicago: University of Chicago Press, 1985.

Kant, Immanuel. *The Critique of Pure Reason*. Translated and edited by Paul Guyer and Allen W. Wood. New York: Cambridge University Press, 1998.

———. *Immanuel Kant: Prolegomena to Any Future Metaphysics that Will be Able to Come Forward as Science*. Translated and edited by Gary Hatfield. Cambridge: Cambridge University Press, 1977.

Lacan, Jacques. *The Ethics of Psychoanalysis, 1959–1960*. Translated by Dennis Porter. Edited by Jacques-Alain Miller. New York: Norton, 1992. Book 7 of *The Seminar of Jacques Lacan*. Translation of *L'éthique de la psychanalyse, 1959–1960*. Paris: Les Éditions du Seuil, 1986. Book 7 of *Le Séminaire*. 1992.

———. *On Feminine Sexuality: The Limits of Love and Knowledge, 1972–1973*. Translated by Bruce Fink. Edited by Jacques-Alain Miller. New York: Norton, 1998. Translation of *Le Séminaire*, book 20, *Encore*. Paris: Éditions du Seuil, 1973.

———. "Kant with Sade." Translated by James B. Swenson Jr. *October* 51 (1989): 55–104.

Levinas, Emmanuel. "The Rights of Man and the Rights of the Other." 1993. In *Outside the Subject*, translated by Michael B. Smith, 116–25. Stanford: Stanford University Press, 1994. Translation of *Hors sujet*. Saint-Clément-la-Riviè: Fata Morgana, 1987.

Locke, John. *Two Treatises of Government*. London: George Routledge, 1884.

Macpherson, C. B. *The Political Theory of Possessive Individualism: Hobbes to Locke*. Oxford: Oxford University Press, 1962.

Marx, Karl "On the Jewish Question." In *The Marx-Engels Reader*, edited by Robert C. Tucker, 26–52. 2nd ed. New York: Norton, 1978.

Marx, Karl, and Friedrich Engels. *The Communist Manifesto: A Modern Edition*. Introduction by Eric Hobsbawm. London: Verso, 1998.

McIlwain, Charles Howard. *The Growth of Political Thought in the West: From the Greeks to the End of the Middle Ages*. New York: Macmillan, 1932.

Merry, Sally Engle. "Law and Colonialism." *Law and Society Review* 25 (1991): 889–922.

Nancy, Jean-Luc. *The Inoperative Community*. Translated by Peter Connor, Lisa Garbus, Michael Holland, and Simona Sawhney. Edited by Peter Connor. Theory and History of Literature 76. Minneapolis: University of Minnesota Press, 1991.

O'Malley, Padraig. *Biting at the Grave: The Irish Hunger Strikes and the Politics of Despair*. Boston: Beacon Press, 1990.

Pashukanis, Evgenii Bronislavovich. *Law and Marxism: A General Theory*. Translated by Barbara Einhorn. Edited by Chris Arthur. London: Pluto Press, 1989.

Pollock, Frederick. "Locke's Theory of the State." *Essays in the Law*. London: Macmillan, 1922. 80-102.

Pound, Roscoe. *Social Control Through Law*. New Haven: Yale University Press, 1942.

Said, Edward. *Culture and Imperialism*. New York: Vintage, 1994.

Salecl, Renata. *Spoils of Freedom: Psychoanalysis and Feminism after the Fall of Socialism*. London: Routledge, 1994.

Singh, Frances. "A Passage to India, the National Movement, and Independence."
    Twentieth-Century Literature 31 (1985): 265–87.
Suleri, Sara. *The Rhetoric of English India*. Chicago: University of Chicago Press,
    1992.
Wagtendonk, K. *Fasting in the Koran*. Leiden: E. J. Brill, 1968.
Weber, Samuel. "Breaching the Gap: On Lacan's *Ethics of Psychoanalysis*." In *Pol-
    itics, Theory, and Contemporary Culture*, edited by Mark Poster, 131–58. New
    York: Columbia University Press, 1993.
Žižek, Slavoj. *For They Know Not What They Do: Enjoyment as a Political Factor*.
    London: Verso, 1991.
———. *The Sublime Object of Ideology*. London: Verso, 1989.

Part III

6 *Recognition as Justice?*

A PROPOSAL FOR AVOIDING
PHILOSOPHICAL SCHIZOPHRENIA

At present, claims for social justice tend to divide into two types. First, and most familiar, are redistributive claims, which seek a more just distribution of resources and wealth. Examples include claims for redistribution from the North to the South, from the rich to the poor, and (not so long ago) from the owners to the workers. Although such claims are no longer as salient as they were a few years ago, they have supplied the paradigm case for most theorizing about social justice for the past 150 years. Today, however, we increasingly encounter a second type of social-justice claim in the "politics of recognition." Here the goal, in its most plausible form, is a difference-friendly world, where assimilation to majority or dominant cultural norms is no longer the price of equal respect. Examples include claims for the recognition of the distinctive perspectives of ethnic, "racial," and sexual minorities, as well as of gender difference. This type of claim has recently attracted the interest of political philosophers, some of whom, moreover, are seeking to develop a new paradigm of justice that puts recognition at its center.

In general, then, we are confronted with a new constellation. The discourse of social justice, once centered on distribution, is now increasingly divided between redistribution talk on the one hand, and recognition talk on the other. Often, moreover, the two discourses are dissociated from one another. The cultural politics of difference is decoupled from the social politics of equality. In some cases, this dissociation has become a polarization. Some proponents of redistribution see claims for the recognition of difference as "false consciousness," whereas some proponents of recognition view distributive politics as an outmoded materialism, which can neither articulate nor challenge many injustices. In such cases, we are presented with an either/or choice: redistribution or recognition? class politics or identity politics? multiculturalism or social democracy?

These, I have argued elsewhere, are false antitheses (Fraser 1995, 1997, 2000, 2003). Justice today requires *both* redistribution *and* recognition. Neither alone is sufficient. As soon as one embraces this thesis, however, the question of how to combine them becomes paramount. I contend that the emancipatory aspects of the two paradigms need to be integrated in a single, comprehensive framework. The task, in part, is to devise an expanded conception of justice that can accommodate both defensible claims for social equality and defensible claims for the recognition of difference.

Morality or Ethics?

Integrating redistribution and recognition is no easy matter, however. On the contrary, to contemplate this project is to become immediately embroiled in a nexus of difficult philosophical questions. Some of the thorniest of these concern the relation between morality and ethics, the right and the good, justice and the good life. A key issue is whether paradigms of justice usually aligned with "morality" can handle claims for the recognition of difference—or whether it is necessary, on the contrary, to turn to "ethics."

Let me explain. It is now standard practice in moral philosophy to distinguish questions of justice from questions of the good life. Construing the first as a matter of "the right" and the second as a matter of "the good," most philosophers align distributive justice with Kantian *Moralität* (morality) and recognition with Hegelian *Sittlichkeit* (ethics). In part this contrast is a matter of scope. Norms of justice are thought to be universally binding; they hold independently of actors' commitments to specific values. Claims for the recognition of difference, in contrast, are more restricted. Involving qualitative assessments of the relative worth of various cultural practices, traits, and identities, they depend on historically specific horizons of value, which cannot be universalized.

Of course, moral philosophers dispute the relative standing of these two different orders of normativity. Liberal political theorists and deontological moral philosophers insist that the right take priority over the good. For them, accordingly, the demands of justice trump the claims of ethics. Communitarians and teleologists rejoin that the notion of a universally binding morality independent of any idea of the good is conceptually incoherent. Preferring "thick" accounts of moral experience to "thin" ones, they rank the substantive claims of culturally specific community values above abstract appeals to Reason or Humanity. Partisans of the right, moreover, often subscribe to distributive models of justice. Viewing justice as a matter of fairness, they seek to eliminate unjustified disparities between the life-chances of social actors. To identify these disparities, they invoke standards of fairness that do not prejudge those actors' own (varying) views of the good. Partisans of the good, in contrast, reject the "empty formalism" of distributive approaches. With a view to promote human flourishing, they insist on the need for an ethical conception of the good life.

These philosophical alignments complicate the problem of integrating redistribution and recognition. Distribution evidently belongs on the morality side of the divide. Recognition, however, seems at first sight to belong to ethics, as it seems to require judgments about the value of various practices, traits, and identities. It is not surprising, therefore, that many deontological theorists simply reject claims for the recognition of difference as violations of liberal neutrality, whereas many theorists of recognition conclude that their concerns require qualitative value judgments that exceed the capacities of distributive models.

In these standard alignments, both sides agree that distribution belongs to morality, that recognition belongs to ethics, and that those two paradigms exclude one another. If they are right, then the claims of redistribution and the claims of recognition cannot be coherently combined. On the contrary, whoever wishes to endorse claims of both types courts the risk of philosophical schizophrenia.

It is precisely this presumption of incompatibility that I aim to dispel. Contra the received wisdom, I shall argue that one *can* integrate redistribution and recognition without succumbing to schizophrenia. My strategy will be to construe the politics of recognition in a way that does not deliver it prematurely to ethics. Thus, I shall account for claims for recognition as *justice claims* within an expanded understanding of justice. The initial effect will be to recuperate the politics of recognition for *Moralität* and thus to resist the turn to ethics. But that is not precisely where I shall end up. Rather, I shall concede that there may be cases when ethical evaluation is unavoidable. Yet because such evaluation is problematic, I shall suggest ways of deferring it as long as possible.

Identity or Status?

The key to my strategy is to break with the standard "identity" model of recognition. On this model, what requires recognition is group-specific cultural identity. Misrecognition consists of the depreciation of such identity by the dominant culture and the consequent damage to group members' sense of self. Redressing this harm means demanding "recognition." This in turn requires that group members join together to refashion their collective identity by producing a self-affirming culture of their own. Thus, on the identity model of recognition, the politics of recognition means "identity politics" (Fraser 2000).

This identity model is deeply problematic. By construing misrecognition as damaged identity, it risks substituting intrusive forms of consciousness engineering for social change. Tending to reify group identity, moreover, it pressures individuals to conform to "group culture" while masking the power of dominant fractions and reinforcing intragroup domination. In general, then, the identity model lends itself all too easily to separatism and political correctness (Fraser 2000).

For these reasons, I shall propose an alternative analysis of recognition. My proposal is to treat recognition as a question of *social status*. From this perspective—I shall call it the *status model*—what requires recognition is not group-specific identity but rather the status of group members as full partners in social interaction. Misrecognition, accordingly, does not mean the depreciation and deformation of group identity. Rather, it means *social subordination* in the sense of being prevented from *participating as a peer* in social life. To redress the injustice requires a politics of recognition, to be sure, but this no longer means identity politics. In the status model, rather, it means a politics aimed at overcoming subordination by establishing the misrecognized party as a full member of society, capable of participating on a par with other members (Fraser 2000, 2003).

Let me elaborate. To view recognition as a matter of status is to examine institutionalized patterns of cultural value for their effects on the relative standing of social actors. If and when such patterns constitute actors as *peers*, capable of participating on a par with one another in social life, then we can speak of *reciprocal recognition* and *status equality*. When, in contrast, institutionalized patterns of cultural value constitute some actors as inferior, excluded, wholly other, or simply invisible, and hence as less than full partners in social interaction, then we should speak of *misrecognition* and *status subordination*.

In the status model, then, misrecognition arises when institutions structure interaction according to cultural norms that impede parity of participation. Examples include marriage laws that exclude same-sex partnerships as illegitimate and perverse, social-welfare policies that stigmatize single mothers as sexually irresponsible scroungers, and policing practices such as racial profiling that associate racialized persons with criminality. In each of these cases, interaction is regulated by an institutionalized pattern of cultural value that constitutes some categories of social actors as normative and others as deficient or inferior: straight is normal, gay is perverse; "male-headed households" are proper, "female-headed households" are not; "whites" are law-abiding, "blacks" are dangerous. In each case, the result is to deny some members of society the status of full partners in interaction, capable of participating on a par with the rest.

In each case, accordingly, a claim for recognition is in order. But note precisely what this means: aimed not at valorizing group identity, but rather at overcoming subordination, claims for recognition in the status model seek to establish the subordinated party as a full partner in social life, able to interact with others as a peer. They aim, that is, *to deinstitutionalize patterns of cultural value that impede parity of participation and to replace them with patterns that foster it.*

This status model avoids many difficulties of the identity model. For one thing, it avoids essentializing such identities. For another, it resists the temptation to substitute the reengineering of consciousness for social change. In addition, by enjoining status equality in the sense of parity of participation, it valorizes cross-group interaction, as opposed to separatism. Finally, the status model does not deliver recognition prematurely to ethics. Conceiving that category in terms of status equality, it provides a deontological account of recognition. Thus, it frees recognition claims' normative force from direct dependence on a specific substantive horizon of value. Unlike the identity model, then, the status model is compatible with the priority of the right over the good. Refusing the traditional alignment of recognition with ethics, it aligns it with morality instead. Thus, the status model permits one to combine recognition with redistribution—without succumbing to philosophical schizophrenia. Or so I shall argue next.

Justice or the Good Life?

Any attempt to integrate redistribution and recognition must address four crucial philosophical questions. First, is recognition a matter of justice, or is it a matter of self-realization? Second, do distributive justice and recognition constitute two distinct, sui generis, normative paradigms, or can either of them be subsumed within the other? Third, does justice require the recognition of what is distinctive about individuals or groups, or is recognition of our common humanity sufficient? And fourth, how can we distinguish those claims for recognition that are justified from those that are not?

How one answers these questions depends on the conception of recognition one assumes. In what follows, I will use the status model to provide a deontological account. Drawing on that model, I shall expand the standard conception of justice to accommodate claims for recognition. By stretching the notion of justice, then, I shall avoid turning prematurely to ethics.

I begin with this question: Is recognition an issue of justice, and thus of morality, or one of the good life, and thus of ethics? Two major theorists, Charles Taylor (1994) and Axel Honneth (1995), understand recognition as a matter of the good life. Unlike them, however, I propose to conceive it as an issue of justice. Thus, one should not answer the question "what's wrong with misrecognition?" by saying that it impedes human flourishing by distorting the subject's "practical relation-to-self" (Honneth 1995). One should say, rather, that it is unjust that some individuals and groups are denied the status of full partners in social interaction simply as a consequence of institutionalized patterns of cultural value in whose construction they have not equally participated and that disparage their distinctive characteristics or the distinctive characteristics assigned to them. One should say, that is, that misrecognition is wrong because it constitutes a form of institutionalized subordination—and thus, a serious violation of justice.

This approach offers several important advantages. First, by appealing to a deontological standard, it permits one to justify claims for recognition as morally binding under modern conditions of value pluralism. Under these conditions, there is no single conception of the good life that is universally shared, nor any that can be established as authoritative. Thus, any attempt to justify claims for recognition that appeals to an account of the good life must necessarily be sectarian. No approach of this sort can establish such claims as normatively binding on those who do not share the theorist's horizon of ethical value. Unlike such approaches, the status model of recognition is nonsectarian. What makes misrecognition morally wrong, in this view, is that it denies some individuals and groups the possibility of participating on a par with others in social interaction. The norm of *participatory parity* invoked here is compatible with a plurality of different views of the good life. It can justify claims for recognition as normatively binding on all who agree to abide by fair terms of interaction under conditions of value pluralism.

Treating recognition as a matter of justice has a second advantage as well. Conceiving misrecognition as status subordination, it locates the wrong in social relations, not in individual or interpersonal psychology. Thus, it escapes difficulties that plague other, psychologistic, approaches. When misrecognition is identified with internal distortions in the structure of self-consciousness of the oppressed, it is but a short step to blaming the victim. Conversely, when misrecognition is equated with prejudice in the minds of the oppressors, overcoming it seems to require policing their beliefs, an approach that is illiberal and authoritarian. For the status model, in contrast, misrecognition is a matter of externally manifest and publicly verifiable impediments to some people's standing as full members of society. And such arrangements are morally indefensible *whether or not they distort the subjectivity of the oppressed.*

Finally, by aligning recognition with justice instead of the good life, one avoids the view that everyone has an equal right to social esteem. That view is patently untenable, of course, because it renders meaningless the notion of esteem.[1] The account proposed here, in contrast, entails no such reductio ad absurdum. What it *does* entail is that everyone has an equal right to pursue social esteem under fair conditions of equal opportunity.

For all these reasons, recognition is better treated as a matter of justice, and thus of morality, than as a matter of the good life, and thus of ethics. And construing recognition on the model of status permits us to treat it as a matter of justice.

But what follows for the theory of justice?

Expanding the Paradigm of Justice

Supposing that recognition is a matter of justice, what is its relation to distribution? Does it follow, turning now to our second question, that distribution and recognition constitute two distinct, sui generis conceptions of justice? Or can either of them be reduced to the other?

The question of reduction must be considered from two different sides. From one side, the issue is whether existing theories of distributive justice can adequately subsume problems of recognition. In my view, the answer is no. To be sure, many distributive theorists appreciate the importance of status over and above the allocation of resources and seek to accommodate it in their accounts (Rawls 1971; Dworkin 1981; Sen 1985). But the results are not wholly satisfactory. Most such theorists assume a reductive economistic-cum-legalistic view of status, supposing that a just distribution of resources and rights is sufficient to preclude misrecognition. In fact, however, not all misrecognition is a by-product of maldistribution, nor of maldistribution plus legal discrimination. Witness the case of the African American Wall Street banker who cannot get a taxi to pick him up. To handle such cases, a theory of justice must reach beyond the distribution of rights and goods to examine institutionalized patterns of cultural value. It must consider whether such patterns impede parity of participation in social life.[2]

What, then, of the other side of the question? Can existing theories of recognition adequately subsume problems of distribution? Here, too, I contend the answer is no. To be sure, some theorists of recognition appreciate the importance of economic equality and seek to accommodate it in their accounts (Honneth 1995). But once again, the results are not wholly satisfactory, as they tend to assume a reductive culturalist view of distribution. Supposing that all economic inequalities are rooted in a cultural order that privileges some kinds of labor over others, they believe that changing that cultural order is sufficient to preclude all maldistribution. In fact, however, not all maldistribution is a by-product of misrecognition. Witness the case of the skilled white male industrial worker who becomes unemployed because of a factory closing resulting from a speculative corporate merger. In that case, the injustice of maldistribution has little to do with misrecognition. It is rather a consequence of imperatives intrinsic to an order of specialized economic relations whose raison d'être is the accumulation of profits. To handle such cases, a theory of justice must reach beyond cultural value patterns to examine the structure of capitalism. It must consider whether economic mechanisms that are relatively decoupled from structures of prestige and that operate in a relatively impersonal way impede parity of participation in social life.

In general, then, neither distribution theorists nor recognition theorists have so far succeeded in adequately subsuming the concerns of the other.[3] Thus, instead of endorsing one of their conceptions to the exclusion of the other, I propose to develop an expanded conception of justice. My conception treats distribution and recognition as distinct perspectives on, and dimensions of, justice. Without reducing either perspective to the other, it encompasses both dimensions within a broader, overarching framework.

As already noted, the normative core of my conception is the notion of *parity of participation*.[4] According to this norm, justice requires social arrangements that permit all (adult) members of society to interact with one another as peers. For participatory parity to be possible, I claim, at least two conditions must be satisfied.[5] First, the distribution of material resources must be such as to ensure participants' independence and voice. This condition may be thought of as *objective*. It precludes forms and levels of material inequality and economic dependence that impede parity of participation. In contrast, the second condition is *intersubjective*. It requires that institutionalized patterns of cultural value express equal respect for all participants and ensure equal opportunity for achieving social esteem. It precludes institutionalized norms that systematically depreciate some categories of people and the qualities associated with them. Both conditions are necessary for participatory parity. Neither alone is sufficient. The objective condition brings into focus concerns traditionally associated with the theory of distributive justice, especially concerns pertaining to the economic structure of society and to economically defined class differentials. The intersubjective condition brings into focus concerns recently highlighted in the philosophy of recognition, especially concerns pertaining to the status order of society and to culturally defined hierarchies of status. Thus, an expanded conception of justice oriented to the norm of participatory parity encompasses both redistribution and recognition, without reducing either one to the other.

This approach goes a considerable way toward resolving the problem with which we began. By construing redistribution and recognition as two mutually irreducible dimensions of justice, and by submitting both of them to the deontological norm of participatory parity, it positions them both on the common terrain of *Moralität*. Avoiding turning prematurely to ethics, then, it seems to promise an escape route from philosophical schizophrenia.

Recognizing Distinctiveness?

Before proclaiming success, however, we must take up our third philosophical question: Does justice require the recognition of what is distinctive about individuals or groups, over and above the recognition of our common humanity? If the answer proves to be yes, we will have to revisit the question of ethics.

Let us begin by noting that participatory parity is an universalist norm in two senses. First, it encompasses all (adult) partners to interaction. And second, it presupposes the equal moral worth of human beings. But moral universalism in these senses still leaves open the question whether recognition of individual or group distinctiveness could be required by justice as one element among others of the intersubjective condition for participatory parity.

This question cannot be answered, I contend, by an a priori account of the kinds of recognition that everyone always needs. It needs rather to be approached in the spirit of pragmatism informed by the insights of social theory. From this perspective, recognition is a remedy for social injustice, not the satisfaction of a generic human need. Thus, the form(s) of recognition justice requires in any given case depend(s) on the form(s) of *mis*recognition to be redressed. In cases where misrecognition involves denying the common humanity of some participants, the remedy is universalist recognition. Where, in contrast, misrecognition involves denying some participants' distinctiveness, the remedy could be recognition of specificity.[6] In every case, the remedy should be tailored to the harm.

This pragmatist approach overcomes the liabilities of two other, mirror-opposite views. First, it rejects the claim, espoused by some distributive theorists, that justice requires limiting public recognition to those capacities all humans share. Favored by opponents of affirmative action, that approach dogmatically forecloses recognition of what distinguishes people from one another, without considering whether such recognition might be necessary in some cases to overcome obstacles to participatory parity. Second, the pragmatist approach rejects the opposite claim, equally decontextualized, that everyone always needs his or her distinctiveness recognized. Favored by recognition theorists like Honneth (1995) and Taylor (1994), this second approach cannot explain why it is that not all, but only some, social differences generate claims for recognition—nor why only some of those claims, but not others, are morally justified. By contrast, the approach proposed here sees claims for the recognition of difference contextually, as responses to specific preexisting injustices, while insisting that *only those claims that promote parity of participation are morally justified.*

For the pragmatist, accordingly, everything depends on what precisely currently misrecognized people need in order to be able to participate as peers in social life. And there is no reason to assume that all of them need the same thing in every context. In some cases, they may need to be unburdened of excessive ascribed or constructed distinctiveness. In other cases, they may need to have hitherto underacknowledged distinctiveness taken into account. In still other cases, they may need to shift the focus onto dominant or advantaged groups, outing the latter's distinctiveness, which has been falsely parading as universal. Alternatively, they may need to deconstruct the very terms in which attributed differences are currently elaborated. Finally, they may need all of the above, or several of the above, in combination with one another and in combination with redistribution. Which people need which kind(s) of recognition in which contexts depends on the nature of the obstacles they face with regard to participatory parity.

We cannot rule out in advance, therefore, the possibility that justice may require recognizing distinctiveness in some cases.

Justifying Claims for Recognition

Up to this point, I have managed to answer three major philosophical questions about recognition while remaining on the terrain of *Moralität*. By construing recognition on the model of status, I have given it a deontological interpretation. And by expanding the standard paradigm of justice, I have treated redistribution and recognition as two mutually irreducible dimensions of, and perspectives on, justice, both of which can be brought under the common norm of participatory parity. Thus, I have so far avoided the turn to ethics and escaped philosophical schizophrenia.

At this point, however, the question of ethics threatens to return. Once we accept that justice *could*, under certain circumstances, require recognition of distinctiveness, then we must consider the problem of justification. We must ask: What justifies a claim for the recognition of difference? How can one distinguish justified from unjustified claims of this sort? The crucial issue is whether a purely deontological standard will suffice—or whether, on the contrary, ethical evaluation of various practices, traits, and identities is required. In the latter event, one will have to turn to ethics after all.

Let us begin by noting that not every claim for recognition is warranted, just as not every claim for redistribution is. In both cases, one needs an account of criteria and/or procedures for distinguishing warranted from unwarranted claims. Theorists of distributive justice have long sought to provide such accounts. Theorists of recognition, in contrast, have been slower to confront this question. They have yet to provide any principled basis for distinguishing justified from unjustified claims.

This issue poses grave difficulties for those who treat recognition as an issue of ethics. According to Honneth (1995), for example, everyone needs their distinctiveness recognized in order to develop self-esteem, which is an essential ingredient of an undistorted identity. On this hypothesis, however, white supremacist identities would seem to merit some recognition, as they promote the self-esteem of poor whites. Unfortunately, cases like this one, in which prejudice conveys psychological benefits, are by no means rare. They suffice to disconfirm the view that enhanced self-esteem can supply a justificatory standard for recognition claims.

How, then, *should* recognition claims be judged? What constitutes an adequate criterion for assessing their merits? The approach proposed here appeals to participatory parity as an evaluative standard for both dimensions of social justice. Whether the issue is distribution or recognition, claimants must show that current arrangements prevent them from participating on a par with others in social life. Redistribution claimants must show that existing economic arrangements deny them the necessary objective conditions for participatory parity. Recognition claimants must show that institutionalized patterns of cultural value deny them the necessary intersubjective conditions. In both cases, too, participatory parity serves to evaluate proposed remedies for injustice. Whether they are demanding redistribution or recognition, claimants must show that the social changes they seek will in fact promote parity of participation. Redistribution claimants must show that the economic reforms they advocate will supply the objective conditions for full participation to those currently denied them—without significantly exacerbating other disparities. Similarly, recognition claimants must show that the sociocultural institutional changes they seek will supply the needed intersubjective conditions—again, without substantially worsening other disparities.

This approach represents a considerable improvement over the "self-realization" standard just discussed, as it provides a basis for condemning the institutionalization of racist values even where the latter provide psychological benefits to those who subscribe to them. Nevertheless, it remains to be seen whether the norm of participatory parity is by itself sufficient to distinguish justified from unjustified claims for the recognition of difference.

Same-Sex Marriage, Cultural Minorities,
and the Double Requirement

The problem is that not all disparities are per se unjust. Theorists of distributive justice have long appreciated this point with respect to economic inequalities. Seeking to distinguish just from unjust economic disparities, some of them have drawn the line between those inequalities that arise as a result of individuals' choices on the one hand, and those that arise as a result of circumstances beyond individuals' control on the other, arguing that only the second, and not the first, are unjust (Dworkin 1981). Analogous issues arise with respect to recognition. Here, too, not all disparities are unjust—because not all institutionalized value hierarchies are unjust. What is needed, consequently, is a way of distinguishing just from unjust disparities in participation. The key question here, once again, is whether the deontological norm of parity of participation is sufficient for this purpose—and whether, if not, one must turn to ethics.

To answer this question, let us apply the standard of participatory parity to some current controversies. Consider, first, the example of same-sex marriage. In this case, as we saw, the institutionalization in marital law of a heterosexist cultural norm denies parity of participation to gays and lesbians. For the status model, therefore, this situation is patently unjust, and a recognition claim is in principle warranted. Such a claim seeks to remedy the injustice by deinstitutionalizing the heteronormative value pattern and replacing it with an alternative that promotes parity. This, however, can be done in more than one way. One way would be to grant the same recognition to homosexual partnerships that heterosexual partnerships currently enjoy by legalizing same-sex marriage. Another would be to deinstitutionalize heterosexual marriage, decoupling entitlements such as health insurance from marital status and assigning them on some other basis, such as citizenship and/or territorial residency. Although there may be good reasons for preferring one of these approaches to the other, both of them would serve to foster participatory parity between gays and straights; hence both are justified in principle—assuming that neither would exacerbate other disparities.

Thus, the case of same-sex marriage presents no difficulties for the status model. Here, on the contrary, the norm of participatory parity warrants gay and lesbian claims deontologically, without recourse to ethical evaluation. Perhaps, however, this example is too easy. Let us consider some presumptively harder cases involving cultural and religious practices. In such cases, the question arises whether participatory parity can really pass muster as a justificatory standard—whether, that is, it can serve to warrant claims deontologically, without recourse to ethical evaluation of the cultural and religious practices at issue. In fact, as we shall see, participatory parity proves adequate here as well—provided it is correctly applied.

What is crucial here is that participatory parity enters the picture at two different levels. First, at the *intergroup* level, it supplies the standard for assessing the effects of institutionalized patterns of cultural value on the relative standing of *minorities vis-à-vis majorities*. Second, at the *intragroup* level, participatory parity also serves to assess the *internal effects of minority practices* for which recognition is claimed—that is, the effects on the groups' own members. Taken together, these two levels constitute a double requirement for claims for cultural recognition. Claimants must show, first, that the institutionalization of majority cultural norms denies them participatory parity and, second, that the practices whose recognition they seek do not themselves deny participatory parity—to some group members as well as to nonmembers. For the status model, both requirements are necessary; neither alone is sufficient. Only claims that meet both of them are deserving of public recognition.

To apply this double requirement, consider the French controversy over the foulard. Here the issue is whether policies forbidding Muslim girls to wear head scarves in state schools constitute unjust treatment of a religious minority. In this case, those claiming recognition for the foulard must establish two points: they must show, first, that the ban on the scarf constitutes an unjust majority communitarianism, which denies educational parity to Muslim girls; and second, that an alternative policy permitting the foulard would not exacerbate female subordination. Only by establishing both points can they justify their claim. The first point, concerning French majority communitarianism, can be established without difficulty, it seems, as no analogous prohibition bars the wearing of Christian crosses in state schools; thus, the current policy denies equal standing to Muslim citizens. The second point, concerning the nonexacerbation of female subordination, has proved controversial. Some French republicans have argued that the foulard is itself a marker of such subordination. Disputing this interpretation, however, some multiculturalists have rejoined that the scarf's meaning is highly contested in French Muslim communities today, as are gender relations more generally; thus, instead of construing it as univocally patriarchal, which effectively accords male supremacists sole authority to interpret Islam, the state should treat the foulard as a symbol of Muslim identity in transition, one whose meaning is contested, as is French identity itself, as a result of transcultural interactions in a multicultural society. From this perspective, permitting the foulard in state schools could be a step toward, not away from, gender parity.[7]

In my view, the multiculturalists have the stronger argument here. But that is not the point I wish to stress. The point, rather, is that the argument is rightly cast in terms of parity of participation. For the status model, this is precisely where the controversy should be joined. As in the case of same-sex marriage, so too in the case of cultural and religious claims: the norm of participatory parity serves to evaluate claims deontologically, without any need for ethical evaluation of the cultural or religious practices in question.[8]

In general, then, the status model sets a stringent standard for justifying claims for the recognition of cultural difference. Yet it remains wholly deontological. Applied in this double way, the norm of participatory parity suffices to rule out unwarranted claims, without any recourse to ethical evaluation.

Ecology Without Ethics?

The question remains, however, whether participatory parity suffices in every case, or whether it must be supplemented by ethical considerations in some. In the latter event, not all claims that passed the deontological test would be justified. Rather, only those that survived a further round of ethical examination would be deemed worthy of public recognition. Thus, it would be necessary, in the end, to turn to ethics.

This prospect arises when we consider cases that are not amenable to pluralist solutions. These would be cases, unlike sex-sex marriage or *l'affaire foulard*, that cannot be handled by institutionalizing toleration. In those two cases, people with different ethical views of the good life could agree to disagree and opt for a regime of live and let live. Suppose, however, we encountered a case in which people's ethical visions were so directly antithetical, so mutually undermining, that peaceful coexistence was an impossibility. In that event, the society would be forced to choose between them, and parity of participation would cease to be a relevant goal. With that deontological standard no longer applicable, it would be necessary to evaluate the alternatives ethically. Citizens would have to assess the relative worth of two competing views of the good life.

Certainly, such cases are in principle possible. But they are not as common as those who assign recognition to ethics believe. Consider the hypothetical case of a society committed to ensuring the integrity and sustainability of the natural environment. Let us suppose that the social arrangements in this society institutionalize eco-friendly patterns of cultural value. Let us also suppose that the effect is to disadvantage a minority of members who identify with eco-exploitative cultural orientations. Suppose, too, that those members mobilized as a cultural minority and demanded equal recognition of their cultural difference. Suppose, that is, that they demanded the institutionalization of a new pattern of cultural value that ensured parity for eco-friendly and eco-exploitative cultural practices.

Clearly, this is a case that is not amenable to a pluralist solution. It makes no sense to institutionalize parity between eco-friendly and eco-exploitative orientations within a single society, as the latter would undermine the former. Thus, society is effectively constrained to choose between them. The question is what can justify the choice. Proponents of ethics assume that the grounds must be ethical. As they see it, citizens must decide which orientation to nature better conduces to a good form of life; and they must justify their choice on such ethical grounds. If citizens opt for environmentalism, for example, they must appeal to value judgments rooted in an ecological worldview; if they opt for antienvironmentalism, on the contrary, they must appeal to antiecological values. Such appeals are problematic, however, for reasons we have already noted. Both invoke justifications internal to a worldview that the other side explicitly rejects. Thus, neither side can justify its position in terms that the other could in principle accept. And so neither can avoid casting the other outside the circle of those entitled to such justification (Forst 1999). Yet that is itself a failure of recognition—of one's fellow citizens qua citizens. In general, then, if no other—nonethical—justification is available, misrecognition, and therefore injustice, cannot be avoided.

Fortunately, the difficulty is less intractable than first appears. In fact, a nonethical resolution is available, as the antiecologists' claim violates the deontological standard of participatory parity—well before ethical evaluation has to kick in. Specifically, it violates the second prong of the double requirement, which holds that proposed reforms must not exacerbate one disparity of participation in the course of remedying another. In this case, the antiecologists seek to remedy their own disparity vis-à-vis their eco-friendly fellow citizens—but they would do so at the expense of future generations. By instituting parity now for practices that would worsen global warming, they would deny their successors the material prerequisites for a viable form of life—thereby violating intergenerational justice. Thus, the antiecologists' claim fails the test of participatory parity. And so this case, too, like same-sex marriage and *l'affaire foulard*, can be adjudicated on deontological grounds. No recourse to ethics is necessary.

The moral here is that one should proceed cautiously before turning to ethics. Ethical evaluation, after all, is problematic. Always contextually embedded, it is subject to dispute whenever divergent evaluative horizons come into contact. Thus, one should take care to exhaust the full resources of deontological reasoning before taking that step. In fact, as this example shows, cases that seem initially to require ethics can often be resolved by deontological means. This is not to say that cases requiring ethical evaluation are impossible in principle. But it is to insist that the determination that one has in fact encountered such a case can be made only at the end of a long line of moral reasoning. To fail to complete that chain is to turn prematurely to ethics. In that event, one embarks on a dubious enterprise. Appealing to substantive horizons of value that are not shared by everyone concerned, one sacrifices the chance to adjudicate recognition claims definitively—in ways that are binding on all.

Conclusion

For this reason, as well as the others I have offered here, one should postpone the turn to ethics as long as possible. Alternative approaches, favored, alas, by most recognition theorists, turn prematurely to ethics. By foreclosing the option of developing a deontological interpretation of recognition, they miss the chance to reconcile claims for the recognition of difference with claims for egalitarian redistribution. Thus, they miss the chance to restructure the conceptual terrain that is currently fostering philosophical schizophrenia.

Given that unpalatable alternative, it is reassuring to see just how far one can get with a deontological interpretation of recognition. And we *did* here get remarkably far. By employing the status model, with its principle of participatory parity, it was possible to handle apparently ethical questions, such as the recognition of same-sex marriage on the one hand, and of minority religious and cultural practices on the other, without in fact turning to ethics. Even the seemingly harder case of environmental ethics proved susceptible to deontological resolution.

In general, then, the argument pursued here supports a rather heartening conclusion: there is no need to pose an either/or choice between the politics of redistribution and the politics of recognition. Rather, it is possible to construct a comprehensive framework that can accommodate both—by following the path pursued here. First, one must construe recognition as a matter of justice, as opposed to "the good life," by replacing the identity model with the status model. Next, one must expand one's conception of justice to encompass distribution and recognition as two mutually irreducible dimensions, both of which are subject to the deontological norm of participatory parity. Finally, after acknowledging that justice could in some cases require recognizing distinctiveness over and above common humanity, one must subject claims for recognition to the justificatory standard of participatory parity. This, as we saw, means scrutinizing institutionalized patterns of cultural value, and proposals for changing them, for their impact on social interaction—both across and within social groups. Only then, after all these steps, *might* one encounter a situation in which it *could* prove necessary to turn to ethics. Apart from such cases, one will succeed in remaining on the terrain of *Moralität* and in avoiding the ethical turn.

It is possible, I conclude, to endorse both redistribution and recognition while avoiding philosophical schizophrenia. In this way, one can prepare some of the conceptual groundwork for tackling what I take to be the central political question of the day: How can we develop a coherent orientation that integrates redistribution and recognition? How can we develop a framework that integrates what remains cogent and unsurpassable in the socialist vision with what is cogent and irrefutable in the new, apparently "postsocialist" vision of multiculturalism? If we fail to ask this question, if we cling instead to false antitheses and misleading either/or dichotomies, we will miss the chance to envision social arrangements that can redress both economic and cultural injustices. Only by looking to integrative approaches that unite redistribution and recognition can we meet the requirements of justice for all.

NOTES

Portions of this essay are excerpted from Fraser (2003). I am grateful for the support of the Tanner Foundation for Human Values, Stanford University, and the New School for Social Research. I benefited greatly from the helpful comments of Elizabeth Anderson, Seyla Benhabib, Richard J. Bernstein, Judith Butler, Rainer Forst, Axel Honneth, Theodore Koditschek, Steven Lukes, Jane Mansbridge, Linda Nicholson, Anne Phillips, Erik Olin Wright, and Eli Zaretsky.

1. Here I am assuming the distinction, now fairly standard in moral philosophy, between respect and esteem. According to this distinction, respect is owed universally to every person in virtue of shared humanity; esteem, in contrast, is accorded differentially on the basis of persons' specific traits, accomplishments, or contributions. Thus, although the injunction to respect everyone equally is perfectly sensible, the injunction to esteem everyone equally is oxymoronic.

2. The outstanding exception of a theorist who has sought to encompass issues of culture within a distributive framework is Will Kymlicka (1989, 1995, 1996). But his approach is problematic. For a critique, see Fraser (2003).

3. Absent a substantive reduction, moreover, purely verbal subsumptions are of little use. There is little to be gained by insisting as a point of semantics that, for example, recognition, too, is a good to be distributed; nor, conversely, by maintaining as a matter of definition that every distributive pattern expresses an underlying matrix of recognition. In both cases, the result is a tautology. The first makes all recognition distribution by definition, whereas the second merely asserts the reverse. In neither case have the substantive problems of conceptual integration been addressed. In fact, such purely definitional "reductions" could actually serve to impede progress in solving these problems. By creating the misleading appearance of reduction, such approaches could make it difficult to see, let alone address, possible tensions and conflicts between claims for redistribution and claims for recognition.

4. Since I coined this phrase in 1995, the term *parity* has come to play a central role in feminist politics in France, where it signifies strict numerical gender equality in political representation. For a critique of that understanding of parity, and an account of its difference from my own, see Fraser (2001).

5. I say "*at least* two conditions must be satisfied" in order to allow for the possibility of more than two. I have in mind a possible third class of obstacles to participatory parity that could be called "political," as opposed to economic or cultural. For an account of this third dimension of justice, see Fraser (2003).

6. I say the remedy *could* be recognition of difference, not that it must be. In

fact, there are other possible remedies for the denial of distinctiveness—including deconstruction of the very terms in which differences are currently elaborated. For a discussion of such alternatives, see Fraser (1995, 2000, 2003).

7. Certainly, there is room for disagreement as to the effects of the foulard on the status of girls. Those effects cannot be calculated by an algorithmic method or decision procedure. On the contrary, they can only be determined dialogically, by the give and take of argument, in which conflicting judgments are sifted and rival interpretations are weighed (Fraser 2003).

8. In general, the standard of participatory parity cannot be applied monologically, in the manner of a decision procedure. Rather, it must be applied dialogically and discursively, through democratic processes of public debate. In such debates, participants argue about whether existing institutionalized patterns of cultural value impede parity of participation and about whether proposed alternatives would foster it—without exacerbating other disparities. For the status model, then, participatory parity serves as an idiom of public contestation and deliberation about questions of justice. More strongly, it represents *the principal idiom of public reason*, the preferred language for conducting democratic political argumentation on issues of both distribution and recognition. For a fuller account of this dialogical approach, see Fraser (2003).

WORKS CITED

Dworkin, Ronald. 1981. What is quality? Part 2: Equality of resources. *Philosophy and Public Affairs* 10, no. 4:283–45.
Forst, Rainer. 1999. The basic right to justification: Toward a constructivist conception of human rights. *Constellations* 6, no. 1:35–60.
Fraser, Nancy. 1995. From redistribution to recognition? Dilemmas of justice in a "postsocialist" age. *New Left Review* 212:68–93.
———. 1997. *Justice interruptus: Critical reflections on the "postsocialist" condition.* New York: Routledge.
———. 2000. Rethinking recognition: Overcoming displacement and reification in cultural politics. *New Left Review* 3:107–20.
———. 2001. Pour une politique féministe à l'âge de la reconnaissance: Approche bi-dimensionnelle et justice entre les sexes. Trans. Brigitte Marrec. *Actuel Marx* 30 (September): 153–72.
———. 2003. Social justice in the age of identity politics: Redistribution, recognition, and participation. In *Redistribution or recognition? A political-philosophical exchange,* by Nancy Fraser and Axel Honneth, 7–109. London: Verso.
Honneth, Axel. 1995. *The struggle for recognition: The moral grammar of social conflicts.* Trans. Joel Anderson. Oxford: Polity Press.
Kymlicka, Will. 1989. *Liberalism, community and culture.* Oxford: Oxford University Press.
———. 1995. *Multicultural citizenship: A liberal theory of minority rights.* Oxford: Oxford University Press.
———. 1996. Three forms of group-differentiated citizenship in Canada. In *Democracy and difference,* ed. Seyla Benhabib, 153–70. Princeton: Princeton University Press.

Rawls, John. 1971. *A theory of justice*. Cambridge: Harvard University Press.

Sen, Amartya. 1985. *Commodities and capabilities*. North-Holland: Elsevier.

Taylor, Charles. 1994. The politics of recognition. In *Multiculturalism: Examining the politics of recognition*, ed. Amy Gutmann, 25–73. Princeton: Princeton University Press.

7 Rethinking the Quotidian

LEGAL AND OTHER REGULATIONS

The Problematic

By 1994, when Alan Hunt and Gary Wickham published their book *Foucault and Law*, the influence of the flamboyant French intellectual on legal scholarship in the United States had peaked. One sensed fewer converts being made in the academy and a decided decrease in scholarly production from a "Foucauldian perspective." After twenty years of rapt attention, by the mid-1990s, the conventional wisdom was that one ought not embark on a Foucauldian project, although one can imagine that quite a few dissertations started at the peak of the phenomenon had yet to be concluded. Perhaps with the shift in fashion, the insights and challenges Foucault still presents for the study of law can be more carefully developed. This essay proposes that the constitutive perspective from which many social science scholars have been working draws on insights developed at least partially in response to Foucault. Although critical of the tendency of Foucauldian legal scholarship to overvalorize the disciplinary practices of everyday life at the expense of the significance of state power, this essay also demonstrates the importance of law's mechanisms for enforcement and its relationship to morality. The essay concludes by transcending the traditional conception of legal pluralism to a constitutive perspective that is in the best tradition of Foucault.

Law and Everyday Life: Foucault's Contributions

Few Western democracies feature public executions anymore, and although executions continue in the United States with considerable publicity and advocates for the death penalty claim that it deters, the rule of law is widely seen as being maintained less by force than by the myriad of social forms that lend authority to conventional practice. Certainly there is ongoing work of the highest order by scholars with links to Foucault such as Alan Hunt (1993), Pat O'Malley (1993), and Marianna Valverde (1998). This work points to the complex social forces, often called governmentality, that determine relations of authority in society. As Hunt and Wickham showed, Foucault's contribution to the study of law, given the sophistication that has come with time, may be more important than ever. Social scientific scholars now speak of power and government differently and treat knowledge self-consciously as a social construction. From these insights, it is now becoming clear that we should see law as one form of regulation among many. This understanding is the source for the title of this essay.

After Foucault and the contemporary movement to study law in everyday life, at least some scholars have tried to avoid the conventional view of the state or government as a sphere outside of society. Under current scholarship, the penetration of legal regulation into culture and social consciousness has been widely recognized. Legal regulation, like other forms of regulation, includes the capacity of judges and various legal commentators to influence the way others think about things. Legal regulation is not simply a matter of rules backed by threats. Legal regulation in society is a matter of understandings, of knowing that things should be done a certain way. For instance, a large part of the thinking that goes into income tax preparation in the United States will be about what is possible. Thus, when a citizen thinks about reporting income on a tax return, he or she must think of life in economic terms and with various unusual categories. To some extent, the implications are about what rightfully belongs to Uncle Sam (or Caesar). But more often, right and wrong have little relevance, and there is actually very little enforcement.

I try to transcend reference to "law" and "the law" as a singular phenomenon and treat this convention as a social artifact. The singularity is partially responsible for the problematic considered here, the difficulty in getting an accurate picture of legal regulation. Much scholarship and some social practices consider "law" as a unitary phenomenon. For Hunt and Wickham, the effort to transcend this unitary claim is the beginning of an inquiry into legal regulation or law as a form of regulation. They argue, "Law is not and never has been a unitary phenomenon, even though the assumption that it is, has played a central role in most legal discourses and theories of law" (1994, 39). What they want to argue instead is that "[L]aw is a complex of practices, discourses and institutions" (39). In their analysis, the imperial mission of state law no longer operates. Thus, seeing law as unitary is linked to a hegemonic view of the state that is not appropriate. They say, "Over this plurality of legal forms 'state law' persistently, but never with complete success, seeks to impose a unity" (39). I will be addressing state law, a speed limit, a "clean water" act, and a sexual harassment code, but as one of many legal regulations. The paradigm of legal regulation in the United States, and generally in Western-style democracies, is in the executive branch of the government. This part of the government includes prosecutors, police, and regulators from administrative agencies. With attention to the more diffuse notion of governance, there is much work to be done in understanding the authorities and practices marshaled around and in support of state law that are not "executive." Seeing law as a form of regulation, I suggest, puts the authority of the state in perspective with other authorities to which it is linked.

The Carrot and the Stick

Part of the constitutive force that makes state legal regulation central is the shadow of various dichotomies such as "the carrot and the stick" or law and morality. This essay works through those shadows and reimagines some of my own work. The sometimes polar, sometimes continuous nature of the regulatory options open to the state have been studied as the carrot and the stick. Regulation may be by means of incentives, like tax breaks or car pool lanes, and/or punishments that range from fines to imprisonment. I use an approach akin to the governance perspective to draw the concept of law away from the positivism of the carrot and the stick and the separation of law and morality (Simon 1988). My goal is to contribute to contemporary sociolegal scholarship by suggesting some affinities between law as a constitutive force and as governmentality. The constitutive becomes a way to develop a notion of governance as a force upon which laws depend. The move from the governance perspective to the constitutive provides a foundation for understanding the function of the carrot and the stick and the attempt to distinguish law from morality. These conventional dichotomies become part of the dynamic of legal regulation in a diffuse system of legal authority.

Policy analysts as well as legal scholars generally concentrate on two ways of gaining compliance with law. These are the polar mechanisms of the carrot and the stick. Traditionally, law regulates behavior through either incentives or punishment. Incentives are used to entice people to behave in a way that is presumed beneficial for social policy (Piven and Cloward 1971). Legal regulation of this sort employs the proverbial carrot as an enticement to desired behavior. Examples of this approach are the lanes on highways and bridges, often designated with a diamond, that are open for use by cars with more than one passenger. This form of incentive was considered a nonintrusive form of environmental regulation begun in the 1960s. In a more characteristic form, law employs sanctions on behavior that we call the stick. Examples of the stick are many. We think of the stick when drunk driving results in a fine or jail time. Similarly, it is the stick when failure to pass a required automobile safety inspection results in a car being prohibited from being on the road.

Both carrot and stick are legal forms of regulation to the extent that they rely on the force of the state—that is, the government—to operate. When the passengers in a confiscated car are left to travel on foot or are transported in a police cruiser because a trooper has arrested the driver, obviously the state is involved. And, although less dramatically, when a driver moves to the diamond lane because the other lanes are backed up and he or she determines his or her car holds the requisite number of passengers, the state is involved. Twenty years ago, observing this polarity seemed like a unique contribution to the jurisprudence of public policy (Brigham and Brown 1980). Traditionally, the stick had been the paradigm for legal regulation. Calling attention to the carrot in the same analysis seemed like an innovative thing to do as part of a sociological jurisprudence.

In retrospect, the analysis a little over twenty years ago seems to have been part of a general widening of the inquiry into the nature of law. It was also a move linked to the emergence of public choice theory, to economic approaches to law. My colleague Don Brown had published with Robert Stover one of the first scholarly pieces using economic analysis to direct the study of law (Brown and Stover 1977). Brown and Stover were clearly interested in approaching law from somewhere other than the "force of the state" framework we had all inherited from positive jurisprudence, along with Walter Murphy (1964), who had used what we now know as "rational choice" to understand the strategic behavior of Supreme Court justices.

The formulation of the carrot and the stick was thought to illuminate the full range of legal tools and help delineate the distinction between law and other types of regulation. In fact, by moving away from emphasis on force, it made it harder to tell the difference between law and other forms of social control. The traditional image of the authority behind law is amplified by attention to incentives that make agency more prominent and call attention to various ways legal regulation operates. The force once thought to be the central feature of legal regulation begins to be subsumed on a larger canvas. This is the case with the diamond lanes on freeways where the penalties for riding in them without the requisite passengers would only seem to be a small part of their meaning in the public eye. The power of the legal sanction is always there. As anyone of us who has been stopped by the police for a traffic violation can attest, it tends to ruin your day. But it no longer seems of overriding significance.

Now we are likely to consider the carrot at least as characteristic of legal regulation as the stick. In contemporary sociology of law, interest in incentives is now often part of inquiry into subtle legal mechanisms and ac-

counting for their significance (Valverde 1998). Recognition of the soft and
the hard edge of legal regulation may, however, simply have been an initial
stage in developing a more sophisticated conception of social regulation. In
the end, we may need to transcend the carrot and the stick. In fact, we need
to see how the polarity once thought novel is itself part of the regulatory
apparatus. Here we suggest that the dichotomous framework of the carrot
and the stick is itself an aspect of law's authority. In this framework, force
is juxtaposed with incentives and coercion with voluntariness in a conception of legal authority that appears complete. The rest of this essay examines that apparent completeness.

Morality and Law

The distinction between morality and law is another dichotomous relationship at the center of the positive tradition that makes it more difficult
to understand the range of legal authority today. Rethinking this puzzling
formulation is at the center of the effort to understand legal regulation in
light of Foucault and the tradition of broad inquiry into the nature of governing structures. The traditional presumption in positive legal theory that
regulation is not a matter of morality is misleading. Positive theory would
have it that driving alone in a car and eschewing the diamond lane is a personal matter, or that making a photocopy of a dollar bill for a work of art is
an aesthetic choice. At least conventionally, regulatory offenses are thought
to be morally neutral. We can think of a time not too far gone in which violation of a mere statute—say, one regulating the maximum amount of elec-
tricity to be produced at a given plant—was understood to be a matter between the regulated and the regulatory agency and not one that had a moral
dimension. Although a manager dealing with an issue of that sort might consult an accountant or a lawyer, he or she is still not likely to consult a priest
or go to confession over a matter of regulation.

The traditional elements of moral content in legal regulation are said by
positive legal theorists to require two things. One is culpability or blame-
worthiness. As *mens rea*, the law identifies a criminal intent. The other is social harmfulness recognized by the society. This means moral wrongfulness,
or that the behavior be viewed as immoral. It is from the latter element that
we get the notion of a distinction in the common law between *malum in se*,
things bad in themselves, and *malum prohibitum*, things that are bad because they are prohibited. Some things that were once merely prohibited,
like dumping the waste products of manufacturing in a river, have become a
social wrong. This makes *malum prohibitum* a key to understanding law. It
is central to the relationship between the approbation that comes from the

sanction in legal regulation and other social approbation. The idea that some things are bad because they are prohibited places legal regulation in the context of other forms of regulation. We expect the criminal law to be associated with *malum in se* and thus limited to things that are bad in themselves, but this is often not the case. For some time in the middle of the twentieth century, driving while intoxicated, which was against the law, was widely tolerated. Drunk driving is now an example of something that has become a social wrong over time (Gusfield 1984). For the most part, actions that are regulated by law are ones that are not bad at the core.

We often hear that criminal law should only be used to prohibit conduct about which the community shares a moral outrage. Many business practices are excluded on these grounds. It would certainly exclude regulatory violations like taking the "Do Not Remove" content identification tags off pillows (Green 1997). This inclination to limit the reach of the criminal sanction is sometimes associated with a claim that extending it too far will weaken the criminal law, or perhaps even all manifestations of law. Herbert L. Packer, in his *Limits of the Criminal Sanction*, believed that rather than "stigmatizing hitherto morally neutral conduct as wrongful," aggressive extension of the criminal sanction to such conduct would likely "decriminalize" the criminal law (1968, 359). Judge Richard Posner has discussed the ambiguously criminal nature of parking violations in his decision in the case, *Van Harken v. City of Chicago* (1997). In his decision, which holds that a challenge to a parking violation does not contain a federal claim, Posner uses a cost-benefit analysis to dismiss a defendant's argument that he should be able to cross-examine the officer issuing a ticket. Although cities might like to have parking violations be seen as administrative, they employ the mechanisms of the criminal law. In responding to Judge Posner, an Illinois appeals court eschewed the economic analysis and used a standard of fundamental fairness instead (*Van Harken v. City of Chicago* 1999).

The desire to connect law and morality calls attention to the seeming excess of laws on the books, the magnitude of offenses anyone could be held accountable for if vigorous enforcement were to ensue. Although one can at least imagine morality coexisting with moral conduct in roughly equal proportion, there always seems to be an excess of law that may be used to govern behavior when it suits the governing authorities. A reaction to that excess of legal regulations and selective enforcement may have been part of the American reaction against the impeachment of Bill Clinton and, ultimately, the failure to convict him on impeachment charges. Scholars such as Stuart Green (1997), and Robert Kagan and Eugene Bardach have written on this subject. In *Going by the Book* (1982), Kagan and Bardach demonstrate the latitude that administrative enforcement agencies have as a result of the surfeit of possible violations that could be imposed on a regulated agency. Ka-

gan and Bardach's work is a critique of regulatory law; Green writes about
what we may legitimately expect from legal regulation.

Here, I suggest that there should be no presumption equating the laws on
the books with regulation. The link instead—or more accurately—needs to
be between the general mechanisms of social order, including morality but
also incorporating institutional structures and conventions that determine
behavior. Just as there is more than a touch of moral condemnation when
the clerk at Kinko's informs me that I can't photocopy money, or the clerk at
Benetton refuses to let Patricia Williams in the door, regulation in its myriad
forms is linked to morality. It is not that this form of regulation depends on
morality. The clerk doesn't have to think I'm a counterfeiter to prevent me
from copying money. He doesn't have to think Professor Williams is going
to rob the store. Those inclinations simply buttress presumptions supported
by codes, regulations, and other conventions of retailing.

Prospects for Jurisprudence After Foucault

The Foucauldian mode of analysis has drawn attention away from
traditional forms of power. In the more doctrinaire circles, the status of legal
regulation suffered. Jürgen Habermas, for instance, comments, "Foucault
leaves the ungrounded impression that the bourgeois constitutional state is
a dysfunctional relic from the period of absolutism" (Hunt and Wickham
1994, 61). This was a significant weakness in Foucault's perspective—or,
more precisely, it is a weakness in the work of those following his lead. A
more appropriate message today should be that bringing out the importance
of little forms of power should not lead us to ignore the very real, and very
big, forces that emanate from government. There is still considerable power
left in the modern state. Clearly, both little and big forms of power must be
incorporated in the description of modern mechanisms of regulation and social control. We should include high courts and surveillance cameras, armies
and clerks at places like Benetton or Kinko's, the Federal Bureau of Investigation and the uniform product code (UPC). Each plays a role in maintaining the social order.

Foucault, with the dramatic image of violence to the condemned that
opens *Discipline and Punish* (1977), also drew disproportionate attention to
the criminal law as the emblematic legal form to be accounted for even while
suggesting that the forces of social control had been transformed. For Hunt
and Wickham, it is "The other faces of law which, in so far as one can safely
quantify law, make up its great bulk of provisions concern the detail of economic and kinship relations and the distribution of social authority" (1994,
60). This observation is particularly significant in delineating the forces of

power in society. The popular news in Western democracies covers crime far more fully than ordinary property transactions, and it covers domestic violence more assiduously than inheritance, although of course crime and property are necessarily linked. It is property and inheritance that are constitutive of crime, domestic relations, and ultimately law's place in society.

This propensity to equate legal regulation with state institutions and the violent transgressions of the criminal law is part of the contemporary configuration of power. This foundation for the reception of Foucault's critique reflects the ideology of legal realism. In legal theory, realism incorporates a picture of an emasculated legal form in its own articulation of power. Set against a formal backdrop that presumes the force of law, contemporary realist legal theory denies that law is a powerful social force. It holds that legal rules are ideas or aspirations and not reality. Here, the politics of law is played out in the domain of positivist epistemology. It is presumed that law can't be both ideal and real. A close reading of the prospects for a postpositivist sociology of law leads us to what it means to take the material world seriously while developing the premises of social construction.

The most salient aspect in Foucault's analysis of power for legal studies was the argument that the central locations of big power, the state and capital, were no longer the defining characteristics of power. Instead, small power located in dispersed sites had become central to the way power is constituted. The queen in her carriage, the president and *Air Force One* were heads of a much diminished state in Foucault's framework. The governing institutions that had once exercised authority as will and displayed their power in the pomp and circumstance surrounding heads of state had been supplanted by new architectures of power, which he called small. These smaller powers are evident in the form of surveillance cameras in stores and sometimes in the street. The smaller powers are more pervasive. They are operated by clerks, like the ones behind the counter at Kinko's with the power to determine what you can copy, or at Benetton, in Patricia Williams' (1991) wonderful example, with a finger on a buzzer determining whether you can enter the store. They are also the UPC that can be scanned at the checkout counter to determine what is being purchased, when and along with which other products. These, for Foucault, amount to forms of discipline. This disciplinary authority is more widely distributed and less obvious than the traditional sites of power.

Foucault did not merely add new aspects of a social power to our understanding of legal regulation. He, and his adherents, tried to change the entire image of modern law from the pomp and circumstance of a state dinner or the macabre drama of an execution to the mundane but far more pervasive regulation produced by the UPC scanner at the checkout counter or the clerk with power to open a shop door. They tried to shift attention from law to "governance." It was a dramatic aspiration and has been a substantial contribution. But its success has often been at the expense of an interest in legal regulation rather than a transformation in the study of law. It has transformed our conception of social control and diminished attention to mechanisms like the police and the authority of heads of state. These old forms are still around and functioning. Hunt and Wickham describe the resulting image of law and the state as "a mechanism that is ineffectual and generally epiphenomenal" (1994, 57). This concern for what has been lost was recognized as mainstream social science brought the state back in to the picture of politics. Here, the governance perspective gives new meaning to law as a form of regulation.

Beyond Pluralisms

Much contemporary sociolegal scholarship looks at law that is not in or on "the books." The perspective is called legal pluralism. Legal pluralism, not unlike the governance perspective, sought to break down the domination of state law by positing other forms of law in society. As exemplified by the *Journal of Legal Pluralism (and Unofficial Law)* under the editorship of John Griffiths and evident in Mark Galanter's essay "Justice in Many Rooms," this perspective saw law in places other than courts, and, of course, in courts but outside the official gaze of the judge. Pluralism, in this formulation, is opposed to centralism, or the view that state law is at the center of the universe of norms. According to Griffiths, "the state has no more empirical claim to being the center of the universe of legal phenomena than any other element of that whole system does" and "courts resolve only a small fraction of all disputes that are brought to their attention" (Griffiths 1981, 48). The pluralist message is essentially the same as the law and society framework. One might find evidence of contracting among businessman or an accounting of liabilities among the elders in a tribe or the homemakers in a neighborhood. One might find all kinds of things like law in places like the corridors of the courthouses.

The best of this scholarship includes "The Law of the Oppressed" by Boaventura de Sousa Santos (1977), which examined the constructions of law in the *favellas*, or squatter settlements of Brazil. He found in the slums of Rio de Janeiro an indigenous normative system, which he described as law and which empowered those who lived outside the mainstream of property and authority. "Marxism and Legal Pluralism" by Peter Fitzpatrick (1983) took on Marxism as an essentialized formulation that missed the variety of power. He found these forms in postcolonial environments. And in her work on disputing, Laura Nader drew heavily on anthropology and developed a field that was sensitive to the cultural aspects of conflict and the power relations in ideologies of authority (Nader and Todd 1978). Summary articles on the contributions of the movement, such as analyses by Sally Merry (1988, 1992), emphasize the discovery of law in formerly unrecognized or unrecognizable places—or, as a recent critique pointed out with some concern, the paradox of finding law in nonlegal places (Tamanaha 1993).

The problem with legal pluralism is evident in academic projects like a conference in 1989 that brought together legal pluralists with democratic advocates of popular justice movements. The call was a utopian reification common in the liberal academy under positivism where attention is drawn from the state apparatus, in a move that seems to deny the legal authority that underlies modern status relations. Certainly there are forms of legal regulation outside the state and thought generated independently of law and the state. But pluralism in legal theory too often turned away from the effect of state regulation on forms of life in society: the family, bargaining, health and wealth. Conversely, recognizing the penetration of state power in movement practice is a good thing. To show how the law of the state, government law, becomes part of the talk, aspiration, and social life of politics—that is, to take a constitutive perspective—is to challenge the positivism in pluralism.

Social scientists have been fascinated by other manifestations of legal regulation's "plurality." Sometimes the work acknowledges the influence of a sovereign legal order, where themes of hegemony and resistance fascinate scholars. One contemporary perspective on dominated groups comes from Antonio Gramsci, who distinguished between the "dominant" and the "subaltern" (Gramsci 1971). The subaltern, also known as "the other," is said to tell us who we are and became a major point for the analysis of western institutions, particularly in what was called a "postcolonial" perspective (Guha 1980). In order to describe the other as a part of the whole, we must place legal regulation in society. In an essay on the cultural appropriation controversy in Canada that focuses on native claims, Rosemary Coombe sees the characteristic feature of the other as representation "that projects upon non-Western peoples qualities and characteristics that are mirror opposites of the qualities the West claims for itself" (1993, 10). A parallel is evident in the language of colonialism. We are being very self-conscious about how much we learn from the parts of society.

The difference between this project and a strict Foucauldian one associated with law and governance begins with the reorientation from the moral relativism of legal pluralism. It requires a move to levels or cultural phenomena as a perspective that both incorporates some state power and unified authority and reconceptualizes power in ways that change how we know such authority. Regulation, not crime or criminal law, becomes the central paradigm for law, but in a new way. Legal regulation continues to

share some of the strictures associated with the state as an authority but-
tressing a centralized structure of power. We have suggested how legal regulation lacks the moral condemnation behind really serious social wrongs,
like homicide, which are governed by the criminal law. Although homicide
is clearly regulated, we don't say this because it is assumed. The very term
regulation seems not strong enough for homicide. Legal regulation seems
more appropriate as a term for filing documents on time, making energy-
efficient cars, or setting up equal opportunity guidelines for employers.
Morality may be involved, but it is not generally the primary subject of regulation. When these behaviors become bad, something that we see with
sexual harassment, it may be at least in part because they are regulated.

Regulation, like pluralism, is not dependent on the state or subordinate
to sovereign authorities. As much as we try and confine legal regulation to
that aspect of regulation associated with government, scholars make this increasingly difficult by extending the notion of governance into everything
from shopping to sports. By emphasizing the reach of regulation into less
formal settings, we come to realize that active state regulation, where the
forces of government are prominent, may be diminishing as a form of social control. Instead, the Foucauldian perspective on legal regulation, rather
than a Foucauldian perspective standing in opposition to law, suggests continuities between the police and the UPC, between the Federal Trade Commission and the kid at Kinko's, or between the judge and the high school
principal. Put that way, it doesn't seem so difficult at all.

Constitutive Law

When looking for legal regulation in practice, common law jurisprudence tends to look past much of what might legitimately be included. Law
was found tucked away in the inner offices of law firms, in difficult-to-access
law libraries, or in obscure professional practices. But legal regulation resides in a much broader range of social and cultural practices. This legal regulation that we don't notice, the kind that is taken for granted and has become a given, is among the most powerful. Legal regulation, usually quite
inconspicuously, marks the boundaries of suburban plots and urban build-
ings. As part of our landscape, legal practices determine whose field the
farmer plows. They tell him whether it is his or if perhaps he works for
someone else. Even when we don't notice legal regulation, we are likely to
be unconsciously aware that large parts of our landscape are legal. In some
cities, it is hard to miss the zones of pornography that support enterprises
with XXX movie ratings, even if we don't generally think that legal regulation plays a role in their creation. And also taken for granted are metropol-

itan residential patterns with distinctive racial meaning that have black people at the center and whites on the periphery. These are partly constituted by the legal regulation that says where children go to school, that specifies how taxes are collected, or that provides the name a community goes by.

Legal regulation in this sense is quieter than the official legal contexts that appear in the chronicles of public life—a trial, a hearing, or an execution. It is also more diffuse, more pervasive, more penetrating. Sociolegal scholars have begun to see rights in legal landscapes for various movements. We should also learn to identify other legal forms such as realism, remedy, and rage as the legal landscapes inhabited by movement activists. Sexuality, positivism, disputing, and pornography, as political practices, are linked to distinctive legal forms that constitute participation in the political process. These forms, like the practice of rights, are ways to do things. Legal forms appear in the practices of distinct communities such as gays in California when they appeal to constitutional rights, or to law professors in Cambridge when they deny the utility of rights. As practices, they frame political interests. These legal frames constitute the identities, guide the aspirations, and fuel the interests that define politics in a legal order.

This is an expression of a "constitutive" perspective on law, what Alan Hunt calls the "hallmark" of the constitutive, the idea that "legal life and everyday social life are mutually conditioning" (1996, 178). The notion that society and law interact in constitutive processes has become an element of the perspective. This interaction is what regulation is all about. Hunt proposes further that "Law enters into the way that life is imagined, discussed, argued about, and fought over; this imagining, talking, arguing, and fighting shapes the law" (179). With property and trespass, ordinary views are constituted at least in part by law that can be traced to traditional sources, but it operates along with the constitutive force of beliefs, like the conventional American perception that to own property is to rule a domain, to be the lord of the manor. Legal regulation incorporates the sophisticated codes and opinions that are property law *and* the conventions that seem at first to all but ignore the formalities. In the end, we can say of domestic disputes over inheritance as well as of land sales that these relations are regulated by law.

This constitutive idea is not quite the same as the idea that the "law is all over," which is often associated with the work of Austin Sarat (1988). Although both positions are linked to the work of the Amherst Seminar in the 1980s and early 1990s, the "law is all over" idea is in response to previous conventions that saw law only in the work of courts and other official lawmakers. Clearly law is more than that, and the Sarat idea is cited on that point. The constitutive perspective is less about the place or setting for legal regulation and more about its dynamics. It incorporates big and little power, state and less imposing examples of authority. Along with the siting of law outside of courts has come the important recognition that courts and traditional legal institutions get their meaning from society as well as offering it themselves.

Constitutive work has developed considerably in the last fifteen years, but statements of the position still both puzzle and inspire. For instance, David Ray Papke quotes Iredell Jenkins to the effect that "Law is like an iceberg: only one-tenth of its substance appears above the surface in the explicit form of documents, institutions and professions, while the nine-tenths of its substance that supports its visible fragment . . . liv[es] in the habits, attitudes, emotions and aspirations of men" (Papke 1992, 3). The constitutive perspective points to the nine-tenths of the iceberg, always with an eye to transcending scholarly fascination with the other part, the one-tenth part, the tip that is most commonly associated with law. In comparative perspective one also sees this phenomenon in the settlement process of undocumented migrants from Guatemala. Here, seemingly powerless people resist U.S. immigration policy, particularly the 1986 Immigration Reform and Control Act, by interpreting the legislation and basing their actions on their own view of the law (Hagan 1997). Or in the case of Muslims in America, the institutions of American law come to alter the meaning of ethnicity in struggles such as those over the siting of mosques, immigration policy, and treatment in prison (Moore 1995). The Amherst Seminar, which I just mentioned, benefited from observations by Brinkley Messick on the meaning of this perspective. His work appeared in *The Calligraphic State: Textual Domination and History in a Muslim Society* (1993), which demonstrates the constitutive significance of written texts in the Muslim society of Yemen.

The message of some of the more recent constitutive work is that legal regulation has a life where courts and lawyers become part of a bigger picture. It is presented across a range of cultures and disciplines that reflect the plurality of legal regulation without necessarily missing the hegemonic power of the state. Helena Silverstein, writing about the animal rights movement, documents the shift from compassion to rights, where rights are formed in a new way. Her book *Unleashing Rights* (1996) helps to explain the constitutive approach to legal regulation. Silverstein gives us a valuable account of what it means to see law as constituting the animal rights movement. She links her approach to law in society. Her framework takes seriously the notion that legal regulation is not just influenced by society, as in the power of movements to change laws. Nor is society simply a receiver of laws, as in the impact of high court decisions on police practices. The point of this book is that legal regulation has a life beyond courts and lawyer's offices. For animal rights activists, law in society is the rights strategies undertaken in the interest of recognizing animals as an oppressed group. As applied to this struggle, her findings run counter to conventional academic wisdom, where rights are presumed to stem from individualistic rather than communitarian perspectives.

One of the earliest treatments that can be identified with this perspective is that of Kristin Bumiller, who studied women who, as victims of discrimination, assumed the mantle handed them in their legal struggles. They became victims. The work was *The Civil Rights Society* (1988), and its early recognition of the problematic status of victim stands as a statement of what might be achieved by empirical investigation and carefully developed theory. Dragan Milovanovic and Stuart Henry are two scholars who have remained focused on the constitutive enterprise for some time. Their survey of the constitutive literature in criminology demonstrates the practical as well as the theoretical punch of the perspective (Milovanovic and Henry 1999). Among the more recent practitioners, Efren Rivera-Ramos has developed the constitutive thesis for the way legal regulation enters into the consciousness and politics of a people in work on the constitution of identity in Puerto Rico (2001). He looks at the insular cases from the early twentieth century, when American courts held that colonialism was compatible with American constitutional law. The result is an ongoing colonial relationship that colors every aspect of Puerto Rican life.

In sum, the constitutive perspective responds to the challenge posed by contemporary readings of Foucault. We understand law as regulation and regulation as embedded in the social fabric. Contemporary sociology of law turns its focus from the state as the singular source of law to how law is constituted in society. The move presumes that the study of culture has been elevated to a mode of analysis and it shifts jurisprudential attention to the plurality of legal form. With this move, law becomes more than a body of rules or norms and less than an imperial governing apparatus. It becomes an aspect of the way we live.

WORKS CITED

Brigham, J., and D. Brown. 1980. *Policy implementation: Penalties or incentives.* Beverly Hills: Sage.

Brown, Don W., and Robert V. Stover. 1977. Compliance with court directives: A utility approach. *American Politics Quarterly* 5, no. 4:465–80.

Bumiller, Kristin. 1988. *The civil rights society.* Baltimore: Johns Hopkins University Press.

Coombe, Rosemary. 1993. The properties of culture and the politics of possessing identity: Native claims in the cultural appropriation controversy. *Canadian Journal of Law and Jurisprudence* 6:249–85.

de Sousa Santos, Boaventura. 1977. The law of the oppressed: The construction and reproduction of legality in Pasargada. *Law and Society Review* 12:5–55.

Fitzpatrick, Peter. 1983. Marxism and legal pluralism. *Australian Journal of Law and Society* 1:45–59.

Foucault, M. 1977. *Discipline and punish.* New York: Vintage.

Gramsci, A. 1971. History of the subaltern classes: Methodological criteria. In *Selections from "The Prison Notebooks."* Trans. and ed. Q. H. Hoare and G. N. Smith. New York: International Publishers.

Green, S. P. 1997. Why it's a crime to tear the tag off a mattress: Overcriminalization and the moral content of regulatory offenses. *Emory Law Journal* 46:1533–67.

Griffiths, John. 1981. Cited in Mark Galanter, Justice in many rooms: Courts, private ordering, and indigenous law. *Journal of Legal Pluralism (and Unofficial Law)* 19:48–72.

Guha, Ranajit. 1980. On some aspects of the historiography of colonial India. *Subaltern Studies: Writings on South Asian History and Society* 1:3–27.

Gusfield, Joseph. 1984. *The culture of public problems: Drinking driving in the symbolic order.* Chicago: University of Chicago Press.

Hagan, Jacqueline Maria. 1997. *Deciding to be legal: A Maya community in Houston.* Philadelphia: Temple University Press.

Hunt, Alan. 1993. *Explorations in law and society.* New York: Routledge.

———. 1996. Law, community, and everyday life. *Law and Social Inquiry* 21:173–85.

Hunt, A., and G. Wickham. 1994. *Foucault and law.* London: Pluto Press.

Kagan, R., and E. Bardach. 1982. *Going by the book: The problem of regulatory unreasonableness.* Cambridge: Harvard University Press.

Merry, Sally. 1988. Legal pluralism: Review essay. *Law and Society Review* 5:869–96.

———. 1992. Anthropology, law, and transitional processes. *Annual Review of Anthropology* 21:357–72.

Messick, Brinkley. 1993. *The calligraphic state: Textual domination and history in a Muslim society.* Berkeley: University of California Press.

Milovanovic, D., and S. Henry. 1999. *Constitutive criminology at work.* Albany: SUNY Press.

Moore, Kathleen. 1995. *Al-Mugtaribun.* Albany: SUNY Press.

Murphy, Walter. 1964. *Elements of judicial strategy.* Chicago: University of Chicago Press.

Nader, Laura, and Harry F. Todd, eds. 1978. *The disputing process—Law in ten societies.* New York: Columbia University Press.

O'Malley, Pat. 1993. Containing our excitement: Culture and the crisis of discipline. *Studies in Law, Politics, and Society* 13:159–86.

Packer, Herbert L. 1968. *The limits of the criminal sanction.* Stanford: Stanford University Press.

Papke, David. 1992. Law in American culture: An overview. *Journal of American Culture* 1 (Spring): 3–14.

Piven, F. F., and R. D. Cloward. 1971. *Regulating the poor: The functions of public welfare.* New York: Vintage Books.

Rivera-Ramos, Efren. 2001. *The legal constitution of identity: The judicial and social legacy of American colonialism in Puerto Rico.* New York: American Psychological Association.

Sarat, Austin. 1988. " . . . The law is all over": Power, resistance, and the legal consciousness of the welfare poor. *Yale Journal of Law and the Humanities* 1:343–70.

Silverstein, Helena. 1996. *Unleashing rights*. Ann Arbor: University of Michigan Press.

Simon, Jonathan. 1988. Ideological effects of actuarial practices. *Law and Society Review* 22, no. 4:771–800.

Tamanaha, Brian Z. 1993. The folly of the "social scientific" concept of legal pluralism. *Journal of Law and Society* 20 (Summer): 192–217.

Valverde, Marianna. 1998. *Diseases of the will: Alcohol and the dilemmas of freedom*. Cambridge: Cambridge University Press.

Williams, Patricia. 1991. *Diary of a law professor: The alchemy of race and rights*. Cambridge: Harvard University Press.

Van Harken v. City of Chicago. 1997. 103 F. 3d 1346.

Van Harken v. City of Chicago. 1999. Illinois Court of Appeals, First District. 1-98-0667.

Part IV

NEW ETHICAL AND PHILOSOPHICAL
TURNS IN LEGAL THEORY

8 Ethics, Normativity, and the Heteronomy of the Law

The question we will address in this essay could be formulated in the following terms: what is the relationship between the ethical (a term that we will try to define later on) and the plurality of actually existing normative orders? Can the latter be derived consistently from the former? And if not, what kind of link could be established between the two? The answer to these questions is highly relevant to a further type of interrogation concerning the groundings of law: if the relationship between the ethical and the normative order was a transparent one, so that the grasping of the nature of the first would give us all we need to choose between the various alternatives at the level of the second, there would be an exact overlapping between ethical subject and subject positions within the normative order of the law. This transparency would be, in that sense, compatible with an autonomy conceived as self-determination. If, on the contrary, the transition between ethics and the normative order presupposes less than a strict overlapping between the two, the institution of law would require a grounding at least partially different from an ethical one; a dimension of heteronomy necessarily inhabits the legal order, and a gap consequently emerges between the ethical and the normative subject.

There is, however, a previous distinction concerning the normative that requires to be deconstructed before we start our exploration: the one grounding the opposition between the normative and the descriptive, between *being* and *ought*. The classical distinction between fact and norm comes from Kant and from his attempt to strictly separate theoretical and practical reason. We do not find any such a stark division in the previous philosophical tradition. The distinction cannot be strictly maintained because there are no facts that are not grounded in the elaboration of our practical relationship with the world. If I try to move to a door at the end of the room, the table opposite me is an obstacle; but if I try to protect myself from an attack, it can become a means of defense. It is only in practical life—that is, in a life governed by norms—that the facts *as facts* can emerge. Even a purely contemplative attitude sees what it sees because it relies on systems of signification that are nothing else than the sedimentation of previous practical experiences. There are no facts without signification, and there is no signification without practical engagements that require norms governing our behavior. So there are not two orders, the normative and the descriptive, but normative/descriptive complexes in which facts and values interpenetrate each other in an inextricable way. What we usually call morality belongs to those complexes.

But if morality belongs to those complexes, what I want to suggest is that the ethical does not. We have to proceed here to a second deconstruction, of an opposite sign to the first one. In the case of the descriptive/normative distinction, we had to proceed to show the mutual contamination of two dimensions that are usually presented as separated. Our second deconstruction has to show the distance between two types of social experience that are usually presented as necessarily linked with each other. What is inherent in an ethical experience? It is initially difficult to answer the question, because our first reaction is to look for a norm more fundamental than the plurality of norms to be found in the various codes of morality. But this type of answer cannot escape the *petitio principii* that inhabits it: that of a ground that is not itself grounded, of a beginning by an irrational fiat, by a *fact* at the root of a normative order that is supposed to be essentially different from the factual one. There is no way of finding the experience constitutive of the ethical if we try to locate it within the positivity of the normative order.

How to go beyond this blind alley? If the *positive* character of the norm is the source of our difficulties in grasping the specificity of the ethical experience, perhaps the way to proceed is to go beyond that positivity, to detect the points in which the positivity fails to constitute itself. Let us concentrate for a moment on the opposition between "being" and "ought to be." If our previous assertion that the normative/descriptive complexes contaminate and subvert the distinctiveness of its two intervening terms stands, in that case, we cannot refer "the ought" to the normative order and "being" to the descriptive—that would simply reproduce the distinction that we were putting into question. There is no advance in opposing the fact of actual behavior to the fact of the norm. There is, however, something that remains if we put aside these two positivities: it is the distance between the two. How to conceive of this distance? It is important to realize that this distance can only be approached if content (positivity) is resolutely ignored. The distance between two positivities can only be conceived as *difference*, and all identity being differential, the identity of one side of the opposition would become the prerequisite of the identity of the other. In that case, distance and proximity would be strictly synonymous. But there is another way of approaching the matter. It is not the *content* of the ought that is opposed to the content of actual behavior, but the fact that the ought expresses a fullness that actual behavior lacks. The ought expresses fullness of being, whereas actual behavior shows *deficient* being. We are not far away from characterizing actual behavior in terms of contingency and finitude. It is this distance between full and deficient being that is, in my view, at the root of the ethical experience.

This still leaves us, however, with the problem of the relation between the fullness of the ought and its own content. For if the experience of the fullness as an ethical command was necessarily attached to a particular content, we would still be prisoners of the positivity of the norm and would have made little progress in our argument. Let us consider, however, the experience of the distance between being and ought in more detail. If the distance between being and ought is not the differential content between two positivities but the one between deficiency and fullness of being, in that case, there is a *lack* in actual being that is the source of the distance. But in that case, the content of the ought appears as essentially split: it is on the one hand a particular normative content, while on the other, this content functions as the representative or incarnation of the absent fullness. It is not the particularity of the content that is, per se, ethical, but that content insofar as it assumes the representation of a fullness that is incommensurable with it. That is why the ethical experience tends to express itself through terms such as "truth," "justice," and "duty"—nobody will deny their ethical character, but their actual realization can be referred to the most different normative contents. We will discuss presently the meaning of such a description. But what we have to emphasize from the start is that if ethical experience is the experience of the unconditioned in a fully conditioned universe, it has to be necessarily empty and devoid of all normative content.

Let us give some examples of what we have in mind in making this distinction. The mystical experience is the experience of the absolutely transcendent. God, being absolutely ineffable, can only be approached by an experience that is beyond any worldly determination and that can only be expressed along the lines of a negative theology. Being God, the locus of a fullness incommensurable with any determination of the *ens creatum* has also to be by necessity absolutely empty—and fullness and emptiness actually become synonymous. It is important to stress the fact that this emptiness, this absence of any concrete content, has nothing to do with any formalism. A formal determination is still a determination and as such has a content. Kant's ethical formalism, for instance, is grounded in the normative content of the categorical imperative. Moreover, abstraction and generality are inherent to any formalism, whereas the mystical experience is absolutely individual and concrete. The emptiness we are dealing with is not simply the absence of content but is itself a content—it is a fullness that *shows* itself through its very absence. Now, the important point is that the mystical experience does not lead to those who have passed through it, to live the recluse life of an anchorite but to engage themselves in the world in a more militant way and with an ethical density that other people lack. Eckhart compares the mystic to somebody who is in love: he will continue to immerse himself in daily activity, but the feeling of being in love will accompany all his actions. It is, paradoxically, the withdrawal of the mystic from the world that is the source of the ethical seriousness of his engagement in the latter.

Something similar could be said of the revolutionary militant. If I participate in a strike, in a factory occupation, in a demonstration just for the concrete objectives of these actions—an increase in wages, a change of the system of authority in the factory, or the demands for some budgetary reform—my militant engagement comes to an end once these objectives have been achieved. If, on the contrary, my participation in all these activities is conceived as episodes in a more universal struggle for revolutionary aims, my identification with the particular aims of those activities will be less complete, but paradoxically, for that reason, my militant engagement in them will be more intense. The revolutionary objective operates as a transcendent "beyond" all particular experience and is, in that sense, the point of identification that allows me to withdraw from the particularism of all concrete experience. This withdrawal, however, is only the prelude to the militant engagement in those very particularistic struggles, which cease to be merely particularistic as soon as they are seen as episodes in the prosecution of more universalistic aims.

Let us take the motto of the "general strike" in revolutionary syndicalism. All particular actions of the working class are seen as steps toward that ultimate event, which is the general strike. Thus, the particular actions are not exhausted in their particularism: all of them are equivalent as far as the *Endziel*, the final objective, is concerned. The final objective splits the aims of the particular struggles and demands: their particularism is simply the bearer of a universalistic aim traversing all of them. It is in this dialectic of withdrawal/engagement where the distinctive feature of an ethical life lies. The experience of the ethical is the experience of that moment of transcendence that takes us beyond all particular aim, norm, or action. What in the mystical experience we see in an extreme form is actually something belonging to the structure of all experience.

Before moving to our next problem, which is the relationship between the ethical and the normative, we have to say something more about the nature of the former. It is crucially important to stress that the equation fullness equals emptiness that we have found as inherent to the mystical experience is not exclusive to the latter but is the trademark of the ethical as such. Let us go back for a moment to the example of the general strike. What is the general strike? According to Sorel, it is not an actual event but a social myth. Social myths, for him, do not have all the precise details of a blueprint of society, such as a utopia, but are restricted to a few, simple images, capable of galvanizing the imagination of the masses. What is the source of this simplification? The answer is to be found in the fact that a myth such as the general strike is no actual event but rather the name of a fullness that is merely the positive reverse of a situation experienced in which such fullness is denied. It is because we live a situation as unjust that we have the experience of "justice" as an actual fullness, but there is no logical transition from injustice as lack to justice as a fullness that would remedy such a deprivation. Many concrete contents can present themselves as the positivization of "justice." In the example that we have been using, "general strike" is not the description of an actual event: its meaning is exhausted in symbolizing—naming—the series of particular struggles and demands that thus acquire their ethical dimension. It is through this equivalential function that the symbol weakens its particularistic meaning and develops the emptiness (that is, its fullness) that transforms it into the name of the ethical experience.

We have now all the necessary elements to address the question of the relationship between the ethical and the normative order (the second deconstructive move that we alluded to at the beginning of this essay). There is here a clear alternative: either we can *deduce* from the emptiness of the ethical moment a normative content that would necessarily correspond to it, or—given the emptiness inherent in the ethical experience—such a deduction is impossible and, in that case, the transition from the ethical to the normative can only take place through something that can only be described as a *radical investment* of the ethical into the normative. Needless to say, the latter is the way that we are prepared to take. If the ethical experience is really the experience of the unconditioned in an entirely conditioned world, of a fullness—as the ground of the ought—that is beyond all determination, there is no way of moving in a straight way from that experience to a norm or injunction. It is only if the latter becomes the symbol of something essentially heterogeneous from itself that a relation between the ethical and the normative can be established at all. This confronts us, however, with a set of theoretical difficulties that we have to address if the nature of this relation is really going to be brought to light.

A first dimension of the relation can be grasped by answering to a possible objection. The objection is the following: if the ethical can only exist invested in the normative, how can we actually distinguish between both? Wouldn't be simpler to speak about ethico-normative complexes in which the distinction between the two sides would become purely analytical? The

answer to this objection can be given at two levels. First, the investment of
the ethical into the normative does not simply consist of a confluence of the
two orders; rather, it is in a structural mutation that the former introduces
into the latter. We have already mentioned what this structural mutation
consists of: the establishment of an equivalential chain between the components of the normative order and the isolation of a set of key terms as signi-
fiers of the emptiness (equals fullness, equals ethical). In that sense, it is not
true that a normative structure is indifferent to the presence or absence of
ethical investment, or that the latter is not altered at all by the former. The
duality between the ethical and the normative is shown in the distinction
within a discourse between those elements that the ethical investment "uni-
versalizes" through an equivalential relation and those who function as
ground of such universalization—that is, as names of the ethical. In our previous example, "general strike" would be a name of the ethical, whereas the
aims of the particular struggles are components of an ethically invested
normative order as far as an equivalential relation can be established between them. The second answer to the objection mentioned above is that
the quality of the ethical life existing in a given society is far from being indifferent to the distinction between the ethical and the normative and from
their differential positivization in the discursive field. If the ethical were *entirely* absorbed into the normative, there would not be distinction between—for instance—justice and what a certain society considers as just at
some point in time. This is the best prescription for totalitarianism. It is only
if justice functions as an empty term, whose links with particular signifieds
are precarious and contingent that something such as a democratic society
becomes possible. There is no democracy without equation of fullness and
emptiness. That is why the reduction of politics to the *contents* of a certain
normative order and the identification of the ethical and the normative are
inimical to democracy, and why the distinction of the ethical and the normative frees both the ethical and the political from their totalitarian fixation
to any aprioristic and all-embracing normativity. I have sometimes been
confronted with the objection that conceiving of the ethical as empty leaves
social normativity without a ground. My answer is that it is precisely that
absence of ground and the possibility of signifying the resulting emptiness
that makes life in society worth living.

Another version, however, of the same objection is frequently presented
in the following terms: if there is no logical transition between the ethical
and a certain normative order, if the presence of the ethical in the normative is the result of a radical investment, why prefer one normative order
rather than another? Don't we end in that case with a normative deficit?
Are we not risking the worst consequences of a pure decisionism? Let us
consider the matter carefully. A pure decisionism would involve the exis-

tence of an omnipotent subject. Only somebody who is not subjected to any limitation could choose without any restriction—except that, as the existentialists would have it, such an omnipotent chooser does not have any reason for his choice. But, most important, such a chooser is a pure fiction. We are always *already* within a certain normative order, and all we can do is to displace through our decisions the areas of that order that are going to be the object of the ethical investment. I have written elsewhere that the subject is the distance between the undecidability of the structure and the decision. This means that an omnipotent chooser would also be an absolute subject—and, conversely, a chooser who is less than omnipotent would also be less than a subject. We live in a world of sedimented social practices that limit the range of what is thinkable and decidable.

This sedimentation of social practices is an *existential* in the Heideggerian sense: it is constitutive of all possible experience. So to the question, why prefer a certain normative order to others, why invest ethically in certain practices rather than in different ones, the answer can only be a contextual one: because I live in a world in which people believe in A, B, and C, I can argue that the course of action D is better than E; but in a totally presuppositionless situation in which no system of beliefs exists, the question is obviously unanswerable. In the case of the mystic, as we have seen, the contact with divinity as an absolute beyond all positive determination is followed by a normative investment that is the source of a militant engagement; but it is clear that the particular normative order that is the object of such an investment is not dictated by the content of the mystical experience—which has no content—but by the positive system of religious beliefs—the sedimented practices—within which the mystic lives. Many times I have been asked if there is not a normative deficit in the theory of hegemony that I have elaborated with Chantal Mouffe in *Hegemony and Socialist Strategy*—the argument being that the theorization of hegemony is an objective neutral description of what is going on in the world, while the book also makes a normative choice (radical democracy) that does not necessarily follow from such theorization. My answer is twofold. First, as I have argued earlier on, there is no such thing as a neutral factual description: the system of supposedly descriptive categories that we have used corresponds to "facts" that are only such for somebody who is living within the socialist tradition and has experienced the set of defeats, social transformation, and renaissance of hopes to which we make allusion. Second, within that normative/descriptive complex, it makes perfect sense to advocate the normative displacement involved in the notion of "radical democracy." The latter is the result of a pluralization of social struggles anchored in the new structures of contemporary capitalism. These displacements are both factual and normative, but it is clear that on both counts, the story that we are telling only makes sense to particular interlocutors who have been part of a certain history, not to an unencumbered spectator. To ask for an absolute grounding of a system of norms would be tantamount to requiring a radical separation between fact and value, and to legislating for humanity in general, independently of all communitarian framework.

Once we have characterized the relation between the ethical and the normative in terms of radical investment, we still have to address two closely related questions: what is the structure of a radical investment? and what determines the terrain of the investment? For our answer—that such a terrain is determined by the ensemble of the sedimented social practices—is clearly insufficient. Even if the ethical investment does not operate in a vacuum—it is not the source of the norm—it changes the latter to some extent, and it is possible at all because of the constitutive dislocations of the normative order. Let us give a couple of examples. A set of social dislocations generates a series of situations that people live as unjust. Between them, a relation of equivalence is established in the way we described above, and as a result, a widespread sense of injustice starts prevailing in that society. As we have seen, justice—as one of the names of social fullness—does not have a content of its own and needs to borrow it from some of the normative proposals that present themselves as incarnations of justice. Let us suppose that a content such as "socialization of the means of production" starts playing such a role. To do so, and to become the signifier of social fullness (an absent fullness, as we have seen), it has to be absolutely empty, and this is only achieved because of the plethora of signifieds resulting from the operation of the equivalential chain. "Socialization of the means of production" not only signifies what it directly designates, but also signifies the end of all injustices present in society: the unfair distribution of income, the unevenness of the access to the means of consumption, unequal opportunities of access to employment, and all kinds of social discrimination. It is in that way that "socialization of the means of production" becomes the signifier of the lack (which equals fullness). This is the moment of the ethical investment in the normative. A certain *order* fulfills the *ordering* function. Because the ordering function fills a lack that is not associated with any actual content, this duality between order and ordering, between the ontic and the ontological, can only reproduce itself *sine die*.

Why is it that a certain order rather than a different one fulfills the ordering function? A first answer is *availability*. It is the order that presents itself as fulfilling the ordering function that will be the object of the ethical investment. This is possible because the gap between order and ordering can never be ultimately filled. In a situation of generalized disorder, people need *some* order, and the concrete order that fulfills this ordering function is only a secondary consideration. It is because of that that the order best located to fulfill the ordering function will be the object of the ethical investment. This cannot be, however, the whole answer, for, as we have seen, there is in all society a normative order governing institutional arrangements, contacts between groups, and circulation of goods. This is what we have called the realm of the sedimented social practices. It is clear that although many aspects of it can be threatened by antagonisms and dislocations, many social practices subsist that are not affected by these traumatic events. Even in periods of deep social dissolution—what Gramsci called "organic crisis"—vast areas of society remain unshaken. So if a certain normative proposal clashes with central aspects of social organization that are not put into question, it will not be recognized as an order able to fulfill the ordering function and will not be the object of a hegemonic ethical investment. This constant renegotiation of the relationship between the ethical and the normative actually constitutes the very fabric of social life.

There is a last point that we have to address. We have said that the relation between the ethical and the normative is one of investment (for there is nothing that could be called an ethical normativity), and that this investment is radical (for there is no way of logically moving from ethical experience to norm). In that case, however, there is a heteronomy of the law that is inherent to social life. For Hegel, for instance, true infinitude, self-determination, and freedom were synonymous. If in passing into the other I only pass into myself, I am entirely self-determined, and the distinction between freedom and necessity collapses. This means that there is going to be a full transparency of the social order to the subject ("the truth of the individual is the state") and that the gap between "order" and "ordering" will be ultimately closed. But if that gap is, as we have asserted in our argument, permanent, then in that case, there is a heteronomous dimension of social life that cannot be eliminated. This does not mean that the category of autonomy (as self-determination) becomes obsolete, but it *does* mean that autonomy and heteronomy are in a more complex relation than what it is usually assumed. If the gap between order and ordering could be rationally closed because there is an order that is (as in Plato) the good society, in that case, order and ordering would exactly overlap, and there would be no need for any ethical radical investment. The world of ethics would simply be the world of specifiable social norms. But there is no possibility of such a rational closing—not because one advocates any irrationality, but because the gap that we have detected is inherent to rationality itself. In that case, there is no order that can claim a monopoly of the ordering function, emptiness is at the heart of the structure, and the distinction between the ethical and the normative becomes crucial—and with it, the notion of investment. To some extent, one reveres the law because it is law and not because it is rational. This opacity of the law and the necessary heteronomy that it involves is perhaps, however, at the origin of another type of freedom, one that no longer conceives of itself as unchallenged self-determination. For the subject that is free because it is entirely autonomous can only be a universal subject for which there is no constitutive exterior; the subject emerging from the undecidable game between autonomy and heteronomy is one inhabiting a more humble but more human environment: one for which there is no universality but universalization, no identity but identification, no rationality but partial rationalization of a collective experience.

9 *Ethics, Norms, and Laws*

LEVINAS, LUHMANN, AND LYOTARD

One of the oldest philosophical problems is the relation of the universal to the particular, and in the sphere of law, that produces a question about the aptness of a law to a particular case. That problem, however, has revived with new vigor because of a dramatic revolution in ethics that makes particular responsibility its center and so disputes the authority of universality. To make ethics so swing to an orientation from particularity requires not a stubborn egocentric existentialism, but rather an attention to the responsibility that I have for others, a relation that finds me addressed and responsible for another person—independent of universal principles, norms, concepts, or laws. Such an ethics of responsibility identifies the origin of ethics in an asymmetrical and unique responsibility—and so criticizes theories of ethics that deduce ethical duties from universal norms.

What, then, happens to law? A law stripped of its generality is no law at all. And because of this objection, many conclude that such an asymmetric ethics is not ethical. Its attack on norms lacks the appeal to a higher universality and so would then be sheer dogmatism, emotivism, decisionism, and so forth. In this essay, I wish to examine how we might reinterpret law and norms, justifying them on the basis of an asymmetric ethics. The shift in ethics, to one of responsibility prior to universality, is not opposed to the rule of law, or indeed to the realm of legal institutions. Rather, it offers a different perspective on law and norms in the hope that the shift in ethics can produce better insight into many key and foundational issues regarding law. I will work with three thinkers who each attack norms and claims of universality as the criteria of ethics: Levinas, Luhmann, and Lyotard. They do not agree with each other, and only Levinas can be clearly identified as trying to write an ethics. But what they share is a richer interpretation of the relation to the other. What emerges in quite different ways is the primacy of the future: that obligation arises in a social relation where I cannot control what will happen. The particularity of my responsibility, then, is bound up with the contingency of what another person will say. But looking from this perspective (the contingency of the future), ethics still requires norms and even laws. The need for norms, as generalized expectations or rules, is legitimated in order to keep that future open. The realm of law, moreover, is then understood not as reduced to a set of universal prescriptions, but rather as a double set of practices: (1) the juridical moment, where the judge must take responsibility before both the defendant and the plaintiff, under and beyond the law, and (2) deliberative legislating, where the possibility of revising and even revoking a law is constitutive in making that law. It is not uncommon to regard the rule of law as a matter of pragmatics (and not just the form of universal propositions), but what appears here is a perspective from which to see the processes of making and deciding law that holds open the future for the sake of the other person. By contesting the self-grounding of universal norms, these authors claim to provide a richer interpretation of how ethics calls for law, and how responsibility in relation to other people justifies the rights of others. Such a strong claim, to supplant the more familiar philosophical justifications of rights and the rule of law based on autonomy with an alternative philosophy of law based on responsibility for others, can only be proposed in this chapter; proof would require the work of a set of books. But in the following pages, I can sketch three different interrogations of norms as well as the constructive implications for philosophy of law.

In this essay, I set up a perspective from Levinas's work, emphasizing how ethics begins with the responsibilities that rest on me in my uniqueness and not through some schematism of norms. My reading of Levinas is a pragmatics interpretation where the other person is interpreter of my utterance—indeed, of me as a sign assigned for the other. The future opens in this unpredictable interpretability—the other as judging me, calling me to speak. My ability to respond arises in the procedural requirement for a hearing—that facing the other solicits my ability to speak. The way back from such rigorous particularity to any general norm or concept opens through an overtaxing of my social responsibilities—owing too much to too many others, we negotiate norms. But the validity of the norm is still permeable to critique from the uniqueness of the other person. The key moment, then, is a juridical moment, when the judge, applying the law in order to serve the general norms, herself still becomes responsible and bound in a hypernormative way severally to each of the parties before her. The judge, too, must face the parties, because justice cannot be rendered impersonally.

Luhmann boldly develops a social theory of law that focuses on the role that contingency and the future play for positive legislation. His definition of norms (as a refusal to learn from disappointment) is surely the most polemical. The differentiation of morals and laws will not be our focus; rather, for my purposes, Luhmann points to a space in law that opens for the future the contrast between juridical interpretation and positive legislation. Legislation, however, also is bound by procedure and by constitution, and so develops a reflexive structure: there is a norm to develop norms. That second-order norm is on the one hand a recognition of a need to learn how to create and to transform norms and not merely use them as a backstop from the past. But on the other hand, its very generativity makes it contrary to Luhmann's own concept of norm—for such a higher-order norm links both past and future.

Lyotard's *Differend* explores a juridical limit. A differend is a wrong that does not count as a damage before a given court. Lyotard interrogates and distinguishes different kinds of phrases or utterances and the gaps between them. In a complex relation to Levinas's thought, Lyotard focuses on the gap between prescriptives and norms, questioning the apparent identity of the legislator and the governed even for democratically determined norms—the making of law both exposes and then forgets the differends between competing groups. His theory redevelops the need for democratic deliberation on the basis of ongoing discussion of what we ought to be and contesting the norm to be what we are. The specific task for philosophy is to discover new rules under which this wrong could appear, to find new ways of responding to the other, particularly beyond the current state of the law.

A tentative conclusion then draws the three thinkers together, with a focus first on the role of pragmatics in interpreting law. The key to the processes and practices, moreover, is the future of responsibility—the holding open of the possibility for another to speak. Finally, the tension between the logics or representation and cooperation (between the judges and the legislators) will clarify the different ways of responsively acting in the present for the sake of the future.

Levinas's Asymmetric Ethics

If we change our point of departure for ethics, heeding the way that I am put in question by another person, then thought arises in the particular, or rather, in an individual, who is indexed in an asymmetrical relation. Ethics begins with me, and that "me" is in question—indeed, under accusation from another person. The "me" who will be able to respond is not her own author but is a responding speaker or writer. The vigor of the demand that such a change of orientation requires characterizes the work of Levinas, but also of many others, as I have tried to explore in my recent *Why Ethics? Signs of Responsibilities*. This contrasts with an ethics of "I," an ethics of a reasoning subject who interprets himself as a specification of a universal concept: the rational self, the moral self, and so on, defined as a case of a universal rational will. This kind of ethics understands each agent as part of a totality, and the subject derives his duties from the universality of a system. But to take up the respondent's position, to discern that we are first called and then speak in response, is to make ethics a matter of being singled out from the totality, and singled out in relation to another person. The other person's call to me precedes the formation of the general term, the formation of the norm. We are looking at a radical uniqueness, one that arises in relation from a specific other—an other who reserves the authority to refuse any classification, who is a principle of an ethical call that refuses all norms (Levinas 1961, 74–75/101). Not because I can recognize the other's belonging to a class of people who deserve my attention (my people, rational animals, my compatriot), but because she contests the intentionality of knowing her. For Levinas, this is a drama displayed in a straining of phenomenology—for the other is enigmatic and does not appear as a phenomenon (indeed, it contests the "as-structure" of phenomenology). And I interpret this as a straining of pragmatics—as an asymmetry of authority. The other has the authority to interpret my utterances—indeed, even to interpret me in my body—in a way where I do not have the parallel authority to interpret hers. I am more able and more beholden to respond than the other is to respond to me. The asymmetry of interpretative authority is the concrete situation of the asymmetry of ethics.

For this essay, the asymmetry appears when Levinas describes a courtroom context. Levinas interprets the agency of the self in terms of the ability to speak, to defend myself before the other's accusation. Levinas is interested in the principle of a hearing: my accuser faces me, and I am called to defend myself for my violence (Levinas 1961, 221/243). I become myself through an indictment, standing on trial, and speaking in response to the charge. My violence has been precisely my refusal to see her uniqueness, the attempt either to subsume the other person under concepts or to judge our relation as subordinate to a norm. The moment when I address the court, responding to the charge, is not a moment of violence, but one of ethical responsibility, where my ability to respond is solicited. Levinas describes "me" as called before the magistrate, who stands above me and demands a response. Appearing before the magistrate is not, however, a totalizing subsumption of me under a norm, for I am engendered to respond to offer my own apology, called to speak in my own name.

This responsibility, however, becomes infinite through a cycling in relation to knowing and responding. For Levinas, I am infinitely responsible for the other: the more I do, the more I am obliged to do (Levinas 1961, 74/100–101). But a comparison between the other as teacher and the other as judge (a comparison made concrete even when Levinas discusses the teacher), shows that the other may teach me the objectivity of the world, but at the same time, because I learn *from* the other, I find myself questioned further. Called to consciousness, called to attention, I attend to the discourse of another but then also find my own efforts to understand and to respond called into question again. Levinas rejects the notion that ethical responsibility is simply opposed to knowledge (and, we would add, to norms), but claims rather that the relation to the other, whose authority is precisely that which contests my effort to know, also sets me to the task of responding and so of knowing. I think and know because I am called before the court, and so the right to a hearing allows me to become a speaker, a knower, responsible in various senses of the word. The particularity of ethics (in me and the other) sets me toward the thematizing and the framing of general concepts and even norms. The norm is not prior to this ethics, but it also is not foreign to it, but rather located within the plot of ethics. The greater my effort to know and to control myself, the greater my sense of being under judgment, and so the greater my responsibilities. Reasoning is not something I do on my own that would thus be my qualification to appear in court: reasoning is something that the procedure of facing another itself requires and empowers me for.

In Levinas's courtroom account, the relation to knowledge is recast as a relation to the straight line of justice—"In reality, justice does not include me in its universality—justice summons me to go beyond the straight line of justice, and from there nothing can mark the end of this step; behind the straight line of law, the land of goodness extends infinitely and unexplored, demanding all of the resources of a singular presence" (Levinas 1961, 223/245). Here is the tension that the teacher creates when knowing becomes justice—justice draws straight lines and also calls us beyond them. And indeed, justice would not be justice without both this measure and this excess. Even were we to insert an artificial distinction calling that excessive justice either *ethics* or even *righteousness*, we would still have a cycling to a limit (a norm) and then beyond it. The justification of norms is before not some higher norm, but on the contrary before another person. And to be under judgment, to become responsible, to become a "me," is to be called beyond any straight line, any universal norm.

What we need here, however, is a justification of law, and indeed of general norms. If the ability to respond knits together my knowing and reasoning with a need to speak to the other, then we also need to see how Levinas can account for the universality of laws. His justification of laws arises from his ethics of responsibility and serves to stabilize and make commensurable the infinite responsibilities I have for others. In a soup kitchen, although each deserves all he can eat, justice doles out equally enough for each. In order to practice my infinite responsibilities, I will depend on laws and legal institutions. The argument is at first quite simple: a third person makes my infinite responsibility for this single other person complicated by other responsibilities (mine for the third, and indeed the others' for the third). Levinas explains that at this point, "There must be justice, which is to say, comparison, coexistence, contemporaneity, assembling, order, thematization, the *visibility* of faces, and through that, the intentionality and the intellect and in intentionality and intellect, the intelligibility of the system, and through that also a copresence on an equal footing in a court of justice" (Levinas 1974, 200/157).[1] The justification for laws and the legal system arises in the surplus of responsibilities. What they require and thus justify is the need for a present moment. The future depends on the moment when people appear together. And the asymmetry of responsibility requires an equality, precisely in court. In the courtroom, equality between the parties is represented by the judge, who should incline to neither. Law in the courtroom is the measure that ethics requires, but the justification of equality is not axiomatic and self-grounding. On the contrary, equality arises in order to serve the complexity of conflicting responsibilities.

We require one more decisive moment to understand what Levinas can provide for our interpretation of law—for law is not itself the rule required to balance responsibilities to thirds, but rather the practices or even procedures. At the center of judicial process is not only the asymmetry of responding to the indictment, but also the role of the judge. Thus we move first from my role as accused, faced by the other and invested with agency, to the rule of law and legal systems, where the parties face each other as equal, to a third moment of facing. If we turn the table of asymmetry and imagine the law in force, the judge making a ruling, we must confront the way that the judge is also a "me," called into question by the one before her. "Justice is impossible without the one who dispenses justice finding herself in nearness . . . The judge is not exterior to the conflict, but the law is in the midst of nearness" (Levinas 1974, 202/159). Laws are applied or enforced through individuals, individuals who seem to be merely serving an impartial role for the sake of all the parties, even for the general interest of the society or the state. But must the judge also be responsible to each unique other before the court? Judgment seems almost impossible, if the judge is also under judgment, is still a responsible "me." But perhaps procedure is not an insulation in the context of enforcement, making the proceedings impersonal so that power can hold sway. Maybe the need for procedure is precisely the vulnerability of the judge who, as "me," is called to respond for plural parties, each infinitely. The others' gaze and questioning pierce the robes and wigs, asking me how I can pronounce judgment.

The bitter truth is that the judge must bear the weight of the ambiguity of law in speaking to, even responding to, the defendant before her (Levinas 1974, 202/159). The judge must stand for impartiality and also for the excessive responsibility to whomever is before her (not simply a combination of plaintiff and defendant, or crown and accused—but to each individually, as unique). The judge upholds the equality of each by shouldering a fundamental inequality of her own responsibilities over her rights. Thus the judge bears responsibility for applying the weight of the legal system—a heavier responsibility—because the judge must see how ethics (or righteousness) may exceed the generality of the law. So that if as defendant I understand myself as called and so enabled to respond, assigned to respond to others, as judge, I understand myself as enabled to respond, even beyond the legal system whose schematism I perform, arriving at the application of violence against the defendant (see Cover 1992). Perhaps one could say that the very ambiguity of language, of law, is performed by the judge who knows herself responsible to each one in the courtroom, and so not only to the law, but also to justice beyond the law. The "me" position then has this defining characteristic: it must respond beyond the straight line of the law—no matter what entanglements it has with norms, and these entanglements have different positive ethical tasks—for "me," ethics requires an excess beyond the norm. The perspective here on the matter of judicial discretion would contrast with some others by focusing on justice requiring a human judge, for a person with a face—that is, a person who can respond to others. Writing an opinion, rendering a judgment, ruling on matters of law—these practices bind the judge to responsibilities to others, and not solely to principles of autonomy or a deductive system. The judge is not free to disregard or even to break the law, but responsibilities to reason and to speak that we first found in the self as accused now appear intensified in the responsibilities to judge others according to the law. The context of juridical reasoning then informs our view of interpretation beyond an argument about the model of phronesis.

The courtroom context then displays the relation between ethics and law. Legal procedure (the right to a hearing, the possibility of equity, the possibility of appeal) offers a context in which to see ethics refracted in "reality." If laws and norms became mere bureaucratic regulations, applied in a mechanical way with no call for a hearing or for a judge who faced the accused, then we would have just the sort of totality that Levinas attacks. But law serves justice, or the justice beyond justice, or ethics, precisely in its universality emplaced in a context where the uniqueness of responsibility is performed.

Luhmann's Positive Law

Luhmann develops a social theory of law under the broader project of a systems theory of society. Luhmann offers an interpretation of how such a systems theory itself functions in contemporary society, but what is clear for us is that systems theory is emphatically not a normative theory, a theory that would try to propose or defend the norms of a society. On the contrary, in this theory, norms appear as functions, and the theory gains its power from a rich descriptive functional interpretation of structures, processes, practices, actions, and so on. Law is a subsystem of the social system, distinguishing between the communications that are counted as legal and those that are excluded. I will offer an interpretation only of Luhmann's fullest statement of theory of law from *A Sociological Theory of Law* (1972), whereas the later work *Soziale Systeme* (*Social Systems*; 1984) moves away from structuralism, because that interpretation will allow me to bring Luhmann into close conversation with Levinas and Lyotard.

In the eyes of someone who holds either that a norm is valid, or indeed, that there is a rational validation for norms, treating a norm in terms of its function is to misgrasp the idea of norms. (And so Habermas never tires of objecting.) But in the context of Levinas's defense of uniqueness both prior to and beyond norms, we may need to see just what norms *do* do, according to Luhmann. At the start, we can consider social expectations—what we expect of others. Society depends on matching our expectations with others' expectations of us. In some discussions, Luhmann has recourse to the double contingency of communication. The expectation of expectation is social, relating me to another, and at the same time it is temporalized in the moment of disappointment. At that moment, my expectations must respond: either I can change my expectations to fit the reality, or I can maintain my expectation and change or try to change the reality. In the former case, I engage in learning and frame a *cognitive*; in the latter, I frame a *norm*, a claim about what ought to be and is not (Luhmann 1972, 42/33).

If we transport this distinction back to Levinas's account of responding to the other person, we find that the other is always able to disappoint my expectation, to contest my current interpretation of her. At that moment I must either respond with a norming reaction: *You should be as I expect!*, or with a cognitive one: *You are my teacher.* For if a norm is merely a stubborn refusal to learn, an insistence on what I already hold as my expectation, then ethics must begin with a criticism of norms. The need to keep learning is precisely the need to submit our thinking and our general conceptual framework to criticism from another, from the unexpectable future. And disappointment of expectation is the drawing near to the other who criticizes me for the inadequacy of my expectations, and indeed, for presuming to determine her expectations.

But if Luhmann can see that norms themselves enable us to confront the experience of disappointment (and so are not simply wicked or inept), that is because a norm is always counterfactual—they mark the gap between what is and what we expect. As a result, they allow us to maintain an expectation independent of what happens. Luhmann defines norms as "Counterfactually stabilized behavioural expectations" (Luhmann 1972, 43/33), and so they posit recognizable, structural *oughts*. The norm addresses the behavior because it concerns the relation between people (and not their internal convictions or struggles). For Luhmann, there is no gap between the facts and the norms (or values), but only between learning and norms—and norms seem in this way to be more like "principles" or "scruples," to verge on the moralistic in their unwillingness to change or to listen in order to learn. They do work in reducing risk, but they do different work from universals in Levinas's account (and Levinas rarely uses the term *norm*), where they coordinate obligations more than they refuse reality in the face of disappointment.

Yet if we take a further step to law, we can see that the stabilized norms can indeed come into conflict. In more complex societies, there are many disappointments and there is an overproduction of norms, because learning cannot serve to respond to every social disappointment. Some counterfactual expectations must be maintained. Law serves to hold a selection of the mass of norms into a congruent whole. It coordinates in much the same way it did in Levinas (although there it coordinates responsibilities to learn from others and not norms to mark disappointment with reality). Luhmann defines law as a "structure of a social system which depends upon the congruent generalization of normative behavioural expectations" (Luhmann 1972, 105/82). Luhmann recognizes that there are various ways of coordinating the range of normative expectations. But the role of *system* is most important, because the sorting of what will count as law depends on its relation to the social system in which the law is a subsystem. Law is not optional for a social system, but it is not the only necessary subsystem either. On the other hand, law is neither simply a normative structure, derived from oughts, nor a coercive structure, derived from the use of force in society. Luhmann carefully negotiates with each of these alternate interpretations of law, and indeed finds that coercion and violence are not foreign to law even though they do not constitute it. Similarly, although law deals with norms, it is the interest of social communication itself that guides law in sorting and coordinating, in generalizing the normative expectations. That interest concerns the future, for the reality of social existence is in the expectations, and indeed, in our expectations of expectations of us. Law concerns expectations and functions to keep the future open. Law holds norms together (which regard disappointment as the world's failure) in a system in order to preserve a space in the future where we can communicate. It does not foreclose the future by determining what must happen, but it also protects social interactions from a collapse when expectations are not met. Thus it keeps the future open by building systems of ways of dealing with failed expectations.

The more familiar justification of law as congruent, generalized norms would be for the sake of maintaining authority (moral or power)—to allow society to stay true to its normative ideals. But Luhmann senses that the optimal openness to the future, to both expectations met and to disappointments from which society can learn and grow, depends on a limiting and coordinating of the closures that norms represent. This seems to offer a richer view of law than Levinas's—although Levinas's justification of law is also to coordinate and in a limited sense control the abundance of "oughts" (responsibilities), his justification is for the sake of responsibility—which, for Levinas, is, again, the opening to the future and not the closure of Luhmann's norm. A constriction of responsibilities serves ethics, but only in between the infinite responsibility of me as accused and the infinite responsibility of me as judge. For Luhmann, the constriction of norms opens the future beyond the normative realm, and that will be clearer in the sharp distinction he makes between juridical law and positive law (or legislation).

Luhmann presents an evolutionary account of law in order to identify the specific way that modern law negotiates with norms for the sake of holding the future open. That theory has three moments: archaic law, premodern high cultural law, and positive law. We have little interest in his narrative here, but we need to focus on the accomplishments of the latter two moments, for the high cultures produced the realm of juridical law, including the fundamental separation of the legal system from political authority. Jurisprudence as the independent system of legal reasoning in courts in order to judge cases and to build up a consistency of precedents and matters of law—all of this comes in the second moment (in Roman law, especially, although we would add in rabbinic law as well, and in common law).

In the modern period, juridical law is retained but the great innovation is the development of legislation, for positive law produces new law that does not rest on old law. Luhmann holds that juridical law becomes more radically separated from legislation, as positive law becomes much more free to conceive of law as independent from natural law. Luhmann does not interpret the separations of powers (an independent judiciary, and so on) as the key to this systemic change. Rather, the key is the grappling with temporality. In its simplest form, the three moments can be mapped onto primacy of the past, of the present and of the future (even though each moment requires a relation to each temporal mode: even positive legislation has need for a past of tradition and precedent). To be a bit crude, in archaic law, the ruling is fate, and there are no other possibilities in the present, much less any serious consideration of how things might change in the future.

But in high cultures and in jurisprudence in the modern period, the judge's task depends on a double possibility in the present (guilty/not guilty). The facts are not the sole determination of that selection—for there are matters of law. The judge is normed in a second-order norm, a norm of making similar rulings in similar cases. Her task is not to promulgate new first-order norms, new laws, but at most to offer new second-order norms on jurisprudence. Moreover, the judge is not personally responsible for the consequences of the judgment, but only for the reasoning involved in the present moment of decision. Appeals reflect the accountability of the judge on matters of law and jurisprudence. The judge selects from previous law to frame a judgment for the present, and the judgment has the possibility of binding future judgments—but in that sense, jurisprudence defines and limits the future for the sake of the present case. In the high premodern cultures, fate is replaced by guilt and atonement—for the individual can be identified as a legal person but also can have his past lifted off his shoulders, thus opening a future (Luhmann 1972, 344/266). The room for positive law is opened, but only slightly, as the fundamental norms are not in question (natural law), but specific future possibilities can be generated, so long as they do not go against that fundamental base.

But when we shift into the modern era and look not at jurisprudence but at legislation, then temporality is radically altered. The governing temporal mode is the future—laws are enacted that are in principle alterable. Positive law is fundamentally experimental and open to revision. Positive law is constituted with its contingency—it not only could be otherwise, it likely will become otherwise. Although courts address past disappointments with application of norms, positive law must hold open the possibility of learning from disappointment, the possibility of new legislation that arises from learning how reality does not meet expectations. The very separation of positive law (legislatures) from juridical law (courts) reflects, according to Luhmann, the need for both maintaining norms and for a creativity for the sake of the future. Constitutionalism arose, according to Luhmann, in the separation and interaction of these two sides of law—as a way for society to challenge the hegemony of politics. In contrast to the judge who maintains the norms, the legislator regards norms themselves as capable of alteration. The legal system depends on both relations to norms. Luhmann does not have the radical rationalist's passion: the legislators must work with the current norms and laws, but laws can be changed when new information or new situations arise in the world. The ideas of an elected legislature, of regular debate, and so on all reflect this new understanding of positive law. Although legislation does make choices, the possibilities that were excluded are not thereby eliminated (Luhmann 1972, 209/161). The other party may come back into power and then try to revise the program they fought against. Deliberative democracy makes decisions that preserve not only the people who opposed the decision, but even the excluded possibility as a possible future option.

Thus at the end of the book, Luhmann accentuates the point about temporality:

The positivity, that is, the principle structural variability of law is only comprehensible if we, in reverse, see the present as the consequence of the future, i.e. as decision. . . . Time itself does not establish the future, although a history has always been shaped within it. It leaves it open, that is, it retains more possibility in its prospect than could ever become present, and therefore, past. (Luhmann 1972, 345/266)

Law can now shift from producing the doubled possibility in the present (guilty/not guilty), to the richer range of possibilities in the future, or rather of holding those possibilities open from the perspective of the future. If positive law struggled merely to determine the present (implementation of norms), or even to make the future conform to a given norm, then we would see, again, a way of forcing the future into the present. But Luhmann's insight is that positive law comes with its own constitutive principle of revision and reform. Positive law itself will be changed, and new norms will come into play. The process is intrinsically one of learning (as opposed to stubborn insistence on today's normative oughts). This prospect for learning, however, means that the norms of the system (often articulated as a Constitution) are second- or third-order norms—they either norm the legal reasoning, which itself is second order in relation to what we would usually call moral expectations (matters of fact versus matters of law), or at least they operate in a parallel way to the legal reasoning norms—as procedural, they norm the choices of making policy. But positive law as a system is intrinsically not about implementing inflexible norms (our basic norms).

Indeed, this interpretation of the futurity of law is precisely amoral. Following both Durkheim and Weber, Luhmann drives home the point that modern law is differentiated from morality. When law abandons the task of making people moral, it is freed for many positive functions in society. Luhmann sees clear systemic advantage from this abandonment of the moral task that law held at other times. One can easily enough imagine this as a Kantian perspective as well. Morality as the development of just and upright individuals, people with inner resources and virtues, is simply outsourced from the realm of law. It is not indifferent to society that people be good, but law asks only that they be lawful, and even that requirement is complicated in relation to the learning that the legislature can do from the disappointments of its normative expectations. The judge, on the other hand, must not ask if people are good, but only if they obey the law. Here we are at a significant tension with Levinas—although it is clear that for Levinas, my responsibility is in no way dependent on whether the other person is good. My struggle to bear the responsibilities that are assigned me in society may produce a law for the sharing out of responsibilities, but adherence to moral goals or rules is not the telos of Levinas's ethics.[2]

There is, moreover, one more striking feature in Luhmann's theory: the reflexivity of norms. Positive legislation does have its own higher-order norm: the norm of norm-making (Luhmann 1972, 215/164). This reflexive structure is a favorite of Luhmann's; other examples are the trusting of trust, the teaching of teaching, feelings about one's own feelings, love of love, and so on. To make the act of instituting norms itself a norm is to make us aware of the activity, and aware that the need to coordinate and transform norms is the source of positive legislation. Creating a legal system, where the legislature will sit and make laws, arises from this norm to norm. Moreover, that higher-order norm about norms itself may well have institutional and procedural content: regular elections, majority rules, equal representation, public hearings, and so on. The legislature should decide which plan to adopt for reducing poverty—even allowing all the bills to die in committee is a decision, and the norm about norming accentuates the choosing. The reflexivity thus also turns the norming activity itself into a learning process—in a different way than having a political scientist study legislative debate (which would be to have a cognitive frame for norming). This hypernorm also seems to me to point to a certain kind of normativity at work in Luhmann's kind of functional analysis—not in any moralistic sense, but rather in terms of the relation between law and the future. Luhmann notes that his sociological approach at this point offers a different perspective on the debate of Hart and Fuller on positive law and morality. To recognize both the contingency of norms in the future and the need to make normative decisions today in relation to the traditions of the past is to interpret the norms as functions, with a power to make a demand upon behavior. It also, however, denaturalizes the norms for the sake of learning from the unexpectable future, making the making of norms itself an opportunity to learn—as well as a norm.

Lyotard's 'Differend'

Lyotard achieves a most radical form of the linguistic turn in his book, *Le différend* (*The Differend*), by restricting his claims to the way that one phrase (or sentence) follows another (Lyotard 1983). Although he would not call it a social system, it bears a strong resemblance to Luhmann's interpretation of social systems, because for Luhmann the system is a set of communications and not a group of people. Moreover, within Lyotard's view of the realm of phrases, there are rules and indeed genres that steer forward to the next selection—and much of the action of the social system is a similar steering. But in this short essay, we need to confine ourselves to a major theme in his work: the relation of prescriptive phrases (imperatives) and normative ones.

Much as Luhmann depends on a distinction between cognitives and norms, so too Lyotard depends on a distinction between cognitive phrases and prescriptive ones. (Although this is not an exhaustive distinction, for phrases also come as interrogatives, exclamations, logical phrases, and so on). Lyotard explores how language is used in a cognitive genre to know the world, to validate claims about the properties things have, and indeed to investigate the existence of entities. None of this applies to prescriptions that work quite otherwise—most of all, they oblige the addressee without seeming to force the addressee to obey. There is no great surprise then that Lyotard draws directly on Levinas's account of responsibility to explore prescriptives. But central to the problem of prescriptives is that they do not identify an addressor. Obligation depends on the "you"—the "me" as addressed, and not on the "I" who speaks to me. Moreover, in the being addressed, I do not learn about the world or about the one who speaks to me. Like Luhmann's norms, there is no learning of content in the prescriptive (Lyotard 1983, 163/111). But Levinas might contribute at this point that the teacher teaches teaching, not a content, or in his terms, says a saying, not a said. For Lyotard, the prescriptive signals a split in the self—the impossibility of taking up obligation without asserting my "I" as a speaker. As obliged "I" must answer, must become an "I." And if I try to understand the command, if I pause and say "Who are you?" to someone who seems to have addressed me, or if I say, "I now feel myself obliged," I have shifted out of the addressee position.

Indeed, the cognitive genre attacks the obligation in a way that is irresolvable: it says "What is the warrant for this prescription?", or even "What are the expectable consequences of obeying?" But it wants a deduction of the prescription, and the prescription is always undeducible (Lyotard 1983, 172/117). If I can take the position of the one who can explain the prescription, then I become the "I" who commands and not the "you" who hears it. I efface my addressee position. Levinas's teaching about the asymmetry of responsibility is here translated into an account of how phrases link onto each other. The tension between cognition and command is irresolvable: there is no reason why we should be obliged, but we are—except that in a cognitive courtroom, we will always look crazy for being obliged without first knowing what we are doing. The validation of a command is to do what is commanded, not to be able to explain the warrant for the obligation—nor to praise the beauty of the command (Lyotard likes the example of the officer who cries "Avanti!" and leaps up out of the trench; the soldiers are moved, cry "Bravo!", but don't budge) (Lyotard 1983, 55/31). Thus the prescriptive interrupts the cognitive (and indeed, other genres as well). Levinas would claim here that the answer "here am I [*me voici*]" offers oneself as all ears, as still addressee and not as the one who understands or who commands. Lyotard is more interested in the impossibility of an ethical linking:

As a sign, the ethical phrase is without sequel, and thus final. But as there is no final phrase, another phrase must link onto it. And, as this linkage cannot be the linkage of an ethical implication—which is an impossibility—this implication, if it is still an implication (a series of consequences), then is not ethical, but cognitive. (Lyotard 1983, 186/127)

Phrases continue into the future, but prescriptives lead beyond themselves, to phrases that betray the position of obligation. The addressee position is vital but also impossible.

We can move to the betrayal that seems most like ethics: the norm. For when the prescriptive is translated from a command ("You should do it") to a norm ("It is a norm decreed by *y* that *x* should do it"), then the prescription is *cited* and some of its obligating force is displaced (Lyotard 1983, 207/143). The norm looks like it identifies a reason why someone should be obliged (because the king or the congress or your mother says so). But that would reduce the immediacy of being singled out by a prescription—for no reason. However, what makes a norm oblige? It cannot depend on a state of affairs or a cognitive regime—for different norms can readily arise from any given situation. A norm obliges where it will, and so what concerns Lyotard is not the validation of norms, but rather how they work with phrases, particularly how they produce law.

"The norm is what turns a prescription into a law" (Lyotard 1983, 206/142). By citing a prescription, the addressor steps forward, identified as the one who will consolidate different stakes of discourse for the sake of justice (what Luhmann might call congruent generalized norms). Those various stakes are not intrinsically coordinatable, but the authority steps up and claims to do so. In the process, the prescription loses its specificity and now obliges a class of people to some act. The addressees of the norm are now some sort of community, people who are equally under the obligation and under it through the norm and not as unique addressees of a command. The interests of justice are not identical to those of knowledge or aesthetics or even of ethics, but rather are a political achievement: the holding together of diverse phrases and the production of a unified set of stakes.

Thus the key question about law, for Lyotard, is the way that the addressees of the law relate to its addressors. Although he advances a strong defense of deliberative democracy, Lyotard refuses the familiar claim that the people are both ruler and ruled in democracy. For Lyotard, precisely because of his insight into the asymmetry of the prescriptive, the normative also must recognize the split of the two "we"s—of the position of norm maker and normed addressee (Lyotard 1983, 145–48/97–99). But deliberative democracy exposes this split—because the ruling party enacts laws for all of the people, and in deliberation, the question of the legitimacy of the norm and of the gap between addressor and addressee is exposed over and over again. Thus deliberative democracy again and again opens the question "What ought we to be?" (and not the norm "Be what you are") (Lyotard 1983, 217/150). The main contrast for Lyotard is with a narrative genre, which through a slipping of the name (We French, We Americans) allows the gap in proclaiming a norm to disappear. But deliberative democracy maintains an empty center where the political conflict between different genres of discourse (different stakes, such as efficiency, profit, and freedom) all can be debated under the question: what should we do?

For Lyotard, like Luhmann, the question of how we make norms replaces the question of how to apply or even to validate norms. Like Luhmann's account of positive legislation, Lyotard's discussion of deliberative democracy places a premium on the openness that cannot be foreclosed in the matter of norms. Deliberative democracy calls into question the very sense of stakes and necessity that seems to link up phrases within a given genre. It is not hard to see how legislative institutions are hereby justified and also held to a higher-order goal.

The question of temporality, however, is taken up more directly in Lyotard's account of the differend, the legal matter that is the title of the book. A damage is actionable in court—there is a tribunal to which one can bring a complaint for a harm done to me by another. But a differend occurs when there is no court, no tribunal, before which I could bring a complaint for some harm done to me. Such is a wrong: a damage accompanied by the loss of the means to prove that damage (Lyotard 1983, 18–19/5). There is no way to find a phrase for the wrong done to me. Lyotard focuses on the difficulty for survivors, especially of the Shoah, to describe to others the unimaginable wrong done to them. Another example he uses is the Martinican who can bring a complaint against any infringement on her rights as a French citizen, but who has a differend if she were to try to bring a case against France for being a French citizen (Lyotard 1983, 49/27).

But the task of philosophy, in particular, is to seek new rules that will allow the wrong to be addressed, to become part of the phrasing. Although the task of the politicians is to debate and to make new norms as laws, the task of the philosopher is to bear witness to differends, to the places where we cannot yet find the words for a wrong. A differend in a linguistic "system" demands an innovation in language itself. There is a strong demand for a new phrase, a new way of speaking or writing to take up the wrong. This ought arises in a clearly different way from either general prescriptives or from normative laws (Lyotard 1983, 29/12). It is a seeking for new rules of linking, and the philosopher's work is to respond to this demand. Language itself is said to summon people: something "asks" to be put into words. Clearly this specific not-yet of the seeking for rules to express differends is an intervention of the future into the present (for the sake of a past wrong that is invisible in the present). But there is then a strange genre, philosophy, whose stakes are to discover rules in the not yet phrasable, to find new rules in order to allow the wrongs to count. It is not endless critique because it does not obliterate the precedents and the previous rules, nor is it an abstract task. Case by case, new rules must be discovered—and this bears a familiar resemblance to common law. This is a kind of justice, but one that goes beyond the current capacities for things to appear or have a present. In the context of this task, the work of deliberative democracy indeed appears future oriented, even future determined, precisely because the empty space of deliberation is also a place where new voices can be heard. The legislature is a place where the differends are exposed, but in the need for a law, a decision, there is a necessary (transcendental) illusion that "we've now resolved that," and so in the moment of decision the differend is also forgotten (Lyotard 1983, 213–14/147). The philosopher, on the other hand, is summoned to open and reopen the differend (Lyotard 1983, 206/142). That contrast allows us again to see the way that legislation overcomes the limitation of norms, precisely by allowing attention to turn to those limitations. But the juridical model, which provides the idea of the differend as a wrong that exceeds the authority of the court, points to a justice beyond justice, a philosophical task that is not simply ethics or prescriptive, but somehow bears a strong affinity to ethics. Just as Luhmann had functionalized norms, Lyotard also displaces the authority of universal norms as a privileged goal of language, but discerns beyond the heterogeneity of diverse genres a different call, even an obligation beyond the obligations that are phrased in prescriptives. One cannot call it ethics or normative theory, but Lyotard's work has its own task, a quasi-ethical or hypernormativity in seeking for the phrase that is not-yet, to find the words for a wrong that does not-yet belong in the jurisdiction of the court.

Future Laws

A theory of law that drew these thinkers into a set would need to explore law as both legislation and jurisprudence. Although Levinas would emphasize the face-to-face in the courtroom and the responsibilities that constitute and exceed the straight line of law, Luhmann and Lyotard both would understand the practices of creating laws as an excess of futurity and as a way of taming the violence of static norms (forgetting differends in Lyotard, refusing to learn in Luhmann). Lyotard's central model, the differend, points to the limits of the courtroom, or rather significantly of any specific courtroom. It points for the sake of justice to a not-yet courtroom, to a future possibility to appear in court—a possibility that is summoning us but that is not yet available. As for norms, from the view of the norm to frame norms (the justification of positive legislation), we can functionalize norms' ability to define oughts. But an irresolvable conflict lies in the tension between the norms' universality and the particularity of obligation. We can begin to frame a tension between the need for generalized norms and the unquenchable vulnerability that general norms must bear. Switching the level of justification for ethics from universality to asymmetrical particular responsibilities does not dismiss norms, but it does displace them. The particularity at the center of this ethics of responsibility itself requires the formation of norms. For the sake of ethics, we must find norms, but ethics also remains critical of specific norms. By changing perspective, and so looking at the justification of norms from the context of particular individuals with asymmetric responsibilities, we see the warrant for norms in a different light.

How, then, does law contribute to a reformulation of this irresolvable tension of universals and particular responsibilities? When norms are justified through autonomous and universal reason, then law, seeking its particular, requires a schematism of some sort. But when the processes of deciding law in court and making law in the legislature are viewed in relation to this tension from particular responsibilities prior to universal ones, then legal processes seem to offer an ethical redress from the norms and the laws as code and statute. A philosophy of law then would lead toward a view of law as pragmatics in the relations of both judges and legislators to the laws they interpret/make. The tensions of making and interpreting laws, tensions that would expose the very futurity of law as well as the interruptive concern for the other, for the unexpectable, for the wrong still in need of accounting—all interlace the role of general norms in the work of justice. But to lean too heavily on the normative, to assume that norms justify themselves in their universality, is to be left with violence that closes the future.

The contrast of jurisprudence and legislating reflects two different ways to keep the future open. In the case of the judge, the judge must decide in the present, making law at this moment—but in bearing responsibility as a "me" before the parties, the judge stands as representative for others, as having the responsibility for the defendant, for the plaintiff, and for society (see Gibbs 2000, 178 ff.). That responsibility singles out the judge, obliged as an individual for the each individual before her, and for all the others. As responsibility, that moment depends on a future that exceeds the "me"s intentions. Even the judge is vulnerable, and the higher justice (beyond the straight line of justice) makes the judge representative for each and for all.

In contrast, the legislator frames laws by deliberating with others, and the future is held open in a more deferred way. The law enacted is not more just than the straight line of justice—that justice is to come. The future casts its shadow over today, lurking. The expectation of revision, of reopening debate, opens a cooperative responsibility—new voices will still have to be heard, new experiences and disappointments will have something to teach us. Our law-making is tentative because we understand that justice depends on a cooperation that lies ahead, not in some present moment, but in an ever-coming future. The legislators make their laws aware that the justice to come will disturb the laws they make today. And the judge interprets the laws determined by past precedent and by the legislature. Both activities, although separate, anticipate the relation with each other—with the result that much of the practices of legal reasoning coordinates over just this contrast of activities. In both activities, we can identify an ethical moment that invests "me" with an excess of responsibility.

If we may make one last tentative conclusion, however, we find that the task of thinking at this theoretical level—the activity of this chapter—helps identify the possibilities for judging law—that is, for an ethical critique of specific norms for the sake of justice. Luhmann's claims for the value for thinking functionally about norms and laws within a legal system depend on the reflexivity of the norm to make norms. Lyotard views the task of philosophy as discovering the new rules that will allow differends to come to language. And Levinas justifies his own theorizing (which must be expressed in general terms) by recourse to a responsibility that rests on me (and not on the "me") to testify to my own responsibilities—like the judge. Such theoretical activity opens new perspectives on the ethical need for laws and norms, offering new ways of reexamining central topics in the study of law. Such theories do not find their justification either in promulgating norms or in knowing in order to know, but reinsert their critical insights into individuating responsibilities back into the complex practices of ethics, norms, and laws.

NOTES

This chapter has greatly benefited from the constructive comments of Lisa Austin, Arthur Ripstein, and Sinkwan Cheng. All translations by the author, but citations are to original pages/available English translation.

1. For a more extensive commentary on this passage, see my *Why Ethics* (2000, 134–39).

2. Although there is significant disagreement here with Drucilla Cornell's interpretation of Luhmann on temporality, that should not obscure the rich and complex agreement and debt of my interpretation throughout this chapter with her work *The Philosophy of the Limit* (1992).

WORKS CITED

Cornell, Drucilla. 1992. *The philosophy of the limit*. New York: Routledge.
Cover, Robert. 1992. Violence and word. In *Narrative, violence, and the law: The essays of Robert Cover*, ed. Martha Minnow, Michael Ryan, and Austin Sarat, 203–38. Ann Arbor: University of Michigan Press.
Gibbs, Robert. 2000. *Why ethics? Signs of responsibilities*. Princeton: Princeton University Press.
Levinas, Emmanuel. 1961. *Totalité et infini*. The Hague: Martinus Nijhoff. Trans. Alphonso Lingis as *Totality and infinity*. Pittsburgh: Duquesne University Press.
———. 1974. *Autrement qu'être ou au-delà de l'Essence*. Dordrecht: Martinus Nijhoff. Trans. Alphonso Lingis as *Otherwise than being or beyond essence*. The Hague: Martinus Nijhoff.
Luhmann, Niklas. 1972. *Rechtssoziologie*. Opladen: Westdeutscher Verlag. Trans. Elizabeth King and Martin Albrow as *A sociological theory of law*. London: Routledge & Kegan Paul.
———. 1984. *Soziale Systeme*. Frankfurt: Suhrkamp. Trans. John Bednarz Jr. with Dirk Baecker as *Social systems*. Stanford: Stanford University Press.
Lyotard, Jean-François. 1983. *Le différend*. Paris: Les Éditions de Minuit. Trans. Georges Van Den Abbeele as *The differend: Phrases in dispute*. Minneapolis: University of Minneapolis Press.

10 Law in the Domains of Death

The affinity, often noted, between law and death is usually put in terms of law's pretension to finality. This is law as determinative, as "the end," as antithetical to "life itself," taking indicative *aperçus* from Blanchot (1981, 16).[1] And when law and death are matched, Blanchot would go so far as to subordinate law: law, we find, is "less the command that has death as its sanction, than death itself wearing the face of law"; this "death is always the horizon of the law" (Blanchot 1992, 24–25). Yet there is another, if strangely muted, tradition which would integrate law into life: "its essence lies . . . in the very life of men."[2] If one is to refine this seeming dissonance and be more nuanced about the relation between law and death, there is an initial and momentous difficulty: within an analytic of finitude, an analytic that sets my engagement here, death does not allow of a position besides itself from which we can observe it as "horizon," as demarcating. It is, however, precisely that difficulty which imbues the present essay and provides the conduit for linking death and law—for bringing out what proves to be, from the perspective of law, a relation of apposition between them, taking "apposition" as a relation in which things can be applied to each other, yet also be opposed.

There is yet another and related difficulty which calls for a preliminary mention. If death allows of no position apart, if it cannot be known to have bounds, how may we delimit its relation of apposition with law? The expedient adopted here is to take a testing situation, one in which law would seek to enter the domains of death, and one where in so doing it finds its horizon. This is a situation in which law purports to deal death with the infliction of capital punishment. The particular instance considered here is made up of judicial discourse on the death penalty in the United States. Perhaps the most pointed outcome of analyzing that discourse is the displacement of the epistemic claims made for legal determination and the consequent revelation of its sacrificial element.

More expansively, then, and starting with the deep affinity between law and death, with death as something like the constituent limit of law, in its supreme stasis, death is often equated with "law itself in its origin, in its very order" (Derrida 1992a, 42).[3] This tends to be put in terms of death as the ultimate or final assertion of law as sovereign, its mundane mode being capital punishment (Locke 1965, 308; Kant 1965, 331–33; Foucault 1979, 49). Borrowing Dean's apt summary, law becomes a "principal instrument" of a transcendent sovereignty whence it is "backed up by coercive sanctions ultimately grounded in the right of death of the sovereign" (1999, 105)— all of which give some force to law's deathly claim to determine absolutely, to fix and hold life, denying its protean possibility. Death in this guise can be found, for example, fully operative in the Benthamite dream of "total and certain order" through law (Lieberman 1989, 281). Or it can be found in the quest of legal positivists for such an order within law itself—a law which, in its achieved autonomy, would not have any essential relation to what is beyond it. Such a self-sufficing law "sever[s] its relation to the life-world by constituting that world of mundane sociality as its outside or other" (Goodrich 1993, 117). In this dimension of it, death, being "always the horizon of the law," is an horizon which cannot be gone beyond, which denies any essential relation beyond it, leaving that which it demarcates to its own immanence, to its self-posited autonomy.

There is, however, a diametrically different sense in which death is the horizon of the law. The horizon now is not a closed finality but the opening to all possibility that is beyond affirmed order. Death denies and dissolves such order and makes something else possible, something unknowable with any assurance beforehand: "it exposes us to the immeasurability of something we can never experience" (Dastur 1996, 4). So to "make a work of death" by regarding its finality only, and by constituting an autonomous law in the image of death, is to deny the importunate mystery of death itself, for death in its determinate predictability is not only the greatest certainty but, in its opening to what is unknowably beyond, also the greatest uncertainty—*and*, what is central to my argument, it is death which makes uncertainty as uncertainty certain (Nancy 1991, 12–13). "Things" are always dying to what they are, and in this dying, the possibility of their being other than what they are is continually created. Law, then, is also this uncertain dimension of death and even, in a sense, primarily so, since law is only called to affirm certainty in the face of uncertainty. Before saying more about these two dimensions of death and the law, and especially about the effect of their combination, I will amplify this unfamiliar dimension of law in familiar terms. One set of terms comes from what is so often seen as a founding account of modern law's power of surpassing determination, Hobbes's *Leviathan*. The other set of terms comes from the operative logics of the rule of law itself.

On first looking into *Leviathan*, what we seem to find is a most complete justification for sovereign power, and something which conforms to the commonplace reduction of this complex work. Life in the natural state, where we find a war of all against all, is so "solitary, poor, nasty, brutish, and short" that there is a primal transfer of "all power and strength" to a singular, sovereign ruler, and in this way, the subject becomes comprehensively committed to all actions of the sovereign "as if they were his own"; subjects are thus inextricably bound to Leviathan, "to him that beareth their person," and so much so that "none of his subjects can be freed from his subjection" (Hobbes 1952, 85, 100–101).[4] Having such an encompassing, such a complete power over life, there would seem to be nothing in the way of Leviathan's taking it away. At this point, however, Hobbes circumscribes the power of Leviathan. Since the primal covenant is entered into for the preservation of life, should Leviathan seek to take life away, he can be utterly resisted (115). So in his very power of determination—determination through laws that are the "command" of the sovereign—Leviathan must have a responsive regard to where that power came from. Hobbes would go even further in Leviathan's regard for life. With this unexpectedly tender side to him, Leviathan has to secure "the safety of the people," but "by *safety* here is not meant a bare preservation, but also all other contentments of life, which every man by lawful industry, without danger or hurt to the commonwealth, shall acquire to himself" (153). So much is this so that Hobbes deduces from it an extensive list of "liberties" of the subject and a most extensive collection of "duties" imposed on Leviathan for ensuring the well-being and improvement of the people (30). Laws, the very command of Leviathan, must be infused with a responsive regard for his subjects (113, 132, 139).

I will now take this perhaps surprising divide in the power and the laws of Leviathan, a divide between determinative force and responsiveness, and extend it to the logics of the rule of law. Countless histories and juridical affirmations would have us believe that certainty, predictability, and order characterize the rule of law. As against the vagaries of an arbitrary and discretionary power, the rule of law clearly marked out an area of calculability in which the individual could now purposively progress. In order for this law, and "not men," to rule, it had to be coherent, closed, and complete. If it were not coherent but contradictory, something else could be called on to resolve the contradiction. If it were open rather than closed, then something else could enter in and rule along with law. If it were incomplete and not a whole *corpus juris*, and if it were thence related to something else, then that something else could itself rule or share in ruling with law. For all of which, law had to be self-generating and self-regulating because if it were dependent on something apart from itself for these things, then again, those things would rule along with or instead of law.

We can, however, take each of these imperative qualities of the rule of law and evoke their opposite "in" the rule of law itself. For law to rule, it has to be comprehensive in its potential range. It has to be able to do anything, if not everything. It cannot, then, simply secure stability and predictability but also has to do the opposite: it has to ensure that law is ever responsive to change; otherwise, law will eventually cease to rule the situation that has changed around it. So how could the rule of law be complete if it must ever respond to the infinite variety of fact and circumstance impinging on it? How could it be closed when it must hold itself constantly responsive to all that is beyond what it may at any moment be? And how could law, in extending to what is continually other to itself, avoid pervasive contradiction? Law cannot be purely fixed and preexistent if it is to change and adapt to society, as it is so often said that it must. Its determinations cannot be entirely specific, clear, and conclusive if it has integrally or at the same time to exceed all determination.

We can also see modern law similarly stretched between stable determination and responsive change in the persistent squabbles that so enliven jurisprudential thought. These intractably polarized debates alternate between law's being autonomous and its being dependent. Taking the latter first, it is readily said that law is dependent on society, politics, the popular spirit, scientific administration, the economy, or the narratives in which it is embedded. In a more diachronic vein, we are told that law has to change along with society or history; otherwise, it becomes increasingly irrelevant and eventually obsolete. The contrary claims for autonomy, although a little more venerable, have not lost any of the force of their assertion. With them, law somehow has to stand apart from the remorseless demands of society, history, and so on, and even to exclude its "own history" (Derrida 1992b, 190). In being so placed, "absolute and detached from any origin" (Derrida 1992b, 194), law not only stands distinctly apart from, say, society, but also orders, shapes, or even creates society—to adopt long-enduring and standard formulations. To the extent that society does not so conform, law yet retains its hold as the measure against which that "failure" and passing imperfection are to be measured. In this, and indeed in all the various applications and changes throughout its history, a law remains insistently that law. Law's autonomous binding force cannot be contained by what it is or has been by its history, but extends to all that it will be. Law is eternally present.

Given this divide and its persistence, perhaps inquiry should be diverted. Rather than seeking law in that which simply conforms to either side or both sides of the opposition, perhaps we could seek a law which "is" in-between the opposed dimensions, which "is" the experienced combination of them, and which has its being because each dimension is inexorable yet unable to be experienced by itself. And perhaps these dimensions are equivalent to the divide between law's autonomy and law's dependence. If so, then it would seem that the condition of being in law is always unresolved and calling for incessant decision and judgment. Nonetheless, we may find prospects for resolution in these dimensions being not only opposed but also somehow integral to each other. A complete determination of position and a responsiveness to what is beyond position are antithetical things, yet there can be neither position without responsiveness to what is always beyond it nor responsiveness without a position from which to respond. In their separation, these dimensions mark the limit of law: the limit as a condition and quality of its contained existence, and the limit opening onto all which lies beyond that existence. These dimensions of law are integral to each other. The separate insistence on each would be death carrying with it either a terminal fixity or a dissolving responsiveness to what is beyond. Law subsists in-between these two dimensions.

Operatively, law so subsists in the decision—the decision of the subject, the judge, and the legislator. The legal decision is always unique. It cannot be rendered beforehand in terms of some empirical reality or in terms of a previous decision. If it could be reduced in either of those ways, there would be no "call" for the decision, no demand for "fresh judgment" (Derrida 1992a, 26). Put another way, the responsibility—or, in terms of an archaic usage, the responsability—involved in judgment cannot be accommodated within the determined or the known. There is always "in" the legal judgment a "secret," a mystery, a "madness" (Derrida 1992a, 26; 1995, 63). The point can be concentrated by way of an example. It is exactly because the political trial eliminates the judicial ability to respond that the judge in such a trial is not considered to be making a legal decision. The trial is "fixed," in both the standard and colloquial senses (Shklar 1986, 149). To be "legal," the decision must be approached in openness. The decision could always have been otherwise than what it is. Yet for a legal decision, the decision *maker* has to gather some fixing elements, some incipiently determinant points of reference; otherwise, the process of deciding would disappear in pure responsiveness. The determinant cannot, however, be complete in itself. Its very persistence as stable, predictable, decided law depends on its constantly responding and adjusting to the impinging difference which ever confronts it. Enduring determination depends, then, on responsiveness. It must sustain an illimitable capacity to be other than what it is, a capacity ultimately compatible with its reversal. Perhaps the most compendious illustration comes from the clash of guiding legal maxims produced in situations of extreme challenge to law where, to translate from the Latin, the responsive clarion to "let justice be done though the heavens fall" confronts the determinant counter that "the preservation of the republic is the supreme law." We also come across numerous ways in which these two dimensions are brought together in law. "Equity" provides a dramatic instance, using the term in its usual association with the common law (but it could be extended to equivalents found in various principles of interpretation and general standards in civil codes). Although usually advanced as a supplement to the common law, mitigating its constrained legalism, the pivotal ability of equity explicitly to combine law's determination with its responsiveness is indicated in the two most common criticisms leveled at it: it was either too much a matter of arbitrary discretion, varying with "the length of the chancellor's foot," or it lost its essential flexibility through a rigid respect for precedent.

Coming closer to my central concern—judicial discourse on the death penalty—let me take the judicial decision as a final general instance. There is a necessary, if usually blithe, acceptance of a radical duality in the judicial role. In sentencing, for example, the judge is supposed to stand constantly, objectively apart from popular sentiment, especially of the more atavistic kind, yet also to have a responsive regard to such sentiment. Conflicting "rules" of interpretation enable the judge to render a statute in a fixedly "literal" way or, alternatively, in a responsively expansive way which has a continuing regard to the purpose or to the "mischief" the statute was supposedly aimed at. Generally, judges are observed more and more to be giving effect to changing times when making their decisions, yet they never do only that. Rather, they always seek to base the decision in what is already given. The resulting duality is reflected in the alternation of criticisms of judges for being too rigid or too loose, too conservative or too liberal, too remote or too involved, too cold or too passionate. What is happening here is the formation of the judicial decision in-between these dualities. It can neither dissipate in responsiveness nor be completely predetermined. In either scenario, there would simply be no decision.

Whilst in this engaged mode, let us plunge straight into the equivalent juridical division in cases on the death penalty in the United States. For a long time now, the judiciary has posited and wrestled with a seemingly intractable division when deciding on the application of the death penalty. The terms of that divide have become quite set. There must, on one side, be a responsive regard for "the uniqueness of the individual" being sentenced. In this same vein, it is said there must be "fundamental fairness." For such things, obviously, there has to be a broad and effective "discretion" in the decision maker. Yet this seeming imperative is accompanied by the refrain that discretion cannot be "unbridled." As it is put again and again, "arbitrariness" has to be avoided. There has to be a determinant "objectivity," "rationality," and "consistency."[5]

The supposed solution has been the guiding of discretion in terms of legislatively specified conditions. In the standard legislative patterning of these conditions, criteria for imposing the death penalty comprising numerous "aggravating circumstances" are to be considered in relation to numerous "mitigating factors." As Justice Powell helpfully described a similar arrangement, "the various factors . . . do not have numerical weights attached to them" (*Proffitt v. Florida* 258). Indeed, a great many of these factors are very broad and, in their terms, import a large discretion. But even if definite numerical weights were attributed to these factors, the combining of the numerous circumstances with the numerous factors would produce a staggering number of possible permutations. Quite apart from all that, there would remain Justice Harlan's observation that "no list of circumstances would ever be really complete"; to which he would add that the prior elaboration of factors "which call for the death penalty" appears to be "beyond present human ability" (*McGautha v. California* 204, 208). Coming inevitably to Justice Blackmun's incandescent dissent in *Callins v. Collins* (1128–38), it is for reasons such as these, combined with his view that it was impossible to reconcile a responsive fairness with a determinant consistency, that he announced his resolve "from this day forward" to "no longer tinker with the machinery of death" (*Callins v. Collins* 1130).

Admirable as the sentiments may be, fundamental problems are raised by the reasoning. There are two such problems. One is to do with the allegedly exceptional quality of the death penalty—with the difference death makes, as the common claim has it, and with what that difference may be. If it does make a significant difference, then the rest of the law may be saved from the disturbingly disparate elements involved in considering the imposition of the death penalty. Even if death does not make such a difference in its own right, perhaps the powerful judicial and other reformist arguments directed specifically against the death penalty may set it distinctly apart and thence distinguish it from the ordinary run of the law and its penalties, and so insulate these from the same disturbing disparity of elements involved in deciding on capital punishment. Obviously, my immediate line of argument is going to be that there is no difference between the decision to impose the death penalty and the legal decision generally. I will now briefly consider these problems. That consideration may incline my thesis toward the death penalty's being aptly of or with-in the law, but I will move on to show how that same argument also orients us toward a position where the death penalty becomes insupportable "in" law. Being at the horizon of the law, death is of the law—it is *law's* horizon—yet beyond it.

First, then, the question of whether the decision to impose the death penalty is exceptional. Justice Blackmun would only go so far as to say: "There is a heightened need for fairness in the administration of death" (*Callins v. Collins* 1132). This does not show whether or how the judgment to deal death is different to any other legal decision. The desiderata that he and others propound—the achievement or the balancing of fairness and objectivity—are obviously not exclusive to decisions about capital punishment; nor is the labeling of such decisions as arbitrary. The scene of legal judgment, as we visited it earlier, is inevitably arbitrary. It does not, and cannot, cognitively, much less coherently, extend to all things that may make the decision what it is. The decision is always a choice and a denial, a "cutting" into the infinite variety of inclination, fact, and circumstance that could possibly inform it (Derrida 1992a, 26). The very terms in which judges engage with the death penalty are, as we saw, indistinguishable from the constituent terms of the legal decision generally.

If in its juridical application the death penalty cannot be treated as exceptional, can the reformist arguments specifically advanced against it be any more successful in setting it apart? That success is vitiated, as we will now see, by the failure of these arguments in their own terms. It has, for example, often been argued judicially that the death penalty should not be imposed on juveniles or on the mentally incapacitated because of their attenuated responsibility (for example, *Thompson v. Oklahoma*). This, however, is inexorably to say that the death penalty should and can be imposed where responsibility is found ample enough. And the original argument, progressive as it well may be in other ways, leaves open the question of degree, the question of how old, how mentally effective one has to be in order to be put to death. In a very strict constructionist vein, Justice Scalia would project us back to the initial publication of Blackstone's *Commentaries on the Laws of England* in 1769, would claim that this somehow informed the making of the Eighth Amendment, and then find in Blackstone's capacious reaches that capital punishment in England could be imposed at the age of seven years.[6] He does not quite have the courage of his convictions. He does not go on to hold that seven seems a reasonable age at which to put children to death. The very debate about infantile or mental capacity imports a resolution as its orienting force—imports an appropriate point at which the child, etc., can be killed. Debates of this kind are often combined with the argument that the death penalty is not justified where incapacity would negate or diminish its deterrent effect. The massive implication of this argument, however, is that where the accused's capacity is sufficient, deterrence can be effective, and on that ground, the death penalty is justified.

Then there are arguments to the effect that, because of limiting or defective or corrupt procedures, or because of incompetent representation of the accused, a wrongful verdict may have been reached or such a verdict is being sustained—and, for good measure, the increasing limitation on review is seen as sheltering these travesties (for example, *Sawyer v. Whitley*). Judges quite often see the failure of the so-called system in these terms and quite often hope, if not always expect, that "one day this [Supreme] Court will develop procedural rules or verbal formulas that actually will provide consistency, fairness, and reliability in a capital sentencing scheme."[7] Again, one could hardly impugn such arguments as far as they go, but they go too far in at least implicitly advancing a realizable truth—a realizable consistency, fairness, and reliability—justifying the imposition of the death penalty. The strongest contribution to this line of argument would deny that the death penalty could ever be imposed with assurance. "The problem," says Justice Blackmun, "is that the inevitability of factual, legal, and moral error gives us a system that we know must wrongly kill some defendants" (*Callins v. Collins* 1130). The trouble with this argument is that, like the others, it is wedded to a positive, realizable truth, a truth that could have prevailed without the error. It allows of a justified imposition of capital punishment where the truth of the situation is perceived as cogent or overwhelming. More significantly, it still allows of irresolvable contention with utilitarian varieties of truth. It may be, as the English nostrum has it, that it is better for ten of the guilty to go free than for one of the innocent to be convicted, but it is arguably preferable for one of the innocent to be executed rather than ten of the guilty go free, an argument which has of late found favor in the Supreme Court (Sarat 2001, 256–57). Furthermore, the Court's insistent elevation of finality—the finality of what cannot be finalized—inexorably imports the killing of the innocent (cf. Sarat 2001, 165).

So if these various arguments against capital punishment do not definitively except the decision to inflict *death*, and if judicial analysis of the death penalty simply reproduces the dimensions of ordinary legal decision making, what—to again borrow the phrase—is the difference death makes? To set that question, I will return to my initial argument advancing law as a putative settlement of the space in-between these dimensions—in-between determinate position and what was ever beyond it. That line of argument was most evidently set against the standard assertions of law's stability, fixity, implacability, or, in the language so often used in capital cases, against law's finality. Even at its most settled, or especially at its most settled, we saw that law could not "be" otherwise than responsive to what was beyond its determinate content "for the time being." Law can and will always be other than what it now "is." There can be nothing enduringly before this law. Yet neither can law dissipate in a pure responsiveness. Hence, there were the contrary yet standard claims as to what law may be outlined earlier—the division between determinant force and responsiveness with-in the rule of law, the combination of Leviathan's awesome assurance with an unexpectedly accommodating side, the jurisprudential division between law's autonomy and its dependence on society, history, and such. How or in what terms can law in this insistent ambivalence have some place, some palpability, some hold? Even if it cannot be positively rendered in terms of existent situations, law is nonetheless necessarily and operatively attached to such situations. It is in the legal decision, in the place of legal judgment, that law becomes so operative. Such decision or judgment itself cannot be reduced to antecedents or to some "factual" truth. There cannot, that is, be a complete comprehending of everything to which a decision has or could have responded or to which it will respond. Law can always be other than what it "is."

To convey the difference freighted with death, let me continue, in what is now leading to a conclusion, to mirror the path of my analysis so far by combining two further judicial arguments which would both except yet implicitly affirm the death penalty. First, an argument which goes some way toward accommodating law's responsive dimension: when looking at standards of responsibility, or at what is "cruel and unusual" in terms of punishment, or at the proportionate relation between crime and penalty, judges have derived meliorative content or assurance from the practices of various societies. The problem with this resort, so far as it is used to counter the penalty of death, is that the practices of societies can become more rather than less draconic, something which Justice Scalia has been quick to observe (*Thompson v. Oklahoma* 865). Yet again the death penalty becomes more embedded in law through reformist discourse rather than excluded from it. For the development of my argument, however, there is a further point this resort to the social tends to emphasize, and this point is, as we have seen, that law, in its essential openness, cannot be bound to or by any specific reference to social practice or in any other way. The quality of openness has to be sustained. The second line of argument starkly makes this point in relation to racial discrimination in legal processes leading to the imposition of the death penalty (for example, Gross and Mauro 1989). Reformist argument here may not appear to be an advance on the others. It could be heard as saying that in the rectifying, actual or potential, of such racial discrimination, capital punishment is being affirmed. Let me now combine these two arguments, one based on evidence of the social and the other on racial discrimination, enfolding the first into the second so as to indicate their undermining effect on the sustainability of capital punishment in law and thence on law's integrally occupying the domains of death.

In the situation of racial discrimination, what difference does death make with its "unique finality," to borrow Marshall J.'s pointed phrase (*Coleman v. Balkcom* 953)? After all, in a certain literal sense, with its "cutting" determination, the scene of legal judgment is inevitably discriminatory. Some modes of existence are elevated in the decision and others suppressed, sacrificed, or ignored. Law, however, maintains its seductive appeal to the excluded through its responsive ability always to be other than what it is. The penalty of death denies that prospect. It denies the protean promise held out by the rule of law to extend equally to all its subjects and to surmount, in particular, all differences of ascribed status. With the imposition of the death penalty, the other is excluded utterly in the name of law itself. The Supreme Court's effort to counter this effect ends up by aggravating it. Here we come inexorably to the much-discussed miasma that is *McCleskey v. Kemp*.

In *McCleskey*, the court faced the dissolution of the whole scene of legal judgment. The defendant McCleskey, described as a black man, had been sentenced to death in Georgia for the murder of a police officer described as white. It was claimed by or for McCleskey that the imposition of this penalty was racially discriminatory and that this discrimination violated the requirement of equal protection of the laws in the Fourteenth Amendment and the prohibiting of "cruel and unusual punishment" in the Eighth. The case turned on the nature of the evidence supporting these claims. This comprised a study, known as the Baldus study, which showed in general statistical terms that defendants charged with killing white victims were much more likely to be sentenced to death than defendants charged with killing black victims. By eliminating the effect of an array of nonracial variables, the study sought to show that race was "a" or "the" decisive factor. This was the relevant evidence, but the study also extended to, and the court was manifestly worried about, other statistical evidence of discrimination in capital cases in Georgia. Henry Louis Gates Jr. summarized matters this way: "The Baldus study was scrutinized and hailed by various prominent statisticians, including the representatives of the National Academy of Sciences, as among the most sophisticated empirical work ever done on criminal sentencing. The experts agreed that the Baldus study proved that capital sentencing in Georgia is a discriminatory process" (1992, 334). The minority decisions in this case accepted the statistical evidence as establishing unconstitutional discrimination. The majority did not. They would not have accepted that any statistical evidence could establish the requisite discrimination.[8] Discrimination had to be intentionally or purposively directed against the defendant specifically. For the majority, statistical probability was not enough, even if for Justice Brennan in the minority the "empirical" quality of such evidence was its strength (*McCleskey v. Kemp* 338).

What the majority propounded, again and again, was the "uniqueness" of each case, of each capital crime, and of each capital defendant. Judges and juries had to be unlimited in their ability to accommodate this uniqueness, to exercise their "fundamental . . . discretion," to "consider" the "varying" and "innumerable factors" potentially involved (*McCleskey v. Kemp* 294, 311). In all this, juries must be allowed to decide matters in their own "unpredictable," "varying," and ultimately inexplicable ways, even if this will involve "some risk" of racial discrimination (*McCleskey v. Kemp* 305, 308, 311). The horrifying alternative summoned up by the majority was the dissolution of the whole criminal justice system. If statistical evidence of racial oppression were given effect, then the like effect would have to be given to "other kinds of prejudice" extending, for example, to "membership in other minority groups and even to gender," or to "the defendant's facial characteristics, or the physical attractiveness of the defendant or the victim," or, it could be added, to the poverty of the defendant; furthermore, this dissipating responsiveness would extend to "other types of penalty" beside death (*McCleskey v. Kemp* 308, 315–17). "Relying" on the Baldus study, then, "questions the very heart of the criminal justice system" (*McCleskey v. Kemp* 314 n. 37).[9] Indeed. It is, however, completely contradictory to elevate utterly an illimitable responsiveness to the specific defendant—elevate it so high as to exclude cogent societal evidence of pertinent oppressions—and then utterly to deny that responsiveness by visiting death on that defendant. Such a death not only freezes forever the range and quality of possible responsiveness to that defendant, it also effects a general denial of law's responsiveness. Law cannot be hermetically trapped in this way and yet be operatively sustained as law.

Short of complete dissolution, it has often been observed, and aptly established, that within the operation of the death penalty the criminal law becomes, as it is put, distorted, and especially where responsiveness to the accused is truncated, and there are also clear indications that the denial of law's responsiveness debases the legal system as a whole (Gross and Mauro 1989). I will end with what are perhaps the two most egregious restrictions on the responsive.

One involves restrictions on the writ of habeas corpus. A leading U.S. authority puts the significance of the writ fairly typically: "The writ of habeas corpus, by which the legal authority under which a person may be detained can be challenged, is of immemorial antiquity. . . . Today it is said to be 'perhaps the most important writ known to constitutional law of England'. . . . Its significance in the United States has been no less great" (Wright 1994, 350). A little more exactly, the modern function of the writ, challenging arrogations of the executive, dates from the sixteenth and seventeenth centuries (Sharpe 1989, chap. 1). Its more general use to challenge the legality of any detention is even more venerable and can be traced as far back as an English case of 1214, from which it is clear that the writ already had a settled existence (Selden Society 1888, 67 no. 115). Habeas corpus, in short, has had a very long history as a responsive mode for the reversal or modification of legal determination. Because of its impertinent effectiveness in challenging death penalty decisions, its general ability to uphold constitutional imperatives has been judicially narrowed (see *Callins v.*

Collins 1137–38). This narrowing has been legislatively matched in various ways, for example by the establishing of a one-year limit on filing petitions for habeas corpus, a limit which comes from the candidly titled Antiterrorism and Effective Death Penalty Act of 1996. It was a string of successful petitions for habeas corpus in *Vasquez v. Harris* which provided further and the most startling denial of law's responsiveness, and thence of law itself. With a manifest petulance, the Supreme Court proclaimed that "no further stays of Robert Alton Harris's execution shall be entered by the federal courts except upon the order of this Court"—a diktat of naked determination aptly described as "lawless."[10] Judge Kozinski commented on that command, with a like disregard for the law, that "the drama had no other possible outcome," and he somehow discerned that "enough is enough" (1997, 51–52).

Foucault once observed that in law we have not as yet "cut off the head of the King" (1981, 88–89). From the aphorism's resonant meanings, we can for now conclude with one: that in law we still seek or at least purport to find a transcendent truth, a truth that is sufficient and entire, a truth which allows us to find and decree an ultimate "enough." To take a stark example, one which resonates with many reforms in progress, a recent and highly critical survey of the operation of the death penalty in the United States concludes: "The steady accumulation of wrongful convictions and death sentences in the United States constitutes a prima facie case that we are dealing with widespread, systemic flaws in the administration of justice. Until those flaws are corrected, we should declare a moratorium on executions" (Berlow 1999, 88).[11] This is to seek a quality of truth in a place—the scene of legal judgment—where it cannot be found. Obviously, there has to be a determinate decision, some limits, some lack of responsiveness, if law is to "be" at all. Granted that, there still remains the matter of how the limits were reached, how the decision was made, how it is to be sustained and regarded; and in all these things, there is a judgment, a choice, a denial of what could otherwise be. Being attuned to the responsiveness accommodated and the responsiveness eliminated in the decision could orient and even impel us toward the recognition of many things—toward the recognition that the legal decision cannot be accorded a complete and positive content, a recognition that such a decision is ultimately unknowable, that it is inevitably partial and arbitrary, that it entails the denial and sacrifice of the other, and the recognition that, to minimize these ineluctable defects, the decision must be made and brought to bear in as open, accountable, and revisable a manner as possible. The death penalty, even as it denies law's necessary responsiveness, pushes us to a limit of law where responsiveness cannot be ignored and where its disturbing implications for the nature of law and the legal decision become insistent.

NOTES

 1. See, however, the injunction in Blanchot (1993, 225).

 2. Savigny as quoted in Agamben (1998, 27).

 3. Cf. Foucault (1981, 144): "Law cannot help but be armed, and its arm, *par excellence*, is death."

 4. What follows on Hobbes and then on the rule of law is summarized from Fitzpatrick (2001, 71–73, 93–95).

 5. Justice Blackmun's dissent in *Callins v. Collins*, 1128–38, provides a good coverage in these terms.

 6. In *Thompson v. Oklahoma* 864. Justice Scalia finds "original" justification in the Constitution for the death penalty itself. Evoking the Fifth Amendment and the inclusion there of capital crime within its protective range, he finds that this "explicitly permits" the death penalty. Simply presupposing the existence of something is not "permitting" it.

 7. *Callins v. Collins* 1138 (Blackmun, J., dissenting). All of which is not to deny the political potency of such arguments, but their ambivalence means that their deployment is not without risk. On this "new abolitionism" generally, see the seminal formulation in Sarat (2001).

 8. This view of the majority opinion was seemingly not shared by one of its members, Justice Scalia (see Dorin 1994). It remained the view of the writer of that opinion, however, even as he came to reject the decision itself (see Jefferies 1994, 452).

 9. And, of course, in terms of my argument, it questions "the very heart" of law generally. It is juridical quandaries like these that underscore law's deific ability to combine determination and responsiveness. It could be then, as Derrida suggests (taking a cue from Freud), that the death penalty in the United States can be sustained as putatively legal because the United States is taken to be "God's own country" (Derrida 2000, 64).

 10. For a general account and this designation, see Caminker and Chermerensky (1992).

 11. The most dramatic recent effect of perception in terms of "flaws" comes from the decision by Governor Ryan of Illinois to commute the sentences of all those awaiting execution in that state; see Sarat (2003).

WORKS CITED

Agamben, Giorgio. 1998. *Homo sacer: Sovereign power and bare life.* Trans. Daniel Heller-Roazen. Stanford: Stanford University Press.

Berlow, Alan. 1999. The wrong man. *Atlantic Monthly* (November): 66–88.

Blanchot, Maurice. 1981. *The madness of the day.* Trans. L. Davis. New York: Station Hill Press.

———. 1992. *The step not beyond.* Trans. L. Davis. Albany: SUNY Press.

———. 1993. *The infinite conversation.* Trans. Susan Hanson. Minneapolis: University of Minnesota Press.

Callins v. Collins. 114 S. Ct. 1127, 1994.

Caminker, Evan, and Erwin Chermerensky. 1992. The lawless execution of Robert Alton Harris. *Yale Law Journal* 102:225–52.

Coleman v. Balkcom. 451 U.S. 949, 1981.

Dastur, Françoise. 1996. *Death: An essay on finitude.* Trans. John Llewelyn. London: Ahlone Press.

Dean, Mitchell. 1999. *Governmentality: Power and rule in modern society.* London: Sage.

Derrida, Jacques. 1992a. Force of law: The "mystical foundations of authority." Trans. Mary Quaintance. In *Deconstruction and the possibility of justice,* ed. Drucilla Cornell et al., 3–67. New York: Routledge.

———. 1992b. Before the law. In *Acts of literature,* trans. Avital Ronell, 181–220. New York: Routledge.

———. 1995. *The gift of death.* Trans. David Wills. Chicago: University of Chicago Press.

———. 2000. *États d'âme de la psychanalyse: L'impossible au-delà d'une souveraine cruauté.* Paris: Galilée.

Dorin, Dennis D. 1994. Far right of the mainstream: Racism, rights, and remedies from the perspective of Justice Antonin Scalia's *McCleskey* memorandum. *Mercer Law Review* 45:1035–88.

Fitzpatrick, Peter. 2001. *Modernism and the grounds of law.* Cambridge: Cambridge University Press.

Foucault, Michel. 1979. *Discipline and punish: The birth of the prison.* Trans. Alan Sheridan. Harmondsworth, UK: Penguin.

———. 1981. *The history of sexuality: An introduction.* Vol. 1. Trans. Robert Hurley. Harmondsworth, UK: Penguin.

Gates, Henry Louis, Jr. 1992. Statistical stigmata. In *Deconstruction and the possibility of justice,* ed. Drucilla Cornell et al., 330–45. New York: Routledge.

Goodrich, Peter. 1993. Fate as seduction: The other scene of legal judgement. In *Closure or critique: New directions in legal theory,* ed. Alan Norrie, 116–41. Edinburgh: Edinburgh University Press.

Gross, Samuel R., and Robert Mauro. 1989. *Death and discrimination: Racial disparities in capital sentencing.* Boston: Northeastern University Press.

Hobbes, Thomas. 1952. *Leviathan.* Chicago: Encyclopedia Britannica.

Jefferies, John C., Jr. 1994. *Justice Lewis F. Powell, Jr.* New York: Scribner.

Kant, Immanuel. 1965. *The metaphysical elements of justice.* Trans. John Ladd. Indianapolis: Bobbs-Merrill.

Kozinski, Alex. 1997. Tinkering with death. *New Yorker* (February 10): 48–51.

Lieberman, David. 1989. *The province of legislation determined: Legal theory in eighteenth-century Britain.* Cambridge: Cambridge University Press.

Locke, John. 1965. The second treatise of government. In *Two treatises of government,* 305–477. New York: New American Library.

McCleskey v. Kemp. 481 U.S. 279, 1986.

McGautha v. California. 402 U.S. 183, 1971.

Nancy, Jean-Luc. 1991. *The inoperative community.* Trans. Peter Connor. Minneapolis: University of Minnesota Press.

Proffitt v. Florida. 428 U.S. 242, 1976.

Sarat, Austin. 2001. *When the state kills: Capital punishment and the American condition.* Princeton: Princeton University Press.

———. 2003. Governor Ryan's decision to empty Illinois death row. FindLaw,

January 28. Available at: http://writ.news.findlaw.com/commentary/20030115
_sarat.

Sawyer v. Whitley. 505 U.S. 333, 1992.

Selden Society. 1888. *Select pleas of the Crown*, vol. 1, *AD 1200–1225*. London:
Bernard Quaritch.

Sharpe, R. J. 1989. *The law of habeas corpus*. 2nd ed. Oxford: Clarendon Press.

Shklar, Judith. 1986. *Legalism: Law, morals and political trials*. 2nd ed. Cambridge:
Harvard University Press.

Thompson v. Oklahoma. 487 U.S. 815, 1988.

Vasquez v. Harris. 112 S.Ct. 1713, 1992.

Wright, Charles A. 1994. *The law of federal courts*. 5th ed. St. Paul, MN: West.

11 *Justice and Truth*

From Plato until today, there is one word that can sum up the concern of the philosopher with respect to politics. This word is *justice*. The philosopher's question to politics is the following: can there be a just political orientation? An orientation that *does justice* to thought? What we have to begin with is this: injustice is clear, justice is obscure. For he who undergoes injustice is the irrecusable witness to this. But who can testify for justice? There is an affect of injustice, a suffering, a revolt. Nothing, however, signals justice, which can be presented neither as a spectacle nor as a sentiment.

Must we then resign ourselves to saying that justice is only the absence of injustice? Is it the empty neutrality of a double negation? I do not think so. Nor do I think that injustice is on the side of the perceptible, or of experience, or of the subjective; nor that justice is on the side of the intelligible, or of reason, or of the objective. Injustice is not the immediate disorder of which justice would be the ideal order.

Justice is a word from philosophy—at least if, as we must, we leave aside its legal signification, entirely devoted to the police and the magistrature. But this word of philosophy is under condition. It is under the condition of the political, because philosophy knows it is incapable of realizing in the world the truths it testifies to. Even Plato knows that for there to be justice, it's probable that the philosopher must be king, but that the possibility of there being such a royalty precisely does not depend on philosophy. It depends on political circumstances, which remain irreducible.

We will call *justice* the name by which a philosophy designates the possible truth of a political orientation.

The vast majority of empirical political orientations have nothing to do with truth, as we know. They organize a repulsive mixture of power and opinions. The subjectivity that animates them is that of the tribe and the lobby, of electoral nihilism and the blind confrontation of communities. Philosophy has nothing to say about all that, because philosophy only thinks thought, whereas these orientations are explicitly presented as nonthoughts. The only subjective element that is of importance to them is that of interest.

Some political orientations, throughout history, have had or will have a connection with a truth—a truth of the collective as such. They are rare attempts, often brief, but they are the only ones under condition philosophy can think about.

These political sequences are singularities; they trace no destiny, they construct no monumental history. Philosophy can, however, distinguish in them a common feature. This feature is that these orientations require of the men they engage only their strict generic humanity. They give no preference for the principles of action, to the particularity of interests. These political orientations induce a representation of the collective capacity that refers its agents to the strictest equality.

What does "equality" mean? Equality means that the political actor is represented under the sole sign of his specifically human capacity. Interest is not a specifically human capacity. All living beings have as an imperative for survival to protect their interests. The specifically human capacity is precisely thought, and thought is nothing other than that by which the path of a truth seizes and traverses the human animal.

Thus a political orientation worthy of being submitted to philosophy under the idea of justice is an orientation whose unique general axiom is: people think, people are capable of truth. Saint-Just was thinking of the strictly egalitarian recognition of the capacity for truth when he defined before the Convention, in April 1794, public consciousness: "May you have a public consciousness, for all hearts are equal as to sentiments of good and bad, and this consciousness is made up of the tendency of the people towards the general good." And in an entirely different political sequence, during the Cultural Revolution in China, we find the same principle, for example in the decision in sixteen points of August 8, 1966: "Let the masses educate themselves in this great revolutionary movement, let them determine by themselves the distinction between what is just and what is not."

Thus a political orientation touches on truth provided it is founded on the egalitarian principle of a capacity to discern the just, or the good, all expressions that philosophy apprehends under the sign of the truth that the collective is capable of.

It is very important to remark that here, "equality" does not mean anything objective. It is not a question of the equality of status, of income, of function, and even less of the supposed egalitarian dynamics of contracts or reforms. Equality is subjective. It is equality with respect to public consciousness for Saint-Just, or with respect to the political mass movement for Mao Zedong. Such equality is in no way a social program. It has, moreover, nothing to do with the social. It is a political maxim, a prescription. Political equality is not what we want or plan; it is what we declare under fire of the event, here and now, as what is, and not what should be. In the same way, for philosophy, *justice* cannot be a state program. *Justice* is the qualification of an egalitarian political orientation in act.

The difficulty with most of the doctrines of justice is wanting to define justice, and then trying to find the means for its realization. But justice, which is the philosophical name for the egalitarian political maxim, cannot be defined, for equality is not an objective of action; it is an axiom of it. There is no political orientation linked to truth without the affirmation—affirmation that has neither a guarantee nor a proof—of a universal capacity for political truth. Thought, on this point, cannot use the scholastic method of definitions. It must follow the method of the understanding of an axiom.

Justice is nothing else than one of the words by which a philosophy attempts to *seize* the egalitarian axiom inherent in a veritable political sequence. And this axiom itself is given by singular statements, characteristic of the sequence, such as Saint-Just's definition of public consciousness, or the thesis on the immanent self-education of the revolutionary mass movement upheld by Mao.

Justice is not a concept for which we have to find in the empirical world more or less approximate realizations. Conceived as an operator for the seizing of an egalitarian political orientation, which is the same thing as a true political orientation, justice defines an effective, axiomatic, immediate subjective figure. It is what gives all its depth to the surprising affirmation of Samuel Beckett, in *How It Is*: "In any case we are within justice, I've never heard anyone say the contrary." In effect, justice, which seizes the latent axiom of a political subject, designates necessarily not what must be, but what is. The egalitarian axiom is present in political statements, or it is not present. And by consequence, we are within justice, or we are not, which also means that the political exists, in the sense that philosophy encounters its thought within it, or it does not. But if it does, and we relate to it immanently, we are within justice.

Any definitional and programmatic approach to justice makes of it a dimension of the action of the state. But the state has nothing to do with justice because the state is not a subjective and axiomatic figure. The state as such is indifferent or hostile to the existence of a political orientation that touches truths. The modern state only aims at fulfilling certain functions, or obtaining a consensus of opinion. Its subjective dimension is only to transform in resignation or resentment the economic necessity—that is, the objective logic of capital. This is why any programmatic definition or state definition of justice changes it into its contrary: justice becomes by it, in fact, the harmonization of the interplay of interests. But justice, which is the theoretical name of an axiom of equality, refers necessarily to a wholly disinterested subjectivity.

This can be said simply: any political orientation of emancipation, or any political orientation that imposes an egalitarian maxim, is a thought in act. But thought is the specific mode by which a human animal is traversed and overcome by a truth. In such a subjectivation, the limit of interest is crossed, so that the political process itself is indifferent to it. It is then necessary, as all political sequences that concern philosophy show, that the state not be able to recognize as appropriate to it anything in such a process.

The state is in its Being indifferent to justice. And inversely, any political orientation that is a thought in act entails, in proportion to its force and its tenacity, serious trouble for the state. This is why political truth manifests itself always in times of trial and trouble. It follows that justice, far from being a possible category of state and social order, is the name that designates the principles at work in rupture and disorder. Even Aristotle, whose goal is entirely a fiction of political stability, declares from the beginning of book 5 of his *Politics*: ολως γαρ το ισον ζητουντες στασιαζουσιν, which can be translated as, "In general in fact, the pursuers of equality rise in rebellion." But Aristotle's conception is still a state conception; his idea of equality is empirical, objective, definitional. The veritable philosophic statement would be rather: political statements bearing truth rise up in absence of any state and social order. The latent egalitarian maxim is heterogeneous to the state. It is then always during trouble and disorder that the subjective imperative of equality is affirmed. What the philosopher names *justice* seizes the subjective order of a maxim within the ineluctable disorder to which this order exposes the state of interests.

Finally, what does making a philosophical statement on justice, here and now, amount to?

It's first a matter of knowing to what singular political orientations we adhere, which are worth our trying to seize the thought specific to them by the resources of the philosophic apparatus, of which the word *justice* is one of the pieces.

In the confused and chaotic world of today, when capital seems to triumph from within its own weakness, and what is fuses miserably with what can be, it is not an easy job. Identifying the rare sequences through which a political truth is constructed, without being discouraged by the propaganda of capital-parliamentary government, is of itself a taut exercise of thought. Still more difficult is attempting within the order of doing politics to be faithful to some egalitarian axiom, by finding timely statements of it.

It is then a matter of seizing philosophically the political orientations in question, whether they be of the past or of the present. The task is then double:

1. To examine their statements, their prescriptions, and uncover the egalitarian nucleus of universal signification.

2. To transform the generic category of *justice* by submitting it to the test of singular statements, of the specific mode, always irreducible, by which they carry within themselves and inscribe in action the egalitarian axiom.

It is finally a matter of showing that thus transformed, the category of justice designates the contemporary figure of a political subject and that it is of this figure that philosophy assures, under its own names, the inscription in eternity that our time is capable of.

This political subject has had several names. He was called a citizen—certainly not in the sense of the elector or of the city counselor, but in the sense the French Revolution gives to the word *citizen*. He was called a professional revolutionary. He was called a grassroots militant. We are probably in a time when his name is suspended, in a time when we must *find his name*.

We might as well say that if we dispose of a history, without continuity or concept, of what *justice* was able to designate, we do not yet clearly know what it designates today. We know this of course abstractly, for *justice* always signifies the philosophic seizing of a latent egalitarian axiom. But this abstraction is useless, because the imperative of philosophy is to seize the event of truths, their newness, their precarious trajectory.

Is the contemporary state of political orientation such that philosophy can engage the category of justice in it? Isn't there the risk of confusing chalk with cheese, of reproducing the vulgar pretension of governments to render justice? When we see so many "philosophers" attempting to appropriate for themselves state schemes with as little thought in them as democracy in its capital-parliamentary sense in Europe, or liberty in its sense of pure opinion, shameful nationalisms—when we thus see philosophy prostrate before the idols of the day—we can obviously be pessimistic.

But after all, the conditions of exercise of philosophy have not always been rigorous. The words of philosophy, because these conditions were not maintained, have always been misused and turned around. There have been in this century intense political sequences. There are faithful followers of these sequences. Here or there, in yet incomparable situations, some statements envelop, in an inflexible and unsubjugated manner, the egalitarian axiom.

The collapse of the socialist states has itself a positive dimension. Certainly, it is a pure and simple collapse. No political orientation worthy of the name played the smallest part in it. And ever since, this political vacuity has not ceased to engender monsters. But these terrorist states were the incarnation of the ultimate fiction of a justice doted with the solidity of a body, of a justice that had the form of a governmental program. The collapse attests to the absurdity of such a representation. It frees justice and equality from any fictive incorporation. It restores them to their Being, both volatile and obstinate, of thought acting from and in the direction of a collective seized by its truth. The collapse of the socialist states teaches us that the ways of egalitarian politics do not pass by state power, that they are matters of an immanent subjective determination, an axiom of the collective.

After all, from Plato and his unfortunate escapade in Sicily up to the circumstantial aberrations of Heidegger, passing by the passive relations of Hegel and Napoleon, and without forgetting that Nietzsche's madness was to pretend "to split the history of the world in two," everything shows that it is not massive History that authorizes philosophy. It is rather "restrained action."

Let us be politically militants of restrained action. Let us be within philosophy those who eternalize the figure of this action.

We have too often wished that justice find the consistency of the social tie, whereas it can only name the most extreme moments of inconsistency. The effect of the egalitarian axiom is to undo the ties, to desocialize thought, to affirm the rights of the infinite and the immortal against finitude, against Being-for-death. In the subjective dimension of the equality that is declared, nothing else is of interest except the universality of this declaration, and the active consequences that it gives rise to.

Justice is the philosophical name of the inconsistency, for the state, of any egalitarian political orientation. And we can here join the declarative and axiomatic vocation of the poem. It is Paul Célan who probably gives us the most exact image of what we must understand by *justice* when he writes this poem, which I conclude with:

> On inconsistencies
> Lean:
>
> flick
> in the abyss, in the
> scribbling in the notebooks
> the world begins to rustle. it all depends
> on you

Keep in mind in effect the lesson of the poet: in matters of justice, where it is on inconstancy that we must lean, it is true, true as a truth can be, that it only depends on you.

— Translated by Thelma Sowley

Part V

THE "INHUMAN" DIMENSION OF LAW:
POSTSTRUCTURALIST ASSESSMENTS

12 Fate ('Schicksal') in Walter Benjamin's 'Zur Kritik der Gewalt'

The topic of this book is the incommensurability among law, justice, and power. No text addresses this incommensurability more directly than Benjamin's *Zur Kritik der Gewalt* ("Critique of Violence") unless it might be commentaries on this essay, such as Jacques Derrida's magisterial *Force de loi*. We hardly need these distinguished works, however, to see the problem. Power, force, or violence, even when ostensibly authorized by law, seems prone to exceed law's authority, as in "police brutality." Laws are devised, necessarily, to apply to many cases. Their enactments are acts of legislation. These are performative enunciations with often dubious authority beyond their own assertion by people in power. Lawmaking is, it may be, a matter of force rather than of justice. Justice, moreover, should be applied to particular, even singular, persons or groups, even though justice needs law for its enforcement, and even though we think of justice as a universal. Does any law ever perfectly fit a given special case, or are special cases (every case is special) always twisted to fit the law, so that a judicial decision can be handed down and enforced?

In a somewhat scandalous assertion, J. L. Austin in *How to Do Things with Words* says that "as official acts, a judge's ruling makes law" (154). The judge does that by deciding, somewhat arbitrarily, that a given law or precedent applies in this particular case and can be applied "justly." Precedents, so crucial in juridical decision, were always particular cases, with their own idiosyncratic circumstances, such as the case of *Roe v. Wade* that led to the Supreme Court decision to affirm a woman's right to choose whether to bear a child. It seems logically illegitimate to make a particular case the basis of a universal law applying to everyone—to all women in this case. But how could law work in any other way but by bending particular cases to fit general laws? Moreover, just as "justified" police violence seems prone to become "police brutality," so judicial decision seems prone to exceed precedent and in effect to "make new law." Sometimes the judge goes beyond using appeal to precedent in making law to make a (political) decision that is without precedent. An example is the Supreme Court's decision in the winter of 2000 in effect to make George W. Bush President of the United States by refusing to allow the full vote recount in Florida. What possible grounds could there be for calling that decision "just," or a manifestation of justice? Because the Supreme Court had in this case no precedent to which to appeal, this makes it even more possible than in cases where precedent can be adduced to view the Supreme Court's decision as a naked, unauthorized, unjust exercise of power.

In all these tensions among law, force, and justice, two perhaps undecidable aporias seem to manifest themselves: (1) the irreconcilability of laws in their generality and the singularity of cases, and (2) the need for decisions, which are always performative speech acts, to have a solid ground in conventions, whereas it can always be shown that they lack such ground. Walter Benjamin's *Zur Kritik der Gewalt*, perhaps better than any other text, facilitates a rigorous confrontation of these incommensurabilities. Benjamin's essay is, however, an extremely difficult text to understand. It is full of surprising turns and enigmatic formulations. It is inhabited by perhaps irreconcilable contradictions within Benjamin's Marxist weak messianism rather than being a text that will allow a transparent identification of the reasons why power, law, and justice seem incommensurable, not able to be measured by a common measure.

I shall by no means offer a full reading of *Zur Kritik der Gewalt*. I propose rather to focus on a single, to me enigmatic and obscure, word or concept in the essay: *Schicksal*—fate, destiny. I propose this focus as a way of approaching toward (*zu*) an understanding of what Benjamin means by *Gewalt*. Although the German word *Schicksal* is in the standard English translation usually given as *fate*, the word *destiny*, because it echoes *destination*, might be better. *Schicksal* is formed from *schicken*, "to send," as when a letter is sent to its destination, and has *schicklich*, meaning "becoming, proper, seemly," and *Schicklichkeit*, meaning "propriety, seemliness," as cognates, an association not possible with "destiny," much less with "fate."

Most of the conceptual terms that generate *Zur Kritik der Gewalt*, however difficult they may be to understand, come in pairs that are, or appear to be, binary opposites: means as opposed to ends, law-establishing violence (*Gewalt*) as against law-preserving violence, political strike as against proletarian general strike, mythical violence as against divine violence, and so on. It should be remembered that the German word *Gewalt*, usually translated into English or French as "violence," also means "authority," "power," and "force." Benjamin's essay advances by a technique of braided rhetoric. Each pair calls forth the next pair and overlaps with it to make a line or rope of argumentation. Whether the rope holds is another question.

Probably not. It may be that *Schicksal* is the weak thread in the sequence of reasoning that makes the whole rope fragment or dissolve before a confrontation with what Derrida, following Montaigne and Pascal, calls the "mystical foundation of authority" (7).

Each word in a given pair is defined by its difference from an opposing one. This gives at least the illusion of clarity, although the term common to the two may thereby slip away from the necessity of clear definition, in a species of circularity. Means, for example, are what are used to attain ends. The end is what means are used to reach. Law-preserving (*rechtserhaltende*) violence maintains law once it has been established by lawmaking (*rechtsetzende*) violence. Derrida has shown, convincingly I think (by recourse to a terminology of speech act theory that Benjamin of course does not use: the concepts of the performative and of iterability), that these binaries tend to break down, one to turn into the other, especially the opposition between law-establishing and law-preserving *Gewalt*. The police, as Benjamin says, are a primary means by which an established state maintains the law, but police violence, a ubiquitous spectral presence in "civilized states," is often or perhaps even always outside the law, and so in a sense is law-establishing. The police are ignominious, even more ignominious in a democratic state than in an absolute monarchy. "[T]his ignominy," says Benjamin, "lies in the fact that in this authority the separation of lawmaking and law-preserving violence is suspended [*in ihr die Trennung von rechtsetzender und rechtserhaltender Gewalt aufgehoben ist*]" ("Critique" 286/*Kritik* 189). The law, as I have said, is general and never exactly fits any particular case. It is only by violence that the judge makes a general law apply in a singular case. Moreover, the judge, with some help from the jury, as Austin saw, makes a man or woman a criminal by pronouncing his or her guilt and passing sentence on a person who until a moment ago was "accused" but still "innocent until proved guilty" (Austin 154). The police are ignominious because, like a lawmaking judge, in police actions, lawmaking and law-preserving are merged. Something law-preserving, Benjamin implies, is present in all law-establishing, something law-establishing in all law-preserving. The breakdown or ruination, one by one, of the binary oppositions that are necessary, according to Benjamin, to make a successful critique of violence is the essential action, one might even say the performative accomplishment, of *Zur Kritik der Gewalt*.

Nevertheless, each member of a binary pair helps to understand the other. Benjamin exploits that help throughout all the turns and surprising deflections of his essay, in spite of consistently challenging received opinion about the relation, for example, between means and ends or between lawmaking and law-preserving. Nevertheless, it remains clear enough that an end is what we employ means to reach, and those means are to be defined as the way to a given predetermined end. That distinction remains more or less solid in Benjamin's essay. Law-preserving violence is used to keep in force a law that has been previously established by a lawmaking violence that took the form of a decision or decree, a speech act breaking with all previous law, making new law, and based on . . . well, based on what? On nothing? On itself, in an act of self-grounding? On "the mystical foundation of authority"? What could that mean, the "mystical foundation of authority"?

Schicksal, in any case, does not seem to work like the binary pairs that are the backbone of Benjamin's essay. What is the opposite of fate? Does it have an opposite? We might think the contrary of fate would be freedom, but Benjamin pours scorn on traditional conceptions of freedom. Moreover, he does not consistently set freedom against fate. *Schicksal* seems to fall outside the table of binary oppositions, or to function equally well on both sides. Nor does Benjamin's essay "Fate and Character," written at more or less the same time as *Zur Kritik der Gewalt*, nor the essay on Goethe's *Die Wahlverwandschaften*, also nearby in time and containing passages about fate, help all that much, beyond complicating matters even further by providing more puzzling uses of the word *Schicksal*. This making more complex, rather than clarifying once and for all, is for me the primary result of the interpreter's sideways movement back and forth from one essay to another in search of illumination, which Benjamin's work invites or demands.

The word *Schicksal* is especially salient in two somewhat widely separated paragraphs in *Zur Kritik der Gewalt*. The first comes just after the introduction of the distinction between lawmaking and law-preserving functions (*rechtsetzende* and *rechtserhaltende*). Conscription seems to fall under the second rubric as a form of law-preserving, but Benjamin says that the criticisms of conscription by most pacifists and activists, not to speak of "childish" anarchists, and including even those critics of conscription who appeal to Kant's categorical imperative against using oneself or others as a means rather than as an end, are powerless to make an effective critique of the power exercised in conscription and the way those conscripted are violently forced to use violence. The reason Benjamin gives for this is odd or unexpected, or at least strikes me as odd and unexpected. It is wholly ineffective, says Benjamin, to attack one particular law. One must attack "the whole legal system root and branch [*die Rechtsordnung selbst an Haupt und Gliedern*]" (285/187). Why? Because the whole system of *Gewalt* hangs together as the "fate" of that particular state or legal order. "Positive law [*das positive Recht*]" claims that it promotes the interest of mankind, as Kant enjoined, by "the representation and preservation of an order imposed by fate [*in der Darstellung und Erhaltung einer schicksalhaften Ordnung*]" (285/187). "[T]here is only one fate," says Benjamin, and "what exists, and in particular what threatens, belongs inviolably to its order. For law-preserving violence is a threatening violence [*es nur ein einziges Schick-sal gibt und . . . gerade das Bestehende und zumal das Drohende unver-brüchlich seiner Ordnung angehört. Denn die rechtserhaltende Gewalt ist eine drohende*]" (285/187–88). Fate, it appears, is the always threatening power enthroned in law as the way in which what in the earthly and polit-ical realms is, is, ineluctably.

In the rest of the paragraph, a cascade of appearances of the word *Schicksal* punctuates the flow of language. These recurrences support the notion that fate is the appearance or incarnation or embodiment within a given law and order system of a power or violence, a *Gewalt*, of which one cannot identify the origin and of which one can only say that when it is em-bodied in legal institutions it is threatening. Part of what is so threatening about the violence of law as the embodiment of fate is its "uncertainty [*Unbestimmtheit*]" (285/188). A given criminal may or may not get caught. It depends on his fate, which is unpredictable, like the question of where lightning will strike (not Benjamin's figure; it might have seemed too "nat-ural" to him).

The unpredictability of fate is especially the case with capital punish-ment. Capital punishment is both essential to lawmaking violence and at the same time, in its arbitrariness of application and in one might therefore say its injustice (certainly this is true of the use of capital punishment in the United States), is a terrifying and unreasonable manifestation of the con-nection of fate to law and of "something rotten in law [*etwas Morsches im Recht*]." This rottenness manifests itself in the way in which fate "imperi-ously [*das Schicksal in eigner Majestät*]" shows itself, in a way appalling "to a finer sensibility [*am . . . dem feineren Gefühl*]" in the fortuitous lightning strike of a death sentence. The purpose of the death penalty, says Benjamin, in what is to me a surprising, even scandalous, sentence, "is not to punish the infringement of law but to establish new law" (286/188). What can this mean? Benjamin must mean that the imposition of the death sentence in a given case is never just or even lawful, but constitutes another unpredictable and fateful intervention of lawmaking violence. Certainly every effort to avoid facing this truth is made by supporters of the death penalty in the United States and by those authorities or executioners who enforce it. A sign beside the road on Deer Isle, Maine, during the 2000 pres-idential election, said "Bush for Executioner." This was a reference to the hundreds Bush had ordered executed as governor of Texas.

Lawmaking violence does not take place once and for all at the begin-ning, at the moment of the founding decision that establishes a new state, often through revolutionary violence, as was the case with the United States. Lawmaking violence goes on happening, fatefully, at unpredictable moments throughout the life of that particular state, as in lawmaking police violence or in the judge's or governor's imposition of a death sentence. The original imposition of law was unjust in the sense of being a ground-less act of violence or *Gewalt*. Any application of that law later on repeats the unjust and unjustified violence by declaring that the law fits this partic-ular case and so makes new law. "Violence, violence crowned by fate," says Benjamin, "is the origin of law [*Ist nämlich Gewalt, schicksalhaft gekrönte Gewalt, dessen Ursprung*]" (286/188). "Majesty"? "Crowned"? What is the force of these monarchist figures of speech? They seem to indicate that even in a democratic state a remnant of monarchy and the absolute power of kings, endorsed by the mystical foundation of authority, exists in the ir-resistible power of fate and the violence it enthrones.

A second paragraph in which the word *Schicksal* is especially salient will help refine further the understanding of what this word means for Benjamin. This is the paragraph that refers to the mythical story of Niobe as told in Ovid's *Metamorphoses*, the story of how Niobe tempted fate by boasting of her unassailable good fortune. She said "*Major sum* [greater than Leto, that is], *quàm cui possit Fortuna nocere*" (*Metamorphoses* 6:195: Naso 115). Mary M. Innes translates this, somewhat loosely, as "I am beyond the reach of Fortune's blows" (Ovid 139). Niobe was then punished by Leto, who set her children Apollo and Diana to kill all seven of Niobe's sons and all seven of Niobe's daughters, leaving her unhurt but so stricken with grief that she turned into a perpetually weeping stone statue. This story of mythical vio-lence is set by Benjamin against the story of divine violence in *Numbers* 16:1, 35. This is the episode of God's judgment on the company of Korah, a set of privileged Levites. In a characteristic use of the strategy of binary op-position I have identified, Benjamin sets Niobe's story against the story of the Korah as bloodletting in mythical violence as against bloodless sacrifice in divine violence. This is a little weird, if one remembers the function of blood sacrifice, at least of animals, in the Old Testament, as in the story of Abraham and Isaac, not to speak of the bloody crucifixion of Christ in the New Testament. Nevertheless, Benjamin needs to say Judaism is bloodless in order to keep the oppositions clear: "Just as," he says, "in all spheres God opposes myth, mythical violence is confronted by the divine. And the latter constitutes its antithesis in all respects. If mythical violence is lawmaking, di-vine violence is law-destroying; if the former sets boundaries, the latter boundlessly destroys them; if mythical violence brings at once guilt and ret-ribution, divine power only expiates; if the former threatens, the latter strikes; if the former is bloody, the latter is lethal without spilling blood" (297/199).

This seems clear enough, but the actual treatment of the Niobe myth in the previous paragraph complicates the matter quite a bit. In the paragraph before the one about Niobe, Benjamin had introduced yet another pair of opposites, law and justice. "How would it be, therefore," Benjamin had asked, "if all the violence imposed by fate [*jene Art schicksalmäßiger Gewalt*], using justified means, were of itself in irreconcilable conflict with just ends, and if at the same time a different kind of violence came into view that certainly could be either the justified or the unjustified means to those ends [the translation seems wrong here; the German is '*nicht das berechtigte noch das unberechtigte Mittel sein könnte*,' which I take it means 'could neither be justified nor unjustified means'], but was not related to them as means at all but in a different way [*irgendwie anders*]?" (293/196). This third kind of violence is a demonstration of the undecidability [*Unentscheidbarkeit*] of all legal problems (293/196; the English misses this and says only "insolubility"). The undecidability derives from the incompatibility between law and justice. "Generalization," says Benjamin, "contradicts the nature of justice" (294/196). Law deals in generalities and submits special cases to fateful judgments. These are unjust in the sense that they do not recognize what is special about the special case. Only divine violence judges the latter justly, but, in another example of the way the concept of *Schicksal* slips back and forth from one side to the other, the story of Niobe illustrates not just mythical violence but also, explicitly, "divine violence [*göttliche Gewalt*]" (294/197).

The action of Apollo and Diana might seem to be a punishment of Niobe for breaking a law, but, claims Benjamin, their violence "establishes a law far more than it punishes for the infringement of one already existing [*ihre Gewalt richtet viel mehr ein Recht auf, als für Übertretung eines bestehenden zu strafen*]" (294/197). First of all, however, that violence functions neither as law-preserving nor as lawmaking, but simply as "a manifestation of their existence [*am ersten Manifestation ihres Daseins*]." The violence that kills Niobe's children and leaves her "all tears" is at once "divine violence" and at the same time a manifestation of *Schicksal*: "Niobe's arrogance," says Benjamin, "calls down fate upon itself not because her arrogance offends against the law but because it challenges fate [*sondern weil er das Schicksal herausfordiert*]—to a fight in which fate must triumph, and can bring to light a law only in its triumph" (294/197).

The law in question appears to be one incapable of generalization or even of reasonable formulation because it manifests the uncertainty and ambiguity of fate, of *Schicksal*, and applies only to the unique, singular case of Niobe's particular defiance of Fortuna. This is why it must be told in a story rather than in a conceptual expression. "Violence," says Benjamin, "therefore bursts upon Niobe from the uncertain, ambiguous sphere of fate [*Die Gewalt bricht also aus der unsicheren, zweideutigen Sphäre des Schicksals über Niobe herein*]" (295/197). It is uncertain and ambiguous because this violence is not punishment for the breaking of any law that existed prior to the violence. How can she justly be held responsible for breaking a law that only comes into existence after the fact of her action? And yet her loss is a fateful punishment for her transgression of a law that did not yet exist. It is an expression of divine violence, *göttlicher Gewalt*, in its uncertainty and ambiguity.

I conclude that *Schicksal* is one name (*Gewalt* is another) Benjamin decides by a species of unjustifiable fiat, a speech act of his own, to use as an appellation for the manifestation, in all forms of *Gewalt* within this lower world, of the permanently mysterious, inscrutable, noncognizable ground that makes things happen as they do happen, something "demonically ambiguous [*dämonisch-zweideutiger*]," to borrow a term from Benjamin's essay (295/198). To put this in a somewhat different way, *Schicksal* is a catachresis for the manifestations of the nameless power that lies behind all identifiable acts of violence, whether they are mythical violence or divine violence, lawmaking, law-preserving, or law-destroying in the name of justice. *Schicksal* is at the boundary, as Niobe's statue serves "as a boundary stone on the frontier between men and gods [*als Markstein der Grenze zwischen Menschen und Göttern*]" (295/197), mute but perpetually weeping evidence of the uncertain, ambiguous sphere of fate. This fate is something incomprehensible, incapable of being reduced to reason. It is a manifestation of something wholly other to human understanding, something that cannot be incorporated into any system of binary reasoning.

Confirmation of this reading, or at least support for it, is given in two remarkable sentences in the last paragraph of *Zur Kritik der Gewalt*. These sentences make a penultimate surprising twist of the rope of reasoning, if it can be called reasonable, that Benjamin has woven. The last twist is in the final sentence that, having said both lawmaking and law-preserving violence are "pernicious [*verwerflich*]" ends by identifing divine violence with sovereign violence [*die waltende*] [300/203]. Just before that come these two sentences: "Less possible and also less urgent for humanity, however, is to decide when unalloyed violence [*reine Gewalt*: pure violence] has been realized in particular cases [*Nicht gleich möglich noch auch gleich dringend ist aber für Menschen die Entscheidung, wann reine Gewalt in einen bestimmten Falle wirklich war*]. For only mythical violence, not divine, will be recognizable as such with certainty, unless it be in incomparable effects, because the expiatory power of violence is not visible to man. [*Denn nur die mythisches nicht die göttliche, wird sich als solche mit Gewißheit erkennen lassen, es sei denn in unvergleichlichen Wirkungen, weil die entsühnende Kraft der Gewalt für Menschen nicht zutage liegt*]" (300/202–3). The phrase "mystical foundation of authority" is justified because it applies to what Benjamin here says about the undecidability and invisibility of divine violence. You can never be sure that you have or do not have a case of it. Its effects are "incomparable [*unvergleichlich*]" not just in the sense that they are of incom-

parable power or *Gewalt*, but also in the sense that no figurative language
or "comparisons" will do justice to them.

I claim to have shown that Walter Benjamin's version of the incommensurability among law, power, and justice is sustained by appeal to a term,
Schicksal, that is the odd man out in the play of binary oppositions that governs or generates his thought in this essay, law-preserving as against lawmaking, mythical violence as against divine violence, Greek against Jew, and
so on. *Schicksal* plays the role of what Montaigne calls the "mystical foundation of authority." The mystical foundation of authority is "mystical" because it is a foundation that can never be confronted as such. The ground of
authority is a foundation immanent to language as speech act, not exterior
to language as something transcending it. This foundation is the immanence,
however, not of a solid ground but of an abyss, an abyss within performative utterances that is covered over by the word *Schicksal*, as in a judge's pronouncement of a verdict for capital punishment that determines the luckless
criminal's fate: "I sentence you to be hanged by the neck until dead," or "I
sentence you to death by lethal injection." In the end, "fate" or "destiny" is
a name for the way things happen as they do happen, even in those judicial
decisions or political acts that may or may not ever manifest "justice," and
even in those, like the proletarian general strike, that appear to make way
for a better political order. The proletarian general strike was, Benjamin believed, a paradigmatic example of law-destroying violence. The proletarian
general strike is destruction of always unjust law. Such a strike, Benjamin
hoped, would move us closer toward that true democracy and reign of justice all long, or ought to long, to attain.

WORKS CITED

Austin, J. L. *How to Do Things with Words.* 2nd ed. Edited by J. O. Urmson and
    Marina Sbisà. Cambridge: Harvard University Press, 1997.
Benjamin, Walter. "Critique of Violence." In *Reflections*, translated by Edmund
    Jephcott, edited by Peter Demetz, 277–300. New York: Harcourt Brace Jo-
    vanovich, 1978.
———. *Zur Kritik der Gewalt.* In *Gesammelte Schriften*, edited by Rolf Tiedemann
    and Hermann Schweppenhäuser, 2:1:179–203. Frankfurt am Main: Suhrkamp,
    1977.
Derrida, Jacques. *Force de loi.* Paris: Galilée, 1994.
Naso, Publius Ovidius. *Metamorphoseon. Opera.* II. London: Bodwell, Martin,
    1815.
Ovid. *Metamorphoses.* Translated by Mary M. Innes. Harmondsworth, UK: Pen-
    guin, 1976.

13 *Rousseau and Law*

MONSTROUS LOGIC

Rousseau's "Law"

> But, then, what is a law? So long as we continue to be satisfied
> with attaching only metaphysical ideas to this word, we will
> continue to reason without coming to any understanding.
> —Rousseau, *Social Contract* (1983, 37)

It is never a mere antiquarian exercise to revisit Rousseau's political
writing. Indeed, in times of political calm, one should probably not reread
Rousseau. If some sunny political day we chance to pick up his *Second Discourse* or his *Social Contract*, we meet with such blinding conceptual clarity and so piercing a rhetoric that it is apt to push us beyond our threshold
of tolerance for enlightenment. Periods that lack a sense of emergency and
political danger always see Rousseau as over the top, vaguely paranoid, and
unnecessarily fierce. His texts, of course, laid the groundwork for modern
democracy and elaborated its most familiar formal features (sovereignty of
the people, separation of powers, the rule of law), but in contrast to other
theorists of the social compact (Locke, for example), Rousseau insistently
colored his reason for inducing the birth of posttheocratic (and post-
despotic) society with intense, emotional expressiveness. The fiery elo-
quence of his works is suspect, his imagery excessive, his rhetoric exorbitant; and his conceptual discriminations are presented without the nuanced,
self-conscious ambiguity we are accustomed to in theorizing today.

Long before Nietzsche skewered Christianity, for example, Rousseau
condemned established state religions in his brief against theocratic orders
in *Social Contract IV*, viii, "On Religion." Denouncing this "so-called oth-
erworldly kingdom [that] became . . . the most violent despotism in the
world" (Rousseau 1983, 98; all references are to this edition of this text),
Rousseau takes Christianity to task specifically because its adherents are
uniquely vulnerable to manipulation by the "falsely pious" largely because
they are supposed to love, and not be suspicious of, their neighbors.[1] The

former citizen of Calvin's Geneva describes Christian citizenship as dual (not of two countries, but of "this world" and "the next"—the "City of God"), rendering Christians alternately society's greatest victims ("enslaved"; 101), and its greatest tyrants[2]: Rousseau writes, "Christian law is at bottom more injurious than it is useful for the strong constitution of the state" (99), reasoning that

the homeland of the Christian is not of this world. He does his duty, it is true, but he does it with a profound indifference toward the success or failure of his efforts. . . . For the society to be peaceful and for harmony to be maintained, every citizen without exception would have to be an equally good Christian. But if, unhappily, there is a single ambitious man, a single hypocrite, a Cataline, for example, or a Cromwell, he would undoubtedly gain the upper hand on his pious compatriots. Once he has discovered by some ruse the art of deceiving them and of laying hold of a part of the public authority, behold a man established in dignity! God wills that he be respected. Soon, behold a power! God wills that he be obeyed. Does the trustee of his power abuse it? He is the rod with which God punishes his children. It would be against one's conscience to expel the usurper. (100–101)

Passages like this make Rousseau almost unbearable to read, especially if one attempts to regard him with a liberal, tolerant eye. Indeed, until recently, I never paid much attention to this particular passage, which appears to have been written in the spirited heat of *philosophe* outrage, standard for the time, against the Church's abuses (recall Voltaire's "*Ecrasez l'infâme!*"). And yet—now that religion is routinely invoked to justify enhanced political powers in our own pluralistic democracies as well as in fundamentalist theocracies, Rousseau's logic once again seems compelling, even compulsory, reading. Political leaders in positions of authority in the world's most advanced democracy, the United States, now claim biblical support for public policy decisions, and the question of separating theology from reasons of state is hypothetical no more. Rousseau's rhetoric, it turns out, is more prescient and realistic, and less outlandishly paranoid, than it first appears; we can no longer afford to consider it merely rhetorical.

It would surely be better if we never *had* to reopen our Rousseau, and in times of only mild political dissatisfaction, we should forgo doing so if we wish to maintain the illusion that the principles of representative democracy he had so strong a role in conceiving have secured a permanent place in our futures. Yet it is undeniable that democracy, a still-fledgling form if you think about it, faces enormous challenges of both a theoretical and practical sort today. The democratic principles Rousseau laid down, such as the importance of the separation of powers, are now being severely tested in the United States, the world's leading democratic exemplar, and they constantly endure subtle and overt challenges that play on nostalgia for medieval forms of governance (corporatism and religion) that seem more predictable. This is due in part to the historical fact that the popular sovereignty and the formal universality of the Law that Rousseau inaugurated left us unprepared for the shocks that followed—the overt violence, wars, and persecutions of the nineteenth to the twenty-first centuries.

The strength of our institutions to withstand the pressures bred by their own contradictions is in question at a practical level. Founding principles taken literally pose unexpected dangers: proponents of "judicial restraint" in the United States, for example, hope to limit the power of courts to redress social imbalances, yet the triumph of such "restraint" (withdrawing the courts from solving "social" problems) may undermine the judiciary's own balancing power within the structure of democratic governance. In the theoretical field, too, we find the renewed popularity of Carl Schmitt (Hitler's political analyst sometimes called the theorist of the Third Reich who made eliminating the legislative branch of government a key component of his "direct democracy") seems symptomatic, an articulation of a "federalism" (in the United States as in Umberto Bossi's Italy) that is a programmatic antipathy to parliamentary governance for the collected American and European states. Western democracies have recently seen the partisan pressuring of legally elected opponents, the physical intimidation of election boards, the disenfranchising of ethnic and racial minorities—the list is long—going hand in hand with economic domineering and other forms of bullying.

Our abysmal collective experience with modern forms of governance—and with those who oppose them so radically—traumatically affects our faith that democratic principles are safeguards against political excesses. Dare we hope that democracy might still draw support against these excesses from Rousseau's own complex passion for it? Yes. If anyone realized that a single concession to bullying, to strong-arming, and to "law-preserving" violence (as Benjamin termed it) is a step in the wrong direction, it was Rousseau. If anyone knew how trespassing against the law removes us instantly to the flawed legal system of predemocracy, it was Rousseau. If anyone opposed the abuse of law as a hidden apology for the right of the mighty, it was Rousseau. He always directed his rhetoric against abuses of power, authority, and the usurpation of "the name of the law." To reread Rousseau is thus to be strongly reminded that the liberating "formality" of the law he inaugurated theoretically is not yet secured for everyone practically.

Times like these—when democratic commitments are wavering—make the fiery rhetoric of Rousseau painfully relevant once more. To reread Rousseau is timely now, for he insistently disturbs the blank assumption that ours remains—in theory at least—the best of all possible democratic worlds. Yet I do not happily find myself having to look again on his fearsome pages, for my act of rereading is an index of the degree to which recent history has shaken confidence in the elastic durability of the democratic system.

Although readers usually overlook his astonishing prescience, Rousseau actually predicted an amazing number of the social paroxysms that were to follow him,[3]. More importantly, he furnished a remarkably subtle understanding of the mechanisms that produce social and political pathology. To look to Rousseau for guidance is inevitably to be taken aback, amazed that he foils our "Kantian" expectations of balanced formality (even though his work introduced formal universality to politics and the law), amazed at the high chimerical quotient to his writing that makes even the most sympathetic reader cringe. He seems always to inject an unsettling element of fantasy into his analyses—and often his writing appears expressly designed for the sake of exposing this fantasy. In the very same places where Rousseau offers his most lucid insights, we also find giants and monsters—the most fantastical figures—springing up, as if Rousseau needed to include his own *malin génie* as counterpoint to his reasoning. Still, in what follows, I wish to argue that the inclusion of fantasy is intentional and systematic and that by means of it, Rousseau conveys literarily that the "irrationalities" of the past are never definitively shut down just because enlightened reason has set to work. The exquisite logic of his concepts could never do this alone. Rousseau forces, so to speak, the realization that fantasy always keeps a hand in the Law.

Fantasy and the Law

Fantasy dominates in Rousseau's *Second Discourse: On the Origin of Inequality Among Men* (Rousseau 1983, originally published 1756). In this text, Rousseau takes a subtle and richly suggestive panoramic tour of human societies, showing them in epoch after epoch as trying (and perennially failing) to institute *justice*. A steady stream of hypothetico-historical societies, depicted warts and all and examined for their benefits and failures, their pains and pleasures, are also Rousseau's "real" societies. That is, they are societies that have been instituted by purely human means, founded on manmade laws without divine intervention. They have developed from an initial zero condition of legislation (the state of nature) into fully elaborated legal states. Although they are founded by purely human means, these states nonetheless share a set of linked metaphysical beliefs: belief in the transcendent *origin* of their laws (in *Nature* or *God*); belief that their foundational laws manifest Natural and/or Divine *Right* or *Order*; and belief that "*Justice*" is the *principle* of the law's institution. Rousseau demonstrates how, given sufficient time, such states nonetheless invariably fail even in their own terms. He cites one optimistic historical example after another (for example, the Roman Republic) being brought low by the flawed foundation of its

Laws, drowned by a torrent of injustice, disorder, and inhumanity that over-
whelms the supposedly well-founded state. Each fully law-bound civil society he depicts, that is, spontaneously spawns, at its height, a monstrous
Thing—a gigantic mouth glutting itself on the very well-being of the state
that has been instituted by "just" laws. This oral monster is a "Despotism
[that] . . . gradually raising its hideous head . . . devour[s] everything it had
seen to be good and healthy in every part of the state" (159).

The eruption of monstrosity cannot be accounted for by any alleged
moral degeneracy in the state. Instead, Rousseau makes clear that the spectral horror has arisen from the very heart of "do-good" civil society (founded
on Right, Justice, and Order). This monster of unparalleled proportions is a
new Leviathan come to gorge itself specifically on the "good" produced by a
wisely and justly administered (Hobbesian) state.

Rousseau's whirlwind tour of social history and its monstrous apocalypse
in the *Discourse* is, of course, meant to illustrate how repressive and restitutive laws alike inevitably (and utterly) fail to check the increasing concentration of wealth and power in the hands of the despotic few at the expense
of the empty-handed many.[4] Why? Human societies, Rousseau explains, are
first organized by informal mores, which naturally favor the better en-
dowed, the more powerful, and the richest. Laws, traditionally conceived,
are regarded as the means of compensating for the unevenness of the societal playing field that custom and mores have shaped. But to Rousseau, Laws
instituted to redress specific local inequities—say, an imbalance in the distribution of social goods—are basically impotent, however well intentioned
they may be. Even when strongly bolstered by metaphysical rationales (like
"justice" and "fairness"), such laws never accomplish the actual instituting
of justice because, according to Rousseau, they are merely "metaphysical."
They do little more than disguise what is a fundamentally flawed organization for society: the simple division into haves and have-nots. Worse, such
laws lay the groundwork for even greater future injustice. The apocalyptic
monster is, then, no mere deus ex machina, nor is it simply a bugaboo created to chastise moral turpitude and political ineptitude in an unworthy society that has lost sight of its values. It is instead *the* cardinal symptom of a
disorder congenital in any order that has designed its laws around preventing the catastrophic return of despotic rule, and the war of all against all.

The impotence of "just" laws is due, that is, to the fact that *disorder* is the
one true principle on which the *order* that opposes disorder rests. Rousseau's
monster is a warning: states that imagine themselves constituted by a principle of repressing disorder will always ultimately spawn monstrous disorder
"trampling underfoot the laws and the people . . . establishing itself on the
ruins of the republic." This is not because of the purely *human* origins of society, with its perfectly understandable *human* failures of equity and justice,

but because society has unconsciously been constructed along an *inhuman* fault line. Its essential, hidden reference is a Thinglike, fantasmatic Other, psychically produced by a fundamentally rivalrous relation to one's brothers. "Metaphysical" social laws are devised to conceal with theological cover-ups an elementary antagonism, but they cannot prevent its eventual return. A monstrous despotism will invariably be unleashed upon the human society (a "republic of citizens") that is so faultily constructed. A "good" society (one lulled into complacency as to its own rectitude) will suffer all the more cata-strophically the greater its naive faith in the "goodness" of its laws and in the love of its neighbors. For the "monster" is, of course, only the return of a so-ciety's own repressed: of its guilty, unconscious knowledge that the corner-stone of civil society is an overwhelming, if concealed, inequality. The despot (a dictator is one who emerges to meet a crisis) is merely one symptom of civil society's original criminality: the fact is that its "leading citizens" are heirs to an original theft of others' freedom and the usurpation of their usufructs, their *jouissance*. Civil society's confidence in the power of "just laws" to attenuate, Rawlslike, the most egregious of a society's problems (through bans on "cruelty" or uneven distributions of socially produced goods) is misplaced. In the end, such Laws prove to be themselves responsi-ble for the shocking return of the absolute injustice and the absolute in-equality that the "monster" represents.

In the *Social Contract*, Rousseau will offer an alternative to the regime of brothers, the *frères ennemis* whose fantasmatic rivalry informs its every law—a complete remodeling of the concept of Law itself. But first let us look at the other fantasy figure in the *Second Discourse*: "Natural Man." Let us turn to him, but in doing so let us finally put to rest the confusion over his real function, which is not to provide a "pure" alternative to des-potism; for his Natural Man is not the Kantian "regulatory ideal" some imagine him to be. On the contrary, Rousseau's Natural Man is the func-tional equivalent of his monster. In Rousseau's hands, both figures are given the structure of the unconscious fantasy—a primal fantasy of total enjoy-ment—that has secretly motivated and shaped the entire elaboration of all our social laws. True, Natural Man is painted in what seems a "positive" light, in opposition to the gluttonous monster; yet once Rousseau sets *le sauvage* into society, it becomes clear that each and every one of his seduc-tive traits (seemingly so blessed in the state of Nature) becomes a horror and a curse. He becomes a despotic menace to his fellow men. Indeed, the fact that Rousseau can only infer the joy-filled Natural Man through the laws enacted against him renders him the structural double of the tyranni-cal monster.[5] Rousseau's image of an inhuman Thing erupting from soci-ety's bosom is the mirror image, that is, of the Natural Man who contains the seeds of destruction of the Nature from whose bosom he erupts.

Of course, it is these figures (signs of the eruption of unbarred *jouis-sance*) that we recall most vividly from the *Discourse*—far more indeed than we recall its complex and subtle argumentation. In Rousseau's *Second Discourse*, then, *Law* becomes inseparable from *Letters*. We shudder aesthetically at its terminator monster just as we shiver with aesthetic delight at its alluring originator, Natural Man—the two figures are irrevocably, literarily twinned. Two conjoined figures of unlimited *jouissance*, monster and Natural Man, both end up increasing the privative powers at work in iniquitous social orders. They are catastrophic figures, conceptually intimate with Rousseau's systematic analysis of the deep structural engines driving "development" (*perfectibilité*) within "civil society" (Freud's "civilization"/ "*Kultur*").

Interestingly, Rousseau initially paints these motive forces of social development with a recognizably human face: they result from a normal "human" passion—the desire to be seen, recognized, and honored by our fellows. This is, he says, the great social spur:

I would note how much that universal desire for reputation, honors, and preferences, which devours us all, trains and compares our talents and strengths; how much it excites and multiplies the passions; and, by making all men competitors, rivals, or rather enemies, how many setbacks, successes and catastrophes of every sort it causes every day, by making so many contenders run the same course. I would show that it is to this ardor for making oneself the topic of conversation, to this furor to distinguish oneself . . . that we owe what is best and worst among men, our virtues and vices, our sciences and our errors, our conquerors and our philosophers, that is to say, a multitude of bad things against a small number of good ones. Finally, I would prove that if one sees a handful of powerful and rich men at the height of greatness and fortune while the mob grovels in obscurity and misery, it is because the former prize the things they enjoy only to the extent that the others are deprived of them; and because, without changing their position, they would cease to be happy, if the people ceased to be miserable. (158)

In the common desire for recognition, however, Rousseau grasps not only its human but also its inhuman quality. Isn't the monster's oral drive derived from (and does it not also model) the very desire that "devours us"—the scopic drive? Once the monster erupts, the natural "social" passion for recognition is profoundly called into question. His appearance reveals that a lurid fear underlies the dream of being a purely scopic object: the fear of becoming an oral object instead. The mania for making oneself seen, it turns out, is only a disguised expression of the unconscious fear of being eaten by the other. The monster (gorging itself on everything) is, after all, the fantasy of the most complete possible satisfaction (*jouissance*) of the oral drive at your expense.

Rousseau pinpoints with acute psychological insight the fundamental fantasy (the fear of being eaten) that underlies classical law. That he deduces it from a simple narrative of human affairs is astonishing. His penetration of the collective's unconscious fantasy recasts social aggregates as nothing more than a search for safety in numbers. Putting everyone under surveillance is a bulwark against the disproportionate (monstrous) advantage that the hidden other will take (Foucault's dream, in a way). Rousseau demonstrates, in short, that in classical notions, the basic structure of society is asocial (antagonistic, rivalrous) in the extreme. To premise the Law of society on the need to defend your own "goods" from your peers' incursions is to found Law on the fantasmatic fear that you will become the object of enjoyment of an overwhelming, monstrous Other that is stubbornly, inalterably opposed to you. The Law's sole *raison d'être* becomes one of sheltering you from the aggressivity of the other.

The asocial society that repressive/retributive laws represent is the flawed product of this fantasy of oral enjoyment—and its producer as well. For the fantasy's social correlate is an actual economy in which the many starve while the few enjoy to excess. Erecting laws on a fantasy of oral *jouissance* inevitably leads to the same baleful outcome: the elementary social passion (the desire to be seen) ends by eating men up. Like Benjamin's angel of history, Rousseau piles up before us the wreckage that classical social "laws" have amassed and, like an uncanny Virgilian escort to the circles of Hell, he confronts us dramatically with that history's "end"—the apocalyptic monster that has secretly menaced it throughout.

Rousseau, of course, wants to put a stop to the eternal return of this monstrosity—eternal return because his *Second Discourse* shows that such an "ending" turns out to be the same thing as society's primal scene—return to Natural Man. Indeed, the figure of a fantasmatic Despot has repeatedly dictated, negatively and positively, the laws of social life (designed to free us from him), and with every narrative of his demise, the cycle recommences. Terminal despotic horror, like some James Cameron–Schwarzenegger Terminator or Ridley Scott Alien, will "be back" to give birth to itself over and over again—and Rousseau knows why. The very pains taken to subjugate it—the ever-stricter laws against despotism's return—ensure the recommencement of its horrific reign.

The sole foundation of repressive law, it turns out, is the unarticulated fantasy of the inescapable cannibal violence of the Other. It is, however a singular violence. Rousseau's fantasy monster is not yet the figure of the ur-violence of Benjamin's "Critique of Violence" (the violence at the origin of law and order); nor is it the figure of a collective guilt for such original violence (for example, against a scapegoat, as René Girard hypothesizes). Rather, Rousseau places the deep engine of social drive in the destructive fantasy itself.

This is surprising, because his social history-making in the *Discourse* had seemed historicist and anthropological, not analytic. Indeed, the *Second Discourse* is a virtual phenomenology of the spirit (of the laws) before the (Hegelian) letter. It carefully unfolds the elementary laws of human association while intentionally forcing us off their programmatic path. Rousseau's whirlwind tour of the "progress" of the spirit of the laws is designed not only to speed us through history but to seduce us into losing our way, into tarrying with whatever utopian moment it personally appeals to us to linger over, before proceeding to the next stage or returning to "reality." Rousseau, that is, lures us into and inevitably forces us past our preferred utopias by dissolving their picture-perfect moments into self-parody or worse—into their own evil twins, clones that degrade and ruin their essence.

The sheer brilliance of Rousseau's method must not be underrated. He whisks us from alluring scenes of egalitarian, albeit isolated, presocial man exercising his liberty to (and through) the successive social forms and political constructions that legally rob him of that liberty (for example, pastoral, agricultural, rural, urban, small town, republic, dictatorship, monarchy). If we imagine we can rest easy once Rousseau dialectically restores man his freedom in civil form (as the citizen of a republic), we are mistaken. For Rousseau snatches this new freedom from him once more as the Despot returns, forcing us to realize that the irrationality of social order (even as civil society) goes far deeper than its surface features announce.

Rousseau's *Discourse* is, then, one of the first dialectical views of social history ever formulated, and it is a dialectic that demands a monster for its "squaring" or quadriplicitous formulation. Well before Freud and Lacan, Rousseau stunningly articulated the unconscious fantasy that analysis is able to precipitate out of an unconsciously distorted narrative, which is here the ordinary tale of human affairs. Yet if Rousseau's monster is the equivalent of Freud's *Ur-Vater*, the figure of a total enjoyment by the One at the expense of the many, it differs from it as well. In Freud, it is the guilt over murder of the mythic and unjust *père-jouissant* by his resentful sons that inaugurates society as the Law (of incest, with its anthropological correlates—bride exchange, organization into clans and families, and even social solidarity—they are all brothers in crime, etc.). The *Discourse* is comparable to the myth of the totemic father in *Totem and Taboo*, but inversely so. For Freud's omnipotent primal father is from the time before time—that is, before society. Rousseau's mythical monster of unfettered enjoyment has a very specific temporality and historicity: it postdates the organization of society and the institution of its Laws. Rousseau abducts the fantasy's monstrous existence from a particular, repetitive patterning of failures in social discourse. This patterning becomes visible only at the end of history (as it is about to become prehistory again), and even then, it can be accessed as fantasy only through its analytic construction (in Freud's technical sense of the term)—that is, the sensitive reading, via tropic reversals and metonymic associations, of a literally unspeakable structure.

What is the specific irrational element in the organization of society that produces the pathological stuttering toward despotism that Rousseau seeks to banish? The equation is simple: Our societies are structured around the single principle of order. Order requires hierarchy; hierarchy inevitably becomes oppressive. Oppression leads to society's ruin—the "return" of the original deadly rivalry that "just" laws were supposed to neutralize. What is less simple is Rousseau's insight that the elaboration of social laws is being driven by the fantasmatic fear of (or dream of?) a total *jouissance* on some One's part (Natural Man/Despot). So long as this fantasy remains unarticulated, the specter of its own apocalyptic destruction ("everything . . . swallowed up by the monster") will haunt each and every society it secretly animates (II, 159). Again *avant-la-lettre*, the contours of Freud's "primal scene" and Lacan's "fundamental fantasy" are the unconscious fantasy of an unbearable enjoyment on the Other's part that commands all of the repetitious failures in the life of the patient—in this case, society itself.

Law and Equality: From Second Discourse to Social Contract

> In fact, to a certain degree, fantasms
> cannot bear the revelation of speech.
> —Lacan (1992, 80)

Fantasy enslaves the subject best. The task of the analyst is to exorcise the power of fantasy by articulating it. Rousseau does this in the *Second Discourse*. But he also sets himself a different task in the *Social Contract*: to recast the very definition of the Law. Rousseau saw Law as framing the conditions of possibility (and impossibility) of acting in a society of free subjects. By demarcating the line between two inherently incompatible regions of legality (freedom and order), he definitively framed—and this really for the first time in history—a Law suited for a society that was not composed of masters and slaves but of subjects mastered by nothing but their own irrational attachments, including their subjective attachment to a lack of freedom: "In their chains, [slaves] lose everything, even the desire to escape. They love their servitude the way the companions of Ulysses loved their degradation" (I, ii, 18–19).

This is why Rousseau creates so dystopian a fantasy at the "close" of social history in the *Second Discourse*. What he first presents as the progressive line of social history proves to be only the long curve of the pathologically repeated failure of society itself. Until this moment in the *Discourse*,

Rousseau simply seemed to be laying out an impressive array of recognizably human and very ordinary failings—competitiveness, envy, greed, and
narcissism—compiling a Voltairian sort of history of *moeurs*, a philosophically bemused study of the common extravagances of mankind. Rousseau's
nontheological view makes men's social traits their sole mark of distinction
from animals (and from Natural Man)—they are responsible for the worst
but also for the best in us. When society collapses, Rousseau pictures its demise as the return of a state of Nature. But postsocial Nature has a horrifi-
cally intensified character. The naive state of nature, with all its sunny qualities, returns at its darkest to display precisely the same despotic features
that once supposedly showed up only in the society of men: "Here everything is returned solely to the law of the strongest, and consequently to a
new state of nature different from the one with which we began, in that the
one was the state of nature in its purity, and this last one is the fruit of an
excess of corruption. Moreover, there is so little difference between these
two states. . . ." (159). The immense irony is that it will have been these
very social traits, shaped by Laws that organize society so as to prevent
their return, that relaunch the reign of Nature with its accelerated, active
destruction of the social contract.

For Rousseau, "equality" is "natural" only when it is absolute—that is,
not relative. Absolute equality is impossible for any *social* being because
once an isolated being is inserted into society, its absoluteness necessarily becomes merely proportionate. What was absolute in isolation (liberty and
equality) becomes, in the group, a point of departure for a deadly rivalry, a
comparison with others: in other words, war. Classical theorists like Hobbes
believed that laws were instituted to quell or pacify the inevitable result of
the entry of solitaries into society, "war of all against all". But Rousseau argues that laws founded on this premise have never really existed, and if they
had, they would not have solved the fundamental problem. Repressive laws
are their own incitement to transgression for the human subject; restitutive
laws are prone to similar abuse, although in a less obvious way. Long before
Nietzsche did, Rousseau found that our bravest historical attempts to make
justice into an a priori principle of the Law—its "spirit"—are pointless. The
real beneficiaries of such Laws are always those who know best to turn them
into instruments "more favorable" to them than to others (199). But make
no mistake: Rousseau's fright-figure is not meant to encourage what conservatives today call "deregulation," anarchy, or even anomie. (He's been accused of all these.) Rousseau's monster simply functions as a signal to us that
the proliferating prohibitions of traditional law suggest we are putting the
accent in the wrong place where the Law is concerned.[6]

To Rousseau, repressive laws are only a symptom of some hidden, unchecked despotism at work in the system. His reasoning is not that we

should therefore do without laws. It is rather that we cannot count on laws that are built on a faulty premise (that they are to prevent the war of all against all) to remedy abuses inherent in any social order. After surveying every type of civil society, it seems obvious to Rousseau that we cannot alter the fundamental unfairness of social order unless we frame our laws differently, which is another way of saying that we have to conceive society on a different model from that of regulating behavior. Yet how could he make it so that the laws could address abuses, and so that the judgments based on them could prevail in the face of indelibly brute force? Of what, in short, does Rousseau's revolution in the Law consist?

For Rousseau, the classical conception of Law is flawed in two ways. First of all, it places a wrong-headed emphasis on social order as its goal. Second, it puts metaphysical concepts in the place of basic principles. The *Second Discourse* has also shown us a third aspect to his thinking: that the Law must now recognize and take into account the factor of fantasy in its own constitution.

Let me explain this last: when Rousseau's despotic monster breaks the poorly forged bonds of social life, it does so simply by staging society's deepest fantasy—its fundamental fear of the ravenous, rivalrous, omnipotent other. The monster's power to act the despot, however, is derived solely from its remaining unrevealed. The despot is empowered only if he can "push the fear buttons" of the subject, who is already driven by an unconscious dread of his fellows.

Rousseau moves to defuse that fear not by preaching brotherly love, but by simply articulating the fantasy—by showing how, at bottom, such fear is unreasonable—an impossible basis for the Law. The monster's return demonstrates that any Law designed purposely to repress the aggression of one against the other, even when framed in the strongest terms as an act of justice, remains vulnerable to the would-be tyrant: let him transgress a single law, or violate a single bond of love or friendship with impunity and the Law in its totality falls. Rousseau, however, does recognize a "natural" limit to tyranny, for even monstrous power eventually bends total mastery itself to the breaking point:

Here is the final stage of inequality, and the extreme point that closes the circle and touches the point from which we started. Here all private subjects . . . no longer have any law other than the master's will, nor the master any rule other than his passions, the notions of good and the principles of justice again vanish. Here everything is returned solely to the law of the strongest, and consequently to a new state of nature different from the one with which we began, in that the one was the state of nature in its purity, and this last one is the fruit of an excess of corruption. Moreover, there is so little difference between these two states, and the governmental contract is so utterly dissolved by despotism, that the despot is master only as long as he is the strongest. (159)

At the *Discourse*'s end, Nature is crowned with the authority and power of
a Divinity who renders all men once again "equal"—which is to say equally
nil—in its eyes: "Here is the final stage of inequality, and the extreme point
that closes the circle and touches the point from which we started. Here all
private individuals become equals again, because they are nothing" (159).
Such a "natural" term to the reign of terror does not satisfy Rousseau, for
all its delicious irony. He wants more: he wants to jam the cyclical alternation of liberty-equality with despotic inequality by recasting the laws themselves, recasting indeed the very way we understand the essence of society
(what it is that draws us into association with each other). If society can no
longer be thought of as a shelter and a way of protecting us from others, it
must be reconceived as something of an entirely different nature. And its
laws must be made to respond to his insight that the classical laws of social
order instigate the very horrors they seek to repress. These horrors, after
all, do not explode as the result of natural violent urges but are the product
of fantasies of enjoyment and of privation (of and by others). For societies
so deeply shaped by fantasies of unlimited *jouissance*, the net effect of their
Laws can never be more than nil. Once Rousseau articulates ("constructs")
their fundamental fantasy, however, he is free to devise an entirely new
strategy for the constitution of their laws.

In the *Social Contract*, therefore, Rousseau will split *Law* from *Order*
and make Justice Law's *object* rather than its *principle*, a principle to be re-
made by detaching it from the spirit that has historically animated it—the
ghost or *Geist* of the Other's obscene enjoyment. He will empty the Law of
this particular "pathological" content (the ineradicable hostility of the
other), and he will then relocate the legal principle outside its traditional
placement (in the metaphysical concepts of "justice," "honor," and "order"). For Rousseau, Law alone becomes the a priori of the Law. In true
Enlightenment materialist fashion, that is, Rousseau reconstitutes the Law
as a conceptless and contentless universal: freedom.

Rousseau is distinguished from his contemporaries by his thoroughly realistic sense of his subject. Very much like Descartes, his primary aim is that
of formulating a rational rather than a fantasmatic basis for the Law. He
nonetheless realizes that a rational acquisition of freedom will not end the
irrationalities of collective history. The fantasms of the *Second Discourse*
will not simply fade from view once the *Social Contract* builds a new stage
for world history. The monster of the old order returns even stronger, more
ravishing and more malignant than ever once it enters the obscure zone between its two deaths, and its second coming is its most dangerous appearance. Rousseau warns: "Freedom can be acquired, but it can never be re-
covered" (II, viii, 385).

Rousseau articulates the fantasms underlying the ideal of social order in order to demystify and break definitively with western society's faith in Divine and Natural Law alike. But his practical analysis of human affairs finds matters less clear-cut. Experientially, there is no simple human way to distinguish the end of the reign of Nature from the beginning of the reign of the gods. Indeed, no caesura marks their terminus. Rather, from a human standpoint, Nature and the Divine stand Janus-faced, a horrid hybrid that masks the real void in the Law framed as either natural or divine. Rousseau marks his break only with a negative, for the important point is not only to be "finally" free of such phantasms, but to preserve vigilantly our potential to free ourselves of them again, once they make their inevitable return.[7]

He thus composes his *Social Contract* strictly from what he will call "the human standpoint." In the *Contract*, Rousseau distinguishes Natural and Divine Law alike from the reign of Law as shaped by reason. Only a turn to reason by the Law will disrupt the tragic dialectic of human society and its vexed relation to enjoyment. The Law he conceives of is a law of freedom that is effectively a freedom from the overwhelming, abusive power that Nature and God represent, and a freedom to turn their power to positive human advantage. Rousseau's legal solution is psychologically sophisticated and ingenious and it gives no grounds for the unreasoning fear of the Other that has driven society up to now, because each member is made to be equally *lacking* in *direct power* over others. Rousseau is the first theorist to conceive of the Law as fundamentally dependent on that factor considered the negative obstacle in all prior theories of social order—the human factor.

Law in the Social Contract

Securing Law from "the human standpoint" turns out, however, to be no easy matter. A crucial section "On Law" in the *Social Contract* finds Rousseau writing:

Whatever is good and in conformity with *order* is such by the nature of things and independently of human conventions. All *justice* comes from God; he alone is its source. But if we knew how to receive it from so exalted a source, we would have no need for government or laws. Undoubtedly there is a universal justice emanating from reason alone; but this justice, to be admitted among us, ought to be reciprocal. Considering things from a human standpoint, the lack of a natural sanction causes the laws of justice to be without teeth among men. They do nothing but good to the wicked and evil to the just, when the latter observes them in this dealings with everyone, while no one observes them in their dealings with him. There must therefore be conventions and laws to *unite rights and duties* and to refer *justice back to its object.* (36–37; my emphasis)

For Rousseau, laws have altered nature in order to produce what we know as "human." To refashion the laws of a society that has itself fashioned human life is to realize that "the effect would have to become the cause" (40). The operation is radically impossible and yet radically necessary. Where can we find the reason (and the imagination) required to frame the laws of a social state if these only appear within a state whose laws and imagination can be framed only because reason already exists there? To this day, the *Social Contract* remains Rousseau's most uncanny achievement, designed as it is to pass between the impossible Scylla of founding law ex nihilo and the Charybdis of the inescapable need to do so.

The *Social Contract* will found a state in which, as Althusser (1972) has so brilliantly explained, the people as sovereign signs with itself its contract: the party of the second part (with which the first party contracts) is "the same" as the first and yet absolutely different from it. Moreover, the first party that the second contracts with has no prior existence outside the contract it signs with the second, which likewise has no prior existence—material or metaphysical—before the contract is fully executed. The cornerstone of all of Rousseau's doctrine on Law is the argument that the sovereignty of the people, self-legislation, and the assumption of legal authority have no metaphysical foundation, no a priori existence; and that they emerge consubstantial with their recognition of each other as the subjects of society: that is, with the emergence of the Law. Rousseau had good reason to attempt to secure the Law on these grounds. For what was the lesson of the *Second Discourse* if not that a Law justified on purely metaphysical grounds is ultimately shaped by fantasy and open to abusive misappropriation? The *Contract* is Rousseau's effort to configure Law and Right in an entirely new and entirely rational way.

But in casting about for a rational basis for the Law, Rousseau finds himself limited by his own thorough realism regarding "the human standpoint." Unlike his classical predecessors, who saw society and its laws as a way of escaping the dread of the other, Rousseau knew from experience that society itself often plays the role of powerful oppressor. He knew that power-seekers are ever alert to take advantage of one's fear of one's neighbors. (Recall how the "law and order conservatives" in the Reagan years terrified United States citizens with the specter of "crime"—which is just another way of saying that you must fear your fellow man and look to us, the police, security guards, and alarms, to guarantee your safety.) To discover a legal solution to the problem of a society founded on fear requires more than reason alone. Irrational fears are deeply rooted, and Rousseau's lawgiver, to be effective, cannot be a stranger to human passions. In his section "On the Legislator," Rousseau criticizes the classical view of the legislator as an alien God who knows human passions but does not undergo them:

Discovering the rules of society best suited to nations would require a superior intelligence that beheld all the passions of men without feeling any of them; who had

no affinity with our nature, yet knew it through and through; whose happiness is independent of us, yet who nevertheless was willing to concern himself with ours; finally, who, in the passage of time procures for himself a distant glory, being able to
labor in one age and find enjoyment in another. Gods would be needed to give men
laws. The same reasoning used by Caligula regarding matters of fact was used by
Plato regarding right in defining the civil or royal man. (II, vii, 38)

How does Rousseau extricate himself from the impasse in which one must
already "know men" in order to frame the constitution of their state from
"the human standpoint" without "altering" men ("I take men as they are,"
he says), as classical theories aim to do? This is exceedingly tricky. Rousseau
has said already that no state has ever yet been founded without recourse to
religion. Rousseau says that the legislator must have no office of "magis-
tracy or sovereignty" (39): his function has "nothing in common with the
dominion over men. . . . [H]e who has command over men must not have
command over laws" (39). As the lawgiver's direct power over others must
be nil (that is, each human must have the same power as any other subject),
his legislative authority must come from a source other than his personal or
political dominance.

Rousseau also bars the would-be legislator from recourse to "force or
reasoning" (persuasive rhetoric), because his power of persuasion usurps
from the people the legislative power that lies exclusively with them. However, since before the institution of the Law, the people are as yet incapable
of reasoning ("the social spirit that ought to be the work of [the institution
of the law] would have to preside over the institution itself"; 40), the legislator's only recourse is to "an authority of a different order, which can com-
pel without violence and persuade without convincing" (40). This is where
religion, even with its penchant for hypocrisy, has played a traditional role
in forming the Law-based state:

This is what has always forced the fathers of nation to have recourse to the intervention of heaven and to credit the gods with their own wisdom, so that the peoples, subjected to the laws of the state as to those of nature and recognizing the
same power in the formation of man and of the city, might obey with liberty and
bear with docility the yoke of public felicity. . . . In the beginning stages of nations
[politics and religion each] serve as instrument of the other. (40–41)

In the long run, though, the realistic Rousseau concludes that the supposed
"interventions" of heaven admit that "any man can engrave stone tablets,
buy an oracle, or feign secret intercourse with some divinity." The real authority of the law comes only from the great soul of the legislator: "the Ju-
daic Law, which still exists, and that of the child of Ismael, which has ruled
half the world for ten centuries, still proclaim today the great *men* who
enunciated them" (40; my emphasis). We must accent the *men*, not the
"greatness," in this phrase.

Conclusion

The best summation of Rousseau's revolution in the Law is contained in his assertion from the *Social Contract* that he takes "men *as they are* and laws as they *might be*" (17). This protocol reverses the classical search for eternal laws to mould human character and guide human conduct on metaphysical and religious grounds. Accepting men as "they are" means taking men as they are already shaped by their sociality and already subjected to society's fundamental laws, which are fewer and yet broader than we imagine. Rather than accenting the repression of the other's demand to enjoy your goods at your expense, this realistic law articulates precisely how fantasy fears have motivated the best and most effective of traditional laws—the Ten Commandments, for example, which enunciate these fantasies under a sign of negation ("Thou shalt not" do what everyone already always does, as Lacan notes). They draw, that is, an incredibly clear picture of the real lives of real people, interested in their neighbor's goods, wives, donkeys, and all, and these laws do not fail to recognize and to mention these passions, albeit in the mode of negation. Rousseau's model for a good law from past times is one that will have taken our unspeakable passions, our fantasies of enjoyment, and turned them into articulated desires. It will have openly *barred* these desires, and yet openly *bared* them at the same time. Fantasies articulated, even negatively, lead the way for the subjective fall of the drives they spawn: "fantasms cannot bear the articulation of speech," as Lacan later put it.

So much for "men as they are"; but what of the "laws as they might be"? Their essence is entirely open: freedom. Rousseau rejects the principle of Law as the framing of *order* (as in classical Aristotelian theory, that is, according to ends defined prior to its institution—for example, justice, harmony). For him, it is instead a principle of *freedom*. Rousseau's Law, that is, is the first to embrace the idea of the Law as a canvas whose blankness permits fantasy to dissimulate itself but also to articulate itself there.[8] He imagines a rational society founded on the absence of harassing fantasms (*fantômes*), haunted by ghosts, but he acknowledges in the greatest possible detail their irrational persistence. For Rousseau, the generality of the Law, its fundamental freedom, works by resisting the perennial temptation to fill the void in Law with our own unconscious, unanalyzed fantasies.

Rousseau thus sits athwart the rational and the irrational, rendering his sense of the energetic conflictual reality of social life different from the "empty" universality that permeates Kant's vision (even though Kant, too, shoos away the *Schwärmerai*). Rousseau articulates the fundamental social fantasy—the oral fantasy of being eaten by one's fellows—with a view to acknowledging it and withering its abusive hold over the conceptual basis of

Law. Rousseau's innovation strips the social canvas of particularity in favor of what I term a negative universal,[9] but the aim is not to purge society of its bad moral content. To *écarter tous les faits* is less to restore original "purity" than to hear with a third ear the deadly clamorings of fantasy that supports its riotous desires. To read Rousseau as primitivist, that is, is to misread him entirely, although this reading persists from Diderot to Pol Pot's expunging of Kampuchea's cultural history in order to purify it. The *Social Contract* offers not moral catharsis but the open possibility of a liberation from fantasy (a hitherto unknown freedom) as the sole principle of the Law. It is not designed to purge men of evil, but to fashion a symbolic place where their ghosts are projected and potentially rejected, where their fantasy fears are "to some degree" exposed to the withering articulations of logic. Rousseau brings fantasy to the bar of symbolic Law—to speakability; it does not root it out (impossible), but rather acknowledges its unwarranted, lethal power. Rousseau thus steps past the naive "natural psychology" of warring dyads underlying theories of Law from Aristotle to Hobbes into its first truly modernized conception.

Unconscious fantasy sets itself against the Rousseauian Law of freedom, for it is a Law that liberates us from domination by unconscious fantasy. Conservatives are constitutionally unable to believe in Rousseau's kind of law, for they remain fantasy-stricken in a structural way that resists all efforts at cure.

Those who continue to appreciate Rousseau's solution seem, sadly, to be diminishing, leaving democracy disappointed.

NOTES

1. Compare Sigmund Freud's remarks on the universal commandment to love thy neighbor in *Civilization and Its Discontents* (Freud 1957, 109–10).
2. See Rousseau (II, 159).
3. See Rousseau (II, viii, 42).
4. In the year 2000, three-quarters of the world's wealth was owned by fewer than three hundred individuals. In *Of Grammatology*, Derrida chides Lévi-Strauss for seeing the west's treatment of nonliterate peoples as exploitation: what Lévi-Strauss calls "*enslavement* can equally legitimately be called *liberation*" (Derrida 1976, 131). By failing to "Distinguish between hierarchization and domination, between political authority and exploitation. . . . [His tone] deliberately confounds law and oppression. The idea of law and positive right . . . is determined by Lévi-Strauss as constraint and enslavement. . . . A classical and coherent thesis, but here advanced as self-evident, without opening the least bit of critical dialogue with the holders of the other thesis, according to which the generality of the law is on the contrary the condition of liberty in the city. No dialogue for example, with Rousseau" (131).

5. The influence of Spinoza on Rousseau is underrated. See Deleuze (1988, 18–19).

6. See Lacan (1992, 84). Rousseau acknowledges that prohibition incites transgression (136) but looks to its deeper fantasmatic root: lethal rivalry with the other.

7. See Lacan (1992, 81).

8. Rousseau argued against slavery, ever mindful that he was formulating this principle for societies (even democracies) whose members were not yet all legally free. (In this regard, Rousseau's critique of Aristotle's defense of slavery in the *Social Contract*, pt. I, ii, 18–19, is of capital importance to his position on Law.)

9. I frame the definition of a "negative universal" in MacCannell (2001, 29–50).

WORKS CITED

Althusser, Louis. 1972. *Politics and history: Montesquieu, Rousseau, Hegel and Marx.* Trans. Ben Brewster. London: NLB.
Deleuze, Gilles. 1988. *Spinoza: Practical philosophy.* Trans. Robert Hurley. San Francisco: City Lights Books.
Derrida, Jacques. 1976. *Of grammatology.* Trans. Gayatri Chakravorty Spivak. Baltimore: Johns Hopkins University Press.
Freud, Sigmund. 1957. *Civilization and its discontents.* In *The standard edition of the complete psychological works of Sigmund Freud*, trans. and ed. James Strachey in collaboration with Anna Freud, vol. 21. London: The Hogarth Press and the Institute of Psycho-Analysis. (Orig. pub. 1930.)
———. 1957. *Totem and Taboo.* In *The standard edition of the complete psychological works of Sigmund Freud*, trans. and ed. James Strachey in collaboration with Anna Freud, vol. 13. London: The Hogarth Press and the Institute of Psycho-Analysis. (Orig. pub. 1912–13.)
Lacan, Jacques. 1992. *Seminar VII: Ethics.* Trans. Dennis Porter. New York: Norton. (Orig. pub. 1986.)
MacCannell, Juliet Flower. 2001. Stage left: A review of Judith Butler, Ernesto Laclau and Slavoj Žižek: Contingency, hegemony, universality. *Umbr@: A Journal of the Unconscious*, 29–50.
Rousseau, Jean-Jacques. 1983. *On the social contract: Discourse on the origins of inequality, and discourse on political economy.* Trans. Donald A. Cress. Indianapolis: Hackett.

Part VI

PSYCHOANALYSIS: JUSTICE OUTSIDE
THE "LIMITS" OF THE LAW

14 *Beyond the Dialectic of Law and Transgression*

FORGIVENESS AND PROMISE

Hannah Arendt is drawn to the main themes of the Augustinian Will. To begin with, Augustine understood that the Will inherited from Paul and the Stoics granted the ego "an *inward* life" that, unlike reason and desire, could respond to an idea that philosophy neither posits nor tries to reconcile: "*Quaestio mihi factus sum*" [I have become a question for myself] (Arendt 1978, 85). Even more important, because there are two wills, one carnal and the other spiritual, and because the Will is an internal capacity for affirmation and negation, when the law addresses the Will (and not the mind, reason, or desires), it is addressing a faculty that functions on its own accord. Augustine was the first person to elaborate on the dialectic between the law and its transgression, a dialectic already revealed by Paul. As Augustine put it, "the greatest joy is ushered in by the greatest painfulness," a notion that prefigures, one might add, the cruelty of Sade as well as of Nietzsche and Artaud (Arendt 1978, 90). But aside from the "sadomasochism" of the Will, a notion that we know Arendt resisted quite vigorously, the power of the Will to regulate itself is what attracted Arendt's attention: every *velle* is accompanied by a *nolle*, although no created being can will against creation. Because the principal will is the Will of creation, it is impossible to refuse unequivocally to will. Accordingly, Augustine does not trust anyone who says, "I'd rather not *be*," because life always implies a desire to continue to be and thus proves to be a form of praise and thanks (Arendt 1978, 91). On the basis of this supremacy of the "will to live" (in the sense that life is *summum bene*, eternal life), the Will, which is inherently tragic and contradictory, is unified through love even though it exposes an interiority that is no longer a dialogue but a conflict.

Arendt removed the dialectic from commandment and freedom, from the law and transgression that underlie the Will; others, for their part, will claim that the dialectic is inherent in the logic of desire necessary for thinking about the human subject as well as political conflicts. Arendt hoped that her meditation on the Will would highlight the distinguishing characteristics of modern metaphysics, particularly its subjectivism, notably Marxist and existentialist, that stipulates violation as a capacity lurking inside us that allows us to claim "to make ourselves" as well as "to make History" (1978, 115). Without relying on moral categories—at least, not in the beginning— Arendt sought to define the character of the political bond by isolating judgment as a distinct capacity of the mind, which, through its specificity as laid out in Kant's *Critique of Judgment*, attests to the way each person is from the outset a member of the human community (see Arendt 1970).

Seduced and yet bogged down by the "frailty of human affairs," Arendt turned her attention to the two pitfalls that threaten judgment—pitfalls that appear to coexist with the linear experience of human time in the process of life and, by implication, in the modern practice of politics: irreversibility and unpredictability.

When time is experienced as being irreversible, it burdens men whose inability to turn it around causes them to succumb to resentment and revenge. Nietzsche once denounced the human "beast" who is "always resisting the great and continually increasing weight of the past" and who—as the mirror image of the animal who never suffers because he forgets everything—suffers to the point of exhaustion because "he cannot learn to forget, but hangs on the past" (cf. Nietzsche 1967, vol. 2, no. 1, 95–96). In place of a ruminative memory that fosters resentment and revenge, the human beast advocates nothing less than the "force of forgetfulness," a power of obstruction, active and, in the strictest sense of the word, positive, that creates "a little *tabula rasa* of the consciousness, so as to make room again for the new." Nietzsche also associates "this very animal who finds it necessary to be forgetful," an animal for which he hopes and prays, with another faculty: the ability to promise. He describes the faculty of promising as "an active refusal" or a "memory of the will" before he exposes some of its formidable ambiguities: the promise is a supreme sovereign in which man can "guarantee himself as a future," but it is also paired with hardness, cruelty, and pain because it inherits the debts [*Schulden*] of an invariably guilty conscience [*Schuld*] in the same way a debtor inherits the debts of his creditor (cf. Nietzsche 1967, 7:251–52, 256.)[1]

To the Nietzschean violence that rises up against the "conscience" and the "contract," however, Arendt contrasts her own serene wager on the potential rebirth of the "who," which is contingent on a renewed relationship with time. Even so, she skirts around the unappealing picture Nietzsche paints of a contractual and indebted conscience that struggles against the throes of the will-to-power, and she considers only what Nietzsche called its "plastic power" (cf. Nietzsche 1967, 2:97). In the end, the feeling of guilt reduces to a figure of impotence—that which engenders linear time. Guilt, which appears to result from a breach of a prohibition or a moral precept, turns out to be deeply bound up with the very experience of temporality— that is, when temporality is coextensive with the life process. Breaking this chain requires an interruption, which in Arendt's view can no longer be forgetting but rather forgiveness. It is impossible to undo what has already been done, and it is impossible to imagine how one can forgive in solitude. Perhaps Arendt believes that forgiveness would be a mere inhibition if it were deprived of the space of appearance and the words of other people. But she can tolerate the idea that men, among themselves and at the heart of the frailty of their actions, free themselves from their doings and past actions whose consequences they had not foreseen or they cannot accept.

Even as she explores succinctly the complex problem of forgiveness, Arendt does not deny that some offenses are unforgivable. "Radical[ly] evil" actions exist (which she acknowledged by citing Kant in 1958, long before the 1963 Eichmann trial), "about whose nature so little is known, even to us who have been exposed to one of their rare outbursts on the public scene. All we know is that we can neither punish nor forgive such offenses and that they therefore transcend the realm of human affairs and the potentialities of human power, both of which they radically destroy wherever they make their appearance" (1958, 241). In Arendt's view, however, "crime and willed evil are rare, even rarer perhaps than good deeds." What is at stake here is merely a "trespass," which turns out to be an everyday occurrence because of "the very nature of action's constant establishment of new relationships within a web of relations." Trespassing thus calls out for "forgiving [and] dismissing, in order to make it possible for life to go on by constantly releasing men from what they have done unknowingly" (1958, 240).

To this limitation on her conception of forgiveness, Arendt adds another: forgiveness is aimed at the person, and not the act. One cannot forgive the murder or the theft, but only the murderer or the thief. By being aimed at *someone* and not *something*, forgiveness becomes an act of love. With or without love, however, one always forgives by taking the person into account. Whereas justice demands that everyone is equal and weighs each act individually, mercy emphasizes inequality and evaluates each person on his own terms. In spite of that difference, however, "to judge and to forgive are but the two sides of the same coin"; "every judgment is open to forgiveness" (1971, 248).

Let us apply this framework to the "judgment" that Arendt rendered in her book on the Eichmann trial. In no way does Arendt forgive this criminal man, precisely because, "by taking into consideration the person," she discovers a nonperson, the absence of a "who" or a "someone," a robotic bureaucrat who was incapable of judging his own acts and who therefore removed himself from the realm of forgiveness. Arendt sees this argument as no less radical than the notion of an "unforgivable crime" or "radical evil" practiced by the very system Eichmann submitted to and that, by destroying the "potentialities of human power . . . dispossesses us of all power [such that] we can repeat along with Jesus: 'It were better for him that a millstone were hanged about his neck, and he cast into the sea'" (1971, 241, citing Luke 17:2). Although Arendt is far from satisfied with this Christlike judgment, she wishes to create an international jurisdiction to punish crimes against humanity visited on the Jewish people. Punishment, to the extent that it is different from vengeance, does not contradict the suspended logic of forgiveness. Like forgiveness, punishment puts an end to something that, without it, could return ad infinitum (1971, 241).

If, on the other hand, a person is able to think and to judge, whatever the modalities and the limitation of that questioning, which itself is always tantamount to an effort to begin again or to be reborn, Arendt agrees to approach him with a judgment fueled by forgiveness. Bertolt Brecht is a good example of this. Did Brecht not condemn himself before anyone else did by inflicting the worst possible self-punishment for a gifted man, which is simply the death of talent? With passion and assurance, Arendt exposes the melancholic beauty of Brecht's work, even though she still judges quite harshly the "irresponsibility" that in her view is endemic to poets, as evidenced by the words that "this poor B. B." composed in a hymn to Stalin. On the basis of this particular "example," Arendt draws a general conclusion: although Brecht never displayed an ounce of self-pity, he still managed to teach us "how difficult it is to be a poet in this century or at any other time" (1971, 249).

In Arendt's judgment, Heidegger deserves forgiveness more than the average person does, not only because of love, "one of the rarest occurrences in human lives" that "possesses an unequaled power of self-revelation and an unequaled clarity of vision for the disclosure of *who*," but also because the revelation of love helps awaken a respect for a thought unique among all others, which she debates and displaces without abandoning the "regard for the person from the distance" (1958, 242–43).

Because this insight was entirely foreign to the Greeks, Arendt credits Jesus with discovering forgiveness, which was prefigured only by the Roman principle of sparing the vanquished [*parcere subiectis*]. Although this Christlike precept of forgiveness was expressed in religious language, it was rooted, in Arendt's view, in "the experiences in the small and closely knit community of [Jesus'] followers [who were] bent on challenging the public authorities in Israel." By thereby judging Jesus' innovation to be eminently political, Arendt zealously advocates her own expansive conception of an ideal politics, and she is clearly going beyond the strict domain of religion. Arendt believes that the correctives Jesus maintains against the "scribes and

Pharisees" are indispensable (1958, 239). Not only is God not alone in His ability to forgive, but it is precisely because humans are capable of forgiveness that God will eventually forgive them. On that score, Arendt cites, among other things, the Gospel according to Saint Matthew: "For if ye forgive men their trespasses, your heavenly Father will also forgive you: But if ye forgive not men their trespasses, neither will your Father forgive your trespasses" (1958, 239, n. 2, citing Matthew 6:14–15). Forgiveness, which also applies to the unconscious ("for they know not what they do") owes it to itself to be consistent, even infinite: "And if he trespass against thee seven times in a day, and seven times in a day turn again to thee, saying, I repent: thou shalt forgive him" (1958, 239–40, citing Luke 17:4).

Arendt's appropriation of religious practice encourages us to submit other modern acts of interpretation to ethics. Psychoanalytic listening and the analyst's speech within transference and countertransference could be considered acts of forgiveness: the donation of meaning with the effect of a scansion. Beyond the madness of the illness, anguish, or symptom and beyond the disintegration of the trauma, the subject is reborn and thus is henceforth capable of reshaping his psychic map and his bonds with other people. To forgive is as infinite as it is repetitive; forgiveness rests on the desire for truth and understanding that is manifested in a subject embarking on an analysis (see Kristeva 1989, 175–218).

On the other hand, in light of the unpredictability of human actions, which underscores our uncertainty about the future, the promise is the only thing that can stabilize without suffocating and that can offer human beings a way out. The promise obviates the obscure need for security that makes us sacrifice our freedoms and that rests on self-domination and on governing other people. Whereas forgiveness is opposed to vengeance, the promise is opposed to domination. Blessed with a long heritage, as is forgiveness, the promise exists in the inviolability of the covenants and treatises of the Romans (*pacta sund servanda*) but it is moored more specifically in Abraham, "whose whole story, as the Bible tells it, shows such a passionate drive for making covenants that it is as though he departed from his country for no other reason than to try out the power of mutual promise" (1958, 243). Arendt denounced the pseudoprophetic manipulations of totalitarian propaganda, which was based on fantastic promises. Skeptical of promises guaranteeing that tomorrow would be a better day, Arendt was willing to concede only "certain islands of predictability" to the frailty of human affairs: in the end, such promises are quite limited, particularly by the mutual and contractual engagement in which "certain guideposts of reliability [such as treatises and agreements] are erected" (1958, 244). Legislation comes to rescue here: Long live the man from Ur, and long live Montesquieu!

To the "identical will" that forges the sovereignty of a group, Arendt contrasts the way men who are connected to one another through a mutual promise "act in concert" (1958, 245, 244). These men dispose of the future as though it were the present, and they live together in the miraculous enlargement of what Nietzsche called the "memory of the Will," which is what distinguishes human life from animal life (1958, 245). As Arendt evokes Nietzsche's concept, she hears only the joyful touches of the superman and detects not a trace of Nietzsche's disdainful tone.

With forgiveness and with the promise, Arendt believes that she has revived two "control mechanisms" of public life (1958, 246), mechanisms that are indispensable and impenetrable to the extent that they are located at the very heart of the most characteristic and dangerous attribute of human life: the faculty of endlessly releasing new, unforeseen, and irreversible processes. Faced with the inexorable mechanization of daily life, forgiveness and the promise render "a sort of judgment" that, in the end, is tantamount to a wager on our capacity for rebirth. In the political context, the ultimate aim of such a judgment is not to return men to their mortal condition but to draw attention to men's faculty for being "beings of birth." This revelation constitutes the miracle par excellence that Christianity refers to as "glad tidings" and that it presents in the form of a narrative. The tale, moreover, is a true "reflective example" and not a "demonstrative" one in the sense that it induces, without generalizing, and that it clears the path for and announces the advent of the "who": "A child has been born unto us" (1958, 247).

Glad tidings indeed! But the good news comes at the cost of inscribing love, which by definition is apolitical and foreign to the world, in that very world—through the intermediary of the child who causes the lovers to engage the community to which their love has chased them. Arendt, who never stops questioning herself, wonders whether the glad tidings are really so welcome. The answer is unclear, because the sheer fact of belonging to the world in some ways represents "the end of love." What to think, then?

Arendt is not done thinking about the difficulties of "human affairs." Without such difficulties, however, who else would seek to understand them? In the end, the life of the mind is what it is all about for Arendt: living while thinking and understanding. Her unique passion remains: "What is important for me is to understand" (1994, 3).

Among the many "difficulties" raised by forgiveness and the promise, the difficulty of their very possibility cannot be overestimated. The radical exteriority that gave rise to Christlike forgiveness and promises as they intervened in the "political world" was known as transcendence and faith. Although Arendt invokes love for forgiveness and legislation for the promise, she does not ignore the need to think about the "Archimedean point" that is unable to establish with certainty that a "who" exists (1994, 248). She calls this point "human plurality," thereby appropriating Kant's notion of a human communicability expanded into a peaceable cosmopolitanism. Arendt appears to discern within that notion the political version of Duns Scotus's affirmation, Nietzsche's Amen, and Heidegger's *Gelassenheit*. The certainty is tenuous at best, but it is still worth trying to attain: by exhibiting taste, by observing, and by telling a story.

In truth, insists Arendt, neither forgiveness nor the promise is a solitary act: no one can pardon himself or promise himself anything with any hope of success. On the other hand, the modalities that allow such acts to be accepted by other people culminate in the sort of forgiveness and promises that concern only the self. Not only do the two faculties "depend . . . on the presence and acting of others," but the roles they play in politics establish a set of principles that are diametrically opposed to the classical "moral" tenets that emanate from the Platonic notion of rule, a notion that is itself founded on the relationship between me and myself (1994, 237). In the end, then, the right and wrong of relationships depends on whatever attitudes are displayed toward one's self (1994, 237–38). Accordingly, the entire public realm is seen in the image of a "man writ large." On the other hand, the moral code deduced from the faculties of forgiving and making promises "rests on experiences which nobody could ever have with himself, which, on the contrary, are entirely based on the presence of others" (1994, 238).

Even if human beings can go mad, as our century has so cruelly shown to be true, the humanity in which Arendt, despite everything, puts her faith, or at least all her confidence, cannot go mad—and must not go mad. Therein lies the transcendence—and the limits—of Arendt's thought. Because humanity, as she understands it, consists of an aptitude for the "enlargement of the mind" and for the ability to communicate common sense, it can be tantamount to language. Humanity and language are Arendt's versions of Being, and language cannot go mad. That is what Arendt believes, and when she was asked what remained for her in pre-Holocaust Germany, she replied, "What is one to do? It wasn't the German language that went crazy" (1994, 13). In the end, once I ask myself, "What should I do?", I will end up believing that a language cannot go mad.

Yet is it really necessary to believe that a language cannot go mad in order to continue to "do"? Imagine that I continue "to do" while asserting that a given language can go mad and that my bond with my community, the "enlargement of the mind," the *sensus communis* of the German or of another people, even of humanity, can go mad, already have gone mad, or could start going mad once again. After all, because a language conditions the subject that inhabits it, it responds *for* the subject, and it carries the possibilities of its own crises: if the discourse of subjects is mad, it is mad *since* language and *of* language.[2] What should be done, then? And how should we go about it?

It is incumbent on us to care for the speech of each person as well as the communitarian bond itself, not so we can restore them to a fixed and sane eternal identity that would find support in our "yes" or our "amen" but so we can usher in some tentative revelations of the "who" without forgetting how tentative they really are. This goal presumes that our hopes for such a revelation are accompanied by a certain pessimism, or at least by our conviction that language, humanity, all forms of identity, unicity, the mother, the father, the subject, and even Being itself are more than just "veiled," "withdrawn," "in oblivion," or "errant." The implication is that each "who" is driven by its inherent impossibility of being: it is nothingness, a crisis, or an illness. From that perspective, the bond with the Other, in the context of this undeniably fragile community, becomes a sort of care that is not an unchecked Will but that nevertheless preserves the miracle of rebirth.

Arendt was far removed from such concerns—and yet she was ever so close. As she reminds us that the "fact of natality" is the "miracle that saves the world," Arendt vaunts "the full experience of this capacity" (1958, 247). A full experience of natality would inevitably include birth, life, an affirmation of the uniqueness of each birth, and continual rebirth in the life of the mind—a mind that *is* because it begins again in the plurality of other people, and only then does it act like a living thought that surpasses all other activities. But the "miracle" also occurs, if only in a single fragment of this "full experience," which justifies the miracle through the promise it provides and the forgiveness it articulates. Arendt shared in that miracle, for she was without a doubt one of the few people of our time to attain the state of bliss in which living is thinking. Did she not write once that, although the rapture of thought is ineffable, "the only possible metaphor one may conceive of for the life of the mind is the sensation of being alive" (1978, 123)?

As for a political action that would be tantamount to a birth and that would shelter us from estrangement, Hannah Arendt—without indulging in too many illusions—invites us to think about it and to experience it in the present, while always remaining inside the realm between promise and forgiveness.

—*Translated by Ross Guberman*

NOTES

1. Nietzsche notes that "even in old Kant: the categorical imperative reeks of cruelty" (1967, 7:258).
2. See Derrida (1998, 84–90), which attributes Arendt's cult of a language incapable of going mad to the bond with the mother, itself cultivated from and defended against "the energy of madness." A true imaginary matricide is a precondition for creating an abyss out of the mother tongue—which can sometimes be accomplished

with serenity (Heidegger) and even joy (Joyce), and which women (Virginia Woolf, Marguerite Duras) approach by subsuming female homosexuality or the loss of the self into melancholia.

WORKS CITED

Arendt, Hannah. 1958. *The human condition*. Chicago: University of Chicago Press.

———. 1970 (Autumn). Imagination. Seminar on Kant's *Critique of judgment*. New School of Social Research.

———. 1971. *Men in dark times*. New York: Harcourt.

———. 1978. *Life of the mind*. New York: Harcourt Brace Jovanovich.

———. 1994. *Essays in understanding, 1930–1954*. Ed. Jerome Kohn. New York: Harcourt Brace.

Derrida, Jacques. 1998. *Monolingualism of the other: or, The prosthesis of origin*. Trans. Patrick Mensah. Stanford: Stanford University Press.

Kristeva, Julia. 1989. *Black sun*. Trans. Leon S. Roudiez. New York: Columbia University Press.

Nietzsche, Fredrich. 1967–77. *Oeuvres philosophiques complètes*. Paris: Gallimard. 14 vols.

Index

The authorized representative in the EU for product safety and compliance is:
Mare Nostrum Group
B.V Doelen 72
4831 GR Breda
The Netherlands

www.ingramcontent.com/pod-product-compliance
Lightning Source LLC
Chambersburg PA
CBHW030644270326
41929CB00007B/195